❧ MAKING
MOROCCO

French Resident General Hubert Lyautey and the Moroccan sultan Mawlay Youssef discussing the progression of military operations at the Taza gap in 1914. MAE, CADN, Résidence générale de France au Maroc, 20MA/201/100 "Avant la prise de Taza."

MAKING MOROCCO

COLONIAL INTERVENTION AND THE POLITICS OF IDENTITY

JONATHAN WYRTZEN

CORNELL UNIVERSITY PRESS
Ithaca and London

This book was published with the assistance of the Hilles Publication Fund of Yale University.

First published 2015 by Cornell University Press

Printed in the United States of America

Library of Congress Cataloging-in-Publication Data

Wyrtzen, Jonathan, 1973– author.
  Making Morocco : colonial intervention and the politics of identity / Jonathan Wyrtzen.
    pages cm
  Includes bibliographical references and index.
  ISBN 978-1-5017-0023-1 (cloth : alk. paper)
  1. Morocco—History—1912–1956. 2. Nationalism—Morocco—History—20th century. 3. Identity politics—Morocco—History—20th century. 4. Ethnicity—Political aspects—Morocco—History—20th century. 5. National characteristics, Moroccan. I. Title.
  DT324.W97 2016
  964'.04—dc23   2015026108

Cloth printing   10 9 8 7 6 5 4 3 2 1

❧ Contents

✍ MAPS, TABLES, AND FIGURES

✍ PREFACE AND ACKNOWLEDGMENTS

In late August 2001, my wife and I were driven in a van from the Casablanca airport and the heat of the Chaouia plain up to the relative coolness of the cedar-clad Middle Atlas Mountains to begin jobs teaching at Al Akhawayn University in Ifrane. As we headed south off the autoroute near Meknes, we saw three Arabic words painted on the foothills at the town of El Hajeb: Allah, Al-Watan, Al-Malik (God, the Nation, the King). This book's origins lie somewhere on that road, which we traversed countless times during our multiple stays in Ifrane, between the Middle Atlas Mountains and the Saiss plain. In subsequent travels, we saw this pithy triptych of state-sponsored Moroccan national identity painted across hillsides from the Rif Mountains in the north to the pre-Sahara in the south. I became intrigued: How did modern Moroccan identity, at least the official version, come to be defined around these pillars? How did the Alawid dynasty, unlike most of its peers in the region, survive European colonization, the independence struggle, and decolonization? And, how and why has Moroccan identity continued to be renegotiated, particularly in the official shift over the past fifteen years from a dominant Arab and Muslim identity to a multiethnic definition of the nation that is formally expressed in the recognition of Tamazight (Berber) as an official national language alongside Arabic in the 2011 Moroccan constitution?

My goal in revisiting Morocco's colonial history is to emphasize the multiple contingencies and critical turning points through which various aspects of Moroccan identity became politically salient during this period, particularly the reification of Arab and Berber ethnicity, the special status of the Jewish minority, and the persistence of the legal and educational status of women as critical symbolic markers of collective identity. This story also encompasses the unlikely survival of Morocco's Alawid monarchy and its continued influence on how Moroccan identity is imagined. Despite the intuitive appeal of explanations that emphasize long continuities in Moroccan history (its dynastic history goes back 1,300 years and the current ruling family has been in power since the 1660s), this book, instead of bracketing the colonial period, carefully examines these decades as a time that had a great impact on the country's post-independence trajectory. The processes traced in this book continue to directly influence how contemporary Moroccan identity is contested and reimagined.

As with all historical projects, this book was conceived, researched, and written within a particular present that left noticeable marks on its contours. I first started teaching at a Moroccan university three weeks before September 11, 2001; I returned to Washington, D.C., to pursue further study in the history of the Middle East and North Africa months after the U.S. invasion of Iraq; I conducted field and archival work in Morocco and France in 2006, during debates about the "surge" and the merits of counterinsurgency and nation-building strategies in Iraq and Afghanistan; and I returned to Morocco to work on revisions in 2011, the year of the "Arab Spring" events and Morocco's historic constitutional reforms. The arc of this decade has strongly shaped the types of questions this book pursues—about Western intervention, indirect rule, anti-colonial resistance and colonial counterinsurgency, state and nation building, the integration of tribal groups, debates over gender and identity, and the political and social role of Islam. This book is thus not just about Morocco's colonial history but also about persistent questions that have returned in the early twenty-first century to the forefront of debates within academic and policy circles and, more important, within the region's public sphere.

Many people have provided invaluable help in this journey. Although the following words of thanks constitute a meager offering, I do want to acknowledge the many people who have helped along the way. For financial support for field and archival research in Morocco and France that made this book possible, I am grateful for support from a Fulbright Student Fellowship, a Fulbright-Hays Doctoral Dissertation Research Abroad Fellowship (Doctoral Book Research Abroad Program), an American Institute for Maghrib Studies grant, and a Yale MacMillan Center faculty research grant. Time to write and revise was made possible by a Georgetown University Fellowship, a Royden B. Davis Fellowship from the Georgetown University History Department, and a Yale Junior Faculty Fellowship.

In Morocco, I owe a great debt of gratitude to numerous colleagues and friends I made at Al Akhawayn University, including Driss Ouaouicha, Mohamed Dahbi, Nizar Messari, Michael Peyron, Abdellah Chekayri, Said Ennahid, Jack Kalpakian, Driss Maghraoui, Peter Wien, Michael Willis, Eric Ross, John Shoup, Nadia Tahraoui, Mohamed Saber, Ben Cox, Kevin and Karen Smith, Peter Hardcastle, Paula Pratt, Bob Mittan, Bob Burgess, and Cate Owens. Thanks to the Mohamed VI Library staff at Al Akha-wayn University for their kindness and assistance. In Fes, I thank Ali Filali for his invaluable help and inside perspective on the medina. In Rabat and Casablanca, I especially thank Mustapha Qadery at the National Library; Mohamed Moukhlis and Abdselam Khalafi at the Royal Institute for Amazigh Culture; Daoud Casewit, James Miller, and Saadia Maski at the Moroccan-American Center for Educational and Cultural Exchange; Evelyn Early at the U.S. embassy; and dear friends Steve and Connie McDaniel and Allan and Deborah MacArthur. I thank Dr. Oudades and Taos Zayd in Aghbala for their tremendous assistance and hospitality. Additionally, I offer sincere appreciation to the library staff of the Bibliothèque Nationale, the Hassaniya Royal Library, La Source, and the High Commission for the Resistance and Veterans of the Army of Liberation in Rabat. In France, my heartfelt thanks go to Hassan Moukhlisse and Bérengère Clément of the Maison méditer-ranéenne des sciences de l'homme library in Aix-en-Provence for their gen-erous assistance with the Fonds Roux and to Amy Tondu of the Fulbright Commission in Paris. The staff at the Service Historique de la Défense at Château de Vincennes, the Ministère des Affaires etrangères archives in Paris, the Centre des archives diplomatiques in Nantes, and the Académie des Sci-ences Coloniales in Paris were also extremely helpful.

I owe much to the tremendous support I received in the Georgetown his-tory department from John Tutino, Kathy Gallagher, Djuana Shields, John McNeill, Alison Games, Judith Tucker, Yvonne Haddad, Richard Kuisel, and Amira Sonbol. This project grew out of conversations and discussions with several of my teachers, advisors, and fellow students. I especially thank those who so generously gave of their time, including Osama Abi-Mershed, Aviel Roshwald, Elizabeth Thompson, and especially John Voll, who has been an exemplary scholar, teacher, and mentor. This study has been profoundly shaped by indirect and direct conversations with Terry Burke. At Yale, I am grateful for an incredibly encouraging intellectual community within and beyond my department. I thank those who gave gracious feedback, including Julia Adams, Phil Gorski, Phil Smith, Jeff Alexander, Peter Stamatov, Ron Eyerman, Rene Almeling, Emily Erikson, Marcia Inhorn, James Scott, Erik Harms, Sara Shneiderman, Adria Lawrence, Ellen Lust, Andrew March, Frank Griffel, and especially Nick Hoover-Wilson and Sadia Saeed. Others who have provided invaluable comments include Julian Go, George Steinmetz, Daniel Schroeter, Aomar Boum, Susan Miller, and Abdellah Hammoudi. I thank the participants in multiple forums in which parts of this project have been presented for their input. These include: at Yale, the Comparative Research Workshop, the Cultural Sociology workshop, the Agrarian Studies workshop, and the Middle East Social Science workshop; the Princeton Near Eastern Studies brown bag; the Social Science History Association; and the Middle East Studies Association. My deepest thanks to Stacey Maples for making this book's wonderful maps. Chapter 3 is a revised version of an article that previously appeared as "Colonial State-Building and the Negotiation of Arab and Berber Identity in Protectorate Morocco" in the *International Journal of Middle East Studies* (2011): 227–249, and I thank Cambridge University Press for permission to reprint it. Finally, at Cornell University Press, huge thanks to Roger Haydon for his encouraging support, humor, and feedback through the publication process; to Emily Powers, Karen Laun, and Kate Babbitt for invaluable editorial and production assistance; and to the anonymous reviewers for making this a much better book.

Finally, I want to acknowledge the incredible support of our families. Thanks to my parents, Dave and Mary, and my in-laws, John and Lestra, for visiting your sojourning children and grandchildren so many times in Morocco and France. I thank my dad and brother, Joel, for multiple readings of this text and for their insightful comments and corrections. I am incredibly grateful for the encouragement of my daughters, Leila and Nora, who have grown up with this project on three continents, and Alia, who arrived near its conclusion, all of whom have given me incredible joy in the midst of my vocation and who have prayed ardently for Baba to "finish his book." It would greatly exceed the bounds of academic propriety to truly express my gratitude to her, so I will end by simply saying to my wife, Leslie, *alf shukran.*

✺ ABBREVIATIONS AND ACRONYMS

AIU-Paris	*Alliance Israélite Universelle, Paris, France*
BN-Rabat	*Bibliothèque nationale, Rabat, Morocco*
CAOM	*Centre des archives d'outre-mer, Aix-en-Provence, France*
CHEAM	*Centre des hautes études d'administration musulmane, Paris, France*
Fonds Roux	*Fonds Arsène Roux, Institute de recherches et d'études sur le monde arabe et musulman, Aix-en-Provence, France*
Hassaniya	*Al-Hassaniya Royal Archives, Rabat, Morocco*
IMA	*Institut du monde arabe, Paris, France*
IREMAM	*Institut de recherches et d'études sur le monde arabe et musulman, Aix-en-Provence, France*
La Source	*La Source Library, Rabat, Morocco*
MAE	*Archives du Ministère des Affaires étrangères, La Courneuve, France*
MAE, CADN	*Ministère des Affaires étrangères. Centre des archives diplomatiques de Nantes, Nantes, France*
Qarawiyin	*Qarawiyin Library, Fes, Morocco*
SHD-AT	*Service historique de la défense. Armée de Terre. Château de Vincennes, France*

❧ Note on Transliteration and Translation

My goal in transliterating Arabic and Berber terms has been to make these as clear and accessible as possible to the non-specialist reader. One of the complications of transliterating Moroccan place and personal names into English is the predominance of French spellings (particularly the use of "*ou*" for a long "u" or a "w" sound). With geographical terms, I have typically used the spelling common in Morocco (Azrou rather than Azru, Tetouan rather than Tetuan, etc.). With personal names, I have used French spellings for individuals best known with these spellings (Mohamed el-Ouezzani, Abdallah Laroui, Abd el-Krim). For others, I have used a simplified version of the *International Journal of Middle East Studies* (IJMES) system. Likewise, with Arabic and Berber terms, I have used the IJMES system but have eliminated diacritical marks except for the 'ayn (') and have used the simpler "-iya" suffix instead of "-iyya." All translations from Arabic, Berber, or French are my own, unless otherwise noted.

❧ MAKING MOROCCO

O mankind! We have created you from male and female and made you into nations and tribes that you may know one another.

—Qur'an 49:13

The modern nation is therefore a historical result brought about by a series of convergent facts.

—Ernst Renan (1882)

"Kifah al-malik wa al-sha'ab haqaq al-istiqlal al-kamil. Al-maghrib dawlata 'arabiya dusturiha al-islam." The struggle of the King and the People has realized complete independence. Morocco is an Arab state, and its constitution is Islam.

—Headline of *Istiqlal* paper *Al-'Alam* on November 21, 1957, in honor of the anniversary of the king's 1955 return from exile

The Kingdom of Morocco, a sovereign Muslim state attached to its national unity and territorial integrity, intends to preserve, in its plenitude and diversity, its one and indivisible national identity. Its unity, forged by the convergence of its Arabo-Islamic, Amazigh, and Saharan-Hassanian components, is nourished by its African, Andalusian, Hebrew, and Mediterranean influences. The preeminence accorded to the Muslim religion in this national reference is consistent with the attachment of the Moroccan people to the values of openness, moderation, tolerance, and dialog for mutual comprehension among all of the cultures and civilizations of the world.

—Preamble to the 2011 Moroccan Constitution

MAP 1. Colonial territorial divisions in northwestern Africa in 1912

Introduction
The Politics of Identity in a
Colonial Political Field

> *Et maintenant nous allons faire le Maroc.*
> And now we are going to make Morocco.
>
> —Comment by Hubert Lyautey, the first French resi-
> dent general, as he watched Mawlay 'Abd al-Hafiz,
> the sultan he had just deposed and replaced, board a
> ship taking him into exile in August 1912
> (Rivet 1996)

In late September 1930, after three months of weekly demonstrations in Morocco's northern cities, a delegation of eight men traveled from Fes to Rabat to meet with the young sultan, Mohamed ben Youssef.[1] The petition they presented him protested *how* the French, in the phrase Lyautey used eighteen years earlier, had been "making Morocco." The catalyst for the discontent was France's so-called Berber policy, a colonial politics of recognition that reified an ethnic distinction between Arabs and Berbers. Since 1914, French authorities had installed a system of tribal courts in the middle and central High Atlas Mountains after these regions, which the French designated as "of Berber custom," had been "pacified" (conquered militarily) and brought under French administration. In the 1920s, they also began to install a fledgling separate educational system of Franco–Berber schools in these same areas, which offered little to no instruction in Arabic or Islam.[2] These ethnically based juridical and educational distinctions provoked little response from the Moroccan public

---

1. Mohamed ben Youssef (Mohamed V) acceded to the throne in 1927 on the death of his father, Youssef, who had replaced 'Abd al-Hafiz in 1912.

2. By 1930, only twenty Franco-Berber schools had been created; they served 700 students (Hart 1997, 13).

until 1930, when the residency promulgated a decree (*dahir*), which the sultan signed on May 16, that put the Berber customary legal system on an equal footing with other jurisdictions and channeled criminal cases into the French courts.

This effort to further formalize a policy of ethnic differentiation catalyzed a firestorm of popular protest that roiled many of Morocco's cities for weeks that summer. In June, a group of young, urban, Arabic-speaking activists began to campaign against what they called the Berber *dahir*. In their eyes the May 16 decree was a fundamental threat to the unity of the Moroccan *umma*, or Muslim community: they claimed it removed the Berbers from the jurisdiction of shari'a[3] and was part of a broader French strategy to Christianize the Berbers. To publicize the danger and rally crowds against the decree, they improvised on the Latif, a traditional prayer used in times of trouble or calamity, standing up in mosques and chanting, "Oh Allah, the Benevolent, we ask of You benevolence in whatever fate brings, and do not separate us from our brothers, the Berbers" (Brown 1972; Lafuente 1999, 190–91). In July, the protests spread from Salé and Rabat to several interior cities, and on August 7, 7,000 Moroccans gathered to chant the Latif at the Qarawayn mosque in Fes (Ageron 1972, 138–39). In response to the escalating protests, the French authorities officially prohibited the prayer throughout the country. The next week, the sultan, under pressure from the French, ordered imams to publically read a letter defending the policies expressed in the May 16 decree and castigating the protestors for politicizing the "religious space" of the mosque. By the end of the summer, the issue had been picked up by Chakib Arslan,[4] a Geneva-based pan-Islamic propagandist, who railed against French neo-crusaderism in his *La Nation Arabe* and began to make the "Berber Crisis" a cause célèbre, energizing anti-French demonstrations and petitions across the Muslim world, from Cairo to Surabaya.[5]

---

3. The 1930 decree is discussed at length in chapter 5. See also Guerin (2011) and Hoffman (2008a).

4. For the most detailed study of Arslan, see Cleveland (1985). Arslan forged a strong personal connection with many of Morocco's young nationalist leaders in the early 1930s. Some of them spent time with him in Paris or Geneva during their studies in France.

5. Cartons F2 and F41 at the Bibliothèque nationale in Rabat contain translations by the French protectorate's Service de la presse musulmane of hundreds of articles from Arabic press about the Berber Dahir and the "de-Islamization" of the Berbers from newspapers in Tunis, Tripoli, Alexandria, Cairo, Beirut, Aleppo, Damascus, Jaffa, Jerusalem, and Nablus and from as far afield as Surabaya,

In late September, protectorate authorities allowed a delegation of protest leaders to meet with the sultan. Their demands, which they presented
in a petition to the sultan and resident general, were clear. Speaking in the
name of the Moroccan people, they emphasized the significance of the Berber Question for the country's religious unity, recounting the history of
the Islamization of Morocco's population, including the Berbers, from the
ninth century. They also reiterated the sultan's sacred obligation, as the duly
constituted Muslim ruler, to ensure that Islamic law was uniformly applied
in Moroccan territory. Appealing to the promise France had made in the
1912 Treaty of Fes to respect the sultan's temporal and spiritual authority,
their concrete policy demands protested France's divide-and-rule legal, educational, and administrative policies and insisted instead on state-led policies
of Arabo-Islamic national assimilation. These included a unified judiciary
that would apply Islamic law to all Moroccans (with the exception of Jews,
who would keep their own courts), a unified educational system that would
teach Arabic and Islam in both urban and rural areas, the adoption of Arabic
as the protectorate's official language, and a prohibition against any official
use of Berber "dialects" or their transcription into Latin characters. Reflecting intense anxieties in the early 1930s about Christian proselytization, the
protestors also called for an end to missionary activity, for Muslim control of
orphanages and schools the Franciscans had established in the Atlas Mountains, and for an end to the protectorate's financial support of the Catholic
Church.[6] Finally, the protestors demanded an end to internal travel restrictions in the French zone and the replacement of obligatory travel permits
with identity cards that would allow free movement between city and countryside (Lafuente 1999, 196).[7] After reading the petition, the sultan communicated his sympathy, but the delegation returned to Fes empty handed, and

---

Indonesia. The international furor over the Berber Decree gained momentum in the summer of
1931 after it was discussed at the Islamic Congress in Jerusalem, which delegations from across the
Islamic world attended.

6. Several factors, including the conversion and entry into a priestly order of the son of a
prominent Fez family, pro-evangelistic rhetoric about the conversion of Morocco's Berbers from the
bishopric of Rabat (reflected in church publications such as *Le Maroc catholique*), the appointment of
Christian Kabyle legal clerks in Berber tribal courts, and the distribution by Paul Marty (a French
education administrator) of Arabic copies of the Gospel had heightened Muslims sensitivities about
proselytization in the late 1920s (Julien 1952, 147–48; 1978, 159–61).

7. Chakib Arslan published a facsimile of the entire Arabic letter in the October 1930 issue of
La Nation Arabe (La Nation Arabe, 1988, 10) and translated it into French.

the protests petered out that fall.[8] Although it seems to have been a failure in terms of immediate goals, the so-called Berber Crisis catalyzed the birth of an urban nationalist movement that developed over the next decade. This cycle of protest also forged a cultural agenda—an insistence on Morocco's Arab and Islamic identity (and the concomitant suppression of its Berber patrimony)—that eventually shaped the identity politics of the post-independence Moroccan state when the nationalist movement leadership came into power in 1956.

This cycle of protests against France's infamous Berber policy in the early 1930s[9] captures key elements of the interactive politics of identity that played out during the country's protectorate period (1912–1956). First, this episode demonstrates that the "we" Lyautey referred to at the onset of the protectorate in his pretentious comment about "making Morocco" did not just include representatives of the French colonial power such as himself. The making of Morocco also involved a constellation of Moroccan actors: the Alawid sultan, the nominal ruler; an urban Arabic-speaking elite that was beginning to mobilize popular support and to make claims about the trajectories of state and nation-building; and, less obviously, groups including Berber speakers and Jews whose marginal ethnic or religious position in society put them at the crux of identity struggles. Second, the 1930 "Berber Crisis" reveals what was at stake. After just two decades of colonial intervention, a set of identity-related issues had become profoundly politicized, including categories of ethnicity such as "Arab" and "Berber," the function of language and religion in educational and judicial systems, the state's control over territory and internal movement, and the appropriate temporal and spiritual roles of the sultan. From this point forward, contention over these concerns dominated political struggles throughout the rest of the protectorate, and they continued to do so after independence.

In this book I address an underlying question brought to the fore by the actors, issues, and interactions linked in the "Berber Crisis" of the early

---

8. Customary courts continued to operate in areas of Morocco up to independence, though a decree dated April 8, 1934, reverted the jurisdiction for appeals to the sultan-appointed Islamic courts (Julien 1952, 133).

9. In the historiographies of the French protectorate and the Moroccan nationalist movement, France's Berber Policy and the protests against the "Berber *dahir*" have received a great deal of attention. On the former, see Burke (1973), Ageron (1972), Hoffman (2008a), and Guerin (2011). On the importance of the "Berber *dahir*" for the nationalist movement, see Halstead (1964), Joffe (1984), Lafuente (1999), and Rachik (2003). In the past decade, the so-called Berber *dahir* has been the subject of substantial revisionist attempts to highlight the nationalists' instrumentalist exploitation and invention of the crisis (Mounib 2002; Wyrtzen 2013).

1930s: How did four and half decades of European colonial intervention in the twentieth century transform Moroccan identity? As was the case for other places in North Africa and in the wider developing world, the colonial period in Morocco (1912–1956) established a new type of political field in which notions about and relationships among politics and identity formation were fundamentally transformed. Instead of privileging top-down processes of colonial state formation or bottom-up processes of local resistance, my analysis focuses on interactions between state and society that occurred in this field. By looking at the formal and informal rules of the game, different styles of play, and the stakes of struggle in this field, I demonstrate how interactions during the protectorate period among a wide range of European and local actors indelibly politicized four key dimensions of Moroccan identity: religion, ethnicity, territory, and the role of the Alawid monarchy. These colonial legacies are significant because these arenas of identity formation continue to be at the center of struggles to defend, contest, and negotiate the legitimacy of Morocco's political order.

In its focus on the politicization of identity in the colonial period, the book makes two substantive interventions. First, it demonstrates that the anti-colonial nationalist definition of Moroccan identity centered on Arabo-Islamic high culture (Gellner 1983) and Alawid dynastic rule—expressed in the cultural agenda of urban nationalists and supported later by the post-independence Moroccan state[10]—was a contingent outcome. It problematizes the notion that this definition of identity represented a direct continuity with precolonial identity configurations and instead demonstrates that it was an outcome of spatial, classificatory, and symbolic struggles that occurred in the colonial political field.

Second, in tracing how and why religious and ethnic markers of identity—Muslim, Jewish, Arab, and Berber—became politicized and how gender was often at the center of struggles over these categories, this book brings to light a plurality of other identity configurations in play in protectorate Morocco—subnational and supranational, ethnolinguistic and non-ethnolinguistic, Muslim and non-Muslim, and nonmonarchic—that were eventually marginalized or elided in the process of anti-colonial nation building. The book examines literate and text-producing Moroccan and European elites, but it also integrates non-elite groups in Moroccan society into its central analysis. By analyzing hitherto neglected primary sources, it brings

---

10. This formulation is neatly summarized in Morocco's post-independence Arabic motto *Allah, al-Watan, al-Malik* (God, the Nation, the King), which was recognized in Article 4 of Morocco's constitution and emblazoned on hillsides throughout the country.

FIGURE 1. The motto "Allah, al-Watan, al-Malik" (God, the Nation, the King) painted on a hillside at El Hajeb, on the route from Meknes up into the Middle Atlas Mountains.
Photo by the author, July 17, 2012.

forth the unique perspectives of rural Berber speakers, Jews, and women who were marginalized by the political elite even though they were symbolically at the center of identity struggles. By locating the origins of an Arabo-Islamic configuration of Moroccan national identity and those it marginalized in the colonial period, this study sheds new light on perennial questions in Moroccan historiography, including the salience of the Arab-Berber distinction, the status of Jews, the position of women, and the survival of the monarchy.

These interventions historicize dominant post-independence narratives of Moroccan national identity and depict the central importance of subaltern, or subordinated, groups in forging this identity. These findings are relevant because they help demonstrate a more complex and nuanced view of Morocco's colonial past. Equally importantly, these four axes of identity—religion, ethnicity, territory, and the monarchy—that were activated during the protectorate period remain the focus of contemporary Moroccan political struggles. This is reflected in ongoing debates over the public role of Islam, religious tolerance, and the memory of Morocco's Jews; recent reforms regarding women's legal status; the monarchy's multiculturalist recognition of Tamazight (Berber) as a national language alongside Arabic; the still-unresolved territorial dispute over the Western

Sahara; and the monarchy's continued symbolic and practical dominance, as Commander of the Faithful, of the Moroccan political field. Finally, by examining linkages among colonial and postcolonial political developments in Morocco, this book isolates and clarifies historical processes that are relevant to numerous other postcolonial contexts.

Writing New Colonial Histories

This study, in revisiting Morocco's colonial past (Maghraoui 2013), contributes to a recent wave of scholarship that reexamines North Africa's colonial period on its own terms in order to better understand longer historical trajectories. It emphasizes 1) that colonial intervention represented a fundamental historical rupture that cannot be parenthesized but instead must be integrally woven into our understanding of contemporary Morocco; and 2) that understanding this rupture requires an interactional rather than a top-down or bottom-up historical approach. Regarding the first point, particularly for a case such as Morocco, which has a very long political history, pre- and postcolonial continuities are not irrelevant. In an initial wave of North African histories written by nationalist elites before and after independence, the obvious underlying apologetic and political goal in "decolonizing history" (Sahli 1965) was to defend the historic unity and continuity of national communities that had been denied in a vast body of French colonial scholarship. As Edmund Burke III (1998, 17) has noted, this orientation was also more and less subtly expressed in later classics, including segmentary explanations of political structure (Gellner 1969; Waterbury 1970) and culturalist analyses of political authority (Geertz 1968; Combs-Schilling 1989; Hammoudi 1997) that, to varying degrees, emphasized continuity rather than discontinuity in addressing aspects of Morocco's post-independence political system.

The uncompleted task for Morocco, and for many other cases, is to write new colonial histories that are both postcolonial and post-nationalist histories that do not reproduce the teleological assumptions in either but instead capture the complexities, contingencies, nuances, and contradictions that were expressed during this critical transitional period. As Burke (1998, 16) observes, this is necessary not only to produce a more accurate understanding of the colonial period itself but also to produce a more accurate understanding of the present: "Unless we re-imagine colonial history as existing in its own right, apart from the progress-oriented narratives that have operated until now, we will be unable to gain much intellectual understanding of post-colonial histories."

Rehistoricizing the colonial encounter in North Africa involves a shift toward "understanding" it rather than "accusing" or "excusing" one side or the other (Rivet 1996, 15). This has involved drawing on newly accessible archival sources in order to reanalyze aspects of colonial rule. Examples include Rivet's (1996) monumental three-volume study on the protectorate and Lyautey's role in shaping it[11] and Burke's (2014) analysis of the creation by French colonial sociologists of a "Moroccan colonial archive" and the institutionalization of this knowledge by an "ethnographic state" during the protectorate. Other scholarship has begun to look at how specific parts of the colonial apparatus worked, including recent studies on the colonial educational system in urban and rural contexts,[12] the impact of colonial policies on the arts and crafts (see Irbouh 2005), the use of linguistic and legal policies based on ethnic differentiation in rural administration (see Hoffman 2008a, 2010; and Guerin 2011), the impact of ecological and forestry policies of the colonial era (Davis 2007; Ford 2008), and the intended and unintended consequences of colonial urban design.[13] Recent research on protectorate Morocco has also refocused attention on colonial military strategies, the importance of colonial intelligence apparatuses, and the lesser-known story of Spain's use of chemical weapons in the Rif War.[14] Comparable scholarship on Algeria examines the metropolitan factors behind French colonial intervention there (Sessions 2011), the logics of colonial violence in the French pacification of the Sahara (Brower 2009), the production of ethnographic knowledge about North African Islam (Trumbull 2009), the influence of native affairs officers of the Arab Bureaus in the formulation of colonial policy (Abi-Mershed 2010), and the assimilationist urban cantonment project of colonial settlers (Prochaska 1990).

Scholarship from another direction has shed new light on North African perspectives. Some ask new questions about the North African nationalist movements, including McDougall's (2006) analysis of how Salafi historians

---

11. On Lyautey and his influence on the protectorate, see also Hoisington (1995).

12. These include Segalla's (2009) book on the influence of French ethnographic assumptions on educational policy during the protectorate, and Benhlal's (2005) detailed monograph on the pinnacle of the Franco-Berber educational system, Azrou College.

13. These include Abu-Lughod's (1981) study of colonial and postcolonial Rabat; Wright's (1991) comparison of colonial urbanism in Morocco, Madagascar, and Indochina; and Rabinow's (1989) study of French modernisms, which devotes substantial attention to Lyautey and urban planning in Rabat and Casablanca.

14. See Gershovich (2000) on the "pacification" and creation of the colonial army, Thomas (2008) on French and British intelligence services in North Africa and the Middle East, and Balfour (2007) on the intimate connections between Spain's involvement in Morocco and developments on the peninsula.

reimagined Algerian identity in the interwar years and Lawrence's (2013) emphasis on how nationalists initially made claims in the framework of the French Empire and only much later shifted to independence-seeking agendas in Morocco and Algeria. Scholars have also begun to address how North African groups outside of or completely overlooked in the dominant Arabo-Islamic urban nationalist narrative experienced, accommodated, manipulated, and resisted the colonial encounter. These studies have brought a focus on rural actors, tribes, peasants, Sufi networks, and regional histories.[15] Telling North Africa's colonial history from below has also brought attention to groups that were neglected in colonialist and nationalist historiography such as colonial soldiers, prostitutes, *haratin* (darker-skinned, lower-caste groups in pre-Saharan oases), and slaves.[16] It has also been expressed in a rich wave of scholarship on North Africa's Jews that has reexamined transitions between the precolonial, colonial, and postcolonial periods; their experiences of colonialism and nationalism; the emigration of the majority of the community; and their position in the postcolonial Maghrib.[17]

There is a tendency, however, in North African studies and the broader literature on colonialism and empire produced over the past several decades to focus on *either* the processes involved in the extension of European power *or* the experiences of the local population impacted by this extension. Well-known examples of the former include the rich literature on colonial power and modes of knowledge (Cohn 1996; Dirks 2001), the legacies of indirect and direct rule (Mamdani 1996; Laitin 1986), and the representational, reordering, and reorganizing effects of modernity (Mitchell 1988). An emphasis on the impersonal macro- or microprocesses (in census taking, cadastral surveys, legal codification, urban planning, and hygienic reform) of colonial governmentality can efface the subjectivities, actions, accommodations, resistances, and interpretations of local actors impacted by these processes. Several recent studies of the impact of colonial intervention on the Middle

---

15. These include an earlier wave of scholarship on peripheral Moroccan groups in the Middle Atlas (Burke 1976), the Tafilelt and Jbel Saghro (Dunn 1977), and the Rif (Seddon 1981). Clancy-Smith (1994) shifts the focus to Sufi elites and networks traversing the border between Algeria and Tunisia, and Aouchar (2002) examines the rural history of Morocco's eastern High Atlas during the protectorate period.

16. On the *goumiers* (North African colonial soldiers) see Maghraoui (1998) and Gershovich (2003). On prostitution generally in North Africa, see Taraud (2003); for prostitution in Casablanca's Bousbir district, see Maghraoui (2013). On black Morocco and the complexities of slavery and race in North Africa, see El Hamel (2013) and Aouad (2013)

17. On Algerian Jews, see Schreier (2010) and Katz (2012). On Moroccan Jews, see Kenbib (1994), Tsur (2001), Schroeter (2003), Kosansky (2011), Boum (2013), and Miller (2013).

East and North Africa, for example, tell us about the British or French colonizing Egypt (Mitchell 1988), inventing Iraq (Dodge 2003), or occupying Syria (Neep 2012) but not as much about what Egyptians, Iraqis, or Syrians were thinking or doing.

The research agenda in a recently resurgent sociology of empire and colonialism (Go 2009; Steinmetz 2013) is similarly biased toward what was going on in the minds and actions of the colonizers rather than the colonized. Scholars have used network theory to analyze Ottoman mechanisms of imperial rule (Barkey 2008), principle-agent theory to examine the decline of the Dutch East India Company (Adams 1994), social network theory to examine the English East India Company (Erikson 2014), and Bourdieu's field analysis to explain variations in native policy in German colonial states (Steinmetz 2007) or to compare the British and American empires (Go 2008b). Others have examined the legacies of colonial experiences and institutions on postcolonial economic development,[18] the relative strength of the nation-state, and the varied gendered rights frameworks that were expressed in postcolonial states.[19] To the extent that individual actors are considered, the focus is overwhelmingly on colonial administrators, on how ethnographic discourse shaped policy decisions or how levels of identification with "native" society impacted taxation strategies.[20] With few exceptions (Go 2008a, Steinmetz 2007), the experience of local actors is rarely, if ever, considered.

This study contributes to recent work that uses postcolonial theory to constructively critique sociology's European metrocentrism and work toward relational theoretical and methodological approaches (Go 2013; Bhambra 2007; McLennan 2003). State-centric sociological analyses of empire and colonialism need to be complemented by approaches that bring both elite and non-elite local actors into the scope of analysis. European colonial intervention undoubtedly had profound effects on colonized societies, but the causal arrow was not unidirectional. Empires and individual colonial units were complex environments of interactions in which local actors were

18. On cases from the British Empire, see Lange (2005); and on cases from the Spanish empire in the Americas, see Mahoney (2010).

19. Centeno (2002) examines how in Latin America a different experience of war-making from the European context led to different state and nation-making outcomes. Charrad (2001) explains how the variation in family law codes in North Africa derives from the relative strength state and tribe in Morocco, Algeria, and Tunisia.

20. Goh (2007) examines the relationship between the production of ethnographic knowledge and native policy in Malaya and the Philippines. Steinmetz (2007) analyzes variation in different frameworks of native policy within the German empire. Wilson (2011) looks at sub-"national" variation in British taxation policies during a critical transition period of colonial rule in India.

equally involved in mediating, accommodating, resisting, and redirecting these processes. It is not sufficient, though, to simply swing the analytical pendulum away from colonial elites to nationalist or subaltern resistance. Frederick Cooper (1994, 1517) clarifies the dilemma involved with writing colonial histories: "The difficulty is to confront the power behind European expansion without assuming it was all-determining and to probe the clash of different forms of social organization without treating them as self-contained and autonomous."

In reintegrating subaltern perspectives into a historical sociology of colonial intervention, the goal cannot simply be to delineate an "autonomous domain" of the "people," as Guha (1988, 37–44) propounds in his critique of elite nationalist historiography.[21] The goal must be to demonstrate the integral interaction of marginalized groups both as contested objects of colonialist and nationalist discourses and as subjects in their own right.[22] What we need to complement existing scholarship on North Africa, colonial studies more broadly, and the historical sociology of empire and colonialism in particular is a framework for analyzing colonial intervention that can address the complex and dynamic interactions that occurred among the various actors involved and hold the larger picture in view regarding macroprocesses such as military conquest, development, state formation, and anti-colonial mobilization while also capturing how these played out at a microlevel in local society.

Identity and Struggle in a Colonial Political Field

Toward this end, this book develops the concept of a *colonial political field* to analyze the space in which interactions between state and society took place, how identity struggles took on distinct forms in this space, and how the stakes of these struggles were defined. The goal of this synthetic approach is to address the importance of institutional structures, critical junctures, and historical sequences in a way that puts actors (colonial and local, elite and non-elite) at the center of analysis. With his well-known concept of the "field" (*champ*), Pierre Bourdieu emphasizes the position of agents, their habitus, the agreed-on rules of the game, and the competition for particular forms of capital in specific social fields. This study evokes that framework

21. The imbrication (rather than autonomy) of subaltern resistance with dominant symbolic and discursive forms of power has been emphasized by O'Hanlon (1988), Abu-Lughod (1990), and Mitchell (1990).

22. For examples of new approaches that examine the complexities of subaltern resistance and negotiation in South Asia, see Chandra (2013) and Shah (2014).

but uses the idea of a political field more expansively to capture a larger space of competitive interaction that extends beyond the scope of any given social field or even the state itself, which Bourdieu construes as an "ensemble" or "intersection" of fields.[23] I distinguish between the state and the political field, intentionally using the latter to capture a wider range of "organization, mobilization, agitation, and struggle" (Zubaida 1989, 145–46) of state and nonstate actors. In developing the concept of a colonial political field, this study is oriented around the three commonsense field characteristics Martin identifies: 1) a topological sense, or the position of agents and institutions in an analytic space; 2) an organization or array of forces; and 3) a field of contestation, or a battlefield (2003, 28–29).

The book analyzes how these three field dimensions were expressed over time during Morocco's protectorate period (1912–1956). The topological sense of the colonial political field corresponds to the protonational territorial space, marked out through two decades of military conquest, in which different actors (colonial and Moroccan) were positioned during the protectorate. The organization of the field or its array of forces corresponds to the symbolic and classificatory logics that formed the rules of the game in that space. Both of these dimensions, the space of the field and the forces that ordered it, are necessary for understanding the colonial political field's third characteristic: how it served as a battlefield of struggle in which collective identities were transformed.

Using this threefold field concept—space, organizing forces, and competition—creates a framework that accounts for the important transformative impact of colonization but can also address multiple mechanisms of causation in terms of what happened in that field over time. It incorporates both the physical and social space in which actors engage, negotiate, and compete. It also emphasizes dynamism and contention in the field rather than stability and continuity and encompasses non-peer interactions including both state actors (colonial administrative and military elites) and a wide range of nonstate actors in the colonized society.[24] This last point is critical.

---

23. Bourdieu restricts the "political field" to "political professionals" involved in the production of political ideas, programs, and concepts (1991, 203–19) and sees the "state" as an "ensemble of administrative or bureaucratic fields" (Bourdieu and Wacquant 1992, 111).

24. In the field framework described by Fligstein and McAdam (2011, 3), external intervention can thus be understood as an exogenous input that creates and shapes a colonial iteration of a "strategic action field," or "a meso-level social order where actors (who can be individual or collective) interact with knowledge of one another under a set of common understandings about the purposes of the field, the relationships in the field (including who has power and why), and the field's rules." As subsequent chapters make clear, much of the interactions within the field focused on disputed understandings of the purposes of, relationships within, and rules governing the protectorate field created in Morocco.

The outcome this book seeks to explain (the range of ways identity was politicized in Morocco by colonial intervention) was produced not by the colonial powers or local parties; it was produced through the interactions among them. The French and Spanish forged a colonial political field in Morocco but did so in the face of local resistance (particularly in remote areas like the Rif and Atlas mountain ranges). The violence this entailed shaped and reshaped both colonial policy and local social and identity structures. Although the end of pacification operations in the 1930s signaled the stabilization of the colonial field as a governance unit, the field was not static: Moroccan challengers to the French and Spanish ruling incumbents continued to struggle for dominance in the field by challenging its symbolic and classificatory rules (i.e., calling for homogenizing Arabization and Islamization policies) or instrumentalizing them toward their own ends (i.e., making claims in the name of the sultan, the nominal sovereign recognized by the Treaty of Fes).

Subsequent chapters trace how, throughout these cycles of struggle against or for control of the expanding colonial political field, actors invoked, imagined, transformed, and, most importantly, politicized group identities. Instead of asking how collective identities function in an ontological, given, sense as causal variables in this context (Brubaker 2004), I focus on tracing identity-related processes that were catalyzed by colonial intervention: how historical, religious, ethnic, gendered, regional, and national identities came to be used by actors as categories of social and political practice (Brubaker and Cooper 2000) in the colonial political field.

These can be differentiated into state- and society-based identification processes (see table 1). State-based processes include internal struggles in the metropole or colonial state bureaucracy over self-representation (i.e., labeling Morocco a "protectorate" rather than a "colony") or over native policy (i.e., debates among French administrators about whether to naturalize Morocco's Jews as French citizens, as had been done in Algeria).[25] These also include external classificatory practices through which the state mapped identities in society (using ethnic, religious, and gender criteria to mark group boundaries). Society-based identification processes can also be external or internal. The former include nonstate actors' efforts to directly contest or redraw state-generated identifications, as demonstrated in the

---

25. See Steinmetz's (2007) comparative analysis of German native policy for the most sophisticated treatment of these state-based processes within and between the metropole and near-autonomous colonial bureaucratic fields.

Table 1   Identification processes in the political field

	INTERNAL	**EXTERNAL**
State-based	Struggles over self-representation (i.e., protectorate vs. colony) or native policy (i.e., whether to naturalize Morocco's Jews as French)	Institutionally reinforced social classifications (i.e., Arab/Berber distinction)
Society-based	Self-understandings and representations and struggles over these (i.e., Atlas Berber speakers' religious, tribal, or regional self-identifications)	Struggles that directly challenge state-based classifications (i.e., protests against *dahirs* and nationalists' framing of Arabo-Islamic Moroccan identity) Categorization/classification of other nonstate groups (i.e., Atlas Berber speakers' conceptions of urban groups, Jews, the French)

Berber Crisis, where Arab urban activists challenged the colonial state's legal and administrative maintenance of a "Berber" ethnic category in the colonial political field. Another external type of society-based identification process involves nonstate actors' classifications and categorizations of other social groups (i.e., how Berber-speaking groups viewed urban populations, Jews, or the "Christian" French, which I analyze in chapter 3). Society-based internal identification processes refer to self-understandings and self-representations of collective identity by nonstate actors (i.e., how the same groups viewed themselves at intratribal, intertribal, regional, religious, etc. levels of identity). This study analyzes contention related to each of these directions of identification, including struggles within groups about their identity.

This case study of Morocco offers what Wimmer (2008) calls a "multilevel, process approach" to analyzing collective identity, integrating insights from studies emphasizing one side or the other of the colonial encounter to build a more sophisticated and more nuanced understanding of complex dynamics.[26] It addresses important state-based practices of identification, classification, and categorization involved in the production of ethnographic knowledge in the colonial field but also takes into account how local actors (including but not

---

26. Wimmer's model focuses mostly on *horizontal* classificatory struggles and negotiations among actors about ethnic boundaries in the national field. This study emphasizes the importance of these same processes during the pre-national, colonial period as "critical antecedents" (Slater and Simmons 2010) that established path-dependent constraints that affected later developments. I highlight a specific aspect of Wimmer's framework, how an exogenous shift such as colonial intervention dramatically reconfigures the institutional order and incentives related to *vertically* defined identity boundaries (ethnic, religious, political), and how both elite and non-elite actors resist, redraw, or accommodate colonial classifications.

limited to elites) actively engaged in identity work, both externally and internally. Instead of a monolithic focus on the colonial state or a binary analysis of colonialist–nationalist opposition, this method of historical sociology targets multiple interacting processes, looking at how state and nonstate institutions and actors developed categories of practice related to identity, how external and self-generated classifications and categorizations developed, how these were contested and refashioned, and how they interacted with each other over time. For protectorate Morocco, this entails examining how the spatial dimensions and ordering powers (symbolic and classificatory) of the colonial political field politicized territorial, religious, ethnic, and gendered markers of identity and how various Moroccan actors then relationally defined multiple levels of identity in this space of political struggle.

Rural Identities and the Expanding Space of the Field

The initial catalyst that triggered these dynamic identification processes was the violent spatial expansion of the colonial political field through military conquest. Between 1907 and 1934, the French and Spanish colonial states completed a "total pacification" of the Moroccan countryside. In North Africa and elsewhere, this type of territorial "enclosure movement" dramatically altered a preexisting political ecosystem.[27] Prior to the colonial period, state-governed and self-governing areas ("state space" and "nonstate space") coexisted in near proximity, belying a Weberian conceptualization of the state as holding a monopoly on the use of force in a bounded territory. Because of the region's topography, which features mountains juxtaposed closely with more easily controlled lowlands and coastal plains, many groups historically retained high levels of autonomy and were able to negotiate the terms of their relationship with the central government or, if they were more remote, totally ignore its administrative aspirations. State space was thus negotiated in reference to a plurality, not a monopoly, of military power and was therefore in constant flux, with social groups submitting to or resisting taxation and military service depending on a shifting calculus of alliances and allegiances.

French colonial scholarship reified these two ideal types of political space, using two local Arabic terms *blad al-makhzan*[28] (the land of government)

---

27. Scott (2009) describes this as a world-historical phenomenon in which empires and nation-states began to systematically eliminate what he calls "nonstate space" in the nineteenth and twentieth centuries.

28. The Arabic root, *khazana*, literally means "to shut up, to preserve, to hoard." *Makhzan* was first used in reference to the iron chest the Aghlabid amir of Ifriqiya (Tunisia) in the eighth century used to store the taxes sent to the Abbasid caliph in Baghdad (Michaux-Bellaire & Buret 1991, 133).

and *blad al-sība*[29] (the land of dissidence). They assumed a binary antagonism between *makhzan* and *sība* that they transposed on more or less static geographies and overlaid a distinction between state and nonstate zones with a host of Arab and Berber ethnic stereotypes. Political space in precolonial North Africa was in fact much more complex. As with other similar geographies that stretch across the Middle East into Central Asia, these two poles of state governance and self-governance, *makhzan* and *sība*, formed a cultural, economic, and political symbiosis. The tribal military potential of the countryside simultaneously was a resource for and a threat to the *makhzan*. Similarly, the *makhzan*'s symbolic and material resources constituted both a resource and a threat to rural power holders.[30] First, the states that emerged in the region, as Ibn Khaldun (2005) first pointed out in the fourteenth century, were typically generated by tribal confederations originally based in the desert or in mountainous "nonstate" periphery. Second, as Mohamed Tozy (1999) insightfully explains, the very existence of the *makhzan* system was predicated on the symbolic ties between the sultan and elites in the peripheries whose privileged connection to the sultan depended on their ability to resist central authority. Their very dissidence gave the *makhzan* the potential for renewal in areas of "controlled dissidence" (63) by developing strategies of neutralization rather than elimination.

The advent of the colonial state in North Africa in the nineteenth century radically altered these patterns of interaction and interpenetration. The French first began to introduce a new territorial paradigm of political space in the 1840s when Governor General Thomas Bugeaud carried out brutal *razzia* campaigns in Algeria. These methods enabled the French to achieve a near-monopolization of the use of force in Algerian territory by the 1870s (Brower 2009). A similar process was carried out in Tunisia in the 1880s. Morocco was spared direct military intervention throughout the nineteenth century because of European diplomatic tensions. After these were resolved in the early 1900s, political space in Morocco also began to be transformed. First, Morocco's ostensible "territory" was subdivided: France took the bulk of the territory in the center and delegated to Spain a zone of control in the north and recognized Spain's tenuous claims in the

---

29. The term *bilad al-sība* probably appeared the first time in an eleventh-century commentary on Maliki law by Abu Imran al-Fassi, a Moroccan scholar based in the Tunisian city of Qayrawan. It was used from the eleventh century on in Andalusia and the Maghrib to refer to the backward rural areas living in a state of *jahiliya*, or ignorance, of the precepts of *shari'a* (Rivet 2012b).

30. This diverges from Scott's (2009) reading of the cultural and economic (but not the political) symbiosis between "hill" and "valley" peoples, or state and nonstate space, in his analysis of Zomia/ Southeast Asia.

far south (including Sidi Ifni, Tarfaya, and parts of the Sahara). Tangier was later declared an international zone in 1923 under the control of Western consuls. Next, from 1907 to 1934, both European powers progressed from seeking limited military control to seeking total military control in their respective protectorate zones. During this process, the French and Spanish authorities extended roads, *pistes* (rough tracks), railroads, and telegraph lines and forcefully disarmed and co-opted the military potential of the so-called *blad al-sība* periphery via the conscription of subdued tribes into the colonial army. In the end, "total pacification" fundamentally transformed Morocco's political ecosystem, defining the space of an unprecedented type of state-dominated political field and violently incorporating a constellation of actors and institutions into it.

The spatial expansion of this new type of political field, in which a state aspired (with much higher degrees of success than the precolonial *makhzan*) to a monopoly on the use of force in a defined territorial unit, entailed a political and cultural paradigm shift for various Moroccan actors. The change was especially radical for rural, mostly Berber-speaking groups living in regions that had historically enjoyed high degrees of autonomy vis-à-vis the central government. As the French and Spanish armies launched successive campaigns to enclose these groups in the colonial political field, these rural populations were forced to militarily resist or submit to a new form of hybrid *makhzan*. This study focuses on two specific sites, the Atlas and Rif Mountains (respectively in the French and Spanish zones), to examine how the colonial military conquest catalyzed transformations in notions of identity in rural Morocco.

In the Atlas Mountains, these groups' processes of external identification concerned state-oriented perceptions of the French invader (framed in a religious binary as the *rumi*, or Christian, enemy of Islam), *makhzan* officials, and the sultan himself. They also included society-directed perceptions about other regions also being invaded or remaining autonomous from the *makhzan*, neighboring tribes, and urban populations that had fallen under "*rumi*." Atlas communities marked ethnic and religious "otherness" in references to the darker-skinned *saligan*, Senegalese colonial troops (*tirailleurs*) the French deployed to assist in the conquest (Echenberg 1991), and to local and Algerian *udayn*, or Jews, with whom they came into contact. These groups also engaged in intense internal identification struggles (both intertribal and intratribal) in the context of disputes about jihad or submission, using sexual, gendered, and religious metaphors to categorize opponents or to talk about their own identity. Analyzing these identity-related process over time—before, during, and after the enclosure of these groups in the colonial political field—offers unique perspectives on the religious, political, and economic ramifications of colonial intervention. This analysis also uncovers explicit reactions, at the ground level, to new everyday practices of governmentality such as confiscating arms, registering the population (including women and children), requiring permits for movement, and conscripting men into the army.

The primary struggle in the Rif Mountains in the northern Spanish zone was also to protect local autonomy from the reach of the colonial state's governance practices, to resist the expansion of the colonial political field. In the early 1920s, though, Mohamed ibn ʿAbd al-Krim al-Khattabi, the son of a Waryaghar tribal chief, transformed what had been coalitional tribal anti-state resistance against the Spanish pacification into a coordinated counter-state-building project. This rural experience differed somewhat from that in the Atlas. In the Rif, notions of identity were impacted both by external pressures from the Spanish ("Christian") invader seeking to expand a state field and by ʿAbd al-Krim's local attempt to resist that process by creating an autonomous state field with its own spatial, symbolic, and classificatory dimensions. Although similar in respects to what happened in the Atlas, the horizontal and vertical identification processes among rural groups in the Rif had a unique trajectory due to the experience and memory of this alternate, albeit brief, political field.

The Field's Ordering Forces and the Politics of Moroccan Identity

For rural groups in the Atlas and Rif Mountains and other remote areas, the fundamental question during two decades of military conquest was whether or not to militarily resist the spatial extension of the colonial political field and what it meant, in religious and political terms, to submit to the Franco-Moroccan *makhzan*. For other parts of Morocco that were more rapidly and firmly brought under colonial control, including virtually all of the urban areas, the colonial political field was an established reality early on, and options concerned what to do in this space. Important Moroccan actors—including the urban Arabophone nationalist movement and the Ala-wid sovereign, Mohamed ben Youssef—accepted the spatial extension of the colonial political field in principle. From the interwar period forward, however, they began to increasingly appropriate and challenge the symbolic and classificatory logics that ordered it. These struggles for control of the field politicized Moroccan identities and had important ramifications for specific marginal groups over whom these battles were waged: Berber speakers, Jews, and women.

Legitimation and Legibility: The Field's Symbolic and Classificatory Ordering Forces

The symbolic and classificatory ordering forces that shaped the colonial political field that the French and Spanish military intervention in Morocco created (and that influenced struggles over collective identity) related to the colonial state's strategies of legitimation and legibility. While most scholars who theorize the colonial state argue that a lack of concern with legitimacy is precisely what signals its exceptional dimension,[31] the evidence in French North Africa demonstrates that colonizing powers were often profoundly concerned with the question of legitimacy and made significant efforts to buttress their claims, both for external audiences and for the local population.

Prior to the colonial period, the *makhzan*'s ideological power was typically more robust than its coercive power. Local Muslim rulers (Hammoudi 1997, 1999; Geertz 1971, 44–50) embodied a combination of religious-charismatic and traditional authority (Weber 2009, 77–79). That authority conflated state and sovereign and could be routinized as symbolic capital by the thin bureaucratic apparatus of the palace. It was also ritualized through the invocation of the name of the ruler during Friday prayers throughout the empire. Periodic *mahallas*—excursions by a mobile royal court and armed guard to mediate disputes, collect taxes, and appoint local *qa'ids* (governors or tribal chiefs)—tangibly projected this power in the countryside. In addition, a form of consent was expressed through the *bay'a*, an oath of allegiance taken by both urban ulama and rural tribal leaders that acknowledged the sultan as the rightful Muslim ruler, which, in turn, functioned as a legitimating mechanism. This religious-symbolic field of influence often extended beyond the spatial field of direct state control. For example, so-called *sība* areas would often paradoxically respect the *makhzan*'s symbolic legitimacy—a testimony to the sultan's religious authority—while actively resisting the central government through military confrontation or a refusal to pay taxes.

When they intervened in Morocco in the early 1900s, the French and Spanish appropriated and reworked some of these precolonial symbolic logics to legitimate the colonial political field. One facet of this legitimacy work concerned the ideological power of the colonial state, or the explicit meaning construction the state used to justify colonial rule and to enhance this schema through "aesthetic" and "ritual" practices (Mann 1986, 22–23).

---

31. For example, in his study of variation in native policy in various units of the German overseas empire, George Steinmetz (2007, 33) recognizes the colonial state's "strong symbolic presence" but asserts it makes no "serious efforts seeking to gain legitimacy in the eyes of its subjects."

As Barkey (2008, 13) observes, empires anchor their rule in some type of "supranational ideology"—their protection of a universalist religious order (i.e., Christendom or Islam), for example, and/or the empire's fulfillment of a universalist "civilizing mission" (religious, cultural, economic, or social). This ideology is used to justify rule over "less-developed" parts of the world to the international community, the metropole, and the autochthonous populations ruled by the imperial power. Under this empire-wide legitimating ideological umbrella, however, a tremendous range of variation is often expressed at the level of the empire's subunits in how control is implemented and formally justified (reflected in the diverse terms—colony, protectorate, mandate, dominion, territory—used to label different administrative units within an empire).

In North Africa, the French first used an assimilationist form of direct rule in Algeria. They attempted to integrate the colony territorially and administratively into metropolitan France while denying Muslim *indigènes* French citizenship. Later they employed an ostensibly associationist form of indirect rule in Tunisia and Morocco that meticulously preserved the nominal sovereignty of local rulers, the Hafsid bey and the Alawid sultan.[32] These formal differences reflected the very different international diplomatic contexts in place when each of these respective units was incorporated into the French empire, metropolitan debates about the most efficient mode of colonization, and calculations about local attitudes about foreign control. This study demonstrates how the initial decision in 1912 by the French to use a protectorate form of colonial intervention in Morocco had a significant causal impact on the colonial political field's symbolic dimensions and the identity struggles that played out in it over the next four decades.

Morocco was spared colonization over the course of the European scramble for Africa in the nineteenth century because of disagreements among European powers over its fate. The dispute, known as the Morocco Question, derived from the country's strategic location on the Straits of Gibraltar, where it controlled access to the Mediterranean and thus to the Suez route to the Indian Ocean, which was so critical to the British Empire.[33] To prevent conflict, European powers refrained from direct occupation, vying instead for economic and diplomatic predominance. In the 1904 Entente

---

32. See Betts's ([1960] 2005) typology of "assimilationist" versus "associationist" forms of colonial rule. For a detailed study of how "protectorate" rule worked out in practice in Tunisia, see Lewis (2013).

33. On the diplomatic history of the Moroccan Question, see Parsons (1976). This situation represented a Moroccan corollary to the Eastern Question that the geostrategic and economic importance of the Ottoman Empire presented (Anderson 1966).

Cordiale, France and Great Britain acknowledged respective zones of control in Morocco and Egypt, removing France's major obstacle to its goal of completing an arc of imperial control in northwest Africa that stretched from Tunisia to Senegal.[34] In 1907, French troops landed in Casablanca and quickly subdued most of its hinterland on the Chaouia plain. From the east, troops under Hubert Lyautey, who had already pressed into Morocco's oases close to Algeria's southern Oranais region, occupied the border town of Oujda. The destabilizing pressure of this foreign military threat catalyzed a Moroccan civil war between the sultan, Mawlay 'Abd al-Aziz, and his brother, Mawlay 'Abd al-Hafiz, who claimed leadership of a jihad to defend Morocco's sovereignty. Hafiz defeated his brother's forces in 1908 and was recognized as the sultan in 1910 by the international signatories of the Act of Algeciras. German claims to Morocco remained an obstacle to French domination until 1911, when the French agreed to exchange a part of the Congo for control of Morocco.

By 1912, France stood poised to consolidate power in Morocco, but a struggle continued in the cabinet in Paris about how to proceed. The colonial lobby, representing French Algerian interests, pressed for a "tribes policy": taking direct control of Morocco from the east by concluding treaties with individual tribal chiefs through negotiation or, more often, by using military force. The Ministry of Foreign Affairs promoted a *"makhzan* policy," which favored preserving the Alawid dynasty and its governing apparatus. The latter option prevailed in the end (Hoisington 1995, 22–45). The French had implemented a similar strategy in Tunisia in 1881; they kept the bey nominally in power and called it a protectorate. The cabinet in Paris considered this associationist policy more diplomatically sensitive and more efficient militarily and economically. They used this protectorate mechanism of imperial incorporation for Morocco when the Moroccan sultan, Mawlay 'Abd al-Hafiz, and the French Republic's emissary, Eugene Regnault, signed the Treaty of Fes on March 30, 1912.

This approach formally preserved the indigenous governmental structure in Morocco—the sultan and the *makhzan*—and legitimized intervention as an attempt to "protect" the failing Moroccan state.[35] In the internationally

---

34. The story of increasing European economic penetration and military encroachment in the nineteenth century and the direct way the French and others undermined internal security and increased the tribal unrest due to the instability produced by this encroachment is the subject of excellent studies; see Miège (1962); Laroui (1977); Dunn (1977); Burke (1976); El Mansour (1990). For a military history of French expansion into Morocco, see Porch (1983).

35. Although the protectorate was a clear precursor to the mandate system used in the Middle East after World War I, a significant difference was that it constituted an agreement between the

recognized Treaty of Fes, the stated purpose of the protectorate (*ḥimaya*) was to "establish a stable regime founded on internal order and general security that will permit the introduction of reforms and will assure the economic development of the country" while preserving the notional sovereignty of the sultan.[36] Expressing a state-building *mission civilisatrice*, the treaty stipulated that in order to develop a modern state apparatus and economy in Morocco, the French protector could institute whatever administrative, judicial, educational, economic, financial, or military reforms it judged necessary. In their "partnership" with the Moroccan sovereign, the French pledged to safeguard the religious respect and prestige accorded the sultan, who retained control over religious institutions (*ḥabūs*, or *awqaf*), and in return the sultan ceded to the French responsibility for maintaining security and order, the right to militarily occupy Moroccan territory, and control over the country's diplomatic representation.

The protectorate framework explicitly legitimated France's colonial intervention in ideological terms as an economic and state-building civilizing mission on behalf of and in the name of the Moroccan sovereign, the sultan, at least formally transferring the precolonial legitimation structure onto the colonial political field. Another more implicit legitimation of state practices was also expressed in the field, what Bourdieu refers to as "symbolic power" or "symbolic violence." This type of legitimation involved the state's power of "official naming" (Bourdieu 1991, 242) and its capacity to "constitute the given" (170). In her work on nineteenth-century Brazil, Mara Loveman (2005) asks how states begin to accumulate this type of symbolic power when they expand into new areas. The four mechanisms she identifies—the innovation of new practices and the imitation, co-optation, and usurpation of existing ones—are applicable to protectorate Morocco, where a new colonial state used a similar combination of strategies in its first decades in an attempt to accumulate and then routinize its symbolic power by naturalizing everyday state practices (the issuance of birth certificates, travel permits, marriage registrations, building permits, etc.) that most Moroccans had never before encountered.

French government and an individual sovereign instead of being (at least theoretically) based on the principle of the self-determination. At decolonization in 1956, it is significant that the abrogation of the Treaty of Fes was again negotiated bilaterally between the French republic and the Moroccan sovereign, not the Moroccan people.

36. The French version of the Treaty of Fes was published in *L'Afrique française* 22, no. 6 (1912): 219–220.

One of the arguments this book puts forward is that the interlinked ideological and symbolic levels of legitimation expressed in the colonial political
field directly influenced the classificatory strategies, what I call the "logics
of legibility," that the colonial power used in it. This claim introduces a
critical new dimension to James Scott's (1998) concept of legibility, which
he describes as the bundle of standardizing techniques modern states use
to simplify governance tasks. I argue that instead of a uniform toolkit of
simplifying, flattening, and homogenizing policies that streamline state practices, legibility strategies are idiosyncratically determined by cultural factors linked to ideological and symbolic strategies of political legitimation:
in sum, "seeing like a state" depends on how the state wants to be seen.
While certain types of modern states clearly do tend to eradicate difference
and local particularity (for instance, liberal democracies legitimated by rights
discourses "see" individual citizens as a primary social unit shorn of kinship,
religious, and ethnic ties), colonial states had a vested interest in preserving
heterogeneous social divisions. "Seeing" like a colonial state usually entailed
preserving, codifying, and, at times, inventing, ethnic, religious, and regional
heterogeneity.[37] Beyond their perceived practical value, these divide-and-rule
tactics were justified in larger legitimating narratives of colonial intervention.

In Morocco, a protectorate imaginary drew together legitimation and legibility strategies that constituted preservationist, ethnographic, and developmentalist modes of rule. The distinctiveness of the protectorate's preservationist linkage of legitimation and legibility is put into relief by contrasting
it with neighboring Algeria, where a nonpreservationist linkage involved
assimilating Algerian territory directly into France, obliterating vestiges of its
Arab and Muslim past, and systematically marginalizing the indigenous population (Prochaska 2004; Hannoum 2008). In contrast, instead of erasing the
past in Morocco, the French assiduously tried to preserve it in various ways.
So-called associationist, indirect rule was legitimated, in part, by historically
documenting how the precolonial *makhzan* constituted a "failed state." Historical data was also catalogued to document the archetypical "traditional"
Moroccan society the colonial power was charged with protecting and preserving. Lyautey, himself a legitimist sympathizer, meticulously maintained
the *makhzan*'s traditional forms and trappings of rule and expended considerable effort to reinvigorate and, in some cases, reinvent the pomp and protocol
of the palace, including a creating new Moroccan national flag and a new

---

37. Many argue that the maintenance of "difference" was one of colonialism's distinguishing
features; see Chatterjee (1993); Young (1994, 232–34); and Steinmetz (2007).

national anthem. Because of the formal symbolic dimensions of the colonial political field, the colonial state "saw" Moroccan society, history, architecture, and culture as static entities that needed to be documented and preserved.

Paradoxically, at the same time, the French legitimized the protectorate as a developmentalist intervention that sought to modernize it economically and politically. In terms of legibility, this involved a strict classification of, and division that separated, the "traditional" native and "modern" European, a distinction Chatterjee (1993, 19) refers to more generally as the "rule of colonial difference." This traditionalizing/modernizing binary (Laroui 1974), what Rivet (1999) calls the protectorate's *"double visage,"* was expressed institutionally by creating separate "European" and "native" schools, courts, and even hospitals; by prioritizing economic investment in modern agriculture, industry, and manufacturing for the European rather than the Moroccan sector; and in urban planning, by designing and laying out cities that preserved the traditional, "native" space of the medina and constructed a modern *ville nouvelle* alongside it for the Europeans.

Equally important is how the state tried to impose principles of "vision and di-vision" (Bourdieu 1989, 19) in the "native" side of this binary. Instead of assimilating the Moroccan population into French or Arabic high cultures and thereby obliterating local heterogeneity, as one would expect of Scott's or Bourdieu's homogenizing modern state, the colonial "ethnographic state" (Dirks 2001, 43–36; Burke 2007, 2014) expended enormous energies researching, cataloguing, classifying, and codifying the ethnic, religious, class, and gender divisions that it believed needed to be preserved in Moroccan society. These logics of legibility constituted what Burke (1972) calls the "Moroccan Vulgate," a series of interrelated binaries that created a colonial ethnographic shorthand for Morocco's complex historical, political, and social realities. This involved reifying opposing Arab and Berber identities as categories of practice and mapping this ethnic binary onto political and geographic divisions that pitted the "land of government" against the "land of dissidence;" plains and coasts against mountains and deserts; and cities against the countryside.

Classification Struggles and the Political Stakes of Moroccan Identities

As French and Spanish intervention forged a new type of political field between 1912 and the early 1930s, these integrated symbolic and classificatory logics (themselves consequences of legitimation and legibility strategies) set the ground rules for the identity struggles that played out during the protectorate period. Although Bourdieu emphasizes the state's "monopoly of symbolic violence" (1999, 72–73), his concept of classification struggles (1984, 479–84) signals that although states may *aspire* to this type of monopoly, there is room from below for actors to challenge its nominative capacity to officially sanction and in some cases reinvent and reinforce social divisions in society.[38] In Morocco and other colonial contexts, the stakes of classification struggles over which groups the state should and should not recognize were intimately connected to deeper questions of political legitimacy in the field, especially as anti-colonial nationalist discourses that emphasized popular sovereignty gained traction after World War I. Questions about national identity and control of the political field forged by colonial intervention became increasingly linked over the course of the protectorate period.[39]

From the 1930s forward, emerging urban nationalists waged a classification struggle against state-sponsored policies that emphasized ethnic, religious, regional, and gendered lines of identification. As highlighted in the opening anecdote, in its initial reformist phase in the 1930s, the Moroccan nationalist movement focused on the colonial state's division between Arabs and Berbers, framing a "countervulgate" that deconstructed colonial ethnographic, historical, and territorial binaries by emphasizing a unitary Arabo-Islamic Moroccan national identity and the symbolic centrality of the sultan. Prasenjit Duara's claims about the historical specificity and relational nature of the inclusionary and exclusionary mechanisms used to define national identity are important here. He explains:

> The multiplicity of nation-views and the idea that political identity is not fixed but shifts between different loci introduces the idea that nationalism is best seen as a relational identity. In other words, the nation, even where it is manifestly not a recent invention, is hardly the realization of an original essence, but a historical configuration designed to include certain groups and exclude or marginalize others—often violently. (Duara 1995, 15)

---

38. Bourdieu (1984) originally used the concept of classification struggles in his work on the cultural dimensions of class formation and later applied it to the construction of regional and ethnic "Occitan" identity in France (1991, 221–24). Goldberg (2007; 2008, 88) has used the concept to analyze efforts to expand or contract the boundaries of citizenship in terms of welfare policies in the United States, and Gorski (2013) has applied the idea of "nation-ization struggles" to the nationalism. This study, building from Gorski's framework, is one of the first to explore how classification struggles play out in colonial contexts.

39. Beissinger (2002, 18) emphasizes the nation as a site of struggle between contested imagined communities in his study of nationalist mobilization in the aftermath of the disintegration of the Soviet Union.

Duara emphasizes that this process involves defining the national "self" in relation to a primary Other, but also that "depending on the nature and scale of the oppositional term, the national self contains various smaller 'others,'" both historical and potential (1995, 15).

In a colonial case such as protectorate Morocco, the historical configuration of the nation that urban Arabophone nationalists imagined as a category of practice during the interwar period was directly shaped by two levels of classificatory logics that the colonial state used to "define and rule" (Mamdani 2013). First, the nationalists replicated the fundamental rule of difference dividing European and native by opposing a Moroccan "national self" against a primary Other, the "Christian" French and Spanish. This "national self" was defined by transposing a precolonial religious notion of collective identity, the *umma*, or Muslim community, onto a national level of Moroccan political identity. Second, the configuration of the nation the urban nationalists defined was also directly influenced by how colonial legibility strategies had increased the political salience of ethnic and religious boundaries (Wimmer 2008, 976–78), highlighting the importance of "smaller 'others'" in Moroccan society. In the colonial political field, these classifications directly influenced what Timothy Mitchell refers to as the "making-other" involved in "distinguishing what belongs to the nation from what does not" (Mitchell 2002, 183).

Morocco's nationalist movement, from its genesis in the "Berber Crisis," challenged the colonial political field's divisionary logics and its underlying legitimacy structure by reifying a unitary religious and political framework of Arab and Muslim national identity. This move created degrees of inclusion/exclusion for various others in Moroccan society, including non-Arab and non-Muslim Moroccans. For urban nationalists, state recognition of Berber markers of group identity constituted a threat to Islam in Morocco and to the unity of the *umma*: instead of being symbolically or institutionally recognized, the ethno-linguistic (Berber) "other" was to be assimilated through state-backed educational and legal practices.

The nationalist Arabo-Islamic classification struggle also focused on the religious other (Jews) and the gendered other (women) in Moroccan society. Over the four decades of the protectorate, Morocco's Jewish religious minority became caught between pressure to assimilate into French culture, Zionist efforts to mobilize Jewish nationalism, and attempts by Morocco's Arabo-Islamic nationalist movement to ensure their loyalty. While French metropolitan actors and protectorate officials struggled over whether or not this population should be naturalized, Zionist activists lobbied for a greater ability to organize immigration to Palestine. Parallel debates played out on the Moroccan side about the quandary of the position of Moroccan Jews in the nation: were they *dhimmi* (protected but second-class members of Muslim society), subjects of the sultan, or fellow citizens with the same rights and duties in the Moroccan nation? Struggles about identity also unfolded in Morocco's Jewish community, highlighting the ambiguity of their position vis-à-vis these three competing loyalties, each of which became increasingly problematic in the last decades of the protectorate because of the Vichy government's anti-Semitic laws, increasing Arab-Jewish tensions related to the establishment of the state of Israel in 1948, and the intensification of the North African anti-colonial struggles in the 1950s.

Gender was at the crux of identity struggles over the legitimation and legibility logics of the colonial political field because it undergirded its symbolic and classificatory structure. In legal and educational practices, the colonial state used women's status to differentiate ethnic and religious groups and as an index of "native" social progress (or backwardness). On the Moroccan side, urban nationalists and later King Mohamed V responded by actively engaging the Woman Question themselves, instrumentalizing gender to challenge these classifications and legitimate their own claims against the colonial state. They justified their call for the unification of a single legal system for "Arab" and "Berber" Muslim Moroccans by pointing out the superior rights shari'a afforded women compared to the Berber customary courts the French maintained. The nationalists and the king also challenged the developmentalist justification for colonial intervention by championing expanded modern educational opportunities for girls. Like Morocco's Jews and Berber-speaking groups, Moroccan women (elite and non-elite, urban and rural) actively engaged in trying to shape these debates.

Along with religion, ethnicity, gender, and territory, the creation of a colonial political field and subsequent interactions in this field politicized another final pillar of Moroccan identity: the Alawid monarchy. Although the endurance of Morocco's Alawid dynasty (it has been in power since the 1660s) is assumed as a given in nationalist historiography and the discourse of the post-independence Moroccan state, it is actually a surprising outcome. Almost no other similar ancien régimes survived both colonization and decolonization in the Middle East and North Africa.[40] The fact that Morocco's dynasty did

---

40. Dynastic rulers in Tunisia, Libya, Egypt, Ottoman Turkey, and Iraq were ousted before or soon after the nationalist struggle for independence. Precolonial indigenous governmental structures in Algeria were obliterated during the 132 years of French colonialism. Oman and (Trans)Jordan are two other anomalies of dynasties that survived colonization. Like the French in Morocco, the British in Oman used the centuries-old Al-Said dynasty to buttress the legitimacy of their de facto rule over

presents a striking, if underappreciated, historical anomaly that this study seeks to explain by plotting its contingent trajectory against the background of the colonial political field. At an initial critical juncture of the creation of the field, the monarchy was preserved by the French decision to implement a protectorate form of colonial rule. From that point forward, the sultan was both constrained and enabled by the formal legitimization framework of this political field, which was nominally under his sovereignty. Over the course of the protectorate, contention among colonial and nationalist actors over these logics, a struggle that eventually the sultan–cum–king himself actively engaged, transformed the monarchy's political role in the field.

The central actor in this story is Mohamed V, who evolved from sultan at his accession to the throne in 1927 to king by his return from exile in 1955. Having charted a careful course in the 1930s between the protectorate authorities and the emerging Moroccan nationalist leadership, Mohamed V asserted himself as a major player after World War II, expanding his autonomy and actively seizing the mantle of national symbol the nationalists had cultivated. By the early 1950s, tensions with the residency culminated in a rupture of the protectorate formula and the exile of Mohamed V in August 1953 to Madagascar. After two years of intensifying urban and rural revolt in Morocco, the French brought the king back to Morocco in November 1955. During the postcolonial transition period from the abrogation of the Treaty of Fes in 1956 to Mohamed V's death in 1961, the monarchy, unlike virtually all of its other peers, was able to consolidate its control over the spatial, symbolic, and classificatory dimensions of the post-protectorate Moroccan political field.

Methodology and Data Sources

Instead of privileging colonial or local mechanisms, this book traces the forces that impacted Morocco's politics of identity back to interactions that occurred during the colonial period, using a field analysis that describes the space in which these took place and the forces in that space that influenced what was at stake in struggles over identity. As a case for examining these processes, Morocco presents a rich array of internal variation (Snyder 2001; Kalyvas 2006). It featured multiple zones and subzones of international

---

the sultanate, whereas in Jordan, the country itself and the Hashemite ruling family were largely a creation of British postwar policy. The Saudi dynasty in Arabia and those recognized in the Trucial States in the Persian Gulf, though not formally colonized, were within Britain's informal zone of imperial influence in the Middle East and benefited from more and less indirect British support.

control in a single colonial unit, more and less direct colonial rule in civilian and military territories, a spectrum of ethnolinguistic and cultural differentiation and similarities in the population, and a variety of armed and nonviolent responses to colonial intervention in rural and urban areas. In addition, the processes this study focuses on were telescoped during a relatively brief period of colonial intervention, just four and a half decades, magnifying their effects. These factors make Morocco not only interesting in and of itself but also a valuable empirical context in which to work out a field-based specification of more general processes related to the politicization of collective identities in colonial contexts. This approach, instead of predicting outcomes, which vary depending on the contingently defined organizing forces of a given field and interactions that play out over time in it, offers a comparative framework for historical analysis that can be extended to examine variation in empires (i.e., different units in the French or Spanish empires) or among them (looking at different trajectories in cases of British, Dutch, and French indirect rule).

This book does not attempt, then, to provide a comprehensive history of protectorate Morocco. Instead, it focuses on describing the creation, construction, and expansion of a colonial political field over a time period that extended from the initial French and Spanish military incursions in 1907 through the completion of pacification operations in the early 1930s, during which the colonial state defined Moroccan territory and extended its reach in it. I then select specific sites (rural and urban, French and Spanish zones) in this field, at different points in time (during its construction from the 1910s to the 1930s and, after its completion, from the 1930s to the 1950s) and involving diverse actors (colonial civilian and military officials, tribal groups, urban elites, religious minorities, women, and the monarchy) in order to qualitatively analyze how the multidimensional identity-related processes described above politicized Moroccan identities during the protectorate period. One of my methodological priorities is to not only trace the identification discourses of the elite (colonial administrators or urban nationalist ideologues) but also to incorporate voices from non-elite groups (including rural Berber speakers, women, and Jews) that are virtually silent in the existing historiography.

This framework required me to gather a wide range of primary data sources in Arabic, Berber, and French that relate to the field's spatial and ordering dimensions and, more importantly, that illuminate the identity-related struggles that played out in it. The following chapters synthesize an extensive amount of more traditional archival data including Arabic and French official and unofficial print sources such as newspapers, journals, books, pamphlets, petitions, posters, administrative decrees, police and military intelligence files, personal correspondence, ethnographic studies, and official reports. They also incorporate more unique, less-traditional sources, including an extensive archive of Berber poetry from the period collected across a wide geography, nationalist songs used in protests, anti-colonial graffiti painted on medina walls, photographs, and oral interviews. In Morocco, I gathered documents from various archives in Rabat including the Bibliothèque nationale, the Institut royal de la culture Amazigh, La Source, the Allal al-Fassi Archive, the Haute commission aux anciens résistants et anciens membres de l'Armée de libération, and the Bibliothèque Royale Hassaniya. In Fes, I collected material at the Bibliothèque Al-Qarawiyin; in Tetouan at the Daoudiyya Archive, the Bibliothèque générale et archives, and the Bennouna family library; and in Casablanca at the Musée du judaïsme marocain. I also conducted oral interviews in Rabat, Fes, and the High Atlas village of Aghbala. In France, I collected materials in Paris from the Service historique de la Défense at the Château de Vincennes, the diplomatic archives at the Quai d'Orsay (now moved to La Courneuve), the Fond Ninard at the Institut du monde arabe, the Académie des sciences d'outre mer, and the archives of the Alliance Israélite Universelle. In Aix-en-Provence, I accessed documents at the Centre des archives d'outre mer and the Fond Arsène Roux at the Maison méditerranéenne des sciences de l'homme. And in Nantes, I used the extensive official collection of protectorate archives at the Centre des archives diplomatiques.

Organization

The book's structure corresponds to the three dimensions of the colonial political field. The first two chapters examine the field's spatial formation and organizing forces, and latter chapters address the battles over identity that played out in it. While there is overlap among the sequences through which these three dimensions of the field were expressed, the following chapters proceed in a roughly chronological order, extending a few years before the protectorate's creation with the signing of the Treaty of Fes in 1912 and after its dissolution with the treaty's abrogation in 1956.

Chapter 1 looks at how colonial intervention forged a protonational territorial space in Morocco. It first explores the physical and human geography of state building in Morocco, contrasting precolonial and colonial conceptions of the state's territorial reach, then examines how the French and Spanish in their respective zones moved in stages from goals of limited to total military control. The chapter highlights how the completion of total pacification by the central government in the early 1930s constituted a historic watershed in the state's achievement of an unprecedented territorial monopoly on the use of force. It also analyzes the tactics, technologies, and organizational strategies employed in these campaigns.

Chapter 2 examines the symbolic and classificatory forces in play that set constraints and opportunities for both colonial and Moroccan actors in the field. Through a tour of the Palais du Maroc exhibit at the 1931 International Colonial Exposition outside Paris, it explores the path-dependent effects of the initial French decision to employ (at least formally) an indirect mode of rule in Morocco. It analyzes the intertwined logics of legitimation and legibility that formed this "protectorate" *imaginaire* and how these influenced the colonial state's representational work and administrative practices, which were expressed in specific ethnographic, preservationist, and developmentalist modes of colonial rule.

The next chapters explore how notions of collective identity were transformed as various elite and non-elite Moroccan actors negotiated the creation of the colonial political field. I first address the experience of rural Berber-speaking groups of the Atlas and Rif Mountains, who bore the brunt of violence during the two decades of military conquest. Chapter 3 thus examines anti-colonial struggle in the Atlas highlands from 1911 to 1934. That resistance attempted to preserve the historic autonomy of these so-called *sība* areas and rejected the legitimacy of the expanding "Christian" colonial state. While these groups have typically been discussed from the perspective of an external French ethnographic and Moroccan Arab nationalist classificatory gaze, this chapter draws on a remarkable archive of Tamazight (Berber) poetry composed during the early protectorate period to explore their own perspectives. It addresses how collective identity and territoriality were re-imagined through this tumultuous period of anti-state resistance and eventual submission to the Franco-Moroccan *makhzan*.

Chapter 4 turns to a second variation of struggle against the spatial expansion of the colonial political field: the construction by the Riffi tribal leader Abd el-Krim of an autonomous rival political field to block Spanish pacification operations in the early 1920s. This chapter examines how rural Moroccan actors mobilized material and symbolic resources in their construction of the short-lived Rif Republic. It traces their remarkable military success in maintaining an autonomous state field and the Rif Republic's ultimate demise in the face of overwhelming French and Spanish military force in 1926. Like the previous chapter, it uses local primary sources to reconsider how these multidirectional processes of state building (externally from the Spanish and internally from Abd el-Krim) catalyzed horizontal and vertical identification processes related to the political, tribal, and religious dimensions of identity among communities in northern Morocco.

The next section shifts the focus away from the countryside and examines how identity processes played out among urban populations. Chapter 5 analyzes the emergence of a city-based anti-colonial nationalist movement in the wake of the 1930 "Berber Crisis." In its initial reformist phase, this movement directed its energies against the colonial state's ethnographic division between Arabs and Berbers. This chapter analyzes how nationalists defined a unitary Arabo-Islamic configuration of Moroccan identity through print and nonprint campaigns against colonial classificatory logics. It also highlights the strategic move the nationalists made during this formative period to subvert the formal symbolic rules of colonial strategic action by using the Treaty of Fes to press the French to honor the sultan's sovereignty rights. The latter part of this chapter examines the nationalists' shift toward the goal of independence after World War II.

The next chapters focus on two other groups in Moroccan society that were at the nexus of classification struggles. Chapter 6 examines how the Jewish religious minority, caught in the colonial political field between competing pressures, faced the choice of assimilating into French culture, emigrating to Palestine, or staying and struggling for Morocco's independence. This chapter examines state-based processes of classification and identification, including the colonial state's maintenance of precolonial legal and educational structures of differentiation, debates among the administrators about the eligibility of Jews to fight for the French in both world wars, and the ambiguities of Moroccan Jews' exceptional legal status during the Vichy period. It also focuses on society-based processes, including external identification debates among Moroccan nationalists and leaders of the community about the religious minority's tenuous position in homogenous definitions of the "nation" and internal processes in the community as tensions mounted inside and outside of Morocco from the 1930s to the 1950s.

Chapter 7 assesses the centrality of gender for the colonial state's attempts to maintain ethnic and religious social divisions, the nationalist struggles to redefine Moroccan identity, and Mohamed V's active engagement with the Woman Question in the 1940s. This study draws upon archival sources that illuminate how the colonial state's classificatory schema—how it "saw" different ethnic and religious identities in Moroccan society—was largely expressed in gendered legal and educational practices. The nationalists and later King Mohamed V similarly focused on women's status in their own classificatory and symbolic struggles in the colonial political field. In addition to highlighting external processes of identification in which gender played a central role, this chapter examines how elite and non-elite urban and rural Moroccan women worked actively to shape the identity politics of the protectorate period.

The last two empirical chapters turn to the final important actor to influence the politics of Moroccan identity in the protectorate political field: the Alawid monarch, Mohamed V. Chapter 8 examines Mohamed V's trajectory and shifting role between his accession to the throne in 1927 and his return from exile in 1955. This chapter charts how the king skillfully navigated between the French authorities and the urban Arab nationalists (both of whom sought to use the monarchy to legitimate claims in the colonial political field) to emerge in the postwar period as the central player in the independence struggle. His increasingly vociferous campaign for Moroccan autonomy led to his exile to Madagascar in 1953. But in 1955, the symbolic capital Mohamed V had amassed as a nationalist hero contributed to the French decision to bring him back from exile so he could broker the decolonization process. Chapter 9 assesses how the king survived decolonization and isolates the mechanisms through which the palace was able to reinforce its control in the Moroccan political field that emerged at independence.

The book's conclusion addresses the broader historiographical and theoretical implications of this case study and briefly discusses how a field approach can explain identity politics in other cases of colonial intervention. It also draws connections between the colonial period and the present in the Moroccan case, assessing how colonial legacies continue to influence struggles over the territorial, religious, ethnic, and gendered components of Moroccan identity in the post-protectorate national political field.

❧ CHAPTER 1

The Space of the Colonial Political Field

When the Treaty of Fes was signed in March 1912 by the French emissary, Eugene Regnault, and the Moroccan sultan, Mawlay ʿAbd al-Hafiz, very little territory of the Sharifian empire that the French were ostensibly taking under their "protection" was directly under any form of state control. Since the death in 1894 of Mawlay Hassan, the sultan who had reconsolidated a level of *makhzan* authority through administrative and military reforms in the 1870–1880s, external economic and military pressures (including creeping territorial expansion into Morocco by France and Spain) had exacerbated internal tensions that debilitated the Moroccan state's ability to exert control in the countryside and even in major cities. These tensions led to a civil war between Hassan's heirs and rival constituencies in 1907–1908.

Although the French had become firmly ensconced on the Atlantic coast and on the eastern border at Oujda since entering the country in 1907, they were nearly overwhelmed by various Moroccan challengers in the interior in the summer of 1912. In the center, they faced a coordinated attack on Fes from nearby Middle Atlas tribes. In the south, Ahmed al-Hiba, a charismatic leader who proclaimed himself sultan in Tiznit, rallied a popular jihad, pushed north over the High Atlas, and occupied Marrakesh in August. Superior firepower enabled the outnumbered French forces to overcome both threats, but at the end of the year, they still controlled little territory beyond the coasts and the primary interior cities of Marrakesh and Fes. For the newly appointed French resident general, Hubert Lyautey, the precariousness of France's foothold in Morocco made pacification the immediate priority.

These operations forcefully expanded the space of the colonial field over nearly two decades (1907–1934), a process that defined a new form of territorial, state-governed, Moroccan political space. In this chapter, I contextualize the impact of colonial military intervention by examining cycles and strategies of state formation and forms of state and nonstate political space in precolonial Morocco. The initial stages of French and Spanish pacification replicated aspects of these prior notions of limited territoriality, allowing for the coexistence of state-governed and self-governed zones. By the 1920s, however, the goal had shifted to total conquest, first for the Spanish and then for the French. When the last pacification operations were completed in 1934 in the far south, this policy had forged a radically new type of political field in Morocco in which a state exercised an unprecedented level of military control in a cartographically defined territorial unit. The last section of the chapter surveys the technologies, military tactics, and organizational policies used through these stages of military conquest, including the colonial powers' co-optation of the military potential of rural groups through the forced or voluntary recruitment of mostly Berber-speaking tribesmen into the colonial army.

State and Nonstate Political Space in Precolonial Morocco

The Physical Geography of State Building in Morocco

One of the historic dilemmas of state formation in Morocco is the challenge posed by its geography (see Map 2). Slightly larger than California, Morocco, like other Mediterranean landscapes, contains a wide range of topographies and climates in close proximity. Morocco's major physical feature is its mountains. A series of three Atlas ranges—the arid Anti-Atlas, the snow-covered High Atlas (which reach 4,165 meters/13,665 feet at Jbel Toubkal), and the cedar-forested Middle Atlas—transverse the country diagonally from the southwest to the northeast. A fourth range, the Rif, stretches like a crescent along the Mediterranean coast; its peaks exceed 2,000 meters/6,500 feet. The mountains divide the Atlantic coast and the central plains of Africa's northwest corner from the Saharan desert to the south and southeast. Precipitation falls as rain on the coasts and plains and as rain or snow on the mountains. It then runs back through several rivers to the Atlantic Ocean and, via the Moulouya River, to the Mediterranean Sea.

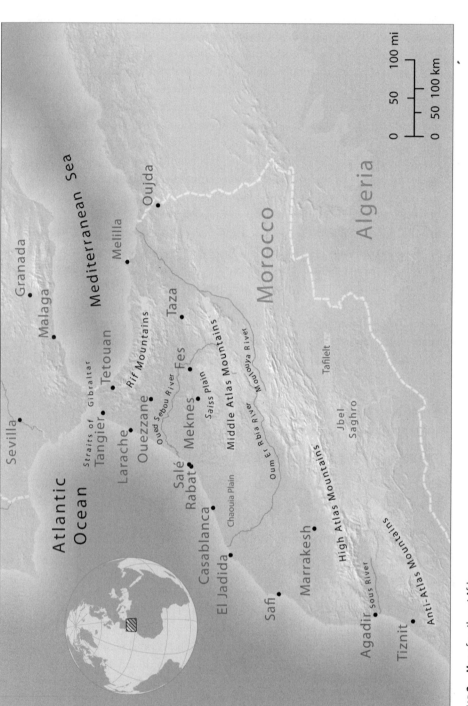

MAP 2. Map of northwest Africa

This geography has structured recurrent relations between state and society in Moroccan history. Certain regions are physically more accessible and
thereby more "legible" (Scott 1998; 2009, 29–33) to state-based governance
while others are much less so. The close physical proximity and dynamic
tension between these two ideal types of state and nonstate political space
constitutes one of North Africa's best-known features. A generation of
scholars has rightly deconstructed the simplistic colonial binary between the
so-called land of government (*blad al-makhzan*) and the so-called land of dissidence (*blad al-sība*) and the overlaying ethnic, cultural, and political stereotypes of this binary. These studies demonstrate through empirical evidence
that a spectrum of cultural, economic, and political relations was historically
expressed between tribes and the central government (see Lahbabi 1958;
Berque 1974; Burke 1976; Pennell 1991; and Hart 2001, 18–19). But a distinction between state governance and self-governance remains analytically
important, as these were viable options for multiple groups in North African
societies up until the colonial period.

Physical constraints such as topography, geography, and resources had a
huge impact on the relative leverage and autonomy different actors had in
their dealings with the central government. State governance was typically
most easily consolidated in the lowland areas, where taxable, fixed agricultural goods such as grains, olives, and wine were produced and military force,
through cavalry and infantry, could much more easily be projected. The
highlands and more remote desert areas usually remained much more autonomous from the tax-gathering and conscription activities of the *makhzan*.
These constituted fluctuating zones of nonstate, or self-governed, space. In
some of these more autonomous regions, transhumant practices including
the herding of highly mobile livestock helped groups evade taxation. In the
High Atlas, where Berber-speaking tribes lived in settled villages and engaged
in permanent cultivation, elevation protected them from much *makhzan*
interference. "*Makhzan*" and "*sība*" were by no means hermetically sealed
or necessarily antagonistic, though; areas of Morocco under state control and
more autonomous regions had dense cultural, economic, and even political
and military ties.[1] The interaction between social groups in these proximate
state and nonstate zones is, in fact, what patterned episodic cycles of state
formation in North Africa, particularly in Morocco.

---

1. Burke (1976, 13) writes of these connections: "There was in fact a wide variety of the kinds
of relations which tribes could have with the *makhzan*, from full-fledged acceptance of government
rule, to the exchange of letters, the periodic sending off embassies to court, the supply of troops at
moments of external threat, and the occasional contribution of gifts at the principal Muslim festivals."

Spatial Scales of Islamic Dynastic State Building

The area that constitutes modern Morocco has historically come under two modes of state-based rule: 1) as a periphery of a Mediterranean- or Middle East–based empire (i.e., the Romans, Byzantines, Umayyads, Abbasids); and 2) as the center of various-sized political units, from smaller regional kingdoms to empires that encompassed North Africa and the Iberian Peninsula (see Map 3).[2] External empires occasionally encompassed parts of Morocco but rarely administered them directly. Outside coastal enclaves and a few interior cities, most of the country remained politically autonomous from Phoenician/ Carthaginian or Roman rule. The rapid western expansion of Arab armies in the seventh century CE that reached the Atlantic and crossed over to conquer much of the Iberian Peninsula introduced Muslim rule to North Africa, but eastern-based Islamic empires, including the Umayyads (whose capital was in Damascus) and the Abbasids (whose capital was in Baghdad) exercised only limited control in the Maghrib. After Berber resentment about discriminatory taxation practices fueled Kharijite revolts against Umayyad rule in the eighth century, Morocco never again came under the rule of an external Islamic empire.

A second mode of state control began in the ninth century CE with the advent of the first Morocco-based states influenced by Islam. In the Tafilelt oasis system, a succession of Sufrid Kharijite dynasties, the Midrari and then the Maghrawa, were founded in the trans-Saharan trade center of Sijilmasa (Love 2010). On the Atlantic coast, Salih bin Tarif established the Barghawata confederation, which lasted until the eleventh century.[3] In the center of the country, a Muslim dynasty was founded in the late eighth century by Idriss ibn Abdullah, a descendant of the Prophet Mohamed's cousin and son-in-law, 'Ali, and daughter, Fatima, who fled Umayyad persecution in Arabia and found refuge among the Berber Awraba tribe near Volubulis. Under 'Ali's son, Idriss II, the city of Fes became a center of commerce and Islamic learning, especially after the arrival of refugees from al-Qayrawan in Tunisia and Al-Andalus (Spain). At its height, the influence of the Idrissid kingdom extended north to the Rif, east to Tlemcen, and south into the High Atlas. As the first "orthodox" Muslim dynastic state, the Idrissids are typically viewed in Moroccan historiography as the country's founders.

---

2. For longue-durée political history of North Africa, see Abun-Nasr (1973, 1987). On Morocco, see Rivet (2012).

3. Salih bin Tarif founded a syncretic religion that combined Christian, Jewish, and animistic practices and relied on a Berber-language holy book influenced by the Qur'an. On the perceptions and interactions between the "heretical" Barghawata and other "orthodox" Moroccan Islamic dynasties, see Iskander (2007).

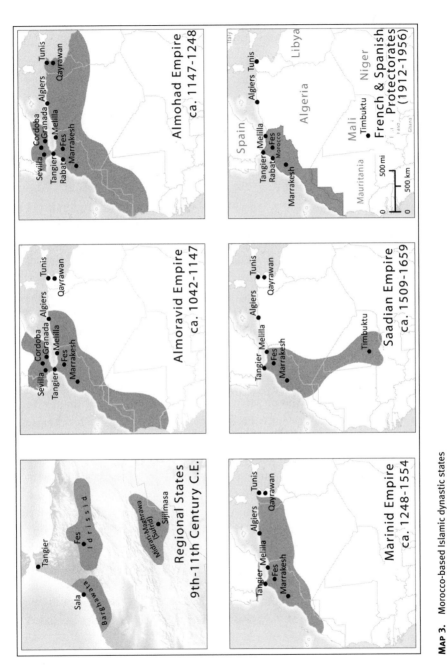

MAP 3. Morocco-based Islamic dynastic states

The scale of the next phase of Islamic state building increased dramatically from local kingdoms to large-scale regional empires. During the eleventh to the fourteenth centuries, three great Morocco-based empires, the Almoravids (1042–1147), the Almohads (1147–1248), and the Marinids (1248–1554), consolidated control over virtually all of the settled areas of the western Mediterranean, including the Iberian Peninsula and all of North Africa west of Tripoli. The Almoravids (al-Murabitun) were a confederation of Sanhaja, Berber-speaking tribes from Mauritania that were unified by a puritanical, revivalist movement led by Ibn Yasin that combined personal piety and military action. They founded the city of Marrakesh around 1070 just north of the High Atlas Mountains, and under the military leader Ibn Tashfin used superior cavalry against the Barghawata confederation on the Atlantic coast. Called to Al-Andalus by the *ta'ifa* (party) kings to aid in the fight against Christian expansion, they extended control over much of the Iberian Peninsula. The Almovarids were ousted a century later by another tribal confederation that originated in the Atlas uplands above Marrakesh. The Almohads (al-Muwahidun) were motivated by another religious reformer, Ibn Tumart, who galvanized a puritanical movement among the Masmuda and neighboring Berber-speaking tribes and attacked the Almovarids for theological and moral laxity. After Ibn Tumart's death, his second in command, 'Abd al-Mu'min, took Taza, Ceuta, Fes, Meknes, and Sale in 1140–1041 and returned to capture the Almoravid capital of Marrakesh in 1147. He then expanded Almohad control north to Al-Andalus and east to Tunisia. An efficient state-builder, 'Abd al-Mu'min ordered a survey of the empire to streamline the taxation system, oversaw infrastructure projects such as irrigation development, and developed sugar and cotton production in the Souss Valley.[4]

In the mid-thirteenth century, the Almohads fell to the Marinids (Banu Marin). This dynasty differed from the previous two dynasties in that it did not originate in revivalist or reformist movement but rather as a tribal group in Morocco's southeast region. The Marinids, using Fes as their capital, controlled a territory that extended east to Tunisia at its zenith in the thirteenth century. However, in contrast to their predecessors, they largely refrained from intervening in Spain. Their inability to forestall the sixteenth-century expansion of the Portuguese on the Atlantic coast led to a crisis of legitimacy and the ultimate collapse of the dynasty, which was replaced by the Fes-based Wattasids in 1472.

---

4. On Almohad state-building see Fromherz (2010).

A "sharifian"[5] phase of Moroccan state formation began in the sixteenth century in response to the threat of Christian expansion on Morocco's coasts (Berque 1982). In contrast to the previous three empires, which spanned across much of North Africa and the Iberian Peninsula, these kingdoms expanded and contracted over an area roughly equivalent to modern-day Morocco. The Saadians, a dynasty that originated in the pre-Saharan Draa Valley, mobilized a jihad against the Portuguese and successfully consolidated state control from their base in Marrakesh in the sixteenth century. At their territorial zenith, after al-Mansur launched an attack on Timbuktu in 1591, the Saadians controlled lands encompassing modern-day Morocco and south across the Sahara to the Sahel. After al-Mansur's death, however, civil war, plague, and famine weakened the Saadian state. In addition, competition from the Caribbean and South American sugar industries and the diversion of the trans-Saharan gold trade to the African coast and Ottoman-controlled ports in the northeast decimated the economy.

In the 1640s, another group that claimed Sharifian descent, the Alawids, began to expand their control from the Tafilelt, another pre-Saharan oasis complex. After the death of Mawlay Rashid in 1672, his brother, Mawlay Ismail, took over leadership. Over the next five decades, he consolidated firm control in northern and central Morocco. Ismail established a vast new capital city at Meknes and built up a janissary-type army, the 'Abid al-Bukhari, by importing sub-Saharan slaves and enslaving *haratin* (free black Muslim populations) in Morocco (El Hamel 2010). Ismail established garrisons along the route from Fes to Marrakesh and repeatedly sent excursions to the south to subdue the Atlas tribes. After his death, the power of the *makhzan* waxed and waned, but subsequent Alawid rulers were able to maintain some degree of territorial control, or at least nominal sovereignty, up to the moment of French intervention by relying on a combination of 'Abid troops; *jaysh*, or army, tribes based on the plains; Arabic- and Berber-speaking tribes allied with the state; and alliances with Sufi networks in the cities and countryside.

Strategies of Islamic Dynastic State Building in Morocco

Over the course of these Morocco-based cycles of state formation, which achieved different geographic scales, a repertoire of strategies was developed to buttress the legitimacy, administrative reach, and military capacity of the

---

5. A *sharif* is a descendant of the Prophet Mohamed.

precolonial *makhzan*. Kably (1986, 1999) identifies five primary sources of authority Moroccan dynastic states used to create legitimacy, often in tandem with each other: 1) Sharifianism, a hereditary charismatic authority based on descent from the Prophet Mohamed; 2) religious reformism, an ideological authority based on purifying and renewing the *umma*; 3) tribal solidarity, relying on kinship ties; 4) Maliki Sunnism, state support for the Maliki school of Islamic jurisprudence (the most widespread of the four principle Sunni legal traditions in the Maghrib); and 5) jihad, tying legitimacy to the successful defense of the Muslim community from external Christian powers or internal purification of "heterodoxy." Nomenclature reveals a cleavage between the ideologically oriented dynasties, for whom internal jihad against dissident and/or heretical factions was an important criterion of legitimacy, and the ancestor-oriented dynasties, for whom descent from the Prophet Mohamed conferred legitimacy. The former include the Almoravids (named after the *ribat*, a religio-military stronghold) and the Almohads (named after the theological tenet of God's unity), while the latter include the Idrissids, Saadians, and Alawids. The Marinids did not claim sharifian descent, but they indirectly cultivated this pillar of legitimacy by patronizing the Idrissid shrine in Fes.

Table 2   Sources of legitimization for Moroccan Islamic dynastic states

	SHARIFIANISM	REFORMISM	TRIBAL SOLIDARITY	MALIKI SUNNISM	JIHAD
Idrissids (ninth–tenth centuries)	X				
Almoravids (tenth–eleventh centuries)		X	X	X	X
Almohads (eleventh–twelfth centuries)		X	X		X
Marinids (thirteenth–fifteenth centuries)	X		X	X	X
Saadians (sixteenth–seventeenth centuries)	X		X	X	X
Alawids (seventeenth century to present)	X		X	X	X

The *makhzan*'s symbolic reach often outdistanced its "infrastructural power," or "institutional capacity . . . to penetrate its territories and logistically implement decisions" (Mann 1993, 59), which was limited by the friction (Scott 2009, 43–50) created by Morocco's geography and topography. The legitimization mechanisms provided in the Moroccan Islamic repertoire—charismatic religious authority, or *baraka* (Geertz 1971, 44–50); sharifian descent; leadership based on jihad; the invocation of the name of the Muslim ruler in Friday prayers; and the *baʿya* oath of allegiance to the sultan the ulama and urban and rural notables took—functioned well in both state-governed and self-governed spaces in Morocco. Areas of political *sība*, or nonstate space, would thus paradoxically usually still respect the sultan's symbolic legitimacy, even when rebelling against the central government through military confrontation or a refusal to pay taxes. An example of this is the honored treatment afforded the sharifian Alawid sultan, Mawlay Slimane, when he was captured during a battle between his *makhzan* forces and the Ait Oumalou Berbers near Tadla in the Middle Atlas in May 1819. As El Mansour relates (1990, 189), the Ait Oumalou tore his tent into pieces and distributed among the tribes "as an invocation of his spiritual power." After three days of captivity, the Ait Oumalou returned the sultan to Meknes and set him free.

In contrast to the reach of its legitimization framework, the administrative capacity of the Moroccan state—its ability to collect taxes, regulate trade, and govern territory—fluctuated widely over time. Only two types of taxes on Muslims are recognized in canonical Islamic law, the *zakat* tax on livestock and the *ushur* tax on the harvest. (Non-Muslims, both Jews and Christians, are required to pay the *jizya* tax.) To supplement revenue from these two taxes, the *makhzan* sometimes imposed a *maks* tax on goods entering the city gates, an extralegal tax (that had to be legitimized in Islamic terms) that was often the catalyst for urban protest.[6] Multiple Moroccan dynasties tried to increase revenue by encouraging and collecting duties on international trade through Tangier or Atlantic ports and, in the sixteenth to the nineteenth

---

6. In 1873, resentment in Fes against the *maks*, which had been instituted because the *makhzan*'s customs revenues were being seized to pay Morocco's indemnity to the Spanish, led to open revolt by the artisan class and the ulama, who refused to offer the new sultan, Hassan, their *bayʿa* (oath of allegiance) until the tax was abolished. Hassan responded by unleashing his cannon and his troops on the city (Laroui 1977, 292–94; Pennell 2000, 95–96). Urban protest erupted again in 1907, with ʿAbd al-Hafiz's succession, over these same tensions (Burke 1976, 114–16). On urban revolts in Morocco, see also Clement (1992).

centuries, by periodically sanctioning privateering against European ships and slaving (Pennell 2001).

Morocco had no single central metropolitan hub (a London, Cairo, Paris, or Istanbul). Instead, the government alternated between the two primary historic capitals, Fes and Marrakesh, which were primary urban centers of culture, trade, and governance. The *makhzan*'s administrative apparatus consisted of a council of ministers, or viziers, appointed by the sultan. The sultan also personally appointed the qadis (Islamic judges), *walis* and *qa'ids* (city or provincial governors), *amins* (tax collectors), and *muhtasibs* (official inspectors), who projected the *makhzan*'s authority by administering justice. The state patronized an Islamic educational establishment that included Al-Qarawiyin University in Fes, Yusufiyah University in Marrakesh, and numerous madrasas to supply this literate class of government functionaries.

The recurrent dilemma for the precolonial *makhzan* was how to ensure the military power necessary to project its authority. Tribal military strength was often critical during the initial phase of state building, but eventually it would prove to be unstable. Facing dissent, dissatisfaction, and decline in their own kinship networks, ruling families turned to a variety of other sources, including 1) paying *jaysh* tribes to fight for the *makhzan* by giving them rights to usufruct and tax exemption (sometimes forcibly resettling them on "fertile" lands);[7] 2) creating a janissary type of professional slave army that was personally loyal to and dependent on the sultan; 3) hiring mercenaries, often Christians from Iberia; 4) calling up an urban militia (*rumat*) for special expeditions; and, 5) organizing a professional salaried army. A chief way for the *makhzan* to project power was in a *mahalla* or *haraka*, a mobile armed court that circulated through Moroccan territory repressing rebellious tribes, extracting taxes, mediating conflict, and appointing government agents (Gershovich 2000, 44–45). Through the *mahalla*, the *makhzan* extended its authority into territories where it had no regular bureaucratic capacity by projecting brute force or through diplomatic skills, playing tribes off of each other (El Mansour 1990, 7). These strategies at times enabled the

---

7. Both Arabic- and Berber-speaking tribes were used as *jaysh*, or military, tribes. The Marinids transferred the Sefiane tribe from Tamesna (along the Atlantic coast south of Rabat) to the Gharb (the fertile plains to the northeast of Rabat), while the Saadians and Alawids both relied on Ma'quil Arabs from the Sahara to subdue to the north and moved *jaysh* tribes from around Marrakesh and Fes to secure the Sahara (El Mansour 1990, 8–9). Mawlay Ismail relied on Rif Berber tribes to secure Tangier and its environs after the English withdrew in 1684 (Hart 2001, 26–27). In the 1790s, early in the reign of Sultan Mawlay Sulayman, the chief of the Ait Ndhir (Beni Mtir) Berber tribe south of Meknes, Ibn Nasir al-Mtiri, served as the commander-in-chief of *makhzan* forces (El Mansour 1990, 102).

makhzan to extend its reach over a vast territory, but state-governed space was typically limited, particularly at moments of succession, when there was often a civil war.[8]

The Alawid Moroccan State on the Eve of Colonial Intervention

As heir and successor to these state-building cycles, the precolonial Alawid state ruled in a territory that had experienced expanding and contracting forms of state-based political unification for over a millennium. Within this political ecosystem, however, the precolonial *makhzan* rarely, if ever, expressed a Weberian form of territorial stateness. Instead of exercising a monopoly, it typically negotiated with a plurality of military and symbolic power holders. In the nineteenth century, the Alawids began to face increasingly direct interventions from Europeans—militarily in confrontations with the French at the Battle of Isly on the Algerian border in 1844 and with the Spanish at Tetouan in 1859–1860 and economically through European commercial expansion and the imposition of disadvantageous trade concessions, starting with the Anglo-Moroccan Treaty of 1856. From the 1870s, Hassan I (r. 1873–1894), the last effective precolonial Alawid sultan, tried to buttress the *makhzan* against these threats through diplomatic protests against abuses of the system of protections and capitulations giving Europeans and their local protégés legal and tax privileges and through attempts to modernize the Moroccan military. He hired European and Ottoman advisors to train the infantry and artillery, tried to create a professional army, and set up a fledgling arms manufacturing industry in Fes.[9] To project his authority internally, Hassan I launched large-scale expeditions, or *mahallas:* in 1882 and 1886 to the Souss Valley, in 1876 to the eastern border at Oujda, in 1889 to Tangier and Tetouan in the north, and in 1893 to the Taflilelt oasis complex in the south. The sultan also mediated his influence by patronizing regional power brokers, including a group of *qa'ids* in the High Atlas who became semi-autonomous warlords in the 1880s.

---

8. In addition to the countryside, cities revolted at times against *makhzan* rule. Fes was in open revolt against Mawlay Sulayman from 1820 to 1822 and proclaimed a rival sultan (El Mansour 1990, 184–208).

9. On Hassan's reform program see Miège (1962, 215–34) and Gilson-Miller (2013, 33–34). Parallel modernization reforms to the Ottoman *tanzimat* were carried out elsewhere in North Africa in the early nineteenth century by Mohamed Ali in Egypt and Ahmad Bey in Tunisia.

When Hassan died in 1894, his successors were unable to build upon this foundation. By the early twentieth century, the *makhzan* had extremely limited financial resources with which to counter expanding European influence in Moroccan territory. Virtually all tax revenue was seized to pay off an oppressive indemnity to Spain that had been negotiated in the wake of the 1859–1850 Spanish-Moroccan War and other debts contracted with European banks over the course of the nineteenth century. French troops had penetrated Moroccan territory on the eastern border and on the Atlantic coast, and urban and rural groups were in revolt against a sultan who had lost legitimacy because of his failure to forestall "Christian" penetration into Morocco. By 1912, these exogenous and endogenous factors had decimated the *makhzan*'s authority and state space under its control had contracted to virtually nothing.

Stages of Colonial Conquest (1907–1934)

The incursion of French and Spanish troops into Moroccan territory in 1907 initiated the construction and consolidation of a type of state-controlled, cartographically defined, territorial political field that was unprecedented in Moroccan history. The next twenty-seven years of colonial military conquest fundamentally reconfigured the precolonial political ecosystem of dynamically interacting zones of *blad al-makhzan* and *blad al-sība*, eventually shifting the balance completely toward state-based governance. This violent "enclosure movement" (Scott 2009, 5–9) eventually eliminated the potential for nonstate space, completely subduing tribal, mainly Berber-speaking groups that had historically leveraged their own military capabilities to threaten or aid the central government and incorporating them into the colonial army. By the mid-1930s, the pacification had achieved a territorial monopolization of force that the central government had never before attained, positioning colonial and Moroccan actors together in a new type of political field. In this field, territory itself—particularly divisions between French, Spanish, and international zones and ambiguities about the eastern and southern border—gained a political salience it did not have before colonial intervention.

The total pacification of Moroccan territory and the cartographic definition of these borders were not necessary or predetermined outcomes or even the initial objectives of colonial intervention. Colonial conquest proceeded in fits and starts and had long periods of stasis as authorities oscillated over whether the complete conquest of Moroccan territory was necessary or whether it was necessary to control just the economically and agriculturally valuable parts. The following sections outline the primary stages (see Map 4)

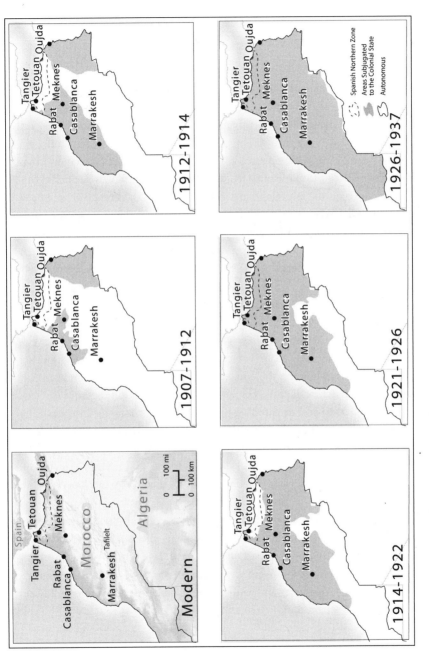

MAP 4. Stages of colonial pacification in Morocco, 1907–1934

in the nonlinear progression of military conquest in Morocco and how fundamental questions about the space of the colonial political field were negotiated.

Securing Coasts, Plains, and Cities (1907–1914)

Moroccan historian Abdallah Laroui (1993, 91) has observed that France's pre-protectorate phase of conquest consisted of opportunistic military incursions justified by various pretexts, such as the death of Dr. Mauschamp in Marrakesh (Amster 2004) and insecurity generated by the Moroccan civil war in 1907–1908. From 1907 to 1911, French forces consolidated their position inland from Casablanca on the Chaouia plain, pressed in from Colomb-Bechar in the southeastern desert, and occupied Oujda and its surrounding areas on the Algerian border. In May 1911, the French consul pressured Sultan Mawlay 'Abd al-Hafiz to invite a large French expeditionary force, including a large contingent of Moroccan *goumiers* (colonial troops), to relieve Fes, which was besieged by a coalition of Middle Atlas tribes. By the end of the summer, the French had occupied Meknes and Fes and effectively expanded their control laterally through the center of the country.

The French assumed formal responsibility for "maintaining order" in Moroccan territory in the 1912 Treaty of Fes. The pacification, which was technically done in the name of the sultan, proceeded according to the needs and capabilities of the colonial state. Right away two uprisings seriously threatened France's hold on the country. In April, Moroccan troops mutinied against their French officers in Fes, looting European businesses and the *mellah* (Jewish quarter) and threatening the rest of the medina until the uprising was put down by an artillery bombardment and a contingent of still-loyal Moroccan troops. The city was besieged again in late May by a Middle Atlas tribal confederation. It took until July for French and Moroccan troops under Colonel Henri Gouraud to break the siege and regain control of the Saiss plain. Later that summer, in August, another uprising was led in the south by Ahmed al-Hiba, who brought an army up from the Saharan Desert and occupied Marrakesh. Colonel Charles Mangin was sent south from the Chaouia region and met Al Hiba's forces at the village of Sidi Bou Outhman. French artillery and machine-gun fire decimated more than 20,000 Moroccans and broke the movement, and Al Hiba and his remaining followers withdrew south of the High Atlas to Sidi Ifni.[10]

---

10. On the Moroccan groups that mobilized during this initial period, see Burke (1976); on the French military actors and strategy, see Porch (1983).

By the end of 1912, the French had secured the Atlantic coastal plain, including the major cities (Rabat-Salé, Casablanca, Safi, Essaouira, Agadir) and the inland plains of the Gharb (northeast of Rabat), Chaouia (inland from Casablanca), Abda-Doukkala (northwest of Marrakesh), and Saiss (around Meknes and Fes). In the High Atlas Mountains and the fertile Souss Valley in the south, Lyautey and his administrators followed the precedent set by Hassan I and relied on the "grand caids" (the Glaoui, Mtouggi, and Gandafi clans) as intermediary warlords. Over the next two years, the immediate priority was to secure critical east-west links from the Atlantic coast to the Algerian border and between Morocco's major interior cities. Operations in 1912–1913 targeted Middle Atlas tribes that threatened the east-west corridor from the mountains south of Meknes and Fes and at the Tache de Taza, a vulnerable gap between the Rif and Atlas Mountains through which transport and communications ran to Algeria. At the same time, colonial units secured the Tadla plain and regions around Khenifra and Azrou that lay on the route that stretched northeast from Marrakech to Fes. By 1914, when the war in Europe put pacification operations on hold, the core lands of the historic *makhzan* had been secured by Franco-Moroccan troops.

In the northern zone under Spanish control, the first stage of pacification also involved securing and expanding coastal footholds. Like the French, the Spanish had already begun to opportunistically seize territorial control in Morocco before the formal imposition of the protectorate. In 1908–1909, the Spanish increased operations against nearby tribes in order to secure a buffer around their eastern enclave on the Mediterranean coast, Melilla. They took the Atlantic coastal port of Larache in June 1911 and pushed inland toward the Jbala range, taking the town of Alcazarqivir (Al-Qsar al-kabir). In 1912, after signing the Treaty of Fes with the Moroccan sultan, the French granted Spain a northern zone of control that stretched from Larache to just east of Melilla. In 1913, the Spanish occupied Tetouan, the primary city of the north, making it the northern capital and naming a relative of the Moroccan sultan as caliph, or designated ruler, for the northern zone. By 1914, the Spanish controlled limited zones inland from their coastal enclaves and around Tetouan but had little to no influence in the Jbala and Rif mountain regions, even though they paid regular stipends to tribal leaders in the interior.

Limited Pacification in the Middle and High Atlas (1914–1922)

During the next phase, the strategic question of total or partial pacification remained unsettled. In the French zone, the demands during World War I for manpower in Europe limited the military capacity of the colonial state:

the goal was holding rather than expanding territory. In the Middle Atlas, the Zaian (Iziyan) confederation posed a significant threat. The French took the strategic town of Khenifra in June 1914 from the powerful Zaian leader Moha ou Hammou, who simply withdrew his troops up into the mountains above the city. In November, an ill-advised sortie by an ambitious French officer, Laverdure, against a camp Hammou had set up fifteen kilometers away at the village of El Herri led to a disastrous counterattack in which over 600 French troops were killed, including Laverdure himself.[11] Despite Lyautey's initials fears the French might lose their whole position in Morocco if the revolt gained momentum, the Zaian did not press their advantage, content to remain in their Middle Atlas strongholds.

For the colonial state, the contiguous highland areas of the Middle Atlas and the central and eastern High Atlas constituted a worrisome block of nonstate space from which tribes such as the Zaian could threaten the fertile Tadla plain and critical internal communications and transportation between Fes and Marrakesh.[12] Similarly, tribes such as the Ait Segrushen in the mountains near the Taza gap threatened rail, road, and telegraph connections from the Atlantic coast through Fes to Algeria. In 1917, Franco-Moroccan *makhzan* forces were able bisect this bloc when they built a road south from Meknes that linked Azrou, Midelt, Rich, and the northern Tafilelt. Military posts were constructed along the route and sorties were regularly sent out to protect this north-south corridor.

Facing increased criticism in the early 1920s from a war-weary French parliament about the costs of military operations in Morocco, Lyautey reframed military objectives in Morocco in terms of "limited pacification." For the metropolitan audience, Lyautey emphasized the distinction between *Maroc utile* (useful Morocco) and *Maroc inutile* (useless Morocco) and pledged that "useful Morocco" would be securely under French control by 1923 (Hoisington 1995, 90). By 1922, the major tribal threats against "useful Morocco" had been subdued and Lyautey could claim that French-controlled state space had been extended to encompass the exploitable, *utile* parts of the country. Only remote pockets of autonomy, what the French labeled *zones de dissidence*, were left in the mountains and distant reaches of the desert (see figure 2).

---

11. On the incident and oral memory among the Zaian, see Gershovich (2003).

12. The authoritative military history on the "pacification" of the Atlas, written from the French perspective by one of the officers involved who later served as resident general, is Guillaume (1946). For details on the participation of Moroccan colonial soldiers (*goumiers*) and partisans in these operations, see Saulay (1985).

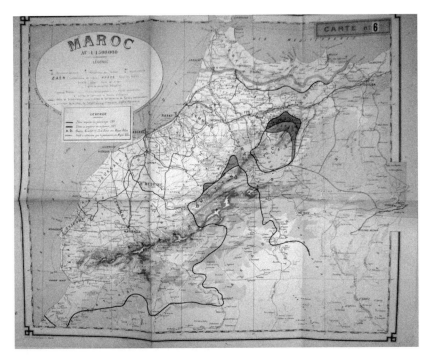

FIGURE 2. Military map indicating the progress of French pacification of Morocco in 1921. The dark lines delineate the boundary between "submitted" and "unsubmitted" zones. The shading indicates the areas that were conquered in the spring and fall. Service Historique de la Défense-Armée de la Terre, Carton 3H 308, Cabinet militaire, Bureau des Cartes.

Total Pacification of the Rif (1921–1926)

France's limited conquest of "useful Morocco" ultimately proved untenable because of developments in the Spanish zone in the mid-1920s. After World War I, during which the Spanish faced numerous tribal revolts (some fomented and financially aided by German agents), they made complete pacification in the north the priority.[13] The first goal was to eliminate the threat posed in the west by al-Raisuni (also known as al-Raisuli), a Jbala-based chief who since the 1890s had alternately served on the Moroccan and Spanish payrolls as a governor, engaged in a lucrative kidnapping operation,[14]

13. On the evolution and progress of Spain's "pacification" strategies, see Woolman (1968, 55–73) and Madariaga (1999).

14. The captives Al-Raisuni held for ransom included the British journalist Walter Harris; the Greek-American millionaire Ion Perdicaris, who published a memoir of his captivity in *Leslie's Magazine* (Perdicaris 1904); and the British military advisor to the sultan's army, Sir Harry "Caid" Maclean.

and led anti-colonial jihads. By 1919, the Spanish had neutralized al-Raisuni and subdued the region inland from Larache, including the Jbala region and parts of the Ghomara region south of Tetouan. In 1920, they pushed further into the Ghomara, facing little resistance to their occupation of the holy city of Chaouen.

The second goal of the Spanish, subduing the eastern Rif region, proved to be much more difficult. Under General Silvestre, they deployed forces southwest from Melilla in 1920 to extend control over Rif tribes. In July 1921, these lines were attacked and they collapsed. Over 14,000 troops were killed in the disastrous Battle of Anoual. Building on the momentum of military success after Anoual, Abd el-Krim, the son of a prominent Ait Waryaghar chief, mobilized a coalition of tribal forces and founded the Republic of the Rif that fall. Chapter 4 analyzes how Abd el-Krim built up his own state apparatus in order to counter Spanish attempts to expand state space into the Rif. He consolidated a territorial zone of control, created a professional army, instituted administrative and judicial structures, collected taxes, and built a primitive transportation and communications infrastructure. The Spanish were not able to regain the upper hand until 1926.

The tide turned because the French, who had intentionally (and somewhat smugly) not yet intervened in the Rif War, were finally forced to enter the conflict when Rif troops overran their defensive positions on the border just north of the Ouergha River.[15] Abd el-Krim's forces came within forty kilometers of Fes, threatened Taza, and tempted the entire northern tier of subdued tribes in the French zone to revolt. Lyautey, under whose watch the situation had deteriorated, came under withering criticism and retired after General Petain, the World War I hero, was appointed in September 1925 to take over military command. That fall, the French and Spanish launched a coordinated counteroffensive. The Spanish landed at Al Hoceima and pushed south from the coast, and the French surged across the Ouergha River to encircle and overwhelm Abd el-Krim's forces. Abd el-Krim surrendered himself to the French on May 26, 1926, and was exiled to Réunion. By 1927, pacification operations in the northern zone were complete. Many Moroccan tribesmen were incorporated into Spain's Army of Africa and in the mid-1930s played a significant role in Spain's Civil War under Spanish commanders, including Ferdinand Franco, who had also served for years in Morocco (Madariaga 1992).

---

15. On the French participation in the Rif War, see Thomas (2005, 215–17; 2008, chapter 5).

Completing Total Pacification in the French Zone (1926–1934)

After the Rif War, the French administration initially resumed the *Maroc utile* status quo, but in the late 1920s, their strategy shifted to total pacification. The reasons for this were twofold. First, the Tadla plain remained vulnerable to raids from unsubdued High Atlas tribes and groups in the Tafilelt region used the oasis as a staging ground for attacks into southeast Algeria. Second, the rising German threat in Europe increased the need to transfer troops from Morocco and elsewhere in the empire to the Rhine. French military planners set a deadline of 1933–1934 to eliminate threats and complete the conquest of Morocco.[16]

Beginning in the late 1920s, annual summer military campaigns were directed at the remaining zones of dissidence in the High Atlas, Jbel Saghro, and Anti-Atlas Mountains. In these areas, tribal groups were mobilized in a defensive jihad by charismatic leaders such as Sidi El Mekki Amhaouch in the Central High Atlas and Sidi Raho in the eastern High Atlas.[17] The French generals' strategy was to encircle the resisting tribal confederations in the High Atlas by cutting a route east from Ouarzazate across the Draa, Dades, and Todra Valleys to the northern Tafilelt and on to the border with Algeria at Bou Denib. The completion of this task in 1927 allowed them to rapidly transport troops in lorries for operations in the High Atlas to the north of the road or in the Jbel Saghro to the south. In 1932, a special command was created for the *confins marocains* (Moroccan borders), including areas on the Algerian-Moroccan border. Its mission was to occupy and put down resistance in the Tafilelt. By 1933, the last redoubts in the High Atlas had been taken by mobile units from Marrakesh and Meknes, and in 1934, the last autonomous areas in Morocco, the 'Ait Atta strongholds in the Jbel Saghro and the Anti-Atlas, were finally subdued.

---

16. The final phase (1931–1934) was recounted by the commanding general of the campaign, Antoine Huré (1952).

17. Mekki assumed the mantle of leadership after the death in 1918 of his father, 'Ali Amhaouch. His father, a marabout, had mobilized the Zaian against the French (Bidwell 1973, 141). In the early 1930s, Mekki, heir to a century of Amhaouch charismatic authority, galvanized a core group of resisting tribes, preaching imminent deliverance for the tribes holding out against the French in fulfillment of prophecies made by his ancestor. He and his followers were finally defeated in early September 1932 after an intense two-week battle at the mountain stronghold of Tazigzaout (Guillaume 1946, 340, 380–87; Peyron 2007). On Sidi Raho, see Gershovich (2000, 105).

Strategies of Colonial Conquest

Over the course of these decades of pacification operations, the French and Spanish employed a range of strategies to expand state space. Some of these replicated those used by the precolonial *makhzan* and others were new. This section examines the key components of the "Lyautey Method" of colonial conquest, *pénétration pacifique* (peaceful penetration) and the *tache de huile* (oil stain). It then focuses on the mechanisms by which the Directorate of Indigenous Affairs extended state administrative practices into the countryside in the wake of military conquest. I also consider the most significant success of the pacification of Morocco: the systematic incorporation of "dissidents," the tribal groups who most strenuously resisted the extension of this colonial iteration of state governance, into the colonial army.

Peaceful Penetration and the *Tache de Huile*

Hubert Lyautey was a high-profile champion of the associationist school in French colonial circles at the turn of the century that lauded the British and Dutch models (Betts [1960] 2005, 35–58) of indirect rule as the key to more efficiently achieving the Third Republic's imperial goals. In the 1880s and 1890s, Lyautey served under Joseph Gallieni in Indochina and Madagascar and had been greatly influenced by his mentor's method focused on military-led pacification and administration.[18] For Lyautey, *pénétration pacifique* was the key principle to colonial state building. In instructions to commanders, Lyautey stressed using every possible means before the military option:

> Political action always precedes and prepares military action, which only enters into play, *ultima ratio*, when all other means have been failed. . . . Political action comes under an infinite variety of aspects and proceeds according to different principles following the political, social, and religious populations in which it is exercised.[19]

The concept of so-called peaceful penetration was entwined with the *tache de huile* strategy. In contrast to the slash-and-burn method of population-centric total destruction Bugeaud had used a century earlier in Algeria, the *tache de huile* was supposed to combine using military force with social,

---

18. In the 1850s, Léon Faidherbe, who had served with General Bugeaud in Algeria, developed a method of less comprehensive use of violence in Senegal that enabled him to enter the region with the help of natives.

19. *Rapport* 25, quoted in Bidwell (1973, 13).

economic, and political means of enticing "dissidents" to cooperate with and submit to the central government. Over time, the zone under the control of the government, the "oil stain," was supposed to gradually spread out and incorporate neighboring dissident tribes (Hoisington 1995, 7–8; Gershowitz 2000, 30, 70–72).

To start the spread of the "oil stain," Lyautey had indigenous affairs posts built on the borders of dissident zones. These military posts included a free health clinic and a weekly market (*suq*) where the French would pay inflated prices for the livestock or other wares nearby tribes wanted to sell.[20] Ostensibly, these economic and public health benefits would entice tribes to submit, gradually expanding the area governed by the colonial state. The political strategy of peaceful penetration also involved exploiting preexisting intertribal and intratribal rivalries and antagonisms, geographically isolating dissident areas, and reducing movement and communications between pockets of resistance.

In the first decade of the protectorate, the French and Spanish both spent considerable energies and funds in attempts to co-opt local tribal leaders through whom they hoped to indirectly control territory. This approach was most successful in the French zone, where the "Grand Caids"—the Mtouggis, the Goundafis, and the Glaouis—were used to impose indirect control over the High Atlas and the Souss region. With the help of French patronage, Thami el Glaoui rose to dominate the south, creating a type of mini-state that he ruled from Marrakesh. The French found no corollaries they could use to subcontract the pacification of the middle and central High Atlas. In the northern zone, the attempt of the Spanish to incorporate tribal chiefs in their administration by paying them a stipend backfired; with no credible punitive threat, the system incentivized resistance, which chiefs used as leverage to increase their stipends.

One of the pacification's most important strategic dimensions, however, was the French military's substantial investment in transportation and communications infrastructure. Before 1912, Morocco had virtually no paved roads, no railroads, and limited port facilities. Military operations required moving large numbers of troops and equipment around the country, usually over extremely rough terrain, in order to overwhelm the highly mobile tribesmen who were accustomed to fighting in their local environs. From 1907 to 1931, the French built over 5,000 kilometers (3,100 miles) of roads

---

20. See Cruchet (1930) for an uncritical celebration of the civilizing benefits brought to the Moroccan countryside by the French "peaceful conquest."

and 588 kilometers (365 miles) of rails (Fédération Française des Anciens Coloniaux 1931).[21] These included primary arteries that linked urban centers and a vast secondary network of *pistes*, or rough tracks, over which transport lorries could move troops and equipment. Major routes built with corvéed Moroccan labor were cut through the mountains, enabling truck convoys to move troops, artillery, and heavy gunnery into position for campaigns in previously inaccessible areas and connect and resupply indigenous affairs posts built in recently subdued territory. These included the north-south corridor that was opened between Meknes and the Tafilelt in 1917 and the routes from Marrakesh through the Tizi-n-Tichka pass to Ouarzazate and through the Tizi-n-Test pass to Taroudant that was opened in 1928. In addition to roads, the French installed thousands of kilometers of telephone lines, which made instant communications between military commands possible.

Although Lyautey touted the hearts-and-minds approach, in reality, the pacification campaigns in the Atlas ranges and the Rif required intensive fighting and an overwhelming use of brutal force.[22] Often, *razzia* strategies had to be used: food supplies were cut off, agricultural infrastructure was destroyed, grain or date cultivation and harvest was prevented in the Tafilelt and other pre-Saharan oases, and livestock were targeted. After World War I, the French and Spanish deployed some of the most advanced military hardware in the world in Morocco, including artillery, automatic weapons, mechanized transport, and air power, for the purpose of colonial conquest. Airplanes gave the colonial state important advantages in terms of reconnaissance and psychological warfare. In the French zone, extensive aerial photography was used to map out the previously inaccessible reaches of the High Atlas, Anti-Atlas, and Jbel Saghro Mountains and the Saharan fringe, which helped in the planning of campaigns against these regions in the 1920s and early 1930s. In the Rif, the Spanish used chemical weapons extensively against Abd el-Krim's forces in the 1920s, dropping mustard gas from airplanes flown from Melilla (Balfour 2002). The Tamazight and Tarifit sources I discuss in chapters 3 and 4 show how aerial bombardment was a powerful tool of psychological warfare against the civilian populations the French and Spanish targeted in remote mountain regions.

---

21. By 1945, there were over 8,161 kilometers of paved roads and over 32,000 kilometers of unpaved *pistes* in Morocco (Gouvernement Chérifien 1946, 155).

22. Porch (1983, 185–88) documents how Lyautey's "method" devolved into *razzia* tactics that used brute force even in his earliest campaigns in the Sud-Oranais in 1906–1907.

Reinventing the Jaysh: Turning the
Blad al-Sība into a Colonial Army

The most critical factor for the success of the pacification, and one of its longest-lasting impacts, was the systematic incorporation of the military potential of the so-called *blad al-sība* into the coercive apparatus of the colonial state. Although both the French and the Spanish used metropolitan troops at first, one of the priorities of colonial intervention was the creation of a loyal and reliable indigenous military force. Between 1907 and the 1930s, the French and Spanish reinvented the *makhzan's jaysh* strategy, which used tax incentives and force to shore up tribal military support for the central government. Both colonial administrations integrated recently subdued tribes as paid regular units into the colonial army or into irregular forces that were given booty rights during operations against other tribes.[23]

Replicating strategies that they had used since the nineteenth century in Algeria, Tunisia, and Senegal, the French formed Moroccan units soon after subjugating the Chaouia plain in 1907. The Spanish also formed native units, the Fuerzas Regulares Indígenas, as early as 1911. After the French took direct command over *makhzan* forces in 1912, multiple categories of Moroccan troops were incorporated into the colonial army. The first level, the *goums*, were auxiliary units that at first were comprised of Arab tribesmen from the Atlantic coast and later almost exclusively of Berber-speaking tribesmen from the Middle Atlas.[24] Three or four of these, around 200 men, were grouped together to form a *tabor*, or battalion. The *goumier* troops were used in the military conquest of Morocco. They were later used abroad and saw action in World War II and in Southeast Asia. Another category was the *mokhzani* units, official troops of the Moroccan *makhzan* that were also under French command; they were used in Morocco to impose order. The final category used during the pacification were the *partisans*, irregular troops that were deployed on an ad hoc basis as the first wave sent against a "dissident" or "insurgent" tribe.

In the late 1920s, the French organized a unit called the *groupe mobile*, an "ad hoc conglomeration of regular units representing a variety of

---

23. On the little-known history of the colonial soldiers who were used to pacify Morocco and who later fought in World War II and postcolonial conflicts in Indochina and even Algeria, see Maghraoui (1998, 2002), Bimberg (1999), and Saulay (1985).

24. The first six Moroccan *goum* regiments were formed in Casablanca in 1908 (Saulay 1985, 30–31). After the signing of the Treaty of Fes, Lyautey ordered the creation of six more *goum* units. By 1924, on the eve of France's entry into the Rif War, twenty-eight units were posted on the edge of *zone de dissidence* (149), and by the end of the final "pacification" operations in Tiznit in 1934, fifty-one *goums* had been formed (456).

arms (infantry, cavalry artillery, engineering, etc.) assembled on an active front and employed, along with irregular troops recruited locally, during a three-four month season of operations" (Gershowitz 2000, 72). In the last stages of the pacification, the French military command scheduled operations in the summer after the harvest so *partisans* could easily be incorporated into auxiliary and regular troops in *groupes mobiles* that were sent out from bases in Meknes, Tadla, and Marrakesh in pincer movements against the remaining strongholds in the High Atlas, the Jbel Saghro, and the Anti-Atlas. Colonial soldiers provided most of the manpower for transporting artillery, heavy gunnery, and supplies and most of the fighting power in these campaigns. For example, troops from the Zaian confederation, which had been subdued in the early 1920s, formed the bulk of the force that was deployed in the later 1920s and early 1930s against the Ait Yafelman confederation in the High Atlas. The latter then fought in 1933–1934 in the Jbel Saghro against the Ait Atta. Troops from the Atlas were also sent to the Spanish zone in the north in 1925–1926 to fight for the French against Abd el-Krim's forces in the Jbala and the Rif. In the early 1930s, tribesmen who had been conquered in the Spanish zone were deployed in Spain itself and played an important role in the Spanish Civil War.

The Role of the Directorate of Indigenous Affairs

The Directorate of Indigenous Affairs (Direction des affaires indigènes; DIA), the bureaucratic arm of the colonial state that was responsible for newly pacified areas, played a key role in incorporating Morocco's tribal groups into the colonial army and projecting the colonial *makhzan's* influence in the *blad*, or countryside. The DIA was an administrative descendant of the Bureaux arabes (Arab Bureaus), an elite corps of native affairs officers formed in the 1840s to administer recently pacified areas in the wake of Bugeaud's brutal conquest in Algeria (Abi-Mershed 2010). These officers, many of whom had trained in the Saint Simonian–influenced L'École polytechnique, were given a great degree of autonomy in administering native policy and wielded a large degree of influence until a civilian administration gained the upper hand in the 1870s. When the French entered Tunisia in the 1880s, the Bureaux arabes were reconstituted as the Service des renseignements. In 1884, however, Resident General Cambon created the Contrôle civile, transferring governance to civilian administrators in most of the country and limiting the Service des renseignements to oversight of Tunisia's southern Saharan fringe.

The Arab Bureaus concept regained ascendancy when the French entered Morocco in 1912. For Lyautey, native affairs officers were the emblematic heroes and idealized vanguard of the protectorate's *mission civilisatrice* in Morocco. In two articles, "The Social Role of the Officer in Universal Military Service" (1891) and "The Colonial Role of the Army" (1901), both published in *La Revue des Deux Mondes*, Lyautey outlined a neo-associationist vision for the military in which the army officer was the key agent of the colonial project. Supposedly skilled in languages, ethnography, and agricultural techniques, these men were to provide the vital liaison between the colonial state and the tribes being incorporated under that state's control.

The first incarnation in Morocco of the native affairs service, the Service des renseignements, or Information Service, was created in 1908 to recruit, train, and command indigenous troops. In 1913, a division of labor was imposed with a civilian administration (Contrôle civile) that was put in charge of areas firmly under French control and the Service de renseignements was assigned unpacified or recently pacified areas on the periphery of state space. In 1917, the name of the Service des renseignements was changed to Direction des affaires indigènes, or Directorate of Indigenous Affairs. Although theoretically all regions were to eventually be transferred to civilian control, in practice the division between civilian and military territories stayed in place through the end of the protectorate, and the DIA played a major institutional role in the colonial administrative apparatus.

Like the officers of the Algerian Arab Bureaus, indigenous affairs officers were given wide-ranging powers in the military zones, most of which were in majority Berber-speaking areas. During the pacification, they conducted reconnaissance, created tribal maps, and attempted to negotiate with resisting chiefs to ensure their submission to the *makhzan*. After a tribe submitted, an indigenous affairs officer was assigned to a post where he administered a *cercle*, the basic administrative unit in the countryside. In a circle, the officer oversaw the tribal councils that had been preserved (or created) to administer customary law in their jurisdiction.[25] DIA officers also were responsible for planning agricultural development projects and, most importantly, for enlisting soldiers for the colonial army.

The Directorate of Indigenous Affairs was under the direct control of the resident general, and DIA officers and their informants provided the eyes and ears of the state in the countryside. They composed *notices* and

---

25. On the complexities of how the administration of customary law through the tribal councils actually looked in practice, see Hoffman (2010).

fiches de tribu (tribal reports containing historical, ethnographic, economic, and political background on the tribes under their control), and submitted regular intelligence reports to their commanders. Although Lyautey's successor, Théodore Steeg, was a civilian, he and subsequent resident generals maintained the DIA's privileged position in the colonial administration. Steeg created an institute in Rabat that put aspiring indigenous affairs officers through rigorous training in languages (Arabic and Berber), law (Islamic and customary), geography, agriculture, and ethnography.[26] In contrast to the Arab Bureaus in Algeria, which declined in importance in the late nineteenth century, the Directorate of Indigenous Affairs remained powerful throughout Morocco's colonial period.

In the long view of the *makhzan*'s waxing and waning power in North Africa, France's occupation of Algiers in 1830 and subsequent pacification operations over the next century were a historic watershed that transformed the spatial dimensions of the political ecosystem. Previously, a plurality of state and nonstate power holders vied for political and military control. State and nonstate spaces were constantly in flux, expanding and contracting in response to multiple factors. These two ideal-type categories of political topography interpenetrated and overlapped each other. Cities sometimes revolted and rural tribes periodically provided the military backbone of the central government. The advent of the colonial state in the nineteenth century indicated a rupture, shifting the balance of power toward a state-dominated political field with increasingly precise spatial boundaries, first in Algeria, then Tunisia, and finally in Morocco.[27]

What factors led to a total rather than a limited conquest in Morocco? As in Algeria, where ad hoc expansion from coastal enclaves developed into a systematic conquest, the pacification in Morocco evolved through multiple stages, not all of which were centrally planned. Having secured the critical productive zones and axes of communication and transport in the protectorate's first decade, Lyautey extolled the completion of the pacification of "useful Morocco" to soothe metropolitan concerns about the costs of colonial war. Within a few years, however, the threat of Abd el-Krim's Rif Republic forced the French to help the Spanish complete the total conquest of the northern zone. Continued raiding from "dissident zones" in the Atlas in the late 1920s, worries these "free" tribes of the *sība* could entice previously

---

26. In the 1920s–1930s, twenty-five to thirty-five officers typically trained at time in the nine-month program before being posted in the countryside (Hoffman 2008, 745).

27. The brutal Italian campaigns to quell Libyan resistance in the 1920s–1930s can be included as part of this larger state enclosure movement in North Africa.

subdued areas back into anti-colonial resistance, and the need to redeploy troops to the European theater eventually pushed French military planners to prioritize total pacification in the early 1930s.

Total pacification transformed state space in Morocco, creating a colonial political field that expressed new forms of territoriality and new modes of legibility. Aerial photography charted the progress of the pacification and helped the cartographic services update annual maps of supposedly subdued and dissident zones. Railroad, road, and telegraph networks linked previously remote areas to the rest of the country. In newly pacified areas, the Director-ate of Indigenous Affairs produced tribal maps, *fiches des tribus*, censuses, and land surveys and carefully researched and codified tribal customary law. The colonial powers also systematically integrated these previously autonomous populations in a paid colonial army. This reinvention of the traditional *jaysh* system equipped the Franco-Moroccan *makhzan* with the elusive depend-able military force that previous incarnations of the precolonial *makhzan* had struggled to secure. By the mid-1930s, these efforts had defined the space of a political field that had a previously unthinkable degree of territoriality, state sovereignty, and administrative penetration.

❧ CHAPTER 2

Organizing Forces of the Field: Legitimation and Legibility

In the first week of August 1931, the Moroccan sultan, Mohamed ben Youssef, and a large delegation of *makhzan* officials that included *qa'ids* from each of Morocco's civil and military regions traveled from Casablanca to Marseille by ship and then on to Paris by train. The state visit's main purpose was to tour the International Colonial Exposition that was staged that summer on the eastern edge of Paris in the Bois de Vincennes. Its organizers promoted the exposition as *"le tour du monde en un jour,"* a tour of the world in one day.[1] The sultan and the entourage were especially interested in the Palais du Maroc at the exposition.[2] On Friday, August 7, the Moroccan entourage was met at the grand entrance, the Porte d'Honneur, by Maréchal Hubert Lyautey, who had been brought out of retirement to serve as the exposition's high commissioner. Flanked by a mounted honor guard of *spahis* and the sultan's own *garde noire*, the vehicles passed by the Metropolitan Section, the Cité des informations, and the Musée des colonies before turning right, past the Madagascar Pavilion's cow skull–decorated Tour des

---

1. See Morton (2000) and Lebovics (1992, 98–134) on the exposition.

2. The sultan, who joined his father on a similar state visit to dedicate the Paris Mosque in 1926, explicitly requested the trip and insisted the two-year-old crown prince, Mawlay Hassan, accompany them. SHD-AT, Carton 3H 304, Lucien Saint to the Minister of Foreign Affairs, A/S: Voyage Officiel en France, de S.M. le Sultan, June 29, 1931. The young emperor of Annam and King Faysal of Iraq were other heads of state that made official visits to the exposition.

FIGURE 3.   Sultan Mohamed ben Youssef and Lyautey passing the pavilion of French West Africa. "Le Voyage en France du Sultan du Maroc," *L'Illustration*, August 15, 1931, 525.

Bucrânes to the Grande Avenue of the French Colonies. The motorcade then proceeded down the primary avenue of the exposition, passing pavilions dedicated to the French imperial possessions of Somalia and Oceania (the Tahitian pavilion); the French enclaves in India, New Caledonia, New Hebrides, French Guyana, Martinique-Réunion-Guadeloupe; and French Catholic and Protestant missions. After pausing a moment in front of a grandiose scale model of the Angkor Wat[3] and the Indochina pavilion, the group continued past the area dedicated to French West Africa and stopped at the bronze Tower of the Army that marked the endpoint of the avenue.

Here, an arched gate styled after the magnificent seventeenth-century Bab Mansour in Meknes marked the entrance to the palace of Morocco. A large crowd pressed in as the sultan, Lyautey, and the rest of the entourage

---

3. The model of the Buddhist temple was 55 meters high and occupied 5,000 square meters. It contained eighty dioramas of life in Indochina.

got out of the cars to enter the exhibit. The *L'Illustration* reporter covering the spectacle gushed,

> A powerful and beautiful vision: the mounted spahis, standing up in their stirrups, their burnouses opened up like wings, saluting with their swords; the *garde noire* rendering honors; and a vague murmur from the crowd, a slow, rhythmic music of song and instrument welcoming the arrival of the Sultan.[4]

Over the next hour, in a surreal juxtaposition of colonial representation and reality, the nominal Moroccan head of state, Sultan Mohamed ben Youssef; the protectorate's founding resident general, Maréchal Hubert Lyautey; and a cortège of Moroccan notables and French officials proceeded on a tour through an elaborate virtual reconstruction of the "Protectorate Morocco" the French had made over the past two decades.

The distilled representation of the protectorate's interlinked logics of legitimation and legibility on display at the palace of Morocco offers a valuable window through which to examine the ordering forces expressed in this colonial political field. In this chapter, the specificity of a protectorate form of colonial rule in Morocco is situated in relation to other frameworks that were meticulously represented in the diverse pavilions along the Grand Avenue of the Colonies. I show how these nominal distinctions (between colony, protectorate, territory)—which were determined based on local, metropolitan, and international factors at the time the subunit was incorporated into the empire—had significant path-dependent effects on what types of organizing logics were expressed in various colonial political fields. For Morocco and other colonial political units, logics of legitimization that were contingently determined at an initial critical juncture directly and indirectly influenced the logics of legibility that were subsequently employed in the field. The following tour through the Palace of Morocco exhibit at the 1931 International Colonial Exposition highlights how these organizing forces were expressed in ethnographic, preservationist, and developmental modes of colonial rule.

Empire on Display at the 1931 International Colonial Exposition

Over seven million visitors passed through the International Colonial Exposition held outside Paris in the summer of 1931. The exposition followed in the tradition of nineteenth-century expositions dating back to the French

---

4. "Le Voyage en France du Sultan du Maroc," *L'Illustration,* August 15, 1931, 525.

Industrial Exposition of 1844 in Paris, the Great Exposition held in London's Crystal Palace in 1851, and the 1889 Paris Exposition for which Gustave Eiffel designed his eponymous structure. As Timothy Mitchell has observed, colonial sections such as the Cairo street reconstructed for the 1889 World Exposition in Paris were key components of these powerful representations of a "European historico-geographic order of culture and evolution, an order reflected and reproduced in the multitude of plans, signposts, and guidebooks to the exposition" (Mitchell 1988, xiv).[5] The 1931 exposition was exceptional because it focused exclusively on representing a European imperial "order of culture and evolution." While previous expositions had included token orientalized spaces such as the Cairo street as exotic contrasts to modernity, the International Colonial Exposition's entire purpose was to map out how the Orient was itself being reordered in a way that blended and preserved the modern and the traditional. The capitalist bottom line of this imperial civilizing mission was also addressed, and substantial space was set aside for private vendors. In addition, information was provided at each colonial pavilion for potential investors.[6]

The explicit pedagogical objective of this colonial propaganda extravaganza was to showcase the grandeur—economic, cultural, and military—of *la plus grande France*, Greater France, for a metropolitan and broader European audience. The exposition's spatial order transitioned visitors outward from the Art Deco exhibition halls dedicated to the empire's modern technological French metropolitan center in a reverse cultural evolutionary descent to the differentiated imperial space of the colonial pavilions, each painstakingly constructed to exhibit "authentic" traditional architectural motifs, ending with the ultimate periphery, the animal kingdom represented in the *jardins zoologiques* (Lebovics 1992, 51–96).

Colony versus Protectorate: Variation in Field Forces in French North Africa

France's treasured North African possessions, Algeria, Tunisia, and Morocco, were showcased at the exposition's midpoint at the Place d'Afrique du Nord. In each pavilion, the respective colonial administrations organized a series of rooms with display cases, mechanized dioramas, posters, maps, slide shows,

---

5. Cairo Street at the 1889 exposition is also the subject of studies by Findley (1998) and Celik (1992).

6. The Louis Vuitton pavilion displayed sumptuous travel gear made from high-end colonial materials such as gold, silver, and leather. "Les Visages de l'exposition: Parmi les pavillons commerciaux," *L'Illustration*, September 26, 1931, Supplément Commercial, xx.

photographs, and artifacts intended to catalog, narrate, and promote the *mise en valeur* (development or enhancement) that had been achieved in the French Empire. Traditional *suqs*, or markets, and Moorish cafes that served mint tea were also included to provide additional local color and refreshment.

Despite surface similarities, the pavilions depicted two very different ideal types of colonial rule: assimilation and association.[7] The Algeria pavilion celebrated the crown jewel of the French Third Republic Empire, what one brochure called "the second metropole." This representation of settler colonialism, direct rule, and territorial assimilation of l'Algérie française, or French Algeria, contrasted sharply with the palaces constructed for the Tunisia and Morocco protectorates. These carefully represented France's associationist nominal partnership with indigenous dynastic rulers, the Husaynid bey and the Alawid sultan. Both pairings of legitimation and legibility were rooted, however, in the early genealogy of French rule in Algeria, which, as the inaugural colony of France's Second Empire, served as the precedent for later expansion in Africa and Asia. A brief exposition of the initial conditions in which Algeria was colonized and the subsequent negotiation of competing associationist and assimilationist logics of legitimacy and legibility provides valuable context for understanding the organizing forces of the colonial political field the French later created in Morocco.

Compared to the later European scramble for Africa, a critical difference of the early nineteenth-century international context was the relative autonomy with which France intervened in Algeria. The initial French bombardment of Algiers and landing at Sidi Ferreuch in June 1830 was the result of a series of bilateral economic and diplomatic contingencies. These involved escalating tensions over unresolved debts for Algerian grain shipped to southern France in the 1790s and a related altercation on April 29, 1827, in which the Algerian dey struck the French consul three times with the handle of a peacock-feather flywhisk.[8] A month after the French entered Algeria, the July Revolution of 1830 swept King Charles X from power and Louis Philippe inherited the Algerian situation. Instead of withdrawing, the

---

7. The classic treatment of assimilation and association in French colonial policy is Betts ([1960] 2005). For a critical reevaluation of an evolutionary reading of a transition over the nineteenth century from assimilation to association based on the Algerian case, see Abi-Mershed (2010). My analysis follows Abi-Mershed's in seeing competing frameworks of native policy in the early to mid-nineteenth century that created an unresolved ambivalence in France's relationship to Algeria.

8. In the 1790s, the Bushnaq and Bacri Jewish merchant families arranged a shipment of Algerian grain to southern France, payment for which remained unresolved over subsequent decades. By the 1820s, Bacri had convinced the Algerian dey that the French had to pay him before he could repay his own debt to the Algerian state (Ruedy 2005, 45–46).

French continued to creep inland over the next two decades. They annexed coastal enclaves at Oran, Bougie, Bône, and Algiers and established a government-general in 1834. In the 1840s, the French deemed political coexistence with autonomous inland Arab rulers untenable, and they appointed a military governor general, Thomas Bugeaud, to "pacify" the interior. This goal was largely accomplished by the early 1870s. Resistance in the Tell Atlas Mountains, and the pre-Sahara was completely reduced by *razzia* (slash-and-burn) techniques that systematically destroyed civilian infrastructure.[9]

The colony's formal status remained unresolved throughout this formative period. The military backed a more indirect associationist rule that would preserve a level of indigenous autonomy and civilian leaders demanded direct assimilation into France. This division was reflected in three zones of rule that were imposed between 1830 and 1870: civilian regions under French metropolitan law, the *communes de plein exercice*; Muslim majority and European minority zones, the *communes mixtes*, where French officials and native chiefs shared administrative duties; and recently pacified military zones with exclusively Muslim populations that were administered by the Arab Bureaus (Abi-Mershed 2010). In 1848, the constitution of the Second Republic declared that Algeria was an integral part of France and the areas under civil control were divided into three departments with representation in the Chamber of Deputies in Paris. The franchise was denied to native Algerians. In the 1860s, during the Second Empire, indirect rule gained favor under Louis Napoleon, who envisioned himself as the patron of an "Arab Kingdom" in Algeria. *Senatus consultes* passed in 1863 and 1865 guaranteed Algerians property rights and declared that Algerians were French but not citizens. To be naturalized, they had to give up their Muslim civil status and come under French civil law. When the Second Empire was defeated in the Franco-Prussian war of 1870–1871, the pendulum swung firmly back toward assimilation. Under the Third Republic, Algeria was formally defined as l'Algérie française, French Algeria, but only "citizens," that is, Europeans and Algeria's Jews (who were naturalized as French citizens by the Crémieux Decree of 1870[10]), benefited economically and politically from its territorial assimilation into France. Muslims were categorized as natives and after 1881 were subjected to a system of summary justice under a repressive *code de l'indigénat* (indigenous code).

---

9. On the violence involved in these phases of colonial conquest, see Brower (2009); and on how local actors alternately resisted and negotiated the conquest, see Clancy-Smith (1994).

10. Schreier (2010) analyzes how Algerian Jews negotiated the imposition of French rule in the decades before the decree. On scholarship on the impact of French colonial intervention on Algerian Jews, see Slyomovics and Stein (2012).

The rival military and civilian claims about Algeria's formal status, associationist versus assimilationist, entailed competing modes of legibility. The so-called indirect rule the military preferred required the production of ethnographic knowledge about the language, customs, religion, and law of the native society. In India, this type of "ethnographic state" was constructed after the 1857 Indian Revolt, or "Sepoy Mutiny," because the British needed to know which natives they could trust. Anthropology thus supplanted history as the dominant "colonial modality of knowledge and rule" in India (Dirks 2001, 43). The sequence was reversed in Algeria. There, the ethnographic mode was initially dominant during the ascendancy of the Arab Bureaus (Abi Mershed 2010). Native affairs officers seeking to structure an "Arab Kingdom" inventoried, categorized, and made Algerian society statistically legible in the wake of colonial conquest.[11] Widespread uprisings in 1870–1871 (the equivalent for the French of the 1857 "mutiny" for the British Raj) and the fall of the Second Empire in France led to the decline of the Arab Bureaus and the ascendancy of the civilian vision of Algeria as a settler extension of the metropole.

Seeing and being seen as "French Algeria," the civilian vision, required a shift toward a historiographic mode of legibility. From the 1870s, what Hannoum (2008) refers to as the "historiographic state" employed a whole infrastructure of societies, journals, and publishing houses to construct a French past for Algeria. This involved an archaeological reclamation of Algeria's Roman and Byzantine Christian past, of which the French claimed to be the direct heir. It also involved reworking Arab North African history. Generations of scholars in the Algiers historical school, including Mercier, Gsell, and Gautier, re-narrated the Algerian past for the period 1880 and 1930. Relying on racialized native categories, these scholars vilified Arabs as destructive invaders and lauded Berbers as freedom-loving autochthones who were related to the Iberians and the Celts.[12] French institutions in Algeria "dressed themselves in the clothes of their classical antecedents and explicitly presented themselves as the heirs and restorers of rational civilization, of a new 'Pax Romana' to a region which had since fallen into barbarism" (Silverstein 2002, 4). This historiographical remapping by the colonial state was also carried out on practical levels through the renaming and francization of Arabic

---

11. Classic ethnographic studies, particularly of Kabylia and the Aurés Mountains, continued to be conducted later in the 1880s by military officers-cum-ethnographers such as Hanoteau, Letourneaux, and Masqueray.

12. On racial stereotyping and the origins of the "Berber myth," see Lorcin (1995, 2005).

place names.[13] The word Algeria (or l'Algérie) itself had been invented as a name for the territories formerly known in Arabic as *al-Jaza'ir*, or the islands (the fertile spots north of the Saharan sea). City and village names were francizied (Algiers, Bougie, and Oran) or given new names (Phillipeville, Orleansville), and new street names referred to classical Roman times (Prochaska 1990). After decades of ambivalence, Algeria's formal status as a colony and an assimilationist mode of legibility had become firmly established by the late nineteenth century.

Later French expansion into Tunisia and Morocco took place in very different conditions. From the onset, two factors shaped the formal dimensions of the colonial rule that was implemented in these countries: changes in the international field by the late nineteenth century and the involvement of French (and other European) financial institutions in loans to modernizing Muslim states in the southern and eastern Mediterranean. Tunisia's fate was directly influenced by European diplomatic maneuvers following Ottoman territorial losses to Russia in 1877–1878. At the Congress of Berlin, the Great Powers decided to maintain the nominal territory integrity of the Ottoman Empire and acknowledge the colonial interests of France in Tunisia and Britain in Egypt.[14] By 1882, both had established de facto colonial rule in these countries but maintained local dynasties to preserve the fictional integrity of the Ottoman Empire. This protectorate form of indirect rule was also convenient because the Tunisian state (like Egypt) had accumulated an enormous debt in the course of modernizing reforms (*tanzimat*) in the 1860–1870s. By legally preserving the Tunisian state, the French, whose banks had major interests in this debt, could continue to have it repaid through tax revenues.

A similar link between diplomatic sensitivities and financial concerns and a strong desire to avoid the "mistakes" that had been made in Algeria, influenced France's decision to employ a protectorate form in Morocco. Morocco had long been shielded from direct colonization because of a strategic deadlock over control of the Strait of Gibraltar and thereby access to the Mediterranean Sea. After the 1904 Entente Cordiale cleared the way for French occupation, an intense debate was waged over whether to proceed with a "tribes policy" of direct conquest in Morocco or with a "*makhzan* policy" of indirect rule. Eugène Etienne, who represented the interests of the Algerian colonial lobby that viewed Morocco as an opportunity to expand

---

13. On the importance of the map as a "totalizing classification" introduced by European colonial states, see Anderson (1991, 171–78).

14. See Shorrock (1983), Perkins (2014, 41–43), and Lewis (2013) on the rivalry between France and Italy in Tunisia.

westward, advocated the former position, while Foreign Minister Théophile Délcassé promoted the latter option (Burke 1976, 69). The Quai d'Orsay's proclivities and the fact that the Moroccan state owed vast sums to French financial concerns from two large debts incurred in 1904 and 1910 clinched the decision.[15] In the end, the *makhzan* policy prevailed in the French government's internal struggles over how to frame intervention in Morocco. It was enshrined in the Treaty of Fes, which imposed a protectorate in which the French nominally preserved the Alawid dynasty. Although assimilation and association rarely were consistently applied practices of colonial rule (they were frequently mixed in varying measures), they did, as ideal types of symbolic legitimization, set up very different organizing forces in individual colonial units. In Morocco, the decision at this initial critical juncture to define colonial intervention in a protectorate framework of indirect rule, formally preserving the monarchy and the structures of the *makhzan*, established a very different legitimation-legibility linkage in this colonial political field than had been put in place in Algeria.

Seeing (and Being Seen) like a Protectorate

The Palace of Morocco at the international exposition, which was built twenty years after the signing of the Treaty of Fes, brilliantly encapsulated this political field's underlying logics of legitimacy—the premise of tutorial state building and economic modernization undertaken on behalf of the sultan and with respect for Morocco's culture, social structures, and religion—and the logics of legibility that flowed from this imaginary. The palace was designed by Robert Fournez and Albert Laprade, two architects Lyautey had used for the urban planning of Rabat and Casablanca. Masters of the neo-Mauresque style that marked French colonial construction in the 1910s–1920s, Fournez and Laprade designed the Palais du Maroc as a series of presentation halls, courtyards, and gardens that were intended to evoke the palaces of Fes and Marrakesh (Morton 2000, 47).

The spaces were arranged carefully to reflect the teleological narrative by which the French understood their project of what Lyautey referred to as "*faire le Maroc*," making Morocco.[16] An official report during the pavilion's planning stages explained that "the places reserved for the different services

---

15. I want to acknowledge Edmund Burke III for making this point in a conversation in 2009.

16. CAOM, Carton ECI 145, "Exposition Colonial 1931, Pavillon du Maroc, Plan de l'ensemble."

FIGURE 4.   Courtyard garden and esplanade of the Palais du Maroc (Dongen 1931, 42)

have been distributed in the Palace in a manner to give visitors as precise and logical an idea as is possible of the succession of different operations that were needed in the pacification, the administrative organization, and exploitation of the riches of our Protectorate."[17] The report added it was not enough to represent French colonial development, or *mise en valeur*: "To measure the work accomplished, it is necessary to show what Morocco was like before our arrival, or at least the state we found it in immediately after the pacification."[18]

The order and flow of the rooms of the Palace of Morocco exhibit at the International Colonial Exposition of 1931 reflected these priorities. From the Avenue of the Colonies, a visitor entered an exhibit hall dedicated to the military pacification and the administrative system that was constructed in newly conquered territories. The next space, "Du Maroc en 1912," empha- sized the "before and after" of French colonial intervention by depicting the undeveloped, "medieval" state of precolonial Morocco on the eve of

17. SHD-AT, Carton 3H 305, Extrait du rapport du directeur de l'office du protectorat de la République Française au Maroc, A/S de la participation du Maroc à l'Exposition Coloniale Inter- nationale de Paris de 1931, 2.

18. Ibid.

French intervention. The third section, a vaulted long hall called the Salle des Arts Indigènes, highlighted France's role in preserving Morocco's traditional culture and displayed traditional Moroccan handicrafts.[19] The final area of the palace showcased the modernizing work of colonial intervention with rooms dedicated to ministries of health, education, industry, agriculture, forestry and water conservation, public works, and mining. In its individual rooms and overall layout, the palace of Morocco carefully reproduced and represented the protectorate legitimacy/legibility dyad—expressed through ethnographic, preservationist, and developmental modes of rule—that shaped the colonial political field.

Ethnographic Logics in the Field

The first exhibit, the Hall of the Pacification, showcased the ethnographic logics colonial administrators attempted to map in the political field. This mode of seeing Moroccan society had its origins in a pre-protectorate "scientific penetration" (Rivet 1988, 20) of Morocco, which included Charles de Foucauld's exploration in 1883–1884, research expeditions sent by the École d'Alger in the early 1900s, and the work of Tangier-based Mission Scientifique du Maroc, which was instituted to gather data on Moroccan society, history, government, religion, and geography. The reports of the latter were published in the *Archives Marocaines*. After the formal imposition of the protectorate in 1912, the colonial state's need for ethnographic knowledge became even more acute as the pacification moved into the Atlas ranges, bringing Berber-speaking groups under colonial rule.[20]

The ground troops needed for this ethnographic mode of rule were supplied by the Directorate of Indigenous Affairs (Direction des affaires indigenes).[21] In 1921, Lyautey founded the Institut des hautes etudes marocains (IHEM) in Rabat to consolidate the production of knowledge about Moroccan society, politics, and history and disseminate this knowledge. Each year, twenty to fifty indigenous affairs officers were selected for the elite and intensive nine-month *cours des Affaires indigènes* in which they were taught by the leading French experts on Moroccan

---

19. The visitor could buy authentic traditional rugs, embroidery, tea sets, and other products in the *suq*, or market, area set up in the main court.

20. See Burke's (2014) definitive study on France's scientific "penetration" in Morocco and the subsequent role of colonial sociology in inventing "Moroccan Islam" and shaping modes of rule during the protectorate.

21. The number of Indigenous Affairs officers posted in Morocco grew from 194 in 1913 to 305 in 1928; a decade later, in 1939, the number was 580 (Méraud 1990, 73).

Table 3   Binaries of the Moroccan vulgate

	BLAD AL-MAKHZAN	BLAD AL-SĪBA
Political	Land of government	Land of dissidence
Geographic	Urban plains and coasts	Rural mountains and deserts
Ethnolinguistic	Arabic	Berber
Religious	Islam	Superficial Islamization overlaying secular/Christian orientation
Gender	Women restricted, veiled, and sequestered	Women free, not veiled or sequestered

history, language (Arabic and Berber), geography, society, culture, religion, and law (customary and Islamic).[22] After being posted in the countryside, these officers submitted biweekly and monthly reports, completed *notices* and *fiches de tribu*,[23] and sometimes published monographs based on extended study. By the mid-1920s, a substantial institutional civilian and military infrastructure had been established that produced a colonial archive of expert knowledge on Moroccan society, much of which was published in journals and series including *Villes et Tribus du Maroc*, *Archives Berbères*, and *Hespèris*.

Burke (1972, 177) labels the distilled colonial wisdom that emerged from these efforts the "Moroccan Vulgate," an analytical paradigm that reduced the complexities of Moroccan history, political organization, and society to a set of interrelated dichotomies.[24] The vulgate's fundamental binary reified a division between the *blad al-makhzan*, the land of government, and the *blad al-sība*, the land of dissidence, then built up a series of political, geographic, ethnic, religious, and gender divisions and stereotypes based on this distinction. These are listed in table 3. The ethnic binary (Arab and Berber) reflected in this attempt to make fluid social categories in Moroccan society legible to colonial rulers soon emerged as a major classificatory strategy of the protectorate administration. Language (Arabic versus Berber) and law

22. On the Direction des Affaires indigènes' recruitment practices and training programs, see Méraud (1990, 73–75) and Hoffman (2008, 745).

23. These reports included information on a tribe's physical location, its history before and after submission to the state, its political situation, its social and economic life, and its administration (Méraud 1990, 186–87). Lieutenant Jean-André Ithier's 1947 *fiche de tribu* and other writings (available at the IREMAM library, Aix-en-Provence, under BE 1.2–5) on the Ahansal *zawiya* in the Azilal Circle served as the basis for much of Ernest Gellner's analysis in *Saints of the Atlas* (1969).

24. Also see Daniel Rivet's excellent discussion of the native policy of the protectorate (1996, Vol. 1, 27–37).

(shari'a, Islamic law, versus *izref*, customary law[25]) were deployed as symbolic markers to enable the French to "see" Arabs and Berbers in Moroccan society, creating an ethnographic logic that politicized these identities in the colonial political field in unprecedented ways.

During the first decade of the pacification, this logic of legibility led to the development of a *politique berbère* based on preconceptions about an ethnic antagonism between the "Berbers" of the mountains and the "Arabs" of the plains. Inspired in part by the "Kabyle myth" (Lorcin 1999) inherited from Algeria, a Moroccan school of French Berber experts emerged who romanticized the "noble savages" of *la montagne berbère* and believed that the Berbers were France's natural allies against the Arabs.[26] As Hoffman (2008) has demonstrated, colonial authorities linked Berber linguistic identity to legal, cultural, religious, political, and even moral identity. Strenuous efforts were made to police the "contamination" of Berber areas (at the onset of colonial intervention, Berber speakers represented an estimated 40–45 percent of the population; Hart 2001, 19) by the Arabization and Islamization these officials feared emanated from the plains and cities. Jacques Berque (1967, 123) describes this policy as an attempt to create "a Berber reserve, a sort of national park which was to be sheltered from the ideologies of the plain, whether Arab or French."

The outlines of this policy were sketched out in the first years of the protectorate. In July 1913, Lyautey sent a letter to regional commanders that emphasized the distinctiveness of Morocco's Berbers, who, although they were Muslims, "remain faithful to their language, traditions, and customs, some of which are opposed to the doctrines of Islam." He affirmed the importance of preserving the institutions and of these groups as they were pacified and incorporated into the French administration and of preventing their Arabization. Comparing them to Algeria's Kabyles, for whom the French created a separate judicial organization, he called for a thorough survey of the status of Morocco's highland groups to determine to what extent they practiced customary rather

---

25. *Izref* is the Tamazight word and *'urf* is the Arabic word for customary law.

26. There was, as Bidwell (1973, 47–55) terms it, a "prolonged honeymoon" between Berber soldiers and their French officers from 1934 to the late 1940s. The latter hoped that their Berber troops would assimilate as Frenchmen. On the Algerian background of French attitudes toward the Berbers, see Lorcin (1995) and McDougall (2006). Morocco's "Berber *blad*," or countryside, was romanticized in the prodigious literary output of a French military officer, Maurice Le Glay, who had fought in the Middle Atlas during the initial stages of the pacification (1923, 1924, 1930, 1932, 1948). Le Glay's novel *Itto* (1923) was made into a film in 1934 with substantial support from the French administration (Slavin 1998). Said Guennoun, a Kabyle who served as an indigenous affairs officer in Morocco, also had literary success writing affectionately about the Middle Atlas Berbers, although his books (1933, 1934) focus on the geography, politics, social organization, and military history of the pacification in the region.

than Islamic law.[27] He commissioned the survey the next summer, sending out a circular letter June 15, 1914, with an eleven-page ethnographic question-naire that indigenous affairs officers were to fill out. The survey ostensibly cataloged the practices of tribes regarding family and civil status, social organi-zation, habitat, agriculture and husbandry, property, law, war (secular and holy), and religion.[28] As the accompanying note clarified, the goal was to measure the "degree of Arabization and Islamization of the ethnic group (tribe)" on social, political, administrative, and religious levels and "to determine, in a word, the category in which to classify the group and its classification in a table, extending from a purely Arab society to a purely Berber one."[29] That same year, Lieutenant Colonel Henrys, the commander of pacification operations in the Middle Atlas, concluded that the resistance of the Atlas Berbers to the French stemmed from a desire to continue practicing their own customary law instead of submitting to the shari'a courts of the *makhzan*. He promised the Ait Ndhir (Beni Mtir) they could continue using their councils (*jama'as*) (Burke 1973, 188–91). In 1914, this legibility strategy for marking Berber identity through designating a tribe's status under customary law took legal form in a decree that provided for the continuance of tribal courts, the *jama'as*, in areas labeled as "of Berber cus-tom." Over the next two decades, French Berberists "invented" (Guerin 2011) a Berber customary system and issued subsequent *dahirs* in 1922 and 1930 that further systematized a Franco-Berber jurisdiction that was distinct from the shari'a courts under the supervision of the sultan-appointed judges.

Language was the corollary marker of ethnic legibility colonial adminis-trators in the field used to mark Moroccan Arabs and Berbers. The French were keenly aware of their role elsewhere in their empire as vehicles of Arabization, which they linked directly to Islamization. Maurice Le Glay, an officer involved in early operations in the Middle Atlas and an early cham-pion of the Berber policy, observed in a 1913 report that

> due to French carelessness, arising from philosophical respect for ideas
> different from our own, and because of snobbery, we have "renovated

---

27. Ministère des Affaires étrangères, Centre des archives diplomatiques de Nantes-Résidence générale de France au Maroc (henceforth MAE, CADN-Mar.), Département des affaires indigenes, Carton 59, Lyautey to Commander Generals in Marrakesh, Fez, and Meknes, "A/S de l'organisation judiciaire des tribus berbères," no. 1667, 30 July 1913.

28. The full text of the "Questionnaire sur la société berbère" was published in the *Archives Berbères* 1915–1916 with an introductory note by Colonel Henri Simon. See Comité d'études berbères de Rabat (1987, 7–20).

29. MAE, CADN-Mar., Département des affaires indigenes, Carton 17, circular from Lyautey to regional commanders, "Mœurs et traditions des populations berbères," June 1914. See Hoffman's (2008, 732–34) extended analysis of the survey.

Arab letters" wherever we stationed our troops. It is our own fault if the Sudan is Islamized today. It is also our fault if, in Algeria, the Berber language is retreating before Arabic. The Arabic language is Islam itself, since the Qur'an is the only book the masses can learn to read.[30]

The French logics of ethnographic legibility that structured the colonial political field heightened the importance of "protecting" Berber linguistic purity and preventing the encroachment of Arabization in regions mapped as "Berber." In theory, documentation for the tribal courts was to be transcribed in Berber and French, not Arabic. To supply needed staff for the court system (and to train sons of rural notables for the colonial army), the French initiated a separate Berber educational system for the sons of rural notables in 1919. In these schools, Arabic instruction was forbidden and French instruction was mandatory. In a 1921 memorandum, Maurice Le Glay explained the intentional Francophone orientation of the system:

> The deep and legitimate concern expressed in our cause demands that the evolution of the mountain populations take place in the French language, the vehicle of our thoughts. The Berber population will learn French and be administered in French. This leads us to this tremendous effort to cover the Berber world with French schools as soon as possible. It is no longer Franco-Arab schools, and it is intentional that we have written French schools *tout court*."[31]

The schools were also strictly laicist in order to prevent Islamization, though this strategy proved to be a failure. In a 1943 report lamenting the rise of Arab nationalist activity at the Berber college in Azrou, Lucien Paye summarized the original political goal of the separate system: "As we know, the particular orientation of education in Berber country was determined by the idea that it was possible to establish and maintain a Berber bloc against the Arab populations and, notably by the activity of the school, to reduce the Islamization that has been observed."[32]

---

30. MAE, CADN-Mar., Département des affaires indigenes, Carton 17, Maurice Le Glay, note 4, "Comment administer les berbères. Mesures préparatoires," 1913.

31. Maurice Le Glay, "L'Ecole française et la question berbère," Direction générale de l'instruction publique, 11–12, quoted in MAE, CADN-Mar., Direction générale de l'instruction publique, Carton 30, report by Lucien Paye, head of Service of Muslim Education, "Note relative au collège d'Azrou à la politique scolaire en pays berbère," 23 January 1943.

32. MAE, CADN-Mar., Direction générale de l'instruction publique, Carton 30, report by Lucien Paye, head of Service of Muslim Education, "Note relative au collège d'Azrou à la politique scolaire en pays berbère," January 23, 1943.

At the Palace of Morocco at the 1931 International Colonial Exposition, the simplifying ethnographic logics of the colonial political field were on full display. Upon entering the pavilion into the Hall of Pacification, a visitor immediately encountered the vulgate's bifurcation between two Moroccos— Arab and Berber, plains and mountains, and cities and countryside. On one wall, a huge relief map of Morocco delineated the military-civilian administrative division between territories under the jurisdiction of the Directorate of Indigenous Affairs and those under the jurisdiction of the Directorate of Civil Control; a dark line and shading denoted unpacified areas.[33] The opposite wall portrayed the different tasks of these two branches of the colonial *makhzan*. On the Directorate of Indigenous Affairs side of this wall, a montage of photos depicted officers performing various duties in Berber zones, including a sortie with a contingent of partisan troops, the submission of a tribe with the ceremonial sacrifice of a bull, and a *jama'a* council meeting at an indigenous affairs post. Immediately below, a sequence of large photos showed indigenous affairs officers conducting reconnaissance missions in the mountains, a doctor performing vaccinations, and a road being built between Marrakesh to Telouet in the High Atlas. A long vertical panel portrayed regional variation among Morocco's tribal peoples with three major sections depicting the Rif-Jebala zone, the Middle Atlas, and the Sahara. Seven mannequins in front of the panel were dressed in regionally specific clothing.[34] The overall effect of the display was to celebrate the role of indigenous affairs officers in bringing "Berber" Morocco, the mountainous *blad as-sība*, under the control of the "benevolent" French *makhzan*.

This wall's other side celebrated the corollary accomplishments of the Directorate of Civil Control in administering the *blad al-makhzan*, the "Arab" cities and plains.[35] In an early circular titled "Muslim Policy," Lyautey emphasized the importance of "partnership" (or at least the appearance of partnership) in the administration of the Directorate of Civil Control:

> The protectorate is the negation of direct administration. Administration must always appear to be supported by the native authorities

33. Service historique de la defense, Armée de Terre (henceforth SHD-AT), Carton 3H 305, Note au sujet de la participation du Service des Affaires Indigènes à l'Exposition Coloniale de 1931.

34. SHD-AT, Carton 3H 305, chief of the Civil Control to the chief of the Commerce and Industry Service, May 28, 1930.

35. The civilian administrators (*contrôleurs civils*) have received much less scholarly attention than the indigenous affairs officers. See Gruner (1984) and Berger (2013), who include information about the career trajectories of several of these colonial functionaries.

under the supreme authority of the Sultan, under our simple control. The heads of municipal services are themselves controllers, placed next to *pashas*, the effective chiefs in the administration of cities (Lyautey 1953, 171).

Snapshots on three large panels depicted this partnership between French administrators and Moroccan civilians. The first panel was divided into two sections, one for urban areas and another for the Atlantic plains. The city section showed a scene from a *makhzan* court session conducted by the local pasha and attended by a French controller. Below, an amalgam of traditional and modern urban life was depicted with photographs of veiled women in a cemetery in Rabat, pedestrians and traffic at the Place de France in Casablanca, and a *mellah* (a Jewish section of a Moroccan city). Different "types" of city-dwellers, including "traditional" and "evolved" natives, were painted in watercolors on the wall below. The second half of the panel depicted the countryside surrounding the major cities on the Atlantic coast and central plains. In the center image, a civil controller on a horse was surrounded by *mokhzani* Moroccan soldiers. To the left, a photograph depicted agricultural development: French administrators were shown battling locust infestations and distributing seeds. Pictures of ancient Moroccan fortresses "used only for war" were juxtaposed with pictures of French-built agricultural villages, "centers of riches and prosperity through which the French domination was implanted."[36]

Although the fundamental binary of the colonial political field was clearly represented in the Hall of Pacification (military and civilian zones, Arab and Berber, *makhzan* and *sība*, Islamic and customary-cum-secular law, and cities-plains-coasts and mountains-deserts), another important ethnographic force in the field was less obvious: a religious classification that reinforced the division between Muslims and Jews. The ethnoreligious distinction of the sultan's Jewish subjects (see chapter 6) was institutionally maintained in the colonial political field through separate legal (rabbinical courts), educational (private and public Franco-Israèlite schools), and administrative (Jewish councils) structures. All of the ethnographic divisions the colonial power attempted to maintain in Moroccan society were imposed on the tradition side of a binary division it tried to police between tradition and modernity in the protectorate framework.

---

36. SHD-AT, Carton 3H 305, chief of the Civil Control to the chief of the Commerce and Industry Service, May 28, 1930, page 2.

Preservationist Logics in the Field

Preservationism, a far-reaching traditionalization policy, was a second force that fused the protectorate logics of legitimation and legibility. In the accounts of precolonial travelers (De Foucauld 1888) and scientific missions (Archives Marocains 1904) that were sent out to study the country, European visitors viewed what journalist Walter Harris (1921) called the "Morocco That Was" as being preserved through its isolation as a pristine, medieval Muslim traditional society. A key feature of this orientalist perspective was its presumption that the object of analysis—whether it was the medina (walled city), artisanal guilds, tribal structures, religious practices, tribal or shariʿa law, or political structures—was static, a fixed entity that could be assessed, probed, measured, and cataloged. This ahistorical bias created a tendency among French scholars to replicate a "before and after" paradigm that ignored any dynamism, fluidity, or agency on the Moroccan side, whether they were talking about Berber political organization (Montagne 1930), the *makhzan-sība* tension in Moroccan history (Terrasse 1949), or the Islamic city (Le Tourneau 1949)[37] before the arrival of the French.

While creating French Algeria required scholars to write Algerians out of history, making protectorate Morocco involved a historiographical project that meticulously documented the country's past. Marking off, codifying, and protecting the indigenous "traditional" Morocco served to legitimate France's colonial intervention there. The political and cultural expressions of this preservationist legitimacy/legibility dyad were obvious in the next two large exhibition rooms of the Palais du Maroc. The room after the Hall of Pacification, called "Du Maroc en 1912," "Morocco in 1912," presented a snapshot of the traditional Morocco the French encountered when they arrived. The space was dominated by a huge diorama reproducing Delacroix's 1845 *The Sultan of Morocco and His Entourage*, in which the sultan is leaving his palace through the massive seventeenth-century Bab al-Mansour gate in Meknes, mounted on a horse and shaded by the imperial parasol.

This evocation of precolonial Alawid rule underscored the importance of political traditionalization in the colonial political field. Under the rubric of indirect rule formalized in the Treaty of Fes, the French pledged to protect the person of the sultan and the institutions of the *makhzan*. In a colonial twist on Ranger and Hobsbawm's (1983) concept of the "invention of

---

37. Abu Lughod (1987) takes apart the *"isnad* of the Islamic city" in orientalist scholarship.

tradition," Lyautey, himself a royalist sympathizer, made considerable efforts to rehabilitate the ceremonial prestige of the Alawid dynasty and the traditional *makhzan* during the first decade of the protectorate. In some respects, this process constituted a "reinvention" (and appropriation) of *makhzan* traditions that had been in use for centuries. For the French, the reign of Hassan I (1873–1894), widely revered as the last great Moroccan sultan, served as an idealized blueprint of the traditional *makhzan*.[38] Lyautey established the custom of paying meticulous attention to the protocol and accouterments of the royal office. The Moroccan sultan had historically projected power by traveling through the countryside with his palace retinue and a large armed force to collect taxes (voluntary or forced), resolve disputes, and receive and give gifts to tribal chiefs. To enhance the reinvented prestige of the *mahalla*, Lyautey assigned the sultan a unit of designated troops, including an artillery contingent, to supplement his personal force, the Black Guard, which dated back to Mawlay Ismail's creation of a slave army in the seventeenth century.[39] This force, along with the palace retinue, would travel from Rabat through the country in automobiles and lorries or in custom-built rail cars to visit royal palaces in Fes and Marrakesh.

The residency also stringently upheld the annual *hadiya* rituals (see figure 5). As Bourqia (1993) explicates, this carefully staged performance constituted an important precolonial symbolic mechanism through which the sultan and his subjects reinforced reciprocal political, religious, and social links. Notables from Morocco's cities and chiefs representing rural tribes traveled to palace's *meshwar*, a courtyard outside the gate, to give the sultan gifts at the three major religious feasts of the year: Mulud (a celebration of the birth of the Prophet), Aid al-saghir (or Aid al-fitr, a celebration of the end of Ramadan), and Aid al-kabir (or Aid al-adha, a celebration of Abraham's willingness to sacrifice his son). Through *hadiya* rituals, urban and rural notables signaled a renewal of their allegiance and obedience to the sultan. At the same time, the rituals created ties of mutual obligation and exchange, allowing notables to make requests of the sultan.

The construction of what I call the neo-*makhzan* also entailed the wholesale invention of new *makhzan* traditions. For example, in 1914, Mawlay Youssef commissioned the director of music for the Moroccan troops, Mr. Zichbauer, to compose a national anthem, the "Sharifian Hymn," which was

---

38. *Kitab al-Istiqsa*, the account of the period of the court historian, Ahmad ibn Khalid al-Nasiri, served as a sort of bible in this respect.

39. The sultan's request that an artillery unit to be added to his Troupes Marocains was granted in 1917. MAE, CADN-Mar. Direction des Affaires Chérifien, Carton 137.

FIGURE 5. Sultan Mohamed ben Youssef, surrounded by the Black Guard, receiving *hadiya* offerings from notables in Rabat in 1930. MAE, CADN, Résidence générale de France au Maroc, 20MA/20/623, "Heddia de l'aïd Seghir, 1930."

played at official ceremonies and at the presentation of the sultan to foreign delegations.[40] In 1915, Lyautey created an entirely new Moroccan flag. The decree creating the flag explained that the old emblem could be confused with other flags (mentioning navy signals in particular) and that the "progress realized by Our Sharifian Empire, in consideration of the great renown it has acquired" necessitated a new symbol to distinguish Morocco from other nations.[41] The new flag was to have a five-pointed green star on a red field. It seems likely that for a European like Lyautey, the six- or eight-pointed stars traditionally used in Morocco were too closely associated with Jewish symbols.[42] For Lyautey, the five-pointed star of Ottoman origin, which had never been used in Morocco before, was a more obviously Muslim emblem.

---

40. MAE, CADN-Mar., Direction des Affaires Chérifien, Carton 137, Note au sujét de la musique du Sultan, April 3, 1914. A later director of music for the Sharifian guard, Captain Leo Morgan, either wrote another hymn or took credit for this one, as he is now known as the composer of the national anthem's music. The current lyrics were written by Mawlay Ali Skalli in 1969.

41. "Dahir du 17 Novembre 1915 (9 Moharrem 1334) portent description du nouveau drapeau de l'Empire," *Bulletin Officiel du Maroc,* November 29, 1916, No. 162, 838.

42. In Morocco, too, these stars had biblical associations via the Qur'an with King David and Solomon and were referred to as *najma Daud* and *najma Sulayman.*

FIGURE 6.   The Salon of Honor at the Palace of Morocco (Nicoll 1931, 168)

Beyond traditional political institutions, preservationist logics were also institutionalized in a sizable bureaucratic apparatus, including the Directorate of Beaux-Arts and Antiquities, which was charged with protecting Morocco's cultural and architectural patrimony. These efforts were celebrated in the next room, about which the exhibition's planning commission wrote: "But if our economic services have been useful in transforming and exploiting the country, our artistic services have, in contrast, guarded its beauty and art. And it is to highlight this effort that we have, with a very wide scope, planned a hall dedicated to indigenous art."[43] The Salon of Honor was the vastest and most ornate space in the entire palace (see figure 6). It featured a vaulted ceiling in the shape of a ship's hull and huge inset bays on both sides that were forty meters long and six meters high. These depicted the two greatest Moroccan imperial cities. On one side, a diorama of Fes offered a panoramic view of the medina and the *ville nouvelle* with the Middle Atlas Mountains in the background. On the opposite wall, a diorama of Marrakesh showed people at *suqs*, including a blind beggar extending a hand requesting

---

43. SHD-AT, Carton 3H 305, Extrait du rapport du directeur de l'office du Protectorat de la République Française au Maroc, "A/S de la participation du Maroc à l'Exposition Coloniale Internationale de Paris de 1931," 2.

alms, a snake charmer playing the tambourine, and a Berber women from the mountains selling carpets in the famous Jma' al-Fna square. The pink minaret of the Koutoubia rose above this scene and the snow-capped peaks of the High Atlas lined the southern horizon.

The two dioramas implicitly affirmed the "protector" role of the Ministry of Beaux Arts and Antiquities, which had created museums of Morocco's cities over the past two decades. In the early years of the protectorate, Lyautey ordered urban planners to protect the medina, or traditional city, and build the modern section, the *ville nouvelle*, adjacent to it in all of the historic urban centers in Morocco. The two worlds, "traditional" and "modern," represented by the two halves of the city were separated by carefully preserved historic walls and a *cordon sanitaire* of wide boulevards or public parks. Abu-Lughod (1980) provocatively argues that this created a de facto "urban apartheid" that hierarchically divided the indigenous Muslim and European sectors of the city.[44] This model froze the "indigenous" section of the city in terms of development and expansion, creating serious problems as Morocco's population became increasingly urbanized. However, instead of hermetically sealing Moroccan and European populations, this urban plan actually created new zones of intercultural interaction at the boundary. As Rabinow (1989, 299) has argued, the "supposed *cordon sanitaire*"—where many cafés, small shops, and the bus terminal were located—"functioned as one of the more socially active areas of the city."

The colonial state's cultural traditionalization policy was also showcased in the Salon of Honor in the wide array of Moroccan rugs, embroidery, engraved metals, tanned leathers, and pottery on display in the center of the hall. These emphasized the colonial power's role in preserving Morocco's "traditional genius." An official publication lauded the achievements of French protector, which, "obeying its tradition to civilize without destroying, knew how to conserve, or more accurately, to save a series of Maghribi techniques that without us would have disappeared completely" (Leclerc 1931, 59). These displays also represented the degree to which this active cultural conservationism entailed an industrial systemization, regulation, and commodification of local arts and crafts (Irbouch 2005), as many of the wares on display had been fabricated in artisanal and craft schools the French had set up.

A room that branched off from the Salon of Honor highlighted the educational initiatives the Directorate of Public Instruction had implemented.

---

44. Also see Gwendolyn Wright's book (1991) comparing French urban design in Morocco, Madagascar, and Indochina.

FIGURE 7.   Exhibit room of the Palace of Morocco dedicated to the Directorate of Public Instruction (Nicoll 1931, 169)

Tellingly, this directorate was a department of the Ministry of Beaux Arts and Antiquities. During the first decade of the protectorate, the French had set up different school systems for Europeans, Muslims, and Jews. While the budget apportioned for "native" education was appallingly small and this system served only a small fraction of the Moroccan population, the classifications the system maintained were symbolically significant, reflecting the ethnographic logic discussed above. Moroccan Muslims and Jews were separated and Muslims were separated into Arab and Berber schools. These were further subdivided by class; the sons (and daughters) of notables and the lower classes went to different schools. Overall, the dominant pedagogical goal was to reinforce traditional roles in Moroccan society and cultivate willing collaborators (Segalla 2003, 2009).

In planning for the exposition, the director of public instruction, Louis Brunot, told his staff that the display would create a sort of "museum of the Moroccan school." This "museum" would provide "a concrete illustration of what we said in *L'enfant marocain*,[45] showing visitors a synthesis of the life

---

45. Co-written with Georges Hardy, *L'Enfant marocain* (Paris: Larose, 1925) analyzed the "typical" Moroccan child.

of our schools, at their homes, in the Qur'anic schools, and in class."[46] The exhibit was arranged carefully according to colonial vulgate logic. There was an "Arab side" and a "Berber side" and a display case on the back wall for Moroccan Jews. In the center of the room was a table with dolls made by Moroccan girls in handicraft workshops that represented all of the indigenous Moroccan types in their "typical dress"—urban, rural, Arab, Berber, Muslim, Jew, *fassi* (Fes dweller), *marrakshi* (Marrakesh dweller), *rabati* (Rabat dweller), male, female, soldier, peasant, bourgeois, and artisan.[47] On the walls, various educational approaches were detailed in displays that described the Qur'anic schools, European and indigenous trade schools, girls' schools, and schools for children of notables. Another set of pictures depicted graduates of colonial schools at work: a teacher, a bank teller, a factory worker, a gardener, an artisan, a librarian, a businessman, and an interpreter working alongside a civil controller.[48]

Developmentalist Logics in the Field

After the succession of halls dedicated to the ethnographic and preservationist logics of the protectorate, the final section celebrated a third mode of rule that shaped the colonial political field, France's role in modernizing Morocco through material development. These last rooms showcased various ministries responsible for the *mise en valeur* of colonial intervention, the development and exploitation of Morocco's economic potential and natural riches.

The first exhibit for the protectorate's administrative services used maps, pictures, models, and films to show visitors how France had developed Morocco's urban centers by constructing the modern *villes nouvelles*.[49] Moroccan cities, particularly Rabat and Casablanca, served as laboratories

---

46. MAE, CADN-Mar., Direction générale de l'instruction publique, Carton 92, "Circulaire au sujet de la participation des écoles de l'enseignement musulman à l'Exposition Coloniale de 1931." In the letter, Brunot emphasized they would be in competition with members of education ministries in other colonies and urged them to do their very best.

47. Brunot sent an eight-page list to the directors of the schools listing the dolls each needed to make, including specific instructions about their clothing and headgear. MAE, CADN-Mar., Direction générale de l'instruction publique, Carton 92, "Exposition Coloniale," February 6, 1930.

48. MAE, CADN-Mar., Direction générale de l'instruction publique, Carton 92, contains correspondence between the directorate and instructors about preparations for the colonial exposition. Many of the textile crafts in the Hall of Indigenous Arts, including embroidered pillows, carpets, tablecloths, and clothing, were created in the French-run training workshops for Muslim girls (see Chapter 7).

49. MAE, CADN-Mar., Direction générale de l'instruction publique, Carton 92, Adjunct Commissioner of Morocco for the Colonial Exposition to the Director General of Public Instruction, Beaux-Arts and Antiquities, "Participation des services du protectorat à l'Exposition Coloniale de Paris 1931," December 21, 1929.

FIGURE 8.   Aerial view of Rabat in 1951 with the modern *ville nouvelle* in the foreground and the traditional medina behind. MAE, CADN, Résidence générale de France au Maroc, cliché Agricolvia, 20MA/102/59, "Rabat, exemple d'urbanisme juxtaposé."

for French urban designers and colonial administrators such as Lyautey who sought to use urban planning as a means of projecting colonial control. The most obvious feature of this plan was the delineation of traditional-native and modern-European space through the separation of the medina and the *ville nouvelle*. The aerial shot of Rabat (figure 8) shows this distinction: the new city is in the foreground and the medina is further west in the background. In direct contrast to Le Corbusier's monolithic modernism,[50] the "techno-cosmopolitanism" (Rabinow 1989, 277–319) Lyautey and his team inscribed in Morocco's cities expressed a hybridized and differentiated colonial modernity. This "protector's style" contrasted starkly with the "conqueror's style" that the French implemented in Algiers (Béguin 1974; Rabinow 1989, 310) in its preservation of the local in motifs, in the patterning of public gardens, and in the juxtaposition and intermingling of the "modern" and the "traditional" in nodal points of interaction in the city.

---

50. Scott (1998, 104–32) discusses Le Corbusier's "high modernist city," specifically his designs for Brazilia and Chandigargh, at length.

From the urban administrative services room, the visitor moved into a space that focused on Morocco's phosphate riches. Before 1912, European prospectors speculated wildly about Morocco's mineral wealth, but surveys revealed only limited deposits of coal, oil, lead, cobalt, and manganese, and many of these were located in remote regions. The resource Morocco has in abundance is phosphates; they were first discovered during World War I southeast of Casablanca. In 1920, the French created the Office Chérifien des Phosphates (Sharifian Phosphates Office) and gave it a monopoly on extracting and selling the natural resource. By 1929, 1,608,150 tons was being exported in a single year through the port of Casablanca and the mineral had become a primary source of revenue.[51]

The activities of Morocco's other industries were detailed in the next room, which was dedicated to the Ministry of Public Works. Here, maps, charts, and photos also described the progress the French had made in building the country's transportation and communications infrastructure, including roads, railroads, ports, telegraphs, telephones, and postal services. It also focused on major projects such as the Si Said Maachou dam, which was intended to supply electricity to vast areas of Morocco and guarantee a water supply for expanded irrigation. The creation of this infrastructure was one of the most radical transformations during the protectorate's first two decades. The first railroad connected Rabat and Casablanca in 1911 and made what had been a two-day trip a matter of hours. The Rabat-Kenitra-Sidi Kacem-Meknes-Fes line, which was completed in 1923, linked the coast to the two largest cities of the central interior. The Tangier-to-Fes line was completed in 1927. The following year, the line from Casablanca to Marrakesh was completed, and the final link to Algeria, the Fes-Taza-Oujda line, was completed in 1934. By the time of the 1931 exposition, the French had built a total of 1,600 kilometers of railroads in Morocco.

The previous chapter emphasized the impact of new roads, which helped move troops and weapons during the pacification. They were built mainly with the forced labor of recently subdued tribes. Primary and secondary roads also linked rural Morocco more closely than ever before with the low-land plains and the coasts where Morocco's cities were located. The roads that brought soldiers into the so-called *blad al-sība* also allowed these populations

---

51. "Le Maroc: Notice Géographique, Economique, et Administrative," *Le Livre d'Or de l'Exposition Coloniale Internationale de Paris, 1931* (Paris: Librairie ancienne Honoré Champion, 1931). It is worth noting that Morocco still controls more than two-thirds of the world's phosphate reserves and that the mineral has bankrolled the central government (and the monarchy itself) since independence.

to quickly traverse the country: a trip from the High Atlas, the Sous, or the Tafilelt to Casablanca, Rabat, Marrakesh, or Fes could be done in a matter of hours rather than days or weeks. Just as importantly, regional markets became major hubs for the rural population and grew into small cities.[52]

This room also highlighted France's investment in ports on Morocco's Atlantic coast. Because of the large number of Europeans present in Casablanca after the landing of troops in 1907, this small fishing village was chosen as the protectorate's primary port, despite the fact that it had no natural harbor and required the construction of a jetty, elevators, and loading facilities. The other main ports were at Safi, which served as an outlet for the export of phosphates and later for the sardine-canning industry, and Kenitra (renamed Port Lyautey), north of Rabat, which was developed as an outlet for the rich agricultural lands of the Gharb plain.

The final exhibit room focused on "Agricultural Colonization" and "Soil Conservation." Information was displayed about France's efforts to maximize soil fertility through irrigation resources and soil conservation. A diorama for the Water and Forest Service (Service des Eaux et Forets) portrayed the vestiges of an ancient forest, the degradation of the soil and desertification, and attempts to combat these threats through soil conservation and reforestation.[53] As Davis (2007) has shown, these policies reflected the dominant colonial theory of desiccation that had been honed in Algeria in the nineteenth century, which linked deforestation and desertification. For the colonial state, conservation and reforestation represented France's environmental civilizing mission to "save" Morocco from destructive native practices of land and forest use. The most important goal of this room, however, was to educate potential investors about agricultural business opportunities in Morocco.

The colonial expropriation and exploitation of Morocco's most fertile land, which had begun in the Chaouia plain soon after the French landed in 1907, then moved inland on the Doukkala and the Saiss plains, was a natural outgrowth of the protectorate's developmentalist logics. Protectorate land tenure policies facilitated the seizure of most of the best Moroccan agricultural areas for European (mainly French) colonization. *Dahirs* in 1913 and

---

52. Eugen Weber (1976) has highlighted the central role the expansion of roads linking isolated villages to larger highways and railway lines played in the integration of France. The economic role of these roads, which allowed peasants to reach new markets, was mirrored in the experience of Morocco's *blad*, or countryside, from the 1920s.

53. SHD-AT, Carton 3H 305, chief of the Commerce and Industry Service to Captain Valhuy, Etat-Major, regarding "Concours pour la fourniture d'un diorama et d'une frise decorative," January 5, 1931.

1915 instituted a Torrens system of land registration, which required owners to produce a title before they could register their land and pay fees for the expenses associated with court adjudication if the land had not been registered. In 1914, the French distinguished between alienable and inalienable lands. *Habus* (*awqaf*, or religious endowment), *jaysh*, and collective tribal lands were declared inalienable and *melk* (private) and domanial *makhzan* lands open for sale. The residency sold off most of the latter to settlers. Much of the private *melk* land was also quickly sold to *colons*. Another round of legislation in 1919 changed the inalienability of communal tribal lands. A commission determined how much land each *douar* (or tent) in the tribe needed, then legalized the sale of the tribe's surplus lands to Europeans. Because the *makhzan* no longer needed *jaysh* tribes to man the *makhzan* army, lands that had been given in exchange for military service were also expropriated. Many of the *habus* properties owned by religious foundations were also sold. From 1913 to 1932, the number of hectares under cultivation by Europeans increased from 73,000 to 675,000. On top of this, a substantial amount of land still owned by Moroccans was rented out to Europeans, including tribal collective lands that decrees published in 1926, 1931, and 1941 declared were legally rentable (Stewart 1964, 71–82).

These policies divided the country's agricultural sector geographically and technologically into two zones: a European zone, in which the best lands were cultivated with modern methods that required substantial capital investment (which the colonial state made easily available), and a Moroccan zone, in which marginal lands were cultivated with traditional methods because of a lack of expertise and lack of access to the capital investment needed for modern methods.[54] Tribes that had formerly used a mixed system, alternately grazing livestock and cultivating crops different times of the year, were forced to settle on and cultivate less productive lands. In an ecological system where agricultural production is uncertain due to inconsistent rainfall, being pushed into even more precarious zones made farming unsustainable for large numbers of Moroccan *fellahin*, or peasant farmers. Although the exhibit at the exposition lauded France's soil conservation and reforestation efforts, the result of the protectorate's policy of favoring European land use was to degrade soil quality in Morocco: much of the rural population was forced into the cities because the *blad*, or countryside, could no longer support them.

---

54. The protectorate founded the Sociétés Marocains de Prévoyance in 1917, but it remained difficult for Moroccans to obtain funding.

After these last rooms dedicated to the development and modernization of Morocco, the visitor moved outside to a long esplanade. This area, which featured two large water basins lined with cypresses and flowers and a fountain at the end, evoked the Andalusian-style Ouadayas garden in Rabat. Rose-covered pergolas provided shade for small boutiques similar to those in the streets of Fes or Marrakesh that had been installed to create a Moroccan *suq* along the walls. Moroccan vendors that had been brought in for the exposition[55] sold embroidery, pottery, rugs, metal wares (brass, silver, gold), and other goods in the boutiques in order to evoke "the type of curious and amusing examples of medieval life one finds in Morocco."[56]

The juxtaposition of petit-bourgeois Moroccan vendors along the esplanade with the stalls of private French enterprises that were active in Morocco just off the courtyard symbolized a pressing dilemma in the dualist colonial economy that emerged within the developmentalist logics of the colonial political field. Morocco's local industries consisted mainly of traditional handicrafts. These had weathered growing competition from European manufactured goods in the nineteenth century, but the inauguration of the protectorate dealt a severe blow. The colonial state's economic policy prioritized subsidizing the planning and financing of new industries but ignored local ones (Stewart 1964, 135). Artisans in Fes, for example, were hurt by the economic downturn (in 1931, the year of the exposition, the global economic crises was being felt acutely in Morocco) and competition from Western products.

In 1918, Lyautey created the Services des arts indigènes to control quality in the handicraft industry and provide training, but these efforts had little impact on the economic viability of Morocco's artisanal classes. On one side, consumer preference inside and outside Morocco switched to Western styles, to the detriment of local manufacturing. In addition, when the colonial state took over the administrative and regulatory functions previously provided by urban cooperatives and guilds and put them under the control of municipalities and the Service des arts indigènes, this further destabilized the traditional socioeconomic structure in the medinas. By the early 1930s, these economic stresses had created a crisis among the artisan class, particularly in Fes, that aided nationalist efforts to mobilize protest (see chapter 5).

---

55. MAE, CADN-Mar., Direction générale de l'instruction publique, Carton 92, adjunct commissioner of Morocco for the Colonial Exposition to the director general of public instruction, beaux-arts and antiquities, "Participation des services du protectorat à l'Exposition Coloniale de Paris 1931," December 21, 1929.

56. René Leclerc, "Le Maroc à Vincennes," in *Le Livre d'Or de l'Exposition Coloniale Internationale de Paris, 1931* (Paris: Librairie ancienne Honoré Champion, 1931), 59.

FIGURE 9. Sultan Mohamed ben Youssef after his tour of the Palais de Maroc, leaving through the reconstituted *"suq* of Rabat" with Resident General Lucien Saint at his right and MAE, CADN, Résidence générale de France au Maroc, document L'Illustration, 20MA/201/156, "A l'exposition coloniale de Vincennes, le sultan du Maroc retrouve les suqs de Rabat," 1931.

This chapter examined how contingent and contextual factors at the outset of France's intervention in Morocco helped determine the entwined logics of legitimation and legibility that shaped this emerging colonial political field. Colonial intervention in Morocco was justified in a protectorate imaginary that held modernization and traditionalization in tension. According to the French, intervention was needed to develop Morocco, but it was to be done (ostensibly) on behalf of the Moroccan ruler and with respect for the country's culture, society, and traditions. This legitimacy-legibility dyad was put into practice through three modes of rule. An ethnographic logic was expressed in classificatory practices that divided Moroccan society according to geographic, ethnic, religious, and political binaries. Instead of homogenizing, the colonial state ossified and at times invented social complexity in terms of ethnic, religious, and cultural differentiation, politicizing Arab, Berber, Muslim, and Jewish markers of identity through these processes in new ways. The preservationist logic of the protectorate involved an elaborate political traditionalization of the monarchy and the Moroccan *makhzan*. It also entailed a careful distinction between the native as "traditional" and the European as "modern" and substantial efforts to protect an "authentic" version of the former that was ahistorical and essentialized. Finally, a developmentalist mode of rule was based on the protectorate's mandate to modernize Morocco. In practice, the economic benefits of this investment flowed almost exclusively to the "modern" European rather than the "traditional" Moroccan. Having examined the spatial parameters and organizing forces of the colonial political field that was constructed in the period 1907–1931, the remaining chapters turn to the contentious interactions, identity struggles, and battles (military and political) that played out among colonial and Moroccan actors.

❦ CHAPTER 3

Resisting the Colonial Political Field in the Atlas Mountains

The power of the colonial state expanded between 1912 and the early 1930s, as we have seen, through the brutal conquest of rural resistance, the construction of an extensive transportation infrastructure, the imposition of an extractive colonial economy, and the extension of a highly articulated administrative apparatus. The focus now shifts to the Moroccan side of this story, examining how the creation of a colonial political field catalyzed external and internal identification processes among rural and urban groups enclosed in the colonial political field. The remaining chapters trace how dimensions of collective identity—local, regional, national, and transnational—were reconfigured in interactions among state and nonstate actors as ethnicity, language, and religion were politically activated in new ways.

The next section turns to identity formation in two rural groups, one in the Atlas Mountains in the French zone and the other in the Rif Mountains in the Spanish zone, as pacification campaigns progressively enclosed them in the space of the colonial political field in the first decades of the protectorate. Historically, these communities rarely contested the legitimacy of the sultan by seeking to overthrow him, but they actively negotiated their material relationship with the precolonial *makhzan* by paying or not paying taxes or assisting or resisting the military, depending on a constellation of cost-benefit calculations. Colonial intervention provoked a qualitatively different type of anti-state resistance. In both cases, the struggle against the central government was interpreted as a jihad, a categorical rejection of the legitimacy of a "Christian" *makhzan*'s attempt to extend symbolic, military, and infrastructural power over Muslims.

This chapter draws on Tamazight (Berber) sources to explore the internal dynamics of the Atlas jihad. In this region, jihad entailed loosely coordinated anti-state resistance, the goal of which was to maintain the relative autonomy of disparate tribes from French (interpreted as "Christian") control. During this tumultuous period, notions of social boundaries (between men and women; among tribes; within tribes; among Muslims; between Muslims, Christians, and Jews; between Moroccan and French) and geographic boundaries (between mountains and plains; between parts of the Atlas; in Morocco; in North Africa) were drawn and redrawn by these groups in the midst of their efforts to resist colonial power and in moments when they were forced to submit to that power. These primary sources provide an unparalleled window into internal struggles over the legitimacy of the state, over whether to submit to or resist the protectorate *makhzan*, over concepts of territoriality, and over notions of collective identity and solidarity in these rural communities.

Understanding the Atlas Jihad on Its Own Terms

There are three major Berber-speaking groupings in Morocco: Tarifit in the Rif, Tamazight[1] in the Middle Atlas and central and eastern High Atlas, and Tashelhit in the western High Atlas, the Souss Valley, and the Anti-Atlas. The ethnographic mode of rule the colonial state employed in the wake of the second stage of the pacification, which was directed at the Berber (Tamazight)-speaking middle and central High Atlas, involved establishing a Berber studies apparatus to research these tribes and train indigenous affairs officers to work in these areas. Ensuring the loyalty of the "Berber bloc," which provided the bulk of the Moroccan troops in the colonial army, quickly became a priority for protectorate officials. Chapter 2 described how a French Berber policy evolved in the first decades of the protectorate. Although far from systematic, this was tangibly expressed, particularly in the middle and central High Atlas, through the creation of separate judicial, educational, and administrative structures intended to "protect" Berber ethnolinguistic identity from the supposed contamination of Arabization and

---

1. In Morocco, Tamazight refers to a specific linguistic group in the Middle and High Atlas. It is also used to refer collectively to all three groups (Tarifit, Tamazight, and Tashelhit) as a more politically correct term than "Berber" (barbarian).

Islamization. This "divide and rule" ethnographic logic eventually became a cause célèbre for Arab nationalists, who mobilized a massive anti-colonial protest campaign against the May 16, 1930 decree that reorganized Berber customary law courts.

Because of its signal importance to the Moroccan nationalist narrative, a great deal of attention has been paid to the Berber Question. Most scholarship focuses on the nexus of colonial ethnography, military operations, and administrative policy that constituted the French Berber policy[2] or the nationalist mobilization against this policy by young urban Arab Moroccan elites (see Halstead 1964; Joffe 1984; Lafuente 1999; and Rachik 2003). Although the rural populations at the center of this intense struggle between colonial administrators and urban Arabophone nationalist elites over ethnic classifications and their relationship to national identity are frequently addressed, these groups themselves are rarely, if ever, heard from in the prodigious colonialist or nationalist sources from the period or in the scholarship that draws upon them.[3]

This chapter examines the neglected perspectives of Tamazight-speaking groups in the Atlas Mountains. It attempts to tell the story of the Atlas on its own terms, asking a series of understudied questions related to how these rural, tribal communities responded to the expansion of the colonial political field in the first decades of the protectorate. How did these groups frame the threat of colonial conquest? How did they mobilize resistance? In light of the supposed distinction between the *blad al-makhzan* and the *blad al-sība*, what were their attitudes about the sultan, urban areas, and other regions in Morocco? How did they express tribal, intertribal, ethnolinguistic, territorial, national, and religious levels of collective identity? And finally, how did they negotiate submission to the Franco-Moroccan *makhzan* and life under the protectorate state?

Answering these types of questions requires a move from the standard base of colonial and nationalist written sources to a unique collection of Tamazight oral poetry that was gathered in the Middle and High Atlas Mountains during the first decades of the protectorate. Because primary source records from nonliterate populations are rarely available or are gathered via

---

2. See Burke (1972), Ageron (1973), Hoffman (2008a), Guerin (2013), Lorcin (1995, 2005), and McDougall (2005) on the "Kabyle policy" precedents in Algeria.

3. The dearth of primary sources from these largely illiterate groups is reflected even in studies on rural resistance in the nineteenth and twentieth centuries that provide invaluable background on this neglected subject, such as Burke's (1976) work on the Middle Atlas tribes and Dunn's (1977) study of the Ait Atta. Ghazal (2010) provides a rare study on the perspectives of Algeria's Ibadi Berber population during the interwar period through an exploration of Arabic Salafi journals.

oral history much later, these poems, which were composed and collected contemporaneously with the events to which they refer, constitute a unique historical source base.[4] Furthermore, as a repository of public discourse, they provide an unparalleled window into how collective identity among these Berber speakers was impacted by the forceful expansion and consolidation of the colonial political field from 1912 to the mid-1930s. Complementing recent scholarship that explores how ethnic identity is contextually situated in the Maghrib (Hoffman and Miller 2010), these sources from a transformative period demonstrate how collective identity, instead of being static, was dynamically negotiated and reimagined among Berber-speaking groups in the midst of a rapidly changing social, political, economic, and military context.

The Creation of a Tamazight Oral Archive

In a footnote to his ethnography of the Ahansal in the High Atlas, Gellner (1969, 94) laments, "If only one possessed all the couplets, with their political and social commentary, invented and sung since the start of the century or earlier, one would have a most vivid account of the social history of the Atlas imaginable." Although he recognized the tremendous possibilities of the region's ubiquitous poetry, Gellner was unaware that a trove of this oral literature had already been collected and transcribed by French Berberists and Tamazight-speaking Moroccan interlocutors during critical stages of the pacification and afterward. While some poems were published in French translation in the 1930–1940s,[5] the most extensive collection is the Fonds Roux, archived at the Institut de recherches et d'etudes sur le monde arabe et musulman in Aix-en-Provence, France. Only recently have parts of it begun to be published.[6]

Arsène Roux was a French soldier who reassigned from Algeria to serve as an interpreter in the first wave of the pacification in the Middle Atlas in 1913. He was stationed in 1914–1918 at the military post in El Hajeb, a

---

4. The importance of poetry in North African oral history is demonstrated in Chtatou's (1991) work on the Rif and Heggoy's (1986) book on poetry collected by French scholars following the Algerian conquest. On the varied ways colonialists and nationalists used Kabyle oral texts as signs of social difference in Algeria, see Goodman (2002).

5. See Reynier (1930) and Paul-Margueritte (1935).

6. Stroomer and Peyron (2003) have performed an invaluable service in their cataloging of the archive. Peyron (Roux 2002) also edited and annotated a volume containing Tamazight poetry that was collected during the resistance period, and Stroomer has published many Tashelhit poems from the archive in the *Berber Studies* journal (2001, 2003, 2007).

market town that controlled the critical transition zone between the plains and mountains south of Meknes. In the early 1920s, he taught Arabic and Berber at the military school in Meknes, and in 1927, he helped create the Berber College in Azrou, where the French sent the sons of rural Berber notables. He served as its director until 1935, then he was assigned to other duties, including directing the elite Collège Mawlay Youssef in Rabat in the 1940s. Throughout this period, Roux's personal hobby was collecting poetry, primarily in Tamazight but also in Tashelhit. While Roux gathered much himself, he also relied extensively on Moroccan assistants, who fanned out to various locations in the Atlas to collect songs, transcribing oral performances in a Latin script form of Tamazight.

In its geographic and chronological breadth, this collection forms a remarkably comprehensive archive, made even more unique in that it was collected almost contemporaneously with the events the poems were composed to describe. Notes typically indicate the author and/or the tribe from which a poem originated and where, when, and by whom a poem was collected. Most of the collecting took place in market centers along the route south from Meknes to the Tafilelt (El Hajeb, Azrou, and Midelt), although Roux's informants also collected poems in Sefrou, Boulemane, and smaller villages.[7] The genre and explanatory notes about the context and performance are also frequently included.

It is difficult to assess the influence of the person who collected and transcribed the poems. It is possible that the authors who recounted poems to a French officer or even to other Moroccan interlocutors practiced self-censorship. One of the poets who visited Roux in El Hajeb, Moha u Bentaher, an Ait Myill (also Ait Njild or, in Arabic, Beni Mguild) poet from the town of Gigou further up in the mountains, provides some insight into the transcription process in a humorous autobiographical poem: "Moha entered the house of the *arumi* [Christian] / He approached the chair and sat down / The *arumi* told him, "Explain your poems to me, I want to write them down in my notebook, but speak slowly! / And the whip was snapped over my head."[8] Like any other oral or written source, the poems must be read with care, but it seems that the individuals who related their poems to Roux and other interlocutors felt free to relate a wide range of perspectives.

---

7. I have retained the French spellings of place names, which are still the most common renderings on maps.

8. Institut de recherches et d'etudes sur le monde arabe et musulman (IREMAM), Fonds Arsène Roux (hereafter Fonds Roux), file 55.1.2.

Although the metaphorical "whip" in the poem above alludes to the power differential between the ethnographer and informant in this process, poets did not seem to be inhibited about relating numerous poems that were highly critical of their "Christian" rulers. In addition, the clear concern about faithfully rendering the lyric on the part of both performer and collector indicates that the transcriptions offer a relatively reliable record of poems in circulation. While transcription is unavoidably an imperfect process of capturing a speech act, the poems are the only extant primary source record from these communities and one of the only means of gaining insight into personal and public negotiations of collective identity in the Tamazight-speaking Atlas during this eventful period.

The Performance Context and Dissemination of Tamazight Poetry

A significant factor that makes the poems such an important source for investigating questions of public perception and opinion is the fact that in its production and performance, North African poetry, like that of other oral cultures, constitutes a highly public, often interactive discourse.[9] One of this genre's most fascinating aspects is the range of its content—from highly intimate to social, political, and theological matters—and the vital function its performance provided for the community as a shared discursive space.

In a discussion of poetry performed in Sefrou, Clifford Geertz (1983, 114) notes how the performance context of popular poetry generates its remarkable power in Moroccan society:

> The performance frame of poetry, its character as a collective speech act, only reinforces this betwixt and between quality of it—half ritual song, half plain talk—because if its formal, quasi-liturgical dimensions cause it to resemble Qu'ranic chanting, its rhetorical, quasi-social ones cause it to resemble everyday speech.

This mixture also creates a strong editorial dimension as poets process, interpret, and didactically comment on society and current events. Hoffman (2008b, 528) observes in her analysis of women's use of Tashelhit poetry in the Souss Valley that an important distinction is made between conversational

---

9. Mammeri (1978) explains that the Kabyle *imusnawen,* a prose and poetic master similar to Morocco's *imdyazen,* plays a role as a spokesperson for the group who helps crystallize its sentiments. On the prominence of oral performance in contemporary urban and rural Arabic-speaking societies, see Cachia (1989), Abu-Lughod (1986), Caton (1990), and Shryock (1997).

speech and poetic singing that sees the latter as more valuable. Most significant for this study's focus, she writes that "collective identity is publicly displayed in these contexts, in contrast to the practices of concealing knowledge prevalent in other discursive domains."[10]

Poems were chanted or sung in the course of everyday activities. For example, *ahellel* poems were composed and sung by women as they performed routine chores such as grinding grain. They were also performed in a wide range of group contexts. Often they were performed in the context of lyrical gamesmanship among local poets during celebrations such as weddings and feasts. These contests often concluded with a large *ahidus* circle in which men and women dancers responded to individual lines as a chorus. In the late 1920s, local poets took advantage of increased security and ease of travel to perform among neighboring tribes. Poems were also disseminated far beyond the local level through the activities of the *imdyazen* (sing. *amdyaz*), wandering bards whom Jouad (1989) has labeled the "rural intellectuals" of the Atlas.[11]

The *imdyazen* profession originated in the Ait Yahia tribe of the eastern High Atlas and spread among the other tribes of the Ait Yafelman confederation.[12] They traveled with a troupe, performing in encampments in the spring and early summer before returning home for the harvest. The *imdyazen* and amateur poets used a poetic lingua franca that preserved a level of linguistic unity in the Tamazight bloc and helped sustain an awareness of common identity by disseminating a shared repertoire of oral literature. The itineraries of the *imdyazen* traversed this linguistic group, from the oases in the Saharan south over the Atlas Mountains to the plains around Meknes and Fes in the north. Traveling *imdyazen* carried news from other regions about the state of crops and herds and, after 1907, the progress of the *irumin*, or Christians, who were invading the country. In addition to linking the rural regions of Morocco, they also linked city and countryside, moving between the mountains and the great urban centers of Marrakesh, Meknes, and Fes, where some even established winter residences.[13]

---

10. Also see her ethnography on space and the language practices of Tashelhit women (Hoffman 2008b).

11. On the activities and roles of *imdyazen,* also see Peyron (2000).

12. Fonds Roux, file 54.2.1, "Légendes sur origines des aèdes"; Fonds Roux, file 53.3, "Le répertoire des imdyazen"; and Roux (1928, 231–51).

13. An *amdyaz* from the Ait Izdeg tribe, Shaykh Mohand 'Ajmi, and his *buganim* (an instrumentalist in the troupe) had winter residences in Fes. Roux interviewed both of them.

Framing, Organizing, and Debating the Jihad in the Atlas

As a repository of public discourse, these poems provide an unparalleled window into the internal dynamics of Atlas tribal communities that faced an unprecedented expansion of state power in their daily lives. A dominant theme is the question of whether to engage in jihad, or defensive holy war, against the colonial state. This issue was tied to a wide range of issues that included perceptions of what constituted legitimate Islamic authority; attitudes toward the sultan and whether tribes were obligated to defend the *umma*, or Muslim community; and debates about the implications of submitting to a "Christian" *makhzan*. In the colonial context, jihad was also directly relevant to existential realities such as hunger, starvation, and the brutality of modern warfare and to more esoteric questions about eschatology, theodicy, and collective identity.

In the period 1911–1934, as the pacification progressed from the Middle Atlas south into the central High Atlas, various indigenous groups used different organizational strategies to respond to the threat. The decision of whether to resist or submit was generally negotiated at the individual tribal level, but periodically that decision was made at the level of larger tribal coalitions. From 1911 to 1913, during the first French penetration into the Saiss plain around Fes and the foothills of the Middle Atlas, tribes including the Ait Ndhir (Beni Mtir), Gerwan (Guerouan), Ait Segrushen, and parts of the Ait Myill (Beni Mguild) coordinated a response that had some early successes but could not sustain resistance against the Franco-Moroccan *makhzan* forces (Burke 1976). This type of temporary alliance among roughly equal tribal chiefs had manifested in 1903 with the Ait ʿAtta and Dawi Mani' alliance in the Tafilelt region (Dunn 1977) and was repeated in the final resistance against the French in High Atlas in the late 1920s. While such coalitions were sometimes remarkably successful in the short run, they fell apart over time as individual tribes or subgroups of tribes would break off and submit to the colonial state. Analysis of the content of poems generated by tribes that continued the jihad, tribes that had submitted, and even by those who were conscripted into the colonial army as partisans or regular soldiers (*goumiers*) presents a fascinating window into military resistance in the Atlas region and its evolution over time.

The earliest poems in the archive were collected during Roux's stint in 1914–1918 in El Hajeb, located about thirty kilometers south of Meknes, on the slope that joined the mountain to the plain. El Hajeb was strategically positioned along the route from Fes to the coast and the route from Fes to Marrakesh, and the French made it into an administrative and market center that they hoped would convince tribes to "peacefully" submit to the state, à la Lyautey's *tache de huile* strategy. Thus, it was an ideal site for gathering poetry from tribes in the transition zone between the plains and the Middle Atlas that had submitted, such as the Gerwan and Ait Ndhir (Beni Mtir), and those located higher up that remained dissident, including the Ait Njild (Beni Mguild) and Iziyan (Zaian). Roux also conducted interviews with touring *imdyazen* from the High Atlas, which was far outside protectorate control at this point. Map 5 shows the location of the tribes referenced in the Fonds Arsène Roux.

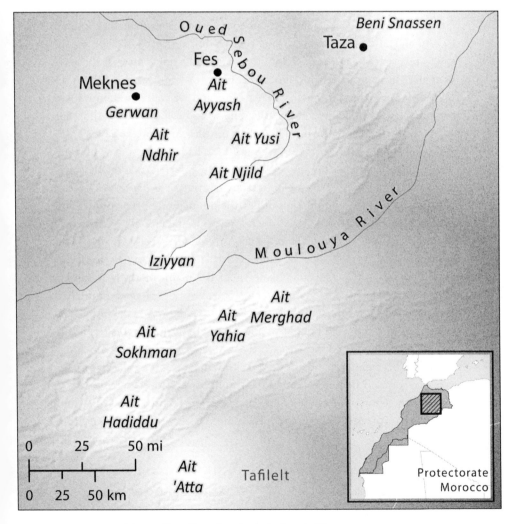

MAP 5.   Tamazight-speaking tribes referred to in the Roux Archive

Poems composed as the French began moving into Morocco reveal the complex relationship between these supposedly *"sība"* nonstate groups and the central government, a relationship that was metonymically and concretely represented for these tribal groups in the person of the sultan. Many poems from the Ait Ndhir tribe, whose territory encompasses both plain and mountains, add historical insight to these dynamics. In the late nineteenth century, this tribe was split between factions that cooperated with the *makhzan* and factions that resisted it. Later, the tribe was intimately involved, along with neighboring Middle Atlas tribes, in the civil war between sultans 'Abd al-'Aziz and 'Abd al-Hafiz in the years just before the French established the protectorate (Burke 1991, 132–44; Vinograd 1974). Several poems comment on the hopes that some placed in 'Abd al-Hafiz, who passed through Ait Ndhir territory in 1908 on his way to receive the *bay'a* oath of loyalty in Fes, and express utter disillusionment after he capitulated and signed the Treaty of Fes. Lyazid u Lahsen, an Ait Ndhir poet, stated: "Mawlay Hafiz came and we welcomed him. / He promised us that once he arrived in Fes, he would call on the Muslims for help. / But, when he settled in, he called on the chiefs of the Haouz[14] to be his counselors. / O Morocco [l-Gherb]! He had already sold you to the *irumin!*"[15] In the poems, the French are generally referred to as *irumin* (sing. *arumi*), or "Christians"; they are only rarely referred to as *fransis*. As was the case among the urban population in Fes, the population in the countryside viewed the treaty as a "bill of sale" by the sultan to the French "Christians" (Burke 1976, 182). Another poet, l-Haj Asusi, chided the 'Alawids: "The Christians have formed their columns and have risen against us from the places they occupy / The sultan sold them the plains of the west under the condition that they come subdue them / We have fought them beautifully / They stated the conditions of their act of purchase; they cited the justness of their claim, that they had bought us and were within their rights."[16] In this case, the poet interpreted the Treaty of Fes as a *jaysh* agreement in which the sultan sold his rights to lands in the fertile western plains to the French in exchange for their help in subduing the troublesome mountain tribes.

While these early poems are highly critical of the failure of the sultan and the *makhzan* to resist "Christian" penetration, they also demonstrate that

---

14. The Haouz region is located just north of Marrakesh, where 'Abd al-Hafiz served as governor before the civil war against his brother in 1907–1908.

15. Fonds Roux, file 59.1, recorded by Roux in El Hajeb, 1914–1918.

16. Fonds Roux, file 59.1, recorded by Roux in El Hajeb, 1914–1918.

these *"sība"* tribes felt solidarity with the so-called *bilād al-makhzan* that the French were invading. The following poem demonstrates a Middle Atlas–based poet's clear awareness of the French encroachment from the Atlantic coast. He referred to the occupation of the Zaer region inland from Rabat and to the occupation of Fes: "The Christian is coming / He has built out-posts in the middle of Zaer country / He has planted his flags over the city of Fes / And he has stretched out his hands to conquer other territories and other riches."[17] Another poem also laments the fall of Morocco's major cities to the *irumin*: "O red city! O Dar Debbibagh![18] The *makhzan* is no more! / The Christians strut about there with total impunity / Cry for the fate of our cities: Fes, Meknes, Agourai, Sefrou, and Tabadout! / Surely the Christians are the cause of our fall! / Fes and Meknes are lost, not to mention Sefrou and Casablanca,[19] / Can one make the crow of the mountains white?" (Roux 2002, 91).[20] The poet l-Haj Asusi linked the *imazighen* (Berbers) to Meknes, which no longer "belongs" to them: "Meknes is no more, O *imazighen*, the Meknes you knew no longer belongs to us. / It is to the Christian that it has gone / As for me, I have given it up. All the nice places to live have been snatched up by the Christian / He has pillaged the treasury of the sultans and my own is also empty."[21] An *amdyaz* of the Ait Yusi tribe in the mountains above Sefrou lamented the fall of nearby Fes, picturing the grief of the medina's major gates: "The Christians have fallen upon the chiefs as the sheep are fallen upon in the cities / Lift up your grief, O gate of Bab-Ftuh, lift up your grief, O Bab-Guissa! / Next to you the sons of pigs have come to wash their coats."[22] These poems clearly demonstrate that tribal groups on the peripheries of urban centers felt a strong sense of solidarity with the occupied cities.

Even when a division was drawn between mountains and plains, a sense of greater territorial unity was present in these poems. A poet from Guigou, an Ait Myill village in the Middle Atlas that had not yet been pacified, feared the progress of pacification: "The General inherited the *gherb* region; God favors him / If he is able, he will go all the way to the pass of Tizi Larays /

---

17. Fonds Roux, file 50.2.10, recorded by Roux in El Hajeb, 1914–1918.

18. The area to the west of Fes al-Jdid, where the French army camped and where the *ville nouvelle* was later constructed (Saulay 1985, 41).

19. The poet uses *l-baida*, a shortened form of Dar al-Baida (meaning Casablanca).

20. Peyron's editorial comment explains that according to legend, the crow used to be white but was blackened by God after it performed a sacred task. In other poems (pp. 137–38), the crow symbolizes a traitor.

21. Fonds Roux, file 59.1 recorded by Roux in El Hajeb, 1914–1918.

22. Fonds Roux, file 52.5, recorded by Moha u Driss al-Yusi in Sefrou, 1934.

Up to the valley of the Moulouya, all the way to the country of U Sidi 'Ali / Then the people of the mountains will submit to him and kiss his hands."[23] This poet used *l-gherb* to refer to the coastal lowland plain to the west. The poet foresaw that the French "General" would inherit the entire land, including the poet's own "people of the mountains." Although the poet views the mountains and plains as distinct, the poet believes they share the same destiny.

The multiple iterations of the root term *l-gherb* provide important insight into conceptions of territory among Tamazight-speaking tribes. The Arabic term *al-maghrib* ambiguously refers to the "west," sometimes the west of the Muslim world (North Africa), and sometimes Morocco itself, "the farthest west," as an abbreviation of al-Maghrib al-aqsa. This ambiguity is also expressed with its Berberized version, *l-gherb*. As shown in poems above, it was used at times to refer to lowland areas to the northwest. At other times, it indicated a larger Moroccan territorial entity. The poet quoted above called out "O l-Gherb! He had already sold you to the Christians [*irumin*]!"[24] In this case the term corresponds to the territory of the sultan's empire, which included the poet's own territory. Another poem about the invading French army further clarified the distinction between l-Gherb and the rest of North Africa: "We see the Christian commander, the Senegalese, the troops of l-Gherb l-wasta, there are even the Jews wearing their black hats."[25] Here the poet broke down the oncoming military contingent into groups that included the French officer (*l-hakem*); the Senegalese (*saligān*) *tirailleurs*, colonial troops that the French deployed from 1907 to serve in the pacification; and Jewish grocers, wearing black kippahs, who followed behind the colonial army selling wares at the encampments of the *groupes mobiles*. The phrase l-Gherb al-wasta, a Berberized form of the Arabic phrase that meant "the middle west," was used in the poems to denote Algeria, a "middle west" that was distinct from the poet's own country, which is presumably "the west," or l-Gherb.

Another important geographical designation in the poems is *tamazirt*, which was used mostly to designate a much closer homeland or countryside. However, the term *tamazirt* also carries the flexible connotations of *patrie*, which was used at times for a much larger Moroccan "country." For example, an Ait Ndhir poet cried out, "The French have received the whole country

---

23. Fonds Roux, file 55.1.2, recorded by Roux in El Hajeb, 1914–1918.
24. Fonds Roux, file 59.1, recorded by Roux in El Hajeb, 1914–1918.
25. Fonds Roux, file 52.5, recorded by Moha u Driss al-Yusi in Sefrou, 1934.

[*tamazirt*] as an inheritance. / Everywhere they have built their military posts and over them they have hung their flags as a sign of victory."[26] The presence of indigenous affairs posts and the French *tricolore* were visual symbols that created dread for the poet, who pessimistically envisioned their total control over the "whole *tamazirt*."

From the perspective of these Tamazight-speaking groups, the sultan's capitulation to the French and the fall of Morocco's cities, coasts, and central plains to Christian control meant that the unsubdued tribes of the Atlas ranges were the final line of defense for Morocco's Muslim community. In contrast to the assumptions of the colonial vulgate that minimized their religious fervor, Islam was the primary category of identity for these Berber groups and motivated their resistance against the colonial state. After nominally submitting to the French in 1911, the Ait Ndhir revolted in 1912 under pressure from tribal confederations to their south. Beginning in 1913, Lyautey directed the military to focus on pacifying the troublesome Middle Atlas tribes who threatened the Rabat-Meknes-Fes-Oujda axis. Facing the pacification, poets affirmed their obligation to mount a defensive jihad against the Christian invader. A poet of the Ait Ndhir cried out to the chiefs of the tribe: "Here is a letter, O messenger! Take it to Driss, to Bugrin, to Moha u Said, the chiefs. / Gather around her Ajammu, L-Ghazi u Gessu, as well as Imalwi and l-Muradi u Mansur. Get U Abli too! / And tell them: The Christian [*arumi*], is it not he that, during his life, the Prophet commanded us to fight?"[27] Another urged Muslims to keep fighting: "Let's go! Rise up, O Cowards, and join the Jews [*udayn*]! / Stand up, O Muslims against the Christians [*irumin*]! Are you already dead?"[28]

These exhortations represent an intense struggle in and among tribes over whether to submit to the "Christian" *makhzan* or continue a religious resistance, or jihad, against it. One Ait Ndhir poet exclaimed, "There is no question of submission / We will fight; if victory eludes us we will move the camp, we will go from country to country / We cannot bear the enemy of the Prophet."[29] Moha u Bentaher, who was from the Ait Myill tribe located the south of the Ait Ndhir, criticized those who submitted: "O you who have submitted / Is it a sultan you follow? / Is it

---

26. Fonds Roux, file 59.1, recorded by Roux in El Hajeb 1914–1918.
27. Fonds Roux, file 50.3.1, recorded by Roux in El Hajeb, 1914–1918.
28. Fonds Roux, file 50.2.10, recorded by Roux in El Hajeb, 1914–1918.
29. Fonds Roux, file 50.2.10, recorded by Roux in El Hajeb, 1914–1918.

a holy person you accompany? / No, it is by a swine that you let yourself be led / But I see no one who is scared."[30] This poet attacked those who submitted to the Christians and the nominal authority of the sultan as being against Islam.

Both men and women also interpreted submission in gendered terms, as a diminution of masculinity. In an *izli*, a couplet form of verse, an Ait Ndhir man declared: "I am going to repudiate the mistress of my tent and leave her to marry Pisani / For I did not know how to fight you enemies of the Prophet."[31] Having failed to resist the Christian invader, the poet felt obligated to forfeit his marital rights to his wife, ceding them to the French officer, Pisani. Another Ait Ndhir man asked the women of his tribe a question that reflected a crisis after the men had submitted: "Women, did you not say you would not admit in your bed a man who does not fight in the jihad? / And now that they kiss the hands of Desjobert, what will you do?"[32]

This interweaving of sexuality, gender roles, and religious identity was explicit in duels between two poets, often from the same tribe, over the choice between submission and jihad. The following exchange was between two Ait Ndhir female poets. 'Aisha Uqessur was the wife of a *qa'id* named Driss who recently had led his fraction of the tribe to submit at El Hajeb. Tabašnut was the wife of 'Alla ou Driss, the leader of a group of Ait Ndhir that continued to fight. In her first lines, Tabašnut taunted 'Aisha's husband, implying that he let the French officer have his way with his wife: "What happens in your heart, O Qa'id Driss, when the French chief orders you to leave your tent so he can enter in?"[33] 'Aisha responded to this insult to her honor by comparing the ease of her present life under the French with the hardships the dissidents faced: "I use the mules to transport the great water skins / I can, O senseless rebels, choose among the springs of the country / You, on the other hand, have been overtaken by misfortune / Your harvest is lost and you fight in vain!" Tabašnut responded by equating submission with prostituting oneself to the French: "I give up the springs of the country, and I leave you to Roux, O Aisha! / Share your bed also with

---

30. Fonds Roux, file 55.1.2, recorded by Roux in El Hajeb, 1914–1918.

31. Fonds Roux, file 50.3.1, recorded by Roux in El Hajeb, 1914–1918.

32. Fonds Roux, file 59.2, recorded by Roux in El Hajeb, 1914–1918.

33. While the poet might be simply slandering her opponent, there were numerous instances of officers taking Berber mistresses.

Pisani."[34] Then she attacked ʿAisha as a collaborator with the Christians: "The large water skins in which you are going to draw water and carry it / Are drying up the thirst of the holy warriors [*imjuhad*] / O ʿAisha, who curses me while you prepare your tent / To let the French chief spend the night in!"[35]

The End of Jihad

In this oral medium of public discourse, the tribes of the middle and central High Atlas fretted over the implications of submission and debated how much resisting tribes should sacrifice. Gender was prominent in these debates, which linked sexual and religious fidelity to jihad against the French. These dilemmas intensified as the pacification entered its final stages in the late 1920s. A large volume of poetry was composed during this period by those who were fighting the Franco-Moroccan *makhzan*; by partisans who had joined or been conscripted into the *makhzan* army that was striving to finish the pacification; and by tribes that had already submitted but were anxiously following the progress of military campaigns against neighboring tribes to the south. Roux was director of the Collège Berbère d'Azrou during these pivotal years, and he gave his students, who were practicing their transcription of Tamazight in Latin script, assignments to write down poetry, legends, and information on local customs during school holidays. Roux's older Tamazight-speaking colleagues also actively collected poetry during these years.

Many poems expressed a sense of apocalyptic doom, resignation, and despair as the last "free" *imazighen* were finally conquered by the Christians. For those still fighting, the technological and organizational superiority of the French army generated a religious crisis. A song collected by Moha u Driss al-Yusi in the early 1930s exclaimed: "What swords! What Senegalese tirailleurs! What organization among the Christians! How can we fight them?"[36] An *izli* from the Ait Hadiddu of the Assif Melloul, which was subdued in 1932, expressed despair: "If the Prophet had had to defend against machines like those that are attacking me / It would have been a long time ago / That the Muslims would have been conquered by the Christians / And that they would have broken their

---

34. Roux notes that he and Pisani were French noncommissioned officers assigned to the Sharifian column stationed in El Hajeb.

35. Fonds Roux, file 59.2, recorded by Roux in El Hajeb, 1914–1918.

36. Fonds Roux, file 52.5.

pacts of mutual support."[37] In this poem, the author evoked the greater Muslim *umma* with a reference to the Prophet Mohamed and intra-Muslim defense alliances against a common enemy. The "machines," or the modern technology warriors were facing, demonstrate the failure of his religious community: even the Prophet Mohamed would not have been able to defeat this foe. Seeing no deliverance in sight as flocks, fields, and families were destroyed in modern warfare, another poet was overwhelmed by the inevitability of defeat: "I look at the land; it is covered with automobiles / I look at the sky, it is full of planes / Where then will the Muslim go who asks himself: / 'What have I to do in the territories governed by the Christian?'"[38]

This disillusionment was also directed at the marabouts and charismatic chiefs (*igurramen*) among the High Atlas tribes that galvanized the last waves of resistance with mahdist, or messianic, promises of deliverance. For many warriors, the juxtaposition of their meager resources and their enemy's vast arsenal led to a sense of betrayal. A poem collected in 1933 from an Ait Yahia poet challenged religious leaders: "Who among our saints would know how make an automobile or build a plane? / Who among them would be capable of setting it on its way, flying it, and flying over you, O Sidi 'Ali?" (Roux 1992, 171). The legendary battle of Tazizaout in 1932 demonstrates the complexities of the disappointment the final failure of the jihad generated. Sidi l-Mekki, one of the *igurramen* whose millenarian rhetoric encouraged the last pockets of resistance, led a group of 1,000 mainly Ait Sokhman and Ait Hadiddu warriors and their families to the stronghold of Tazizaout, located east of Imilchil. After heroically holding out for more than a month against three French army columns, Sidi l-Mekki negotiated a surrender in late September. L-Mekki was despised by many of his former followers when his deal-making with the French later led to his appointment as a *qa'id* over the Ait Sokhman (Peyron 2007).

Finally falling under the control of the "Christian" government, which involved relinquishing weapons and being registered by indigenous affairs officers, was interpreted as a religious cataclysm. Sidi Mohand, a warrior of the Ait Merghad tribe, composed the following self-searching poem after

---

37. Ibid.
38. Ibid.

surrendering at the Keba'a military post[39] in 1933: "Can he that has passed in front of the post (l-biru) / And has been registered by the Christian / Become a Muslim again? / Is the post better than Islam / In the eyes of the subjugated / Who have forgotten the Prophet for the French?"[40] Here the poet equated submission with apostasy.[41] Elsewhere the pacification was interpreted as desecration. In another poem collected in the early 1930s, an Ait Yusi poet grieved, "What sorts of prayers are left? / The Qur'an is mishandled, and the Christians [irumin], wearing their képis, trample on our sanctuaries."[42]

Northern tribes that had been pacified earlier also agonized over the last stages of the pacification to the south in the High Atlas, mixing hope and an expectation of doom for these last bastions of autonomy: "The imazighen hope that the Saint Sidi Yahia u Yusuf will turn back the Christians. / But then, look, the Senegalese are camping close to the sanctuary."[43] As news about French victories in the High Atlas spread, poets in lower-elevation regions expressed intense disappointment and anxiety. In a poem collected in 1932, a poet in Azrou rhetorically asked the Ait Hadiddu tribe if the airplanes had reached their mountain fastnesses: "Question the pilot, O man of the Ait Hadiddu, and ask him if he is coming to bomb / Has he reached all the way to the Ait Hadiddu? Has he succeeded in subduing them?" (Roux 1992, 171). In another poem collected that year, a member of the Ait Ayyash of the Saiss plain near Fes grieved the fate of a region 200 kilometers to the south, "Why did you submit? O Assif Melloul!"[44] These poems display an awareness of events transpiring across a wide region, a circulation of poems back and forth across the line of dissidence, and a growing awareness of the encroachments of the modern state via telegraph lines, air power, artillery, and roads. Poets clearly identified this evidence of what the French saw as modernization as the cause of their defeat.

---

39. The indigenous affairs outpost was called l-biru in Tamazight, a Berberized form of the French word bureau, indicating the legacy of the Arab Bureaus first implemented in Algeria in the nineteenth century. When I met with present-day imdyazen in Aghbalou in the High Atlas, they still referred to the site of the old DAI office as l-biru.

40. Fonds Roux, file 57.1.1, recorded by Mawlay Ahmed in Kebab, 1933.

41. A 1932 poem by Houssa ou Moah, recorded near Azrou at Ougmes, makes the same equivalence between submission and apostasy, using a similar lyric (Roux 2002, 69).

42. Fonds Roux, file 52.5.

43. Ibid.

44. Fonds Roux, file 57.5.1, recorded among the Ait Ayyache south of Fes, 1932.

Figure 10. Moroccan colonial troops saluting the French tricolor after installing a radio tower close to Taourirt in 1911. MAE, CADN, Résidence générale de France au Maroc, 20MA/201/62, "A Taourirt devant le poste de télégraphie sans fil."

Life under the *Irumin*

By the end of 1934, the entire Tamazight-speaking region had been enclosed in the colonial political field. A large number of poems in the archive comment on life under the "Christians," the injustices and the inconveniences the protectorate administration brought. Occasionally, they speak of the benefits of the new order. Some criticized the colonial state as an unwelcome imposition that interfered with daily life. One poet complained: "I am going again on the route without being granted a travel permit / Today the Christians were without pity and gave me a fine."[45] However, the *amdyaz* Smaʿil n-Hammami appreciated the increased security: "From now on, fear is unknown / The French authorities have banished it / Go then, O travelers, follow your route without any shred of fear / No one will question you / The paths will be without obstacle for you."[46] Although travelers needed to get a travel permit in the colonial political field, at least the roads were safe.

Ambiguity was also expressed in attitudes about the protectorate's administration of justice. Some applauded the French: "I tell you, the Christians are good / Without them, the rights of orphans and widows would be trampled by injustice."[47] Another poet, Buhali l-Burezzuni l-Mtiri, praised them in a poem composed early in the protectorate: "The French are worth more than our sultan / They do not love injustice / They follow a straight path and do not turn from it."[48] However, the same poet, also noted the cost that these benefits entailed: "The battles of days gone by have now been taken to the military outpost / The blows the tongue carries are more effective today / Than the shots of the rifle of yesteryear / That is now the lot of the *imazighen* / But it is also the general lot of everyone."[49] The last two lines poignantly reflect the bard's awareness of a new reality in which the decision to use violence to settle conflicts had been ceded to the modern state.

Buhali was highly sensitive to other profound shifts in the colonial political field. His oral culture was pitted against the hegemony of the written word in the new bureaucratic system. In another poem, he asserted: "It is in the spoken word that I will write the number two / I have no notebooks and, even more, I am illiterate / But it is in my memory that I inscribe my reports."[50] The census operations of the indigenous affairs officer reflected a deeper ordering, a tangible expression of Bourdieu's "symbolic violence" that was felt not just in the countryside, but in the whole of Moroccan society. Buhali expressed a general ambivalence about this process in another

---

45. Fonds Roux, file 52.5, songs of the Ait Youssi.

46. Fonds Roux, file 52.1.3. The poems in this file were prepared for a présentation Roux made at the Congrès de la musique marocaine in Fes in 1939.

47. Fonds Roux, file 50.2.10, recorded by Roux in El Hajeb, 1914–1918.

48. Fonds Roux, file 59.1, recorded by Roux in El Hajeb, 1914–1918.

49. Ibid.

50. Ibid.

poem: "The Christian chief registered the women in his log / I attended the operation / It was my lawful wife at the head of the line."[51]

Another poet, Lyazid u Lahsen, also lamented the new order under the Franco-Moroccan *makhzan*, contrasting it with life before: "In the past, the mosquito himself did not dare attack our teams of horses / No one dared approach my herd of cows / Today, we ourselves have been harnessed to the plow / The yoke has been made to our measure / And the spur is pressed on our flanks / Us? We are subdued!"[52] A poem collected in 1934 from the Ait Ayyash uses the metaphor of a flour mill to describe life under the protectorate: "The *qa'id* is like a mill / The French commander [*hakim*] plays the role of the canal that brings him water / And the poor guys [*msakin*] are like the kernels of grain that are crushed under the grindstone."[53] Here, the *makhzan*-appointed *qa'id* is viewed with antagonism, the French chief enables the exploitation, and the poor normal folks are exploited.

For the Tamazight-speaking block, one of the most significant transformations during these years was the incorporation of many tribesmen into the colonial army. Several poems offer first-person reactions to the type of microprocesses of modern governmentality Mitchell (1988) describes in his discussion of the Egyptian army's *tanzimat* reforms. After being put through a series of military exercises, one soldier composed these lines: "Where could I have learned to do this drill? / What do these orders mean—'At arms!' 'At ease!' or 'To the right!' / Is it not true that the Christians break us like one breaks an ox with a yoke to train it for the plough?"[54] Fighting on the side of the *irumin* could generate a great deal of ambivalence among colonial soldiers. One early poem ridiculed Moroccan soldiers under the French: "O wearer of the blue burnoose / O dogs of the 'kicking officer' / O servants of the Christian! / When you hear the bugle call announcing the raising of the flag / You salute, putting your hand over your ear."[55] As the pacification progressed, more and more Tamazight-speaking soldiers were incorporated into the forces sent against neighboring tribes in the Atlas. The campaigns of the late 1920s and early 1930s in the Upper Moulouya and the Assif Melloul (two of the last redoubts in the High Atlas) relied heavily on Iziyan (Zaian) partisan forces (*l-bertiza*) who had fought the French fiercely the decade

51. Ibid.
52. Ibid.
53. Fonds Roux, file 57.5.1, recorded among the Ait Ayyash south of Fes, 1932.
, 54. Fonds Roux, file 52.5, recorded by Moha ou Driss el Youssi in Sefrou, 1934.
55. Fonds Roux, file 50.3.1, recorded by Roux in El-Hajeb, 1914–1918.

before. A soldier who was called up to fight in 1931 expressed reluctance: "When they gave us our turbans / I understood that we were close to departing for the operation / I was hoping that he would discharge us back to our tents."[56] Another soldier asked: "Why should I attack the *zawiya* of Sidi Yahya u Yusuf? / Why should I curse the poor people I oppress?"[57]

On the other hand, some poems expressed pride in the *imazighen* troops and the fact that the French relied on them. The Ait Ndhir poet Sma'il n Hammani composed an *izli* that boasted: "If the French need something, it is to me they look to help them / We, O *imazighen*, we are used to glorious bravery and will never desert them / Again, when they mobilized us to go in columns / Did not all of the Ait Ndhir leave to subdue the countryside stirred up in rebellion?"[58] A poem by Hammami about intervening in the Spanish zone in the 1920s during the Rif War celebrated the bravery of Ait Ndhir soldiers: "We have conquered you, O post of 'Ain 'Aicha / But the Qa'id Haddou and the *khalifat* Moha were wounded there / The Ait Ndhir have always been courageous." Another poem that was composed by Moha u 'Abid and collected in 1932 hints at the role auxiliary troops played in quelling urban nationalist protests. In the poem, a young man's mother buys him a horse and he goes to the bureau to join as a *mokhzani*. After resolving the issue of his lack of a travel permit, the officer gives him a blue burnous and a sword as long as a pole. He asks "But who am I going to hit with this saber? It will overload my horse." The final line of the poem answers the question: "Rejoice O jackal! I'm going to prepare you a feast of the bone marrow of the rich inhabitants of Fes!"[59] Given the date of the poem, it seems likely that the young Berber poet was being sent to quell the Arab nationalist protests against French Berber policy in Fes.

Although Tamazight-speaking colonial troops were successfully incorporated into the French colonial army, it became evident by the late 1930s that a cantonment policy to separate Arabs and Berbers was a fantasy, primarily because of processes the French themselves had set in motion, including the pacification itself and the construction of a transportation and communications infrastructure. The French were also not unaware of their own role in facilitating the Arabization and Islamization of the Berber areas they were striving to maintain the pristine integrity of. In 1928, Georges Surdon (1928,

---

56. Fonds Roux, file 56.3.4, recorded by Houssa ou Moha in Ougmes, 1932.
57. Ibid.
58. Fonds Roux, file 52.1.3, recorded by El Ghazi u 'Umar es-Saddni in El Hajeb, 1939.
59. Fonds Roux, file 51.1.2, gathered by Moha ou Abid in El Hajeb, 1932.

10), a former interpreter in the French colonial army and a commissioner in the Sharifian government, observed:

> Unfortunately, it seems that the Arabization of the Berber country is in danger of being rapidly accomplished, for various reasons which it would take too long to develop here. One can, however, state that to Arabize is, for the Berber, a manner of self-defense against us and, above all, that we are the vehicles for Arabization by obliging the Berbers to express themselves, in their dealings with us, in Arabic. If we do not take caution, we will have broken our promises and created an impassable abyss between the Berbers and us.[60]

By the early 1940s, many of the Atlas notables were either refusing to send their children to the Franco-Berber schools, demanding instead that they go to the Arabic schools in the major cities, or pressuring local Berber schools (in Sefrou, El Hajeb, Khemisset) to offer more Arabic and Islamic instruction.[61] Upward mobility in the colonial political field was tied to Arabization (and to knowledge of French), and Tamazight speakers wanted access. From the 1920s to the 1940s, service in the army, interaction with a French- and Arabic-dominated government administration, increasing economic activity conducted in Moroccan Arabic in market centers, and, above all, massive migration to cities were inexorable factors that further integrated these communities into a Moroccan field in which Muslim, Arab, and Berber identities were beginning to have new political implications.

This chapter's analysis of Tamazight oral primary sources from the period of the colonial pacification and just after that time reveals a nuanced and complex negotiation of collective self-identification among groups in a Tamazight-speaking bloc in the Atlas Mountain ranges. On one level, this shared repertoire demonstrates how an illiterate, transhumant population imagined a broader political-religious community beyond a local or regional scale.[62] This corporate identity was crystallized by the threat of a foreign invasion by the French army. The primary distinction that emerges from this poetry is between Christians and Muslims. For the Atlas Tamazight

---

60. Surdon later laments that the lack of Berber-speaking French officers created perennial problems for the administration, as most had much better Arabic skills.

61. MAE, CADN-Mar, Direction d'Instruction Publique, Carton 30, report by G. Germain, director of Collège Berber in Azrou, July 1943.

62. This reveals nonprint mechanisms other than the mass literacy that Benedict Anderson (1991) emphasizes that can sustain nation-sized levels of imagined community.

population, Muslim identity was primary, and many viewed themselves as
the last true defenders of a Moroccan community defined in Islamic terms.
Significantly, the most intense struggles were waged over whether or not
to continue to fight to preserve this community. In the Middle and High
Atlas, proponents of jihad rejected the legitimacy of the Franco-Moroccan
makhzan. This defensive anti-state resistance was carried out mostly at tribal
and subtribal levels; only sporadically and briefly was resistance express in
larger coalitions.

These Tamazight-speaking groups did identify with a distinct "Morocco-
sized" territorial and social entity (l'Gherb), but this level of imagined community was only one of many in play. *Imazighen* also expressed individual
tribal identity and intertribal solidarity. This level of collective identity as
"Berbers" is implicit in the use of various external classifications to distinguish among Algerian Arabs, Jews, and the despised Senegalese colonial troops
the French deployed in Morocco. A shared oral literary tradition unified the
identity of these Tamazight-speaking groups, but language did not constitute
an impermeable "ethnic" boundary between them and Arabic-speakers, as
French colonial theorists and policy makers ardently hoped it would. With
the completion of the pacification in 1934, the Berber-speaking areas colonial administrators had formerly labeled the *bilad al-sība* became more and
more integrated into the colonial political field through the increased ease of
travel, the enlistment or conscription of much of the male population into
the colonial army, and economic upheaval that encouraged, or forced, much
of this population to migrate to the cities.

✿ CHAPTER 4

Creating an Anti-colonial Political Field in the Rif Mountains

In comparison to the pace of pacification in the French zone, Spain's extension of a state-controlled political field proceeded slowly. It was not until after World War I, in 1919, that they began to launch concerted pacification operations to subdue the interior mountain ranges of the northern zone. These efforts were relatively successful in the Jebala range in the west but encountered concerted resistance in the eastern Rif. This was coordinated by a charismatic leader of the Ait Waryaghar tribe, Mohamed bin 'Abd al-Krim al-Khattabi (Abd el-Krim),[1] who dealt the Spanish a catastrophic defeat at Anwal (Anoual) in 1921. Over the next five years, Abd el-Krim effectively constituted an autonomous anti-colonial political field, the Republic of the Rif. He successfully waged war against a European colonial power, consolidated control over close to 80 percent of the northern zone, collected taxes, administered justice, and initiated educational reforms.[2] In 1925, Abd el-Krim tried to extend this field to the south. He overran French military posts on the border and came within forty kilometers of Fes. These ill-fated gains provoked

---

1. "Mohamed the son of 'Abd al-Krim al-Khattabi." His father's name was 'Abd al-Krim, and the Ait Khattab are a clan of the Waryaghar that claims descent from 'Umar ibn al-Khattab, the second caliph (Hart 1976, 370). Henceforth, I will refer to him as Abd el-Krim, the name by which he is best known historically.

2. In emphasizing its "stateness" (Nettl 1968), I am following Pennell (1986), which remains the authoritative study of the internal state-formation processes of the Rif Republic.

the French to mount a counterattack, which they coordinated with the Spanish. They deployed an overwhelming force of more than 200,000 troops to crush the Rif army and force Abd el-Krim to surrender.

Because the territory of Morocco was subdivided, the Spanish zone offers an opportunity for subnational comparison. Colonial intervention in the Spanish zone politicized Moroccan identities in ways that were both similar and different from the way this process happened in the French zone. Like the Atlas jihad, the Rif resistance focused on blocking the spatial expansion of the colonial political field. However, while the anti-state resistance in the Atlas region sought to defend tribal autonomy from state controls in any shape or form, in the northern zone, Abd el-Krim's anti-state resistance involved creating those controls himself. He consolidated a Rif-based state to defend the autonomy of the region. The following sections examine the relationship between state and nonstate space in the Rif before colonization and how Spanish intervention began to impact this area in the early 1900s. The focus then turns to the processes through which Abd el-Krim constructed a nascent anti-colonial political field that had its own symbolic and organizational logics in response to accelerated Spanish pacification operations. Finally, the chapter explores why the Republic of the Rif eventually fell to a joint Franco-Spanish offensive. Like the previous chapter, this analysis draws on previously underutilized local primary sources to explore the external and internal identification processes that played out among rural populations as they navigated the brutal clash between rival state-governed political fields.

State and Nonstate Space and Society in the Precolonial Rif

Outside of the Atlantic coast and a sliver of the Ouergha valley, the Spanish protectorate consisted of mountainous territory that had only rarely been under any form of regular administration under the precolonial *makhzan*. Geologically distinct from the Atlas, this mountainous crescent—including the Jbala, Ghomara, and Rif—hugs the Mediterranean coast, reaching elevations above 2,400 meters (8,000 feet). Rainfall decreases from west to east as air moves from the Atlantic to the leeward side of the Rif Mountains. Very few rivers flow through this topography of steep mountains cut by deep ravines. The flora consists mostly of maquis, although there are isolated pockets of Aleppo pine, fir, and cedar at higher elevations (Pennell 1986, 22–24; McNeill 1992, 41–45).

Given this topography and ecology, the primary settlement pattern was scattered villages in mountain valleys where grain, vegetables, and fruit could be grown. The most fruitful areas of the eastern Rif lay on its edges, including the plain inland from Al Hoceima Bay on the northern coast and the Ouergha plain to the south (Pennell 1986, 24; McNeill 1992, 208). The large towns are Tetouan, which is close to Ceuta and the Mediterranean coast, and Tangier, which served throughout the nineteenth century as Morocco's diplomatic capital and was designated as an international zone in 1923. In the interior, the only major urban center was Chaouen, a holy city sixty-five kilometers south of Tetouan that was settled in the fifteenth century by Andalusian Muslim and Jewish refugees.

The economy, particularly in the mountains, was largely self-contained, although there was limited trade with Fes to the south and with the Spanish enclave of Melilla to the north. In the mid-nineteenth century, laborers began to migrate seasonally to French farms in western Algeria (Hart 1976, 88–92). In the Rif, weekly local markets played a major role in economic life and served as the primary public social space where news was disseminated and tribal councils met.[3] Linguistically, the northern region is split; in the western Jbala, Arabic is spoken, and in the Rif, Tarifit (a regional variety of Berber) is the primary language. Cultural and religious transregional ties linked the Rif to urban centers such as Fes or Tetouan.

Politically, the mountainous north was semi-autonomous. Although relations with the *makhzan* were maintained and *qadis* (Islamic judges) were periodically appointed, the primary organizing structure was the tribal council (*jama'a* in Arabic and *agraw* in Berber). As in the Atlas, these councils resolved disputes through customary law. However, the nonstate space of the mountainous interior bordered closely with the territories under the more direct control of the Moroccan *makhzan* and Spanish military enclaves on the Mediterranean coast. In the decades leading up to the protectorate, the Rif became even more autonomous because of the rapidly declining capacity of the *makhzan* to project its power. Rif groups frequently attacked Spanish garrisons. In addition, there was intensive feuding between and within tribes, which the Spanish tried to capitalize on by financing rival parties.[4] Multiple local warlords, such Ahmad al-Raisuni[5] in the Jebala and Abu Himara (a *rogui,*

---

3. See Hart's (1976, 69–92) extended discussion about the sociocultural and political role of markets among the Ait Waryaghar, including their designation of separate women's markets.

4. This period of relative anarchy between 1898 and 1921 was referred to locally as the *ripublik,* not to be confused with the Rif Republic State (*Dawla jumhuriya rifiya*) that Abd el-Krim declared in 1923 (Hart 1976, 356, 377).

5. Raisuni was a *sharif* who traced his ancestry to the Idrissid dynasty. Between 1903 and 1904, his predations near Tangier and his kidnapping of Walter Harris, a (London) *Times* correspondent, and Ian Perdicaris, a Greek-American millionaire, brought international attention, including threats from President Roosevelt (Hart 1976, 390–93; Porch 1983, 136–46).

or pretender, to the Alawid throne)[6] in the eastern Rif, carved out local fief-doms. At times these warlords resisted the Spanish and at other times they cut deals with them.

After attacks on their mine and railway concession at Wiksan in 1909, the Spanish began to move south from Melilla, using the *razzia* techniques of burning villages and dynamiting houses to collectively punish northern tribes. In 1911, they landed troops on the Atlantic coast at the port city of Larache and moved inland. After formalizing their position with the 1912 treaty, the Spanish settled for a limited pacification of these lowland areas, opting to influence the interior indirectly by bribing tribal chiefs. It was not until after World War I that the Spanish shifted to a more aggressive policy that prioritized total pacification. It was this postwar shift that provoked the anti-state jihad movement Abd el-Krim led in the 1920s.

Spanish Colonial Intervention

Given their historic interest in Morocco (which stretched back to the Recon-quista and the minimally successful African Crusade),[7] the Spanish were among the European powers that were eager for a piece of Morocco in the nineteenth-century colonial scramble for Africa. This interest was kept in play after the Spanish-Moroccan war of 1859–1860, a conflict in which the Spanish sent an expedition south from Ceuta, in response to tribal raiding, to occupy Tetouan. The British brokered a treaty between the Spanish and the Moroc-can sultan in which the latter agreed to pay an indemnity of 20 million duros (pesetas) and acknowledged Spanish territorial claims in the south at Ifni.[8] In the diplomatic wrangling over Morocco's fate in the early 1900s, the British steadfastly defended Spain's claims because of their own interest in preventing France from occupying the southern shore opposite Gibraltar. Even before the formal establishment of the protectorate, the Spanish military had begun to expand into Moroccan territory from enclaves at Melilla in 1909 and Larache in 1911). Eight months after the signing of the Treaty of Fes in March 1912, French and Spanish negotiators agreed to the Treaty of Madrid, creating a

---

6. Abu Himara ("the man with the she-ass") had been driven from his base in Taza in 1903 by *makhzan* forces and relocated to Selwan (Selouan), near Melilla, in 1904. Over the next six years he carved out a mini-*makhzan*, raising revenue through taxation, customs duties, the importation of firearms, and the sale of mining concessions to Franco-Spanish business interests (Hart 1976, 361–68; Burke 1976, 62–64; Dunn 1980; Venier 1997).

7. On the African crusade and Spain's expansionist aspirations in North Africa, see O'Callaghan (2011).

8. See Zunes and Mundy (2010, 99–102) on Spain's further expansion in the south.

"sub-protectorate" (Pennell 1986, 166) that included a strip north of a line that stretched from the port of Larache in the west to the Moulouya River's exit into the Mediterranean and a zone in the far south around Tarfaya. The Spanish retained control over areas they had previously occupied, including Ifni on the Atlantic Coast and Ceuta and Melilla, their two Mediterranean enclaves.

With this arrangement, the French retained the lion's share of the agriculturally productive areas of Lyautey's *Maroc utile*, leaving the Spanish the markedly *inutile* parts of Moroccan territory (Ayache 1981, 8, 16–18). The northern zone, which stretched 362 kilometers (225 miles) from west to east and 48–80 kilometers (30–50 miles) north to south, encompassed 20,000 square kilometers (8,000 square miles). The vaguely defined border between the French and Spanish zones arbitrarily cut through little-explored mountainous areas, splitting tribal groups such as the Beni Bu Yahi, Metalsa, and Geznaya in half (Woolman 1968, 16). However, this did not become a problem until a decade later, in the 1920s, when both colonial powers attempted to systematically map out their zones when they shifted to a policy of total pacification.

The Franco-Spanish agreement did not formally create a separate protectorate. The territorial units under Spanish control theoretically still remained under the Moroccan sultan's sovereignty. After the Spanish occupied Tetouan and made it the northern capital in 1913, the sultan's nominal sovereignty was acknowledged with the designation of a cousin as his *khalifa*, or deputy, in whose name decrees were issued. A parallel native *makhzan* administration was also kept in place to administer the Islamic courts and *habous* (*awqaf*) religious foundations. In practice, however, the two protectorate zones functioned autonomously, as neither colonial power was willing "to come to blows over the provisions of the Treaty of Fes" (Woolman 1968, 15–16). The Spanish appointed their own high commissioner, who was parallel with the French resident general, and created a replica of the French system of an indigenous affairs administration, the Oficina de Asuntos Indigenas, to oversee tribal areas. Compared to the French, however, the Spanish invested very little in infrastructure.

Constrained by limited resources, the Spanish had minimal initial objectives. Military planners prioritized direct control over the much smaller "useful" areas close to the coast. In the interior, they attempted strategy of indirect control, relying on a network of tribal leaders who were on their payroll to project influence in their areas (Pennell 1986, 48–52). During World War I, most of the military budget was spent on these monthly pensions. In the west, the Spanish identified al-Raisuni, a local warlord who had built up his power base in the turmoil leading up to the protectorate, as a grand caid they could work with in the Jbala region. Although he resented that he was not named *khalifa*, al-Raisuni accepted an appointment as pasha in Asilah. From this position, he further consolidated his power base in the mountains around Tazruft, alternating between lukewarm service to and open resistance against the Spanish. This alternating strategy gave him leverage to increase his salary. In the east, however, the Spanish found no single chief they could deal with; instead, they cultivated multiple clients to create a *leff*, or tribal coalition, to try to counterbalance the most powerful Rif tribe, the Ait Waryaghar. They also tried to sow divisions within this tribe by offering some, but not all, leaders monthly pensions (Madariaga 1992, 68).

The fatal flaw of this system of indirect rule was that in the absence of a credible military threat to inflict consequences for disloyalty, it incentivized tribal leaders who were eager to increase their pensions to engage in unrest and did not provide a long-term formula for stable control. After World War I, the Spanish government shifted to a new policy of total pacification, attempting to extend a military monopoly of control in their zone. In 1919, a new high commissioner, Dámaso Berenguer, was appointed, and troops, supplies, and air support were designated for expanded operations.[9] In the west, Berenguer successfully occupied the holy city of Chaouen in October 1920 and trapped al-Raisuni in his base at Tazruft in early 1921. Lieutenant-General Manuel Fernandez Silvestre directed a Spanish offensive on the eastern front that pushed to the south of Melilla, reoccupying the Wadi Kart. He then deployed troops westward up into the foothills of the Rif, trying to link up with Spanish forces in the Jbala and open an east-west corridor, as the French had done a decade earlier between Rabat and Oujda. Silvestre's troops were poised to break through the central Rif in the spring of 1921. That summer, however, a tribal coalition anchored by the Ait Waryaghar launched a counterattack that completely destroyed Silvestre's forces (and killed Silvestre) and threatened the entire Spanish foothold in the northern zone.

Framing and Organizing Jihad in the Rif Mountains

Beginning in the late nineteenth century, Spain's steady expansion from its coastal enclaves at Ceuta and Melilla provoked a range of reactions from the tribal groups in the north that included collusion, accommodation, and

---

9. Before the war, in 1913, the Spanish were the first to use an airplane in North Africa and were among the first to drop bombs from airplanes. They used airplanes extensively for aerial photography on reconnaissance missions in the north of Morocco (Abellán García-Muñoz 2005, 10). During the expanded pacification campaigns after the war, they used air power to conduct numerous nighttime bombing raids in the Jbala in the campaign against Al-Raisuni in 1919 (40). They used these tactics in the Rif also, including the extensive use of chemical weapons in the 1920s (Kunz 1990; Balfour 2002, 123–56).

resistance and strategic alternation among all three. Typically, individual tribes or subgroups of tribes negotiated their relationship with the Spanish. The outcomes of these negotiations depended on geography, relative military strength, and the individual calculations of chiefs. There were also examples, as in the Atlas, of periodic broader coalitions that mobilized against Spanish military operations. One of these coalitions was mobilized against Abu Himara, a *rogui* (pretender to the throne) claiming to be the sultan who had moved north from the Taza region and set up a mini-*makhzan* based at Qasba Silwan in the eastern Rif, where he collected taxes, appointed judges, and received oaths of allegiance. In 1907, Abu Himara sold the Spanish Compania Espanola de Minas del Rif a 99-year lease on iron deposits at Jabal Uksan (Sp. Monte Uixan) and the right to build a railroad to link Jabal Uksan to the port at Melilla twelve miles north. The next month he sold a similar lease to lead mines at Jabal Afra to a Franco-Spanish company (Woolman 1968, 38–39). However, resentment about Abu Himara's sale of concessions to the "Christian" Spanish and his ongoing attempts to pacify regions further to the east led nearby tribes, including the powerful Ait Waryaghar, to mount an attack against his power base and force him to flee to the south in 1909 (Hart 1976, 361–68).[10]

When the Spanish responded to these attacks with harsh reprisals, the jihad shifted into a new phase, gaining momentum under the leadership of Sharif Mohamed Amziyyan, a Banu Bu Ifran chieftain in the eastern Rif. As in the Atlas, a large corpus of Tarifit poetry of resistance was composed and passed down in the Rif about this and later episodes of anti-colonial resistance.[11] Several of these early poems refer to the leadership of Amziyyan, or "Sidi Muhand": "The wind blew / In the kettle of the *rumi* [Christian] / God has assailed him / With the brave Rifian / It is Sidi Muhand / Who is fighting against the *rumi* / Numerous telephone poles / Down in the plains / O free fighter! / Phone to the Spanish / Tell them to increase the number of their soldiers / Tell them that Spain is ruined" (Khalafi 2002a).[12] As did the Atlas poetry,

---

10. In August 1909, the *rogui*'s forces were defeated north of Fes by the sultan Mawlay 'Abd al-Hafiz's *makhzan* troops. Abu Himara was taken captive and eventually promenaded through the streets of Fes in a wooden cage, tortured, thrown into a lion pit, and finally executed on September 12 (Porch 1983, 210–13; Woolman 1968, 41).

11. While no parallel to the Roux archive exists, a limited number of Berber poems from the Rif have been published. Although Chtatou (1991) and Khalafi (2002a, 2002b) have emphasized the historical potential of these primary sources, they are doubly marginalized by the fact that they oral sources and are from the Rif, one of the most marginalized regions in Morocco.

12. In 2002, Khalafi published two articles on Rif poetry from the 1890s to the 1920s in the online Tamazight journal *Tawiza*: "La poésie de résistance au Rif: 1893-1926," 63 (July 2002), http://tawiza.x10.mx/Tawiza63/Khalafi.htm; and "La poésie de résistance au Rif: 1893-1926 (2ème partie)," 64 (August 2002), http://tawiza.x10.mx/Tawiza64/Khalafi.htm.

this poem highlights the importance of communications in the minds of Rif tribesmen. It also displays the bravado of Rif fighters, who tell the Spanish soldiers down on the plains to phone news of their defeat back to the metropole.

Hostilities quickly subsided after Amziyyan died in battle in 1909. By 1912, the Spanish had stabilized the front at Wadi Kart, but they left the higher elevations of the Rif alone. For the tribes, this very light footprint offered hope of a much less intrusive form of colonial intervention than was developing in the French zone, one that would preserve the status quo of high levels of local autonomy from state-based rule. Several leaders, including Mohamed bin 'Abd al-Krim al-Khattabi and his father, had hopes that the Spanish infrastructure would benefit the local population. But they became disillusioned with Spanish colonialism with the postwar shift toward total pacification and direct control.

In the Rif, as in the Atlas, the initial goal of anti-colonial jihad was to preserve local autonomy. In the early 1920s, however, this anti-state mode of resistance was transformed into a much more ambitious anti-state-building project under the leadership Abd el-Krim, the eldest son of an Ait Waryaghar *qadi* who took on the leadership of the tribe after his father died in 1919. The elder al-Khattabi had been among the "friends of Spain," tribal leaders or informants who were paid regular stipends (Pennell 1986, 49). He sent both of his sons to study in Melilla in 1906. The elder son, Mohamed, who had also earlier received training in Islamic jurisprudence at Qarawayin University in Fes (1903–6), worked as an interpreter and clerk for the Spanish Oficina de Asuntos Indigenas, as editor of the Arabic supplement for the *El Telegrama del Rif*, and as *qadi* in Melilla. Eventually the Spanish appointed him Qadi Qudat (Supreme Qadi) in the Kart valley on the eastern edge of the Ait Waryaghar's territory. His younger brother, Mahammad, was sent in 1917 to study engineering at the School of Mines in Madrid (Ayache 1981, 158; Hart 1976, 371–73).

In the early 1920s, a series of bad harvests caused widespread starvation and Spain's expanding pacification operations created increasing hardships. This produced very strong pressure in the eastern Rif from tribespeople against any accommodation of Spanish control by their leaders. This anti-Spanish sentiment was particularly acute in the Waryaghar tribe, which controlled access to the west from Melilla. The elder 'Abd al-Krim al-Khattabi, seeing that there was no longer any significant advantage in maintaining his role as a client of the Spanish, broke off relations with them and wrote to his older son Mohamed in Melilla[13] and his younger son Mahammad in Madrid,

---

13. Though Mohamed had been jailed in 1916 for writing articles critical of Spain's expansion from its enclaves and broke his leg in an escape attempt, he was reinstated as a *qadi*, or judge, and remained in Melilla up to 1919 (Hart 1976, 372).

who both returned to the Ajdir area to begin to lay the groundwork for renewed anti-colonial resistance from the Ait Waryaghar.

The event that catalyzed this transformation to anti-state resistance in the north came during the Spanish offensive in the spring of 1921. Starting in 1919, the Spanish had pushed with pincers from the west and east with the goal of unifying a contiguous state-controlled political field. In 1921, the Ait Waryaghar tribe stood between the two Spanish lines. In the east, the front consisted of an extended line of isolated small fortifications that were often located on high points far from a water source. In May, the Rif enjoyed the best harvest in fourteen years, creating a surplus that freed tribesmen for a sustained large-scale assault on these lines (Pennell 1986, 73). This assault began with attacks in early June on two forward posts, Dahar Ubarran and Igheriben.[14]

Seven weeks later, in the heat of the summer, the son, Abd el-Krim, launched a coordinated general assault on the front.[15] The Waryaghar tribesmen focused on Anoual, the primary forward Spanish base, and the commanding general of Spanish troops in the east, Manuel Silvestre, ordered a general retreat. This devolved into a total rout as the Spanish front collapsed and the other tribes of the eastern Rif rallied to join the Waryaghar. In the end, Anoual constituted the worst defeat of a European colonial power in the twentieth century: the Spanish lost over 13,000 lives, 20,000 rifles, 400 machine guns, 129 cannons, large quantities of ammunition, and large quantities of canned food (Ayache 1981, 147; Pennell 1986, 91). While the Atlas jihad discussed in the previous chapter was never an existential threat to the French colonial state, Abd el-Krim's victory at Anoual was a near-fatal blow to Spanish aspirations. It also presented a critical opportunity for a Rif state to emerge.

Constructing an Autonomous Anti-colonial Political Field

In the post–World War I milieu in which European colonial powers and local actors such as Ataturk, Ibn Saud, and Reza Shah actively reshaped political units across North Africa and the Middle East, Abd el-Krim, though less well known, was remarkably effective at merging military, political, and cultural state-building strategies. The victory at Anoual provided him with weapons,

---

14. Hart (1976, 374–75) highlights the symbolic importance of these first battles in the popular imagination of the Rif and even to the west in the Jbala, particularly Dahar Ubarran, which was celebrated in *izran* poems sung by girls over the next five years.

15. For a detailed account of the battles in June and July 1921, see Woolman (1968, 83–102).

ammunition, Spanish prisoners, and, perhaps most critical, symbolic power and legitimacy. After pushing the Spanish back to coastal enclaves in the summer of 1921, Abd el-Krim and his Rif forces consolidated an autonomous anti-colonial political field in the hinterland that included seventy to eighty tribal groups in the northern zone (Hart 1976, 383) (see Map 6). That September, Abd el-Krim proclaimed the creation of the Republic of the Rif, and over the next months, he began to centralize authority in this territorial space by rationalizing the judiciary, tax collection, the administrative bureaucracy, and the army. The Rif Republic expressed its own logic of linked legibility and legitimacy.

Legal Islamization was a primary mechanism Abd el-Krim used to consolidate this political field. He centralized and monopolized control of the juridical system by banning tribal customary law (*izref* or *'urf*) and unifying a shari'a-based judiciary.[16] Customary law functions as a system of nonstate-based governance that relies on means of collective enforcement that include oaths, a fine system (*haqq*), and, in a worst-case scenario, the feud (*'adhawth*).[17] Abd el-Krim's campaign to eradicate customary law in the Rif and replace it with shari'a, a system that uses individual evidence, testimony, and punishment, undercut local tribal autonomy and centralized state control in a hierarchically organized system of government-appointed judges. To enforce this legal monopoly, the Rif state abolished collective oaths and executed or imprisoned those who took part in blood feuds or vendettas (Hart 2001, 200).[18] To set an example, Abd el-Krim refused to take vengeance on the individual who had poisoned his father.

As it took shape in late 1921 and early 1922, the Rif state began to have an increasing impact on society through a range of everyday state practices. Social discipline was enforced by fining people for smoking *kif* (a cannabis product grown widely in the Rif), for not trimming beards, and even for not wearing footgear in public (Hart 1976, 390–91). It also paid informants and appointed *muhtasibs*, or governmental inspectors, to regulate weekly markets (Pennell 1986, 145–46). Many legal reforms directly affected women. Under Islamic law, in contrast to Berber customary law, women gained legal rights and duties, including the right to own property and inheritance rights.

---

16. Hart (1976, 389) observes that one of Abd el-Krim's lasting accomplishments was the eradication of customary law in the Rif.

17. On these social mechanisms within Rif society, see Hart (1976; 2001, 57–66, 70–71).

18. The three prisons Abd el-Krim constructed were a novelty in the Rif, which previously had not had any (Hart 1976, 383–88). Hart (2001, 200) also relates that Abd el-Krim ordered the destruction of household *ishbrawen*, or mud and stone "snipers' enclosures," which were used during feuds.

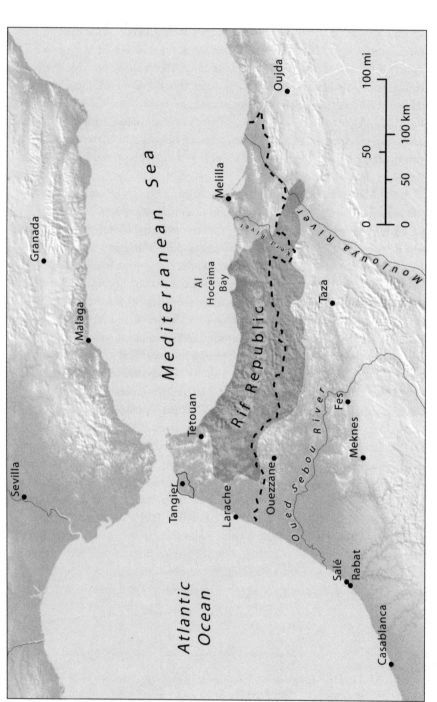

MAP 6. The Spanish northern zone. The shaded area shows the greatest territorial reach of Rif Republic.

Women and men were also both required to perform the five daily prayers. The penalty for not doing the prayers for men was to be sent to the battle-front; for women, the fine was a chicken (Hart 2001, 203; Pennell 1986, 148). Married women, widows, and divorcees were prohibited from singing or dancing, and the length of wedding celebrations was reduced from seven to three days. Poems from the period indicate resistance to these reforms. One poet pleads with Abd el-Krim: "God put you on the right path / That you would give us the freedom to sing and dance / Oh Sidi Muhand / Why is your heart so hard? / You must know that your homeland is the origin of song and dance" (Khatami 2002b).

Abd el-Krim tried to create a monopoly on tax collection and fines. The state imposed a poll tax and a tax on produce. It also collected fines from recalcitrant tribes that refused to fight against the Spanish. Customs houses were set up to tax goods going back and forth into Spanish-controlled areas that generated 5,000 pesetas a day (Ayache 1981, 221). Customs duties were also collected on the borders with the French zone and Algeria. Another strategy for generating revenue was selling mining concessions. Abd el-Krim pitched this idea to a Spanish businessman, Horacio Echevarrieta, and to the French company Le Tellier, but these never resulted in tangible investment. What did work was the ransoming of Spanish prisoners captured at Anoual in 1923. This raised four million pesetas and enabled Abd el-Krim to finance a professional army.[19]

The administrative structure of the Rif Republic blended patrimonial and rational-legal bureaucratic forms. The central administration was based in Ajdir, the principal town of the Ait Waryaghar and de facto capital of the Rif Republic. Abd el-Krim appointed close relatives or extended family members to virtually all of the cabinet posts. He also instituted a hierarchical bureaucratic structure that began with the local *jama'at*, tribal councils, which were transformed into military-executive bodies. Each was required to elect a *qa'id* who was then appointed commander of military forces and required to provision and lodge troops. Above the *jama'at*, the Rif Republic had a consultative body, the *majlis al-umma*, or national parliament, although decision-making centered on the person of Abd el-Krim.

Over the next five years, the Rif state succeeded at repelling Spanish intervention primarily due to Abd el-Krim's skill at military organization and tactics. Replicating traditional practices used by the *makhzan* and by French

---

19. The Spanish government, using Echevarrieta as an intermediary, paid 3 million pesetas for the prisoners and 1 million for damages the Rif forces suffered (Hart 1976, 376).

and Spanish colonial armies, he put together a Rif version of a *mahalla*, or hybrid military expedition that combined regular and irregular troops. The core *nizam* army, which was drawn from the Ait Waryaghar and a handful of Europeans, was paid a salary. It included former Moroccan colonial soldiers in the Spanish *fuerzas regulares* who had specialized artillery training. These were organized into *tabors*, or units, of three to five hundred men, then subdivided into smaller commands of one hundred, fifty, twenty-five, and twelve men (Pennell 1986, 130–32; Hart 2001, 202). With a total strength of six to seven thousand, the regular army fought the Spanish but also projected the Rif *makhzan*'s authority among other tribes, particularly as the Rif state pacified territory to the south and west. This regular force was supplemented by partisan, or irregular, troops numbering up to 60,000 that were periodically enlisted on a tribal basis through coercion or the promise of booty (Hart 1976, 388).

As this autonomous political field expanded westward into the Ghomara and Jbala regions with further victories over the Spanish, the Rif Republic's authority was projected through the creation of a network of military command posts, or *mahkamas*, which resembled the indigenous affairs posts Lyautey used as the cornerstone of his expanding colonial administration in the wake of pacification in the French zone. The Rif state was also physically manifested in infrastructural development projects, the most significant of which was the construction of roads, or more accurately dirt tracks (*pistes*), that radiated outward from Ajdir and linked *mahkama* posts throughout the mountains. To overcome the topographical challenges to state space in the north, Abd el-Krim also prioritized the construction of a telephone/telegraph network that connected Ajdir to these posts. To do so, he bought or stole wire from the French and the Spanish (Hart 1976, 387; Pennell 1986, 143).

Imagining the Rif Republic from Above and Below

The construction of the autonomous political field of the Rif Republic entailed substantial symbolic work to legitimate the nascent state apparatus and sustain anti-colonial jihad. A national anthem was composed and a national flag was designed that had a red background, a centered white diamond, and a green six-pointed star and crescent. In January and February 1923, tribal leaders across the zone gave a *bay'a*, or traditional Islamic oath of allegiance, hailing Abd el-Krim as amir of the Rif. The immediate precedent was the 1908 *bay'a* the ulama in Fes had given to Mawlay 'Abd al-Hafiz, on the condition that al-Hafiz carry out jihad against the French. The text of the Rif *bayʿa*, which was similar to the 1908 *bayʿa* (see Pennell 1986, Appendix 3), made the legitimacy of Abd el-Krim's rule as amir conditional on his enforcement of shariʿa and his continuation of jihad against the Spanish. Anti-colonial armed resistance was framed in the Rif as defensive jihad, but instead of the episodic coalitions mobilized by the Atlas tribes, Abd el-Krim attempted to channel and sustain jihad through state-like institutional structures and an active public relations campaign.

One of the legitimization strategies the Rif Republic used was to enlist *imdyazen*, or itinerate troubadours, to perform pro-regime propaganda in weekly markets. As in the Atlas, in this largely oral culture, the performance of poems served the critical functions of relaying news, engaging in public debate, and imagining collective identity. During the war, Abd el-Krim commissioned songs that supported jihad, glorified the Rif *mujahideen* (those fighting in the jihad), and celebrated victories over the Spanish (and later over the French). At the weekly markets, the local *qaʾid* would read out the latest news from the front, then the *amdyaz* and his troupe would perform before the circle of spectators. Both the longer *raqsiyat* genre, which consists of a refrain of two or more rhymed couplets that is repeated after each verse, and the shorter two-line *izran* (singular *izri; izlan/izli* in Tamazight) were composed to legitimize Abd el-Krim's rule (Chtatou 1991, 197–202).

Mohamed Chtatou, who collected and translated multiple Tarifit poems about this period among the Gzennaya tribe, relates one of the *raqsiyat* that entered the Rif canon in the aftermath of the war. The verses recount Rif successes against the Spanish and French colonial armies: "We gained independence and kicked out colonialism / I will die for two things: my country and my sweetheart / Take your rifle and get up early / Take enough ammunition and go to the hill / If you want to crush the treacherous people" (Chtatou 1991, 198). Another poem, which celebrated the Rif forces' occupation of Chaouen in 1924, was modified to become the lyrics of the national anthem:

> On to the war, off we go / We will come back home victorious
> O friend ask history / It will inform you that we are the best victors
> We fought so many battles / And left the enemy baffled
> They left behind castles and buildings / And hurried in their defeat
> Today the red flag is fluttering / High over the victors' heads
> Praise to God the Almighty / And curses to all the traitors.
>
> *(Chtatou 1991, 201)*

Here the Riffis are putting themselves in the historical record, citing great deeds done against the European enemy, including their successes in battle and their taking of the "castles and building" left behind in the city of Chaouen. The prominence of the "red flag" in the poem, the national symbol of the Rif Republic, clarifies its fittingness as the national anthem.[20]

Other poems laud Abd el-Krim's military and religious virtues in an attempt to maintain high levels of morale:

> Abd al-Karim is the hero of heroes / He fears nothing / Neither the mountains, nor the lions
> Abd al-Karim is a Muslim / To whose aid God has come / The Spanish, our enemy / Hunts the Riffis in the mountains
> Sidi Mohamed / Is a political leader / He has sworn to expel the French to the borders! 'Abd al Karim is a dove of the sky! We wish him a long life!
> The Rumi attacked Anwar and A'arwi / Mohammed 'Abd al-Karim / Oh! The Freedom Fighter!
> The airplane flew over the mountain / Sidi Mohammed is the hero who defends the religion.
>
> (*Khalafi 2002b*)

In this song, the precarious geographical and strategic context of the Rif state, caught between two colonial powers is obvious, but the author puts hope in Abd el-Krim, their religious, military, and political leader.

Sung poetry was used to rally the public to fight the holy war, to defend the homeland and their families against the Spanish: "Oh young Riffis / Defend your homeland / The Spanish attack us / To possess our women!" (Khalafi 2002b). Another poem refers to a total mobilization of Rif society for defensive war: "Our grandfather! / When you asked us to war / Everyone mobilized / The shepherd and the farmer / The *faqih* who left the mosque / The old women who broke their pots / Look at the warrior / How many weapons he carries with him / Look: the sharp dagger / Look: the sword of the farmer / The rifle in his hand / Has felled the enemies" (Khalafi 2002b). Here the plowshares are being beaten into swords as shepherds and farmers take up arms to join in the war.

These sources also reveal insights into the experience of fighting a highly asymmetrical war, one in which the Rif tribesman daily confronted an enemy with superior military technologies. Often the poets tease the airplanes passing by: "Oh my dove / Oh plane that flies / And deposits no more / Pass on a

---

20. Chtatou (1991, 201) includes the original poem composed at Chaouen and the abridged version used as the anthem cited in Ouezzani (1981, 455) and Kridia (1986, 79).

greeting to the president of the nations / Tell him to drop bombs on us / 'Abd al-Karim is very strong / Omar N Rmadani / Is a fighter without equal / He fights with his pistol /And his sword" (Khalafi 2002b). Another tells the plane to pass on a message encouraging the French president to agree to a treaty: "Oh my dove / Who flies where he wants / Pass on my greeting / To the president of France / Tell him to agree to a link of friendship with 'Abd al-Karim / Otherwise, be sure that 'Abd al-Karim is dangerous!" (Ibid). Here, the lyrics refer to diplomatic overtures by Abd el-Krim to ensure French neutrality, which was imperative for maintaining supply links to the east into Algeria and south into the French zone and for avoiding the opening of multiple fronts. But as with the previous poem, a clear awareness of the international implications of the anti-colonial struggle is combined with a dismissive bravado when confronting European colonial powers.

Other sources, however, reveal struggles to keep discipline in Rif society. As we saw with the dueling Atlas poets who debated the merits of submission or continued resistance, the primary temptations the colonial state offered were material: food, money, and safety. The following poem attacks the poet's "aunt" and "uncle" for selling out to the Spanish across the front lines: "Have you filled your silo with grain, my aunt? / Your husband is an insolent man / When he is out of work / He rushes to rejoin the *rumi* / The face colored / He goes out to steal / On his back he carries bread and tea / His wife waits to bring him something to eat / Him, he loves wine / Be sure he will be pierced like a dog! / What have you gained? / Oh you who spies on your village? Have they given you a salary / So that you exploit the reaper?" (Khatami 2002b). Here the poet refers to the significant contraband activity across the front lines and differing opinions about trade with the Spanish enemy.

Although these sources celebrated Rif victories and the prowess of Abd el-Krim, many others sung poems expressed deep ambivalence about the human costs of the jihad. Like their Atlas analogues, many expressed dismay about the horrors of modern warfare, particularly aerial bombing: "The airplane flies in the skies above Tizi 'Ezza / O my God / It has left the nation of Islam consoling itself / The airplane flies in the sky above the region of Iyyar Mawas like smoke / It killed humanity / It killed Mohamed / And has cut him in two" (Khatami 2002b). This poem offers a firsthand reaction to the increasing use of air power as the Rif War progressed. From 1924, the Spanish began to use mustard gas against the civilian and military targets (Balfour 2002), often in psychologically devastating nighttime bombing raids (Abellán García-Muñoz 2005, 40). In the fall of 1925, when the French joined the Spanish offensive, the cost of the Rif War escalated sharply as civilian and military populations in the Rif faced widespread starvation that winter when a blockade cut off supply lines to the east and south.

The Rif War and the Fate of the Rif Republic

In 1921, in the immediate aftermath of the stunning victory at Anoual, Abd el-Krim refrained from pressing the attack all the way into Spain's coastal stronghold at Melilla. He instead established a line of defense at the higher elevations above the Wadi Kart, allowing Spanish reinforcements to reoccupy the lowland areas below. In 1923 and 1924, Rif forces shored up defenses on the eastern and southern fronts and began to expand west into the Ghomara and Jebala. On the Spanish side, General Primo de Rivera, who had taken power in the fall of 1923, was convinced by officers in the Army of Africa, including Francisco Franco, to not abandon Morocco. Instead, the Spanish staged a limited withdrawal from 400 posts in the interior to stronger defensive positions near the coasts. The retreat from Chaouen in the fall of 1924, however, turned into another devastating loss. Rif forces killed between 17,000 and 20,000 withdrawing Spanish troops and recovered huge amounts of abandoned supplies (Woolman 1968, 132–41).

For the Rif state, the difficulty was holding on to newly gained territory in the west after the Spanish withdrew. Although Abd el-Krim enjoyed popular support initially, he soon faced stiff opposition from local tribes, including the Akhmas, who resented Waryaghar intrusion, and Sufi leaders, including 'Abd al-Rahman al-Darqawi, who were eager to protect their autonomy against Abd el-Krim's expanding state. Anti-Riffi sentiment only increased in the Ghomara as hunger increased in 1924. Abd el-Krim was forced to deploy the regular army to maintain order in the Ghomara and the Ouergha valley to the south. As conditions in the Rif Republic worsened, these troops were increasingly viewed as outside occupiers.

By 1925, the combination of crop failure in the north and restricted cross-border movement into and trade with the French zone forced Abd el-Krim to expand operations into the south.[21] The Rif state's main strategic need was the rich agricultural zone in the Ouergha (Wargha) valley. On April 12, Rif forces attacked parts of the Banu Zeroual tribe, taking 400 hostages and confiscating livestock. The hostages and livestock were released when

---

21. On the material and symbolic pressures that influenced Abd el-Krim's decision to open up the southern front with the attack against the French zone, see Pennell (1986, 182–84).

the tribe paid fines. Two weeks later, 3,000 Rif troops crossed the Ouergha River and attacked French outposts on the border (Thomas 2008, 140). By early June 1925, Rif forces had overrun French defensive positions and progressed as close as forty kilometers north of Fes. Abd el-Krim sent letters to the ulama of Fes, defending his legitimacy as rightful ruler because he was administering shari'a and criticizing the Alawids for relying on Christian support to sustain their rule. However, the Fassi ulama, clearly aware that the French still had firm control in their zone, did not publicly throw their support behind him (Pennell 1986, 189–90). By the end of the summer, the French had shored up their northern front, but hostile Rif forces were still positioned very close to the vital east-west axis of the French protectorate zone at Fes and Taza.

Rif expansion into the French zone catalyzed a crisis in the French protectorate. Before this, French and Rif representatives had negotiated to have a customs office on the border, approved trade agreements, and come to a de facto understanding about movement across the Rif Republic's southern border with the French protectorate and its eastern border with Algeria (Ayache 1981, 183). Lyautey hoped that this policy of accommodating the Rif Republic gave him a back door through which the French could extend influence into the north. However, the Rif advances overrunning French forces in the summer 1925 forced the issue. When the French government transferred military command to Maréchal Pétain, Lyautey retired as resident general and returned to France.

French and Spanish military planners met in Madrid in June to coordinate a joint strategy that involved pincer movements from the north, south, and east. The Franco-Spanish counterattack was launched in September 1925. Close to 123,000 troops were deployed against 12,000 Rif forces (Pennell 1986, 214). On September 8, the Spanish landed an amphibious attack at Al Hoceima Bay, close to the Ait Waryaghar heartland and the Riffi capital of Ajdir. This expedition involved 16,000 men, sixty-three ships, and one hundred airplanes (199). The forces found it easy to disembark, but they faced stiff resistance from the 5,000 Rif fighters who were dug into the hills immediately inland. It took more than a month for the Spanish forces to advance nine kilometers to Ajdir. The French attacked on September 10, quickly reoccupying the lands of the Banu Zerwal and moving north toward Wadi Kart, where they linked up with Spanish troops at Timsaman. This maneuver sealed off the south and east frontiers of the Rif at the onset of winter. The blockade increased pressure on the Rif state as food and salt grew scarce and people could not tend their fields because of the threat of air raids.

The cataclysmic costs of the war generated questions about the trajectory of the jihad and Abd el-Krim's leadership. One poet asked: "The house in the mountains / O my sweetheart / Where is your master? / Why isn't he here? / Is he sick? / Tell me, where has he gone? / Is he dead? / If so / Ask God to comfort you / O my mother / How I have mourned when the village was emptied of its inhabitants / Comfort my heart, cry no more / Comfort like the mountains that resist the clouds / Oh Mawlay Mohand / What path do we take? / The path that leads to our country / Is now full of *rumis*" (Khatami 2002b). Although the core army continued to fight, a sense of exhaustion was expressed in the general public: "O Sidi Mulay Muhand! Our patience is exhausted / The bomb comes from the sky! And the bombardment comes from the sea!" (Khatami 2002b).

Abd el-Krim, who had steadfastly rejected French and Spanish efforts at mediation the previous year, put out feelers about negotiations in the spring 1926. His conditions included internal autonomy in the northern zone under the nominal authority of the sultan. Abd el-Krim would be named amir, the capital would be located in Tetouan, and several Ouergha and Jebala tribes currently in the French zone would be transferred to Rif control. In addition, the Rif would have an open door to trade with Europe (Pennell 1986, 211). The Spanish and French rejected this proposal and pressed forward with a spring campaign. Unable to maintain the forces needed to defend the Rif Republic on two fronts, Abd el-Krim, who was losing domestic support, initiated truce negotiations with the French in April. On May 27, 1926, he surrendered to the French at Targuist and was exiled to the island of Réunion. With the Rif war over, the Spanish were able to consolidate control in the northern zone over the next year and did not face another serious threat for three decades. Indeed, the Army of Africa successfully incorporated a significant number of Moroccan troops during and after the Rif War which were then deployed in the peninsula in the early 1930s. These crack units later played a significant part in the Spanish Civil War between 1936 and 1939, fighting under the command of Franco and other nationalist officers. More than 70,000 Moroccan troops eventually fought in Spain (Hart 1976, 416; Madariaga 1992).

This chapter and the previous one tapped an untraditional source base, poems authored by rural tribesmen and women, to provide new insights into the perspectives of nonstate actors about colonial intervention and the expansion of a colonial political field. These sources shed light on the identification processes that were catalyzed during this period. They reveal how the ideological paradigm of jihad was used to frame resistance, how fierce internal struggles were waged over whether to resist or submit to the state, and how these subaltern actors experienced the brutal expansion of colonial state space. Subnational comparison also revealed an important typological distinction between two different modes of defending the autonomy of historic nonstate spaces. The goal of the anti-state resistance of the Atlas was to block the intrusion of the colonial political field through individual tribal jihad and loose confederative military jihad. The goal in the Rif was the same, but the means differed: in order to block the colonial state's pacification campaign, Abd el-Krim built a state himself, coalescing the northern tribes in a defensive jihad against the Spanish and French. Although his anti-colonial political field was ultimately eliminated by the overwhelming military onslaught of two industrialized European powers, the legacy of the Rif Republic and collective experience of autonomy, state formation, and military resistance reinforced a firm sense of separate Rif identity for subsequent generations.

✋ CHAPTER 5

Classification Struggles and Arabo–Islamic National Identity

> Oh God, the Benevolent, we ask of You benevolence in whatever fate brings, and do not separate us from our brothers, the Berbers.
>
> —Modified Latif prayer

The early 1930s proved to be a pivotal midpoint of Morocco's colonial period. At the very moment the French and Spanish were eliminating the last military resistance to the spatial extension of the colonial political field in the so-called Berber countryside (the Rif War in the north ended in 1926 and final pacification campaigns against autonomous tribes in the High Atlas and southern regions of the French zone took place in the late 1920s to early 1930s), the colonial *makhzan* began to face a significant challenge from the heart of the "Arab" medina that Lyautey's colonial urbanism had so carefully preserved. This urban *sība* originated in Morocco's northern cities—Fes, Rabat, Salé, and Tetouan (in the Spanish zone)—historic centers for the Arabic-speaking intellectual and commercial elite. In the early 1930s, a group of young nationalist activists based in these cities began to frame and mobilize a popular movement that challenged the classificatory logics of the colonial political field and co-opted its symbolic forces. At first these activists attempted to reform the field, but when these appeals failed, they demanded complete Moroccan independence.[1]

Unlike the rural resistance in the Atlas and Rif Mountains that rejected the colonial political field tout court, the urban nationalists ostensibly accepted

---

1. On the periodization of reformist versus independence-seeking Moroccan nationalism, see Halstead (1967, 4), Spadola (2008), and Lawrence (2013).

the political legitimacy of the protectorate project that was embedded in the Treaty of Fes, namely that a sovereign nation could play the role of tutorial state builder in another country. What they rejected was *how* and *to whose benefit* the French (and, to a lesser extent, the Spanish) were doing it. During their initial reformist stage, the goal of the nationalists was to get the residency to treat Morocco like a protectorate instead of like a colony. Through demonstrations, petitions, and an international press campaign, nationalist leaders tried to pressure the French to abide by the stipulations of the Treaty of Fes, the formal rules of the game that were supposedly in force in this colonial political field. They asked the French to respect the sultan's sovereignty, incorporate more Moroccans into higher levels of the administration, and share the benefits of economic development with Moroccans instead of channeling them solely to *colons*.

In tandem with these material demands, the urban Arabic-speaking nationalists engaged in a dynamic form of identity politics that directly contested the linkage between legitimacy and legibility that undergirded the colonial political field. In protests and in the press, they framed a nationalist countervulgate that emphasized Morocco's Arabo-Islamic dynastic history as evidence of long-standing national unity and reinforced claims about the inviolability of Moroccan sovereignty. While Morocco's past was relevant, the real stakes of struggles between the nationalists and colonial authorities over the classificatory and symbolic logics of the political field concerned the present and the future: how collective identity in Moroccan society *should* be imagined and the state's role in reinforcing or threatening this vision through juridical, administrative, and educational policies. Instead of preserving or inventing divisions in Moroccan society in line with the colonial *imaginaire* described in chapter 2, urban nationalists demanded that the colonial *makhzan* enact policies that bolstered ethno-religious, or Arabo-Islamic, national unity. The failure of the nationalists to achieve reforms related to the material or symbolic trajectory of nation-state building in Morocco in the 1930s and the exile of much of the Moroccan nationalist leadership on the eve of World War II led to a strategic shift in the early 1940s toward the goal of independence.

This chapter focuses on identification processes that were catalyzed during this formative period as urban anti-colonialists defined a new category of Moroccan political identity, *wataniya* (nationalism), that mediated between local levels of identification (tribe, village, city, region) and the translocal *umma*, or global Muslim community. From the 1930s forward, as Hassan Rachik (2003, 85–88) has emphasized, Moroccan nationalist began to speak "in the name of the nation" in calls to protest, to boycott French goods, to strike, or to contribute to the nationalist cause. In analyzing how these Moroccan actors waged identity-related struggles over and against the colonial political field's logics of legitimation and legibility, the following sections address several questions. Why did urban nationalists emphasize Islam and Arabic language and culture and marginalize other certain dimensions of Moroccan collective identity, including Berber or Jewish markers of identity? Second, why and how did they make Mohamed V (the young sultan the French put in place after his father, Mawlay Youssef, died in 1927) the fulcrum of their claims? And finally, how did they use these three dimensions of Moroccan identity (Islam, Arabic, and the monarchy) to mobilize popular protest?

This chapter starts by revisiting the Berber Crisis in the early 1930s, describing how this formative episode shaped the ideological and symbolic parameters of the nationalist classification struggle in the colonial political field. The next sections trace how Arab, Berber, Muslim, Jewish, and gendered dimensions of Moroccan identity were defended and contested in the nationalists' print and nonprint, performative struggles against colonial classificatory policies. I also analyze how the nationalists co-opted the very symbols the French had cultivated to legitimate the protectorate, including the flag and, most important, the person of the sultan, in their own celebration of Moroccan *wataniya*, or national identity. The conclusion assesses how the crystallization of the nationalist's core Arabo-Islamic and monarchy-centric definition of the Moroccan nation represented a contingent configuration that was related to how Moroccan identity had been politicized in the colonial political field.

The 1930 Latif Protests: Crafting a Moroccan Repertoire of Contention and Performing (and Defining) the Nation

On May 16, 1930, the French residency promulgated a *dahir*, which the sultan perfunctorily signed, that reorganized the separate customary legal system that the French first set in place in 1914 in certain so-called Berber regions under the control of the Direction of Indigenous Affairs. The decree put the customary system on the same legal footing as French and Islamic courts and stipulated that criminal cases be judged under French law rather than under Islamic law. In the summer of 1930, Moroccan Arab nationalists began to hone a definition of national identity in urban areas by repurposing a traditional prayer, the Latif, to mobilize protests against the decree.[2] For the nationalists, the Berber *dahir* constituted an integral threat to a Moroccan imagined national community unified for over a millennium by Islam and by Arabization. Between June and August, young activists used the Latif prayer as a "contentious social performance" (Alexander 2004; Isaac 2008) to communicate this impending threat against Morocco's ethno-religious national unity. They mobilized thousands in anti-colonial demonstrations by stoking fears that the French were dividing "Berbers" from "Arabs" and attempting to Christianize them.[3]

This cycle of contention centered on Berber, Arab, and Muslim Moroccan identities and constituted the seminal moment from which the urban nationalist movement developed. Instead of reinforcing a nationalist narrative teleology in which the Latif protests serve as a signal event in a progression toward Moroccan independence, my analysis unpacks how this critical juncture shaped the identity configuration the urban nationalists made dominant during their anti-colonial struggle and after independence. In the two decades after 1930, the Latif prayer became both a "classic" mode of protest in the Moroccan repertoire and a ritualized framing device, as the refrain "Oh God, the Benevolent, we ask of You benevolence in whatever fate brings . . . and do not separate us from our brothers, the Berbers!" was repeated over and over in demonstrations. The Moroccan nationalist movement remained profoundly shaped by this initial classification struggle that critiqued logics of legibility that differentiated between Arabs and Berbers and insisting on a

---

2. Halstead (1967) is still the best study of urban Arab nationalist leadership. He was able to interview most of these leaders extensively in the late 1950s, gathering vital firsthand documentation that was not preserved in writing because of the fear that it would be intercepted by protectorate security forces. Halstead focuses primarily on the first phase of the movement, 1930–1937. Allal al-Fassi (1948) also provides a firsthand, though not unexpectedly often teleological, account of the urban nationalist movement's steady progress towards independence. This section also draws upon the major French histories of the interwar period (Julien 1952; Berque 1967; Ageron 1972).

3. The following discussion reanalyzes the well-known Latif protests through the lens of Jeffrey Alexander's six-part model. The first element is collective representations, the background cultural references or the "universe of basic narratives and codes and the cookbook of rhetorical configurations from which every performance draws" (Alexander 2004, 550). Choices about specific meanings performers wish to project form the "script" of the performance. The trick is for this improvisational selection to remain authentic and ring true for the audience. The second component is the actors, the flesh-and-blood embodied performers who project the meanings of the script. The third element is the multiple observers/audiences involved in the performance, including participant-observers and broader audiences not in direct attendance. The fourth component is the means of symbolic production, including the physical props and the space(s) where performance takes place. Fifth is the mise-en-scène, the temporal sequencing and spatial choreography involved in the performance. The sixth component is the social power involved, including the material power to allow or prohibit performance and the interpretive power to determine its meaning (530–33).

unified judiciary that applied shari'a, Islamic law, under the authority of the Moroccan sultan. The Berber Crisis thus tied questions of ethnic, religious, and national identity to a specific Arabo-Islamic identity configuration from the very genesis of the nationalist movement.

The Urban Arab Nationalist Elite in the Interwar Period

In the late 1920s, a rising generation of young urban Arab men that had grown up under French rule began to meet in informal secret societies in Fes, Rabat, Salé, and Tetouan. They gathered in homes a couple of times a week to read and discuss Arabic and French newspapers, journals, and books from Algeria, Tunisia, Egypt, Syria, and Europe, including Islamic reformist writings by Mohamed Abduh, Rashid Rida's journal *al-Manar*, and Ibn Badis's journal *Al-Chihab*. Most of these men were educated in the traditional system or the modernized Arabic curriculum offered in the Moroccan-run free schools (al-Fassi 1954, 161–63) and had gone on to study at the Qarawiyin University in Fes, the millennium-old bastion of Morocco's educated elite. There, they studied with several professors whose teaching urged the revitalization of Moroccan Islam and resistance to assimilation into French culture.[4] Influenced by the late nineteenth-century *salafiya*, a reformist movement that focused on a return to the "pure" Islam of the first Muslim generations (*al-salif al-salih*), these teachers emphasized the development of a modernized system of Islamic law, the revitalization of the Arabic language, and the purification of heretical expressions of Islam in the country's widespread Sufi brotherhoods, or *zawiyas*. Others had received or were in the process of receiving a Western education in one of the Franco-Moroccan schools. A few of them had pursued university studies in Paris. The membership in each group meeting in the various cities numbered between fifteen to twenty (Halstead 1967, 166–72).

In the late 1920s, this loosely linked network of urban young men educated in Arabic and French institutions focused on revitalizing the cultural, linguistic, and religious dimensions of Moroccan nationalism. The protonationalist groups in Fes clandestinely published a monthly journal in Arabic, *Umm al-Banin*, which they secretly distributed in Fes, Rabat, Marrakesh, Tangier, and Tetouan (al-Fassi 1954, 116). Other groups were involved in Arabic theater troupes that used performances to speak about the need for

---

4. On the introduction of *salafi* influence in Morocco in the late nineteenth century, its impact at the Qarawiyin, and its role in the formation of segments of the Moroccan nationalist movement's leadership, see Abun-Nasr (1963) and Munson (1993, 77–114). On Salafiya more broadly in the Middle East in the early twentieth century, see Lauzière (2010).

reform (Halstead 1967, 170). Young men involved in closely linked theatrical and literary clubs in Rabat and Salé had also begun to use a discourse that involved the concept of *wataniya*, or nationalism (Rachik 2003, 62–66). It was the May 16 decree about the Berber customary court system that catalyzed a transformation toward political claims and gave these young men a strategic opportunity to act on their beliefs about Moroccan national identity.

For the young urban Arab nationalists, the 1930 decree fused the political, ethnic, and religious dimensions of Moroccan collective identity by threatening to further systematize a state-sanctioned classificatory division between Arab and Berber based on different legal systems: shariʻa, or Islamic law, for the former and *izref*, or customary law, for the latter. Partly due to their orientation toward *salafism*, in which the defense and renewal of Islamic law was a central concern, Moroccan activists seized on the issue of Berber customary law as a critical issue related to the future trajectory of Moroccan national identity. The 1931 census counted 5,067,800 Muslims, 124,500 Jews, and 172,400 foreigners (Gouvernement Chérifien 1946) in the French zone,[5] and the Berber-speaking population was estimated at 40–60 percent of the total Moroccan Muslim population (Lafuente 1999, 37–38). For the nationalists, therefore, the stakes of state-sponsored identity policies related to language and law increased significantly in the early 1930s as the colonial state neared completion of its pacification operations enclosing Berber-majority regions in the colonial political field.

Although most of the Arab nationalists had few or no personal links with the rural populations the French Berber policy affected, a decree that further formalized a territorial division based on the colonial state's ethnic classifications represented a threat to their own vision of consolidating Arabo-Islamic national identity by furthering the Arabization of the countryside and reforming (and co-opting) Sufi-oriented Islamic practices. Although they overemphasized the religious dimensions of the French Berber policy, the leaders of the Latif protests rightly diagnosed the ethnographic, preservationist, and developmentalist modes of colonial rule the French were implementing in Morocco.[6] Colonial policy explicitly attempted to discourage the spread of

---

5. This was the second census under the protectorate. The first census was taken in 1926.

6. The official policy of the predominantly laicist residency did not encourage the mass conversion of the Berbers to Christianity, but various factors heightened the religious dimensions of the colonial conflict. These include open calls in Catholic journals such as *Le Maroc catholique* and the *La Revue d'histoire des missions* for increased evangelism in Morocco's Berber areas; the distribution by a French official, Paul Marty, of copies of an Arabic-language book titled *Life of Jesus*; and the appointment of converted Algerian Kabyle court clerks in several of the Berber *jamaʻas*. The 1928 conversion and entry into priestly orders of Mohamed Ben ʻAbdeljelil, son of a Fassi notable family and brother of a future nationalist leader, also disturbed the nationalists (Julien 1952, 147; 1978, 159).

Arabic and Islam in the *blad* in order to prevent Arab-Berber national unity, and seeing difference through law and language was a mechanism through which the colonial state exercised symbolic power (Bourdieu 1991, 1999).

In 1930, these young Moroccan elites were in place, had a growing sense of national identity, and now had a *causus belli* for anti-colonial protest. The question was how to communicate it and get the masses into the streets to protest. Examining the Latif cycle of contention that played out from late June to early September shows how these actors improvised on preexisting cultural representations to create a new political script for a religious ritual, how they staged this in the strategic space of the mosque and the medina, and how authorities wielded social powers in the colonial field to manage and eventually shut down the protest.

Improvising on Moroccan Collective Representations in the Latif Script

The French did not choose a propitious time to announce what became known as the Berber decree. Locusts had devastated the crops of the Souss Valley in the south in 1929, and an autumn drought had destroyed one-third of the cattle and one-fifth of the sheep. The locusts returned in spring of 1930. In addition to the agricultural stresses, Morocco began to feel the effects of Great Depression as the demand for phosphate exports decreased. Several factors, including the conversion and entry into a priestly order of the son of a prominent Fes family and pro-evangelistic rhetoric from the bishopric of Rabat, had heightened Muslim sensitivities about the protectorate in the late 1920s (Julien 1978, 159–60). French actions early in the spring further escalated tensions. In April, authorities revealed a plan to divide the waters of the Fes River, diverting most of the water to French settlers. The revelation triggered a demonstration of 10,000 people on May 9 that caused Resident General Lucien Saint to withdraw the plan. Only a week later, the residency issued a decree reorganizing the Berber customary law system, taking it fully out from under the authority of the sultan-administered Islamic courts.

Abdellatif Sbihi and Mohamed Lyazidi, two Moroccan translators working for the protectorate administration who were also members of the protonationalist cultural associations in Salé and Rabat, were among the first to become aware of the *dahir*.[7] Sbihi resigned in protest after the decree was signed by the sultan and was published in the *Bulletin Officiel* on May 16. Over the next several

---

7. Lyazidi had worked as an interpreter in Rabat at the Land Registry for four years (Halstead 1967, 181), and Sbihi, also a translator, actually had the *dahir* cross their desks in May (Brown 1972, 209).

weeks, his warnings of the impending geographical division of Morocco failed to move either students or the older generation in Rabat, Salé, and Fes (Lafuente 1999, 198–88). Ahmad Maaninu, a member of the early Salé group, relates that Sbihi's warnings about the decree were finally able to evoke a strong response when he shifted from using the word *turab*, or soil, to warning that "Islam is being violated in its very being ('*Islam yumass fi jawharih*')" (Brown 1972, 209). This shift in framing, which conflated Berbers' legal status, territorial integrity, and the religious unity of the Moroccan Muslim *umma*, began to resonate among Sbihi's small network of cultural nationalists. It took until the end of June, though, for these men to translate these grievances into mass protest.

The strategy they hit upon was repurposing a ritual Muslim prayer, *Ya Latif*. The Latif was traditionally used in times of calamity, such as pestilence, locust plagues, drought, floods, or famine, to pray for divine relief. In such times of disaster, at the large Friday gatherings at the mosque, the imam or someone in the congregation would call out "Oh God, the Benevolent, we ask of You benevolence in whatever fate brings!" The assembly of the faithful would then join in the prayer.

During the third week of June of 1930, one of Sbihi's friends, 'Abd al-Karim Hajji, suggested using the Latif prayer in the mosque to raise awareness about the May 16 decree. That week, Sbihi and other youths pressured imams at mosques in Salé to recite the Latif on June 20 at the Friday noon prayer, the largest gathering of the week, because of the threat of the Berber decree (Lafuente 1999, 190–91). Maaninu relates that at the Grand Mosque, the old imam's cracking voice calling out the Latif "electrified all those present," including a large group of women who had congregated on the roof to listen to the prayers, and that "it was as if something very heavy had descended on all of us" (quoted in Brown 1972, 212). As a social performance, this repurposing of the Latif to focus on the purported threat of the Berber decree transformed the congregation into participant observers through a familiar prayer ritual that conflated intense religious emotion with a nascent sense of Arab-Muslim national identity. The resonance of the fusion that the Latif achieved "electrified" the Salé audience with the gravity of the threat against the unity of an imagined Moroccan Muslim community, reinforcing this level of collective identity. Over the next days and weeks, the performance of the Latif proved to be remarkably portable; it was replicated in mosques all over Salé and Rabat and eventually in most of Morocco's major cities.[8]

---

8. Demonstrations were also staged in Tetouan in the Spanish zone, not against the Spanish protectorate administration but against the French, who were responsible for the Berber *dahir*.

Means of Symbolic Production and the Mise-en-Scène of the Latif Performance

After the first performance on June 20, congregations in multiple mosques in Rabat and Salé chanted the Latif again on June 27 and 30. The prayer was typically scheduled for the Friday service, and speeches explaining the Berber Crisis to the large gathering would follow it. An intelligence report of the Directorate of Indigenous Affairs relates that Sbihi went to Marrakesh on July 6 to organize a Latif performance there. He instructed his collaborators to go to multiple mosques for the noon prayer, then cry out "*Ya Latif, ya Latif!*" When they were asked what the imminent danger was, they were to respond, "For our Berber brothers who are deprived of Muslim law and who can no longer live under the law and customs of their ancestors." These collaborators would then call on the audience to fast the next Sunday (Lafuente 1999, 192). The effort to diffuse the Latif beyond Rabat-Salé began to bear fruit; it spread to Fes on July 4 and to Casablanca on July 18.

In July and August, the contentious cycle gained steam as the Latif became diffused as a "collective action performance" (Isaacs 2008), generating demonstrations against government authorities in almost every major city in the country. Beginning in July, Fes proved to be the most active hotbed of anti-French agitation. As the spiritual capital of Morocco and the home of the venerable Qarawiyin University, Fes offered a substantial urban population of over 100,000 (Fédération Française des Anciens Coloniaux 1931) that included many students, small-scale artisans under economic duress due to the Great Depression and the influx of global manufacturing competition, and other petit bourgeois elements with a high potential for mobilization. After the Latif was chanted in Fes on July 18, crowds from multiple mosques converged at the tomb of Mawlay Idriss, the patron saint of the city, and proceeded in a street demonstration to the pasha's residence to voice their concerns. The pasha told the organizers to return the next day, then had Mohamed el-Ouezzani and Hashemi al-Filali arrested and publicly whipped. Two other young nationalist protest leaders, Allal al-Fassi and Abdelaziz Bendriss, were arrested and released after a brief imprisonment (Lafuente 1999, 194). The Latif protest reached its peak in early August as crowds increased during the annual *moussem* (saint's day) for Mawlay Idriss and more than 7,000 participated in prayer performance on August 7 in Fes (Ageron 1972, 138–39).

Moroccan nationalists were able to escalate and spread the Latif social performances because they could exploit important spatial and human resources related to what Alexander (2004:532) calls the "means of symbolic production." One of the most important of these was the mosque, which provided a strategic space for staging the performance. Soon after the founding of the protectorate, the first French resident general, Hubert Lyautey, issued a decree prohibiting all non-Muslims from entering mosques in Morocco (Rivet 1996, 175). This decision protected mosques as freer spaces for political speech due to the fact that French personnel could not enter them (though they did position informants in them). This space fuses the religious and the political, as prayers are said in the name of the ruler of the community, an Islamic equivalent to a pledge of allegiance. Historically, changing the name of that ruler has been a political statement tantamount to declaring a revolution.[9] The Friday sermon, the *khutba*, is another political instrument, as it constitutes a way to communicate to a large audience and thus inherently lends itself to mobilizing the community to action.

In Morocco, as in the rest of the Muslim world, mosques have functioned historically as a primary locus of public association in urban areas. Although hard numbers on how many participated in the Latif are not available (except for the estimate of 7,000 for the August 7 event in Fes), a significant majority of the male population and a lesser number of the female population (for whom prayer at the mosque was not viewed as obligatory) attended the Friday prayers. The Latif was performed multiple times through July and August in Rabat (population 38,000), Salé, Tetouan, Fes (100,000), Marrakesh (149,000), and Casablanca (107,000), and it is likely that a large majority of these urban Moroccan populations experienced the performance or heard about it from others who were present. Staging an anti-colonial nationalist protest in the mosque gave the nationalists the largest possible mass impact in urban Morocco.

Another structural-spatial advantage the nationalists exploited was the bifurcation of urban space between the modern European and traditional native quarters. The segregation of these populations created more freedom of activity for the Moroccans in the medina, the historic walled area of the city. The Fes medina, the largest in the world, presented an intimidating labyrinth to French security forces (both French and rural Moroccan colonial soldiers, many of whom were Berbers from the countryside who also did not know their way around) that gave the nationalists an advantage

---

9. In the tumult of Morocco's civil war (1907–1908), prayers were successively said in the name of Mawlay ʻAbd al-Aziz, in the name of Mawlay ʻAbd al-Hafiz, and then, in the south, in the name of El-Hiba, depending on the fluctuating political allegiances of the moment.

because of their familiarity with the layout of streets and the fact that they could find refuge in multiple locations throughout the city. The nationalists also benefited from institutions such as the Qarawiyin mosque-university complex at the center of the medina, which served as a central meeting place that could accommodate crowds in the thousands. Qarawiyin University provided an important networking node that created strong ties between al-Fassi activists and like-minded youth in Marrakesh, Tetouan, and Tangier who had spent time studying Islamic sciences in the 1920s.[10] Qarawiyin also linked urban centers and parts of the countryside, as a majority of the students at the university were actually *tolbas* (students of Islamic sciences) from the *blad* who boarded in the many madrasas encircling the main complex of the mosque-university.[11]

The young nationalists used these informal networks and those that had developed among the like-minded secret societies that had grown out of relationships developed at Qarawiyin University, at French-run *collèges musulmans* in Fes or Rabat, or through family and business connections. Several of the activists exploited their diplomatic immunity as protégés, or naturalized citizens of foreign governments (primarily Britain, Italy, and the United States), to travel among cities and openly organize the Latif with the assurance that the protectorate authorities could not imprison them for long. Some of the most effective protest organizers were British protégés and Moroccans who had gained Italian citizenship who used their legal immunity as an advantage with the local police forces that tried to arrest them as they spread the protest to Marrakesh and Casablanca. The Bouayad family (British protégés) and the Douiri family (naturalized Italians) were particularly active in organizing demonstrations in Fes, Casablanca, and Marrakesh. The diplomatic protections afforded to these activists gave them greater ability to travel, organize meetings, print and distribute tracts, gather funds, and maintain contacts outside Morocco. This made them particularly effective in the first years of the nationalist movement (Kenbib 1996).

The nationalists' staging and sequencing of the Latif protests from mosques enabled them to frame an emotionally resonant appeal about a

---

10. These included Mokhtar Al-Soussi from Marrakesh (who was imprisoned for his nationalist activities in the 1930s); Mohamed Daoud, Abdessalam Bennouna, M'hammed Bennouna Abdelhalek Torrès from Tetouan; and Abdellah Guennoun from Tangier.

11. In 1935, only 150 of the 800 to 900 students at the Qarawiyin came from Fes. The rest, the *afaqiyun* (people from the far horizon), were from the *blad* (Berque 1967, 177). Eickelman's (1985) social biography of a rural Moroccan judge demonstrates the parallel influence of the Yusufiyah mosque-university in Marrakesh.

threat to Morocco's Muslim community to a large urban population. The marches that resulted from these appeals were highly public contentious performances that featured the shouting of slogans, the singing of songs, and the chanting of the Latif. These marches served the dual functions of broadcasting grievances against the government throughout the medina and educating the population at large about the anti–Berber *dahir* cause. Through large-scale participatory social performance, the nationalists fused religious ritual and political protest in ways that began to make the solidarity of a Moroccan national community that was unified by Islam and Arabic language and culture an embodied experience for thousands of urban Moroccans.

The Social Power of the Moroccan Nationalists, the Sultan, and the French Colonial Authorities

This social performance was staged in a context in which multiple actors other than the nationalists, including the French administration and the Moroccan sultan himself, retained high levels of social power to mitigate and control its impact. The French authorities tried to forestall the initial recitation of the Latif in Salé by arresting Sbihi on the Thursday before the first recitation on June 20 (Brown 1972, 211). After the street demonstrations in Fes in mid-July, the police arrested twenty-four agitators. The following Friday, units of the Foreign Legion were stationed around the medina and police actually entered the mosque to make arrests (Halstead 1967, 182). After the huge crowds that gathered in Fes and in other cities on August 7, the French recognized that the Berber protests in Moroccan cities had begun to pose a significant threat to public order and a more serious threat to the legitimacy of the protectorate partnership.

Resident General Lucien Saint's response was to enjoin the sultan to issue a letter that called for the protests to end and chided the young activists. The letter, which was read in the mosques across the country on August 11, criticized the nationalists' attempt to drum up passions about French missionary activity and warned against politicizing mosques:

> Some young people, lacking any type of discernment and unaware of the full range of their reprehensible acts, would have one believe that these measures that we have decreed have no goal but the Christianization of the Berbers. They have thus induced the crowds to believe this error and convinced people to gather in the mosques to recite the Latif prayer after the ritual prayers, transforming prayer by this process into a political demonstration that troubles peoples' minds. Our Majesty

absolutely condemns the transforming of mosques, which God made as places of prayer and piety, into halls for political gatherings where hidden political agendas and negative tendencies are given free range. (Lafuente 1999, 196)

On August 13, French authorities officially prohibited the Latif in Morocco, but the sultan agreed to receive ten delegates to hear complaints about the May 16 *dahir*. The memorandum they presented the sultan and resident general (which is described in the opening anecdote of the Introduction) laid out the stakes of the identification struggle that was playing out in the colonial political field. It encapsulated the urban nationalists' counternarrative to the colonial vulgate's Arab-Berber binary, emphasized the centuries of Islamization and Arabization processes in Morocco, and urged state-based actions that would further this trajectory. These included creating a unified judiciary to apply Islamic law, creating a unified Arabic and Islamic curriculum for the educational system, and recognizing Arabic as the country's official language. The nationalists asked that teaching in Berber "dialects" and using such "dialects" in administrative records be prohibited; that all missionary activity and all government subsidies for evangelistic efforts, payment of priests, and church construction cease; and that Muslim alternatives be supported instead of Christian orphanages and vocational schools. To the activists' great disappointment, the memorandum achieved no immediate effect; the May 16 decree remained in effect. Although a 1934 decree returned criminal cases to the jurisdiction of the sultan, customary courts continued to operate until 1956 (Hoffman 2010, 856). There were Latif performances on August 31 and September 2, but the French arrested many of the organizers. That fall, the prohibition against the Latif was strictly enforced, and the streets of Fes, Salé, Rabat, Marrakesh, and Tetouan calmed down.

Chakib Arslan and the Internationalization of the Berber Crisis

Even though the Berber issue stalled in Morocco, it gained momentum abroad that fall as the front shifted to Paris, Geneva, Cairo, and Jerusalem. The main tactician responsible for transforming the Latif protests into a transregional pan-Islamic movement was Chakib Arslan, a Lebanese Druze amir, poet, and journalist based in Geneva who was one of the Arab world's most vocal anti-colonial political activists in the interwar period. In Paris in the 1920s, Arslan had come in contact with Moroccan students, including Mohamed al-Fassi, Ahmed Balafrej, and Mohamed el-Ouezzani. In the summer of 1930, Balafrej and al-Fassi accompanied Arslan on a tour of Spain, then arranged for him visit to Tangier and Tetouan for ten days in August, at the height of the Latif protests in the French zone (Cleveland 1985, 90–114).

Arslan returned to Geneva and launched a campaign against the French press through his French-language journal *La Nation Arabe*. He also wrote articles about the Berber issue in several of Cairo's major Arabic periodicals, including *al-Manar*, *al-Fath*, and *al-Zahra*. The issue was picked up by newspapers in Tunis, Tripoli, Beirut, Jaffa, and Damascus, editorialists castigated the French as an "enemy of Islam."[12] In November 1930, the French began to take heat for the Berber decree in Cairo. Exiled Tunisian Dustur leaders there sent a letter to the French president protesting France's attempt to "separate the great Muslim Berber people from Muslim law and society,"[13] and the Universal Association of Muslim Youth, which was headquartered in Cairo, planned a demonstration in front of the French consulate.[14] By January, the anti-French movement had extended to the eastern edge of the Islamic world as twelve Muslim associations met in Java to create the Muslim Committee for the Defense of Berbers.[15] Two Moroccans, Mekki Naciri and Mohamed Bennouna, were sent as delegates to the Islamic Congress held in Jerusalem in December 7–17, 1931, where they distributed pamphlets and presented the plight of Moroccan Berbers to the general assembly (Ageron 1972, 141–42). At its conclusion, the congress passed a resolution demanding that the French government rescind the decree.[16]

For this brief moment in the early 1930s, the "Berber Crisis" moved Morocco, the peripheral "farthest west" of the Arab world, to the center of pan-Islamic and pan-Arab concerns. Its anti-French struggle was considered the front line of a conflict between Islam and Christian Europe. With its emphasis on defending Arabo-Islamic culture, the anti–Berber

---

12. SHD-AT, Carton 3H 247, Office de Liaison, Rabat, Renseignement, A/S manifestation anti-française en Lybie à l'occasion du dahir du 16 mai 1930 du Sultan du Maroc.

13. SHD-AT, Carton 3H 247, Office de Liaison, Rabat, Renseignement: Protestations d'éléments destouriens du Caire a/s de l'indépendance religieuse accordée aux berbères du Maroc, November 27, 1930.

14. SHD-AT, Carton 3H 247, Office de Liaison, Rabat, Renseignement, Sujet: agitation de l'Association Universelle de la Jeunesse Musulmane à l'occasion du Dahir du Sultan du Maroc sur les tribus berbères, November 10, 1930.

15. "Echos de la question berbère dans les Iles Nederlandaises," *La Nation Arabe* 1 (February 1930): 5.

16. Bennouna family archives, Tetouan, pamphlet titled *Muqarrarat al-mu'tamer al-islami al-'am*, December 1931.

dahir campaign also tied Moroccan nationalists more closely to anti-colonial nationalist peers in the Arab East. The Moroccan movement developed an important transnational base for activism in the Mashriq and enjoyed support in Egyptian and Palestinian newspapers, which continued to rail against the Berber policy.[17] Cairo began to emerge as an important center for publishing North African nationalist propaganda in Arabic. This was significant, since Arabic publishing was for the most part banned by the French in the protectorate.[18] These links to the Arab world proved increasingly important after World War II. With the founding of the Arab League in 1945 and the rise of Nasser as the leader of the pan-Arab movement in the 1950s, Cairo transcended Paris as a base for expatriate Moroccan nationalist activity.

Formal and Informal Nationalist Organizational Structures

In Morocco, after the Latif cycle of contention died down, the nationalists faced the question of how to create a sustainable movement that could achieve the material and symbolic reforms they desired. The next steps were to develop a more formalized organizational structure, expanding the means by which they could propagate their framing of Moroccan national unity and the dangers of colonial classifications that undermined that unity and implement contentious strategies to gain more leverage against and responses from the colonial state.

In the years after the Latif protests, the tiny circle of loosely connected young activists developed into a more tightly networked and disciplined leadership structure. Despite their *salafiya*-inspired anti-Sufi polemical stance, they drew extensively on Morocco's deep Sufi traditions. They also drew on the cellular structure of communism and the secret society strategy of

---

17. The campaign in the Arab press continued strong for several more years. A 1932 article in the Cairo paper *Al-Fateh* emphasized Morocco's attachment to the Arab world and criticized the French attack on the country's "Arabo-Islamic unity" and ties to other Arab and Islamic countries with an assimilationist policy in the countryside that were trying to covert Berbers to Catholicism and French culture. SHD-AT, Carton 3H 247, Report from Col. Margot, Service de la Presse Musulman, to Chef du Cabinet Militaire de Monsieur le Résident General, A/S, articles d'*Al Fateh* sur le Maroc, June 16, 1932.

18. For example, in June 1932, French intelligence services in Morocco reported that a tract against the Berber Dahir published by the Association of Muslim Youth in Cairo had been sent via English post to Abdelaziz Aboutaleb, manager of the Imprimerie Moderne in Fes. He received 500 copies. Mohamed Akalai in Tangier received 150, and Mohamed Bennouna in Tetouan received 350. SHD-AT, Carton 3H 247, Office de Liaison, Rabat, Renseignements: A/S Propagande nationaliste, June 23, 1932.

Freemasonry, developing a uniquely Moroccan hybrid organizational structure.[19] The inner circle appropriated a Sufi-oriented name, calling themselves
the Zawiya.[20] Outside this inner circle, they created a ring of membership
called the Taifa, or group, and in 1933, a public arm of the movement was
created, named Kutlat al-amal al-watani, the National Action Bloc (Comité
d'action marocaine).[21] Membership in the Taifa required an oath of allegiance and the payment of dues. For the oath, a copy of the Qur'an was
placed on a table, the prospective member put his finger on the Qad-sami
chapter and said, "I swear by God and the Qur'an that I will follow the orders
of the Wataniyin."[22] The movement also developed Sufi-like overtones of a
master-disciple relationship, especially in rural areas, where it competed with
the Qadiriyya and Tijanniya orders. After a split in the movement in 1936,
those who followed Allal al-Fassi were often referred to as the Allaliyin, and
al-Fassi was called Sheikh Allal or Haj Allal (Julien 1952, 138).

Although the nationalist leadership in Tetouan in the Spanish zone coordinated their activities to an extent with the Kutla, they created parallel
organizational structures. In 1932, the Spanish republican regime allowed
the creation of the Hispano-Muslim Association (Al-Jamiya al-Isbaniya al-
Islamiya), which was led by Abdessalem Bennouna, Mohamed Daoud, and
Abdelhalek Torrès. The nationalist leadership in the two protectorate zones
developed different trajectories due to fluctuations in the relative liberality
of the French and Spanish colonial states, although the two groups remained
in close contact throughout the 1930s and 1940s.

---

19. Connections between freemasonry, early Salafiyah, and Egyptian nationalism have been
explored in more depth than similar connections in the Maghrib (Kudsi-Zadeh 1972; Wissa 1989).
Freemason orders had been established in Morocco since before the protectorate was established (in
Tangier in 1891 and in Casablanca in 1910). Several Tetouani activists joined the Freemasons in the
1930s, though I have not found evidence that any in the French zone joined. Moroccan nationalists
from the French zone studying in France were in contact with members of the French Communist
Party in the 1920s and 1930s. However, the Moroccan nationalists were not as closely connected
to communist groups as the Algerian nationalist, Messali Hadj, and the early Etoile nord-africaine
in the 1920s.

20. *Zawiya* literally means "corner," referring to the corner of the mosque where a teacher
would teach his pupils. The word came to signify the physical building, or lodge, of a Sufi movement and even the movement itself when it was used along with *tariqa* (or way). All of these levels
of meaning were implied by the Moroccan nationalists.

21. Halstead (1967, 191–97) includes detailed lists that break down the membership and activities of the Zawiya leadership in different Moroccan cities.

22. Wataniyin (nationalists) was the name given to the main branch of the movement that
followed Allal al-Fassi following the split with Ouezzani in 1936. The description of the oath was
given during interrogations following riots in Fes in 1937. SHD-AT, Carton 3H 250, "Extraits des
déclarations du nommé Taieb Ben Hassan Janati," November 1, 1937.

Another nationalist organizational initiative in the interwar period focused on Moroccan youth. Although the free school movement (meaning free of government control) was not formally affiliated with the Kutla, it was an important recruiting structure. The free schools, the first of which was opened in 1919, competed as an alternative to the Franco-Muslim schools founded by the Direction of Public Instruction. These schools, which taught Arabic and Islam as a part of a modern curriculum, played an important role in cultivating a sense of national identity among urban youth.[23] The political dimension of the free schools has perhaps been overemphasized, but they played an important role in providing a parallel Arabic educational system (which by the 1940s had come under the administration of the grand vizier) and laying a cultural foundation for nationalism by "instilling national spirit—feeling of patriotism and a sense of Moroccan nationhood—in the students" (Damis 1970, 242).[24] Many of early nationalist leaders had been involved in founding free schools and had taught in them. By the 1940s, several of the new generation had been educated in them.

Alongside the free schools, the nationalists also helped create a Muslim corollary to the Éclaireurs Français; they founded the first Moroccan scout troop in Rabat-Salé in the summer of 1933.[25] The Moroccan scouts provided the nationalist movement with motivated ground troops for protest. They marched through streets singing nationalist hymns, distributed tracts, and wrote anti-French graffiti on walls.[26] The nationalists also had strategic ties with the leadership of the Moroccan alumni organizations of the official protectorate-run elite *collèges musulmans* in Fes and Rabat, which provided another important networking structure.

----

23. In the mid-1930s, 5,000 Moroccan students were enrolled; by the late 1940s, this number had increased to 25,000 (Damis 1970).

24. Damis (1970) disagrees with Halstead, Rézette, and Julien, arguing that the free schools were not used to politically indoctrinate or recruit members but that they did have a vital role in propagating a cultural frame of Moroccan nationalism.

25. The Moroccan Scouts were started by Ahmed ben Maati Bouhlal in August 1933 in Rabat-Salé and initially had ninety members. For French analysis of the "threat" of Moroccan scouting from the perspective of the mid-1940s, see M. Goidan, "Le Scoutisme musulman au Maroc," *CHEAM* 944 (October 1946). The Centre des Hautes Etudes d'Administration Musulmane (CHEAM) functioned as a type of colonial think tank in Paris where current and former colonial administrators, soldiers, and politicians met to discuss policy issues. A wide range of fieldwork was presented at the center as papers.

26. *L'Action du peuple* reported in its September 15, 1933, edition on the scandalous treatment of the Moroccan Scouts who had gathered to welcome the sultan back from trip to France at the Trois-Portes in Casablanca. The residency sent the motorcade through another gate. The scouts were also frequently mentioned in security reports about nationalist demonstrations in Rabat, Salé, and Fes.

The Nationalist Print Campaign against the Protectorate's Logics of Legibility

While they strengthened their organizational infrastructure in the 1930s, the Moroccan nationalists also continued a two-pronged action strategy: they honed a configuration of Arabo-Islamic national identity and framed the colonial threat to it; and they used popular protest to create pressure on the colonial state. This section focuses on the print campaign the nationalists launched against the logics of legibility in the colonial political field through a handful of nationalist journals and newspapers. The next section turns to nonprint strategies that focused on the symbolic expression of national unity through the invention of public commemorative spectacles and the staging of mass protests.

Although nationalist newspapers and journals offer a rich documentary trove, several qualifications must be made about the actual dissemination and reception of these texts. In relationship to the type of mass reading public that Anderson (1991) argues constitutes an important precondition for imagining a national community, the nationalist print campaign in Morocco was severely handicapped by major factors: an illiteracy rate of 94 percent for women and 90 percent for men in the interwar period (Ennaji 2005, 201); and the residency's strict restriction of the freedom of the press through heavy censorship or outright banning of Moroccan publishing. Protectorate administrators had no interest in fostering a mass Arabic reading public. They did not fund the expansion of Arabic education, and they set up legal barriers to Arabic-language publishing that was not controlled by the state.[27] For more than twenty years, these policies prevented virtually any Arabic language periodicals from being published in Morocco.[28]

Because of these strictures, the inner nationalist leadership circle, the Zawiya, launched its first major periodical, *Maghreb*, in Paris in 1932. A

---

27. An April 27, 1914, *dahir* provided the legal foundation for the residency's expansive powers over the press. The edict forbade "any attack on the rights and power of the French Republic in the Sharifian Empire" and gave the residency the right to forbid the circulation of any foreign journal. Arabic-language publications, even if published in Morocco, were considered "foreign" press that could the resident general could prohibit by special decree. In 1920, another *dahir* stipulated that the founding of an Arabic-language publication required an (always revocable) vizierial order, creating another hurdle to the creation of the Arabic press (Aouchar 1990, 18). Later *dahirs* (June 26, 1937, and October 18, 1937) gave the residency additional power to forbid any publications that threatened order and security.

28. The exceptions included *Al-Jarida al-rasmiya,* the Arabic version of the *Bulletin Officiel,* and the bi-weekly *As-Sa'ada,* which was under the control of the Directorate of Indigenous Affairs (Souriau 1975, 86–87).

major goal of the revue, the editorial board of which included sympathetic French leftists such as Robert Jean Longuet, was to argue the case of the Moroccan nationalists to a French metropolitan audience that was largely unaware of and indifferent to events in the empire. The journal was also distributed widely in Morocco before it was banned there. In 1933, a second paper (also in French because the residency denied permission for an Arabic version) was founded in Fes, *L'Action du peuple*, with Mohamed el-Ouezzani as editor-in-chief. *L'Action du peuple* was aimed at three audiences: Moroccans (French-speaking), protectorate authorities, and French *colons*.[29] Moroccan nationalists also aired opinions in other Paris-based journals that were smuggled into the country, often through the British post, via a network of nationalist friends in Tangier and Tetouan that included Abdel Khalek Torrès and Mohamed Daoud.[30] These activists in the northern zone enjoyed a much more liberal publishing environment, and Spanish authorities there authorized the creation of several nationalist papers in Arabic and Spanish. In Tetouan, the first nationalist periodical, *Al-Salam*, appeared in October 1933. It was joined by *Al-Hayat* in March 1934. Both of these were circulated clandestinely in the French zone, where the freedom of the Moroccan press had been revoked. *Maghreb* was first banned in September 1932, and the residency permanently banned its circulation in the protectorate in 1933 (the journal was discontinued in January 1935). The Fes-based *L'Action du peuple* was shut down immediately after the controversial reception of the sultan in the medina during his official visit in May 1934.

During the brief window of opportunity when they were able to openly print newspapers and journals, the nationalists critiqued the French administration on material and symbolic levels. Numerous articles denounced the exploitation of Moroccans and the favoring of French *colons* in terms of taxation, agricultural credit and financial assistance, and education expenditure. The majority of the print space, however, was dedicated to attacking the colonial state's intertwined historiographic and ethnographic logics of legibility and legitimacy. Nationalists mounted a cultural and religious defense of Moroccan national identity in the journals and criticized France, the supposed "protector" state, for undermining it. This print campaign emphasized three intertwined themes: a historiographic defense of Morocco's Islamization and Arabization; an attack on the moral basis of Berber customary law

---

29. Mohamed el-Ouezzani, "A nos lectures," *L'Action du people*, August 4, 1933.

30. SHD-AT, Carton 3H 247. Office de Liaison, Rabat, Renseignement: A/S Correspondance des Nationalistes Marocains d'Europe avec le Maroc, February 2, 1933.

and a corollary justification of the superiority of shariʿa; and an argument for state-supported Arabization and Islamization policies expressed through a unified education system and judiciary.

Numerous articles outlined a countervulgate that glossed over ethnolinguistic distinctions in Moroccan society by arguing that Berbers had been almost completely assimilated by Arabic and Islam for centuries. An article titled "The Berbers and the Gauls" attacked the suggestion in colonial scholarship that the Berbers were racially related to the Gauls. It identified a "double perfidy" that asserted that Berbers were independent of Arabs and Islam, using a quote from Gautier's colonialist history of North Africa, *L'Isalmisation de l'Afrique du Nord* (1927), to show that even colonial historians such as him accept their Islamization and Arabization:

> For ten or twelve centuries the Berbers have been Islamized and, for the most part Arabized, in their manners and language. This is evidenced in the upsurge of the Islamic faith which, since the first years of the Arab occupation of North Africa, carried the Berber armies of the general Tariq (Tariq ibn Ziyad) to Spain across the strait that bears his name, "Gibr-al-Tar."[31]

Another author, Mohamed Lyazidi, a member of Zawiya from Rabat, rebutted the residency's assertions (in defense of the May 16 decree) that allowing the continuance of Berber customary law instead of enforcing Islamic law in the countryside was consistent with historic precedents set by the precolonial *makhzan*. Lyazidi pointed out that Berber tribes welcomed Idriss I, the founder of the first Moroccan *makhzan*, as a descendant of the Prophet Mohamed and that they then served as his soldiers in conquering Morocco and spreading Islam. Lyazidi emphasized that the most glorious historical periods of Islamic civilization in Morocco were instigated by Berber dynasties (the Almoravids and Almohads) rather than Arab dynasties and that the Almohads were the first to achieve the political and religious unification of the country.[32] Lyazidi argued the colonial vulgate's logic was historically applicable only to the decades immediately before 1912:

> The division of this country into *blad al-makhzan* (the submissive zone) and *blad al-sība* (the unsubmissive zone) can only be applied to

---

31. Rolland Elissa-Rhais, "Les Berbères et les Gaulois," *Maghreb*, November 1932, 7–8. Rhais was among the French sympathizers who contributed to the journal.

32. Mohamed Lyazidi, "Divers aspects de la politique berbère au Maroc," *Maghreb*, May–June 1933, 8.

a relatively recent time period, that is to say, the era when the Great
European powers began to foment troubles with scheming plots in
order to justify their intervention.[33]

Attacking the French justification that their intent was simply to protect
tribes' historic rights by not imposing the "foreign" jurisdiction of Islamic
law, he reiterated the nationalist claim that the Berber *dahir* was part of an
overall plan to assimilate Berbers into French culture and reflected a Catholic
influence that encouraged proselytization.

The colonial state's *politique berbère* and the Catholic Church's aspirations in Morocco were frequently conflated in the Moroccan nationalist
press. In 1934, *L'Action du peuple* reprinted quotes that fused Catholic hopes
for the conversion of the Berbers and French imperial interests in North
Africa from the September 1927 issue of the Paris-based *Revue d'histoire
des missions*:

> Let Christianity act on the Berber soul as it formerly acted on our soul,
> not by helping its action through brutal means, not even by official
> means, but just by not frustrating it. This would without doubt make
> the dissolution of the Arab bloc much easier, and by extension the
> Islam of our North Africa, to the aid of our civilization and our race.[34]

A piece by Mohamed el-Ouezzani titled "The Twentieth Anniversary of the
Berber Policy (1914–1934)" also warned against the colonial religious threat.
He called the Berber *dahir* a "war machine" against treaties between France
and Morocco, against the sultan and the Moroccan government, against Islam,
against Arabic culture, and against order and unity in Moroccan society. He
wrote: "This is nothing but a Machiavellian colonial project. It symbolizes
the abominable crusade carried out by the imperialists and priests against
Islam and Arab culture. It constitutes a war engine against Sharifian power
and the Moroccan people."[35] In the midst of the vitriol against the decree,
however, he continued to defend the sultan who signed it, explaining that the
residency had outmaneuvered him.[36]

---

33. Ibid., 9, 11.

34. "La Croisade contre l'Islam," *L'Action du Peuple*, January 5, 1934, 2.

35. Mohamed el-Ouezzani, "20eme anniversaire de la politique berbère (1914–1934), *Maghreb*,
May–June 1934, 10.

36. Another example of this sentiment was a letter to the editor of *Maghreb* by a Moroccan
who stated, "We are convinced that the young leader of the Muslim community did not grasp the
heavy responsibility which was put on him." "Pour le France et le Maroc contre le dahir berbère,"
Maghreb, December 1932.

The nationalist print campaign also directly attacked the protectorate's use of separate legal jurisdictions as a classificatory mechanism that distinguished between Arabs and Berbers. The focus of this stream of articles was discrediting the moral basis of tribal "Berber" customary law and demonstrating the superiority of Islamic law. A 1932 article titled "Consequences of the Berber Dahir" related the plight of a *mokhzani* soldier whose daughter married a man in Khenifra, a Berber town in the Middle Atlas. After the son-in-law died, the father was told that his daughter's probate status had been determined according to the "prehistoric customs of the Berbers that do not recognize the right of the wife to inherit any of her husband's or his parents' property." The article's author protested:

> Thus, thanks to the Berber policy of Mr. Saint, a woman of Fes, a city which is not part of the Berber sector, finds herself dispossessed of her rights on the basis of the heritage of her husband, who is a Muslim like her. This is the organizational logic of the justice system in which there is a dual jurisdiction between Arabs and Berbers in a country in which all of the elements of the country intermingle and can in no way lead isolated lives![37]

A frequent theme in these attacks was the unequal treatment of women under Berber tribal law and the superiority of shari'a in giving women more rights.

Other writers took aim at the divisive logic of the colonial state's legal classifications that designated separate courts for Moroccan Jews and for French and other Europeans in the country. One contributor commented, "We do not want any differentiation according to race. We have, at present, jurisdictions for Jews, for Berbers, for Arabs, and for the European elements, in addition to the consular jurisdictions [for protégés]. The Arab, in the face of this diversity of tribunals, loses his head and does know not where to go."[38] For this nationalist author, the clear solution was to unify the judiciary framework, reform shari'a, and apply it uniformly in Moroccan territory. In a letter reprinted from a French paper, *Le Cri marocain*, the pseudonymous author "Muslim" attacked the residency's attempt to expand the jurisdiction of the French legal code in Morocco and limit the application of Islamic law. The author of the letter then called for a modern reform and codification of shari'a, saying:

> Our law is neither archaic, nor absurd. On the contrary, it agrees perfectly with the spirit of modern times. Our justice only needs to be

---

37. "Conséquences du dahir berbère," *Maghreb*, October 1932, 6–7.
38. "La politique berbère," *L'Action du Peuple*, August 18, 1933.

brought up to date and cleared of certain influences that paralyze its action and soil its reputation. Muslim law needs to be studied carefully. It needs to be codified. Only a truly competent, truly independent commission could conduct such a noble enterprise.[39]

The other clear demand of the nationalists was that Arabic become the official language of the protectorate. Arabic was the cultural and linguistic twin pillar of the national "high culture" of Islam that the Kutla ideologues wanted the colonial state to sponsor. An article from January 1933 complained that the "Franco-Arab" schools the Direction of Public Instruction had founded over the past decade were basically just "French." Only one to two hours a week were devoted to Arabic instruction. The author also observed that the French zone in Morocco functioned almost exclusively in French, from the post office to the bank to road signs to city names that had been changed (i.e., Sidi Kacem to Petit Jean and Kenitra to Port Lyautey). The article concluded: "It is enough to say that a foreigner traveling in Morocco would have no idea that he was in a country for which Arabic was the mother tongue of its inhabitants."[40]

In making the case for implementing educational, administrative, and judicial policies that consolidated the nationalists' vision of Moroccan Arabo-Islamic national identity, they appealed to the formal legitimization logic that undergirded France's state-building civilizing mission in Morocco. In a 1933 article, Mohamed el-Ouezzani pointed out that the Berber *dahir* contradicted the fundamental logic of the Treaty of Fes in which the French pledged to protect the authority of the sultan. The point of the pacification should have been to increase the reach of the sultan's authority, but in regions the French labeled "of Berber custom," he was not allowed to appoint *qadis* to apply Islamic law. For Ouezzani, the French excuse that they had an obligation to respect the rights of the tribes that submitted to them was ludicrous, since the pacification had been a "formal commitment made by the French government to aid our *makhzan* in reestablishing order and tranquility over dissident provinces." It made no sense to sanction the customs of the "insurgents." The only reason these customs were still in existence was because the situation had been "unfavorable to the installation of an institution applying Muslim law there as in the rest of the country."

---

39. Letter to the editor of the Socialist paper *Le Cri Marocain*, republished in February 1933 edition of *Maghreb* and titled "En Marge du dahir berbère," 36, 38.

40. Abou Abdillah, "Comment le protectorat respecte notre langue," *Maghreb*, January 1933, 30–32.

Ouezzani pointed out that the only justifiable raison d'être of the protectorate and the pacification was to extend the authority of the sultan and the *makhzan*, not undermine it.[41]

On the third anniversary of the 1930 decree, Ahmed Belafrej summarized the nationalist critique of the Berber policy, arguing that both past history and the current forces the French had unleashed indicated that a transcendent Moroccan "national spirit" unified by Islam would only grow stronger:

> History offers us proof of the existence of a national Moroccan spirit which was formed in the course of trials and in battle against the Christian Portuguese and Spanish kingdoms and against the Turks, Muslims who nevertheless harassed the country without respite. . . . Why choose to use the principle of race in order to break us up and divide us? We are all more or less Berbers, some more Arabized than the others; the Arab element in Morocco is tiny. But one fact is certain— that all of Morocco is Muslim. . . . One cannot assert that Morocco is a Berber country colonized and oppressed by the Arabs and that France has arrived today to charitably liberate it. For Muslim Morocco has always been independent.

He concluded with an incisive and prophetic analysis of the Berber policy and its link to Arabization: "The Berber policy can have but one result which is to give Moroccans themselves a consciousness and unify them in an instinctive defense reaction. For they now feel the danger that menaces them. The 'Berber mountain' is not a farm laboratory where the imperialists can experiment with their dangerous theories. There is an economic factor that trumps them. Sooner or later the Berbers will come down to the plains and learn to speak Arabic."[42]

The nationalist print campaign culminated in December 1934 with the presentation of a formal reform program to the French foreign minister, the resident general, and the sultan. The "Plan de réformes marocaines" was drafted by a committee that included prominent members of the Zawiya such as Mohamed Lyazidi, Omar Ben Abdeljalil, and Mohamed Hassan al-Ouezzani. It summarized their reformist agenda, which still accepted and assumed a Franco-Moroccan protectorate framework but appealed to the

---

41. Mohamed el-Ouezzani, "La politique berbère et le statut du Maroc," *Maghreb*, May–June 1933, 20–26.

42. Ahmed Belafrej, "Et maintenant?," *Maghreb*, May–June 1933, 50–51.

"protector" to do a better job of fulfilling the mandate of the Treaty of Fes.[43] After opening with a list of grievances that critiqued French colonial policy in Morocco as racist, unjust, anti-liberal, colonizing, and assimilationist, the authors explained that implementing the reform plan could fix the broken protectorate partnership (Comité d'Action Marocaine 1934, i–xvi). The plan then outlined recommendations for political, judicial, social, and economic reform. One of the last sections turned to identity-related cultural and religious reforms, calling for the elimination of the Berber policy, a ban on Christian proselytization, and the institution of Arabic as the protectorate's official language. The "Plan de réformes" received a tepid response from the French protectorate administration and gained no traction in Paris. With the complete failure of this reformist strategy and the shutdown in 1935 of all of their press outlets, the nationalist leadership faced a crisis in the mid-1930s. It was in this context that nonprint framing, popular mobilization, and contentious tactics moved to the forefront.

Co-opting the Field's Logics of Legitimization in Nationalist Performances

Print media was a questionable strategy for mass mobilization because of colonial censorship and Morocco's low literacy levels. As evidenced in the Latif cycle of contention, the staging of large-scale demonstrations was in many ways far more important than newspaper articles for conveying elite definitions of Moroccan national identity to urban audiences. As we saw earlier, various components of urban space were critical for performing the nationalist countervulgate. Protests were orchestrated and mobilized in mosques and marches, demonstrations, boycotts of French products, the circulation of petitions, and strikes were carried in the "traditional" space Lyautey had delineated in the medina. More than through a print community, these performances of collective protest, both the occurrences themselves and the dissemination of reports about them, provided the means for a national Moroccan community to be imagined, particularly in urban areas, during the 1930s-1940s.

---

43. Allal al-Fassi (1954, 140) explains: "The reform program was an ingenious stratagem to reconcile the existing treaties with the interests of the country, in the economic section, for example, the Kutla advocated the open-door policy and free trade, in accordance with the resolutions of the Algeciras Conference. This platform was designed to appeal to the support of the left-wing parties in France and to the signatories of the Algeciras international conference; at the same time, it was agreeable to the best interests of Morocco under the circumstances."

In performing the nation on this public level, the nationalists countered the ideological and symbolic power of the colonial state by co-opting the symbols and rituals Lyautey had reinvented for the *makhzan*, including the redesigned Sharifian flag and the national anthem, and inventing their own symbols of Moroccan national unity. Beginning with annual commemorations of the Berber *dahir*, the nationalists began to craft a national liturgical calendar of dates affiliated with national identity and resistance.[44] They marked May 16 by organizing large gatherings at mosques to perform the Latif prayer, closing stores in medinas, circulating petitions, and sending scores of telegrams protesting the Berber *dahir* to officials in Rabat and Paris.

The most significant of these national holidays was the Throne Day celebration that Moroccan nationalists "invented" (Hobsbawm and Ranger 1983) in 1933.[45] Throne Day (Aid al-'arsh in Arabic and Fête du trône in French) commemorated the anniversary of the accession of Sultan Mohamed ben Youssef (Mohamed V) on November 18, 1927. In late October 1933, Mohamed al-Ouezzani, published a large picture of the sultan on the front page of *L'Action du Peuple* and announced an initiative to celebrate Aid al-'arsh. An organizing committee was formed that included the *salafi* former minister of justice, al-Dukkali, and nationwide celebrations were planned that included the decoration of streets and markets with Moroccan flags, the closure of government institutions, and official ceremonies.[46] Despite a meager turnout the first year, Throne Day took off in 1934 and became the major nationalist holiday. When colonial administrators attempted to co-opt the event by making it an official holiday, the nationalists exploited the opportunity to use officially sanctioned banquets and gatherings to propagate their anti-colonial message.

One of the most important path-dependent outcomes of the nationalists' early emphasis on Throne Day in the early 1930s was that it tied their construction of Arabo-Islamic Moroccan national identity to the Alawid monarchy and the fortunes of Mohamed V. Allal al-Fassi reports that part of the motive for creating the Throne Day was a desire to reaffirm the nationalist movement's allegiance to sultan in order to counter the residency's efforts to restore Mohamed V's uncle, Mawlay 'Abd al-Hafiz, to the throne (al-Fassi 1954, 132). In inventing Throne Day, the nationalists

---

44. For a broader treatment of the creation and politics of national holidays in the Middle East, see Podeh (2011).

45. On the central importance of Throne Day in symbolizing Moroccan national identity, see Rachik (2003, 102–12).

46. In true Moroccan fashion, a ceremonial tea was scheduled for 4 p.m. in Fes.

also empowered the sultan, to whom them they began to refer with the more modern title of "king."[47] Although these decisions were purely symbolic at this point, they gave the king potential resources he would later tap in his own efforts to frame and mobilize the nation after World War II. It became a Throne Day tradition for the king to give a speech to the nation, which was published in the Arabic government journal, *Es-Saada*, and in the French press. From the late 1930s, the speeches were broadcast live on Radio Maroc.[48] In the 1940s, when the king took an active role in the independence movement, these Throne Day speeches became an increasingly important platform for him to communicate directly to the Moroccan nation.

The symbolic potential of the king for the nationalist cause was clearly demonstrated during an official visit of the king to Fes in May 1934 for the *moussem*, or festival, of the city's founder and patron saint, Mawlay Idriss. Massive crowds turned out on May 10 to line Mohamed V's flag-festooned route to the Mawlay Idriss mausoleum in the center of the medina. French officials were disturbed by the crowd's enthusiasm, which they expressed with shouts of "Long live the King! Long live the Crown Prince! Long live Morocco!" and "Down with France!" and the singing of a nationalist hymn composed for the occasion. According to al-Fassi, when the king reached the *hurm* (the sacred space around the mausoleum), the crowd "broke into tumultuous applause joined with nationalist chanting" (al-Fassi 1954, 133). Reportedly, after the sultan returned to the palace, a group of young demonstrators waving Moroccan flags marched to the regional office of the Direction of Indigenous Affairs shouting "À *bas la France!*" and pulled down the French flag.[49] When

---

47. From this point forward, I use "sultan" to refer to Mohamed V when referencing French usage and "king" when referencing the title the nationalists used. Although this can be confusing, it avoids an anachronistic projection of the title "king."

48. The French administration carefully tracked the number of radio receivers Europeans and Moroccans owned in their zone. A 1939 report said that in April, Europeans owned 32,791 radios, Moroccan Muslims owned 5,339, and Moroccan Jews owned 2,116. SHD-AT, Carton 3H 1413, Direction des Affaires Politiques, "Situation politique et économique," April 1939. In the late 1930s and during World War II, French security services carefully monitored German and Italian propaganda broadcasts in Arabic and Berber from Radio Seville, Radio Tetouan, and Radio Bari. See MAE, CADN-Mar., Direction de l'Intérieur, Carton 188.

49. MAE, CADN-Mar., Direction de l'Intérieur, Carton 892, delegate minister of the resident general to the minister of foreign affairs, "A/S des événements du 10 Mai 1934 à Fès et de leurs conséquences," May 21, 1934. According to the French report, the enthusiastic demonstrators overwhelmed the guard around the sultan, separating him from the other viziers. When the pasha tried to intervene, he was thrown to the ground. The latter detail is entirely plausible, as no love was lost between the nationalist activists and Pasha Bargache, who had thrown many of them into jail and had several others beaten.

the residency insisted that the sultan be surrounded with colonial troops the next day on his walk down the Tala'a l-kbira, the main artery through the medina, to say prayers at the Qarawiyin mosque, the sultan reportedly refused because he worried that the presence of troops would lead to a violent confrontation with the crowd. He returned instead to Rabat. The residency publicly declared that the sultan disapproved of the troublemakers and issued a statement castigating the nationalist element in Fes.

In response to French attempts to portray them as rabble-rousers who had threatened the well-being of the sultan, nationalist leaders quickly issued a statement reaffirming their loyalty that the nine leaders of the movement signed and sent as a telegram to Resident General Ponsot and the sultan. The front page of the next week's *L'Action du Peuple* was dedicated to revealing the true facts about the royal visit on May 10 and carried a copy of the nationalists' telegram, which said, "We confirm our confidence in the medina, assuring you that it intends for the Sovereign to remain the friend of France."[50] On May 14, the king met with the Kutla leadership to assure them he had left the city to prevent a violent confrontation in the medina, not in anger.

The residency, however, cracked down on the nationalist movement by suspending publication of *L'Action du Peuple* in Fes and prohibiting the entry of the journal *Maghreb* from Paris, effectively shutting down the nationalist press. Forbidden Arabic- and foreign-language periodicals continued to be smuggled into the country, however, and sold under the table.[51] The nationalists also sneaked a printing press into Qarawiyin University to print brochures and pamphlets, though many were still reproduced by hand.[52] In the medinas of Fes and Rabat, the nationalists posted handbills on the city walls at night, exploiting this major print space by also writing pro-Moroccan and anti-French graffiti in chalk or charcoal. These forms of written propaganda on the walls of the medina, like mass demonstrations that filled the medina streets, visually reinforced the anti-colonial national collective identity the nationalists sought to mobilize.

---

50. The telegram was signed by all of the major leaders of the movement: Mohamed el-Ouez-zani, Mekki Naciri, Allal al-Fassi, Omar Ben Abdeljalil, Ahmed Mekouar, Ahmed Bouayad, Driss Berrada, Abdel Aziz Ben Driss, and Hachemi Filali. *L'Action du peuple*, May 13, 1934.

51. It is important to note that written propaganda was disseminated to a larger audience than just the literate population, which was small in Morocco. Newspapers, tracts, and other materials were read aloud, though discreetly, in cafés, which by the 1920s had become significant public spaces for men in Morocco's cities. Later, radio broadcasts (which became more prominent in the mid-1930s) could be listened to within this important communal space in the large and small cities where cafés were ubiquitous. On café culture in North Africa, see Carlier (1990).

52. Interview with director of Qarawiyin University Library, October 20, 2006.

National identity was also physically represented in distinctive forms of locally produced dress—the *tarbouche* (feš) or turban as headgear and the black and white *djellaba*—in protests and in ceremonial contexts.[53] The nationalists projected forms of social discipline "in the name of the nation" in calls to boycott foreign products, including textiles and tobacco, and to close down shops or strike on certain days. Similarly, public indignation about violations of public morality, primarily alcohol and smoking, was also channeled into an anti-colonial nationalist framework. In 1933, an activist in Fes, Abdesalam ben Messaoud was arrested and sent to jail in Mogador for organizing a boycott against the French state-owned monopoly.[54] Eighty-seven others who protested his arrest were subsequently jailed.[55] In Salé, a group filed a complaint about the ubiquity of black-market alcohol and the related problem of public drunkenness but received no response from the civil controller. A group of 300 Moroccans frustrated about the lack of action then attacked seventeen small *hanuts* (corner stores) that sold alcohol, breaking all of the bottles of wine in stock. In an article defending the demonstrations, Omar Ben Abdeljalil argued that clandestine sales of alcohol had gotten out of control in recent years, citing stores that sold it near private homes and in front of mosques, and said that bands of drunks had even attacked pregnant women. He explained that the true story in Salé was that a group had spoken with the vendors, some of whom voluntarily drained bottles of wine in the street, after which the group paraded through the streets to the cheers of the neighborhood.[56]

Another area in which the nationalists sought to project social discipline was in repressing certain Sufi practices. Emilio Spadola (2008; 2014, 28–46) has shown how the nationalists were keenly aware of the competition posed by certain Sufi orders, namely the Isawa and Hamadsha,[57] that engaged in ecstatic

---

53. Rachik (2003, 92–83) relates that the Hajji family, textile merchants in Salé, set up a network of workshops to produce Moroccan *jalabas* in Fes, Ouezzane, and Chaouen and sell them at reduced prices. In the 1940s, first young women and then their mothers began to don the *jalaba*, instead of the more constrictive *haik*, to symbolize their nationalist political convictions and expand their own public roles in Moroccan society (Mernissi 1994, 119).

54. Georges Hertz, "Les troubles de Fès," *L'Action du people*, August 18, 1933.

55. The nationalists argued that Messoud had simply distributed a tract citing an injunction against smoking by the Fassi ulama because of health risks and that his actions were not political. "Les derniers événements de Fès," *Maghreb*, September 1933, 3.

56. Omar Ben Abdeljalil, "Contre l'alcoolisme au Maroc," *L'Action du Peuple*, May 4, 1934. Ben Abdeljalil's piece responded to a Rabat newspaper article about the incident that claimed the 300 Moroccans attacked 17 liquor stores owned by Spanish, Senegalese, Algerian, and Moroccan proprietors.

57. See Crapanzano (1981) for a comprehensive ethnography of the Hamadsha order.

displays of religious devotion including self-mutilation, sword swallowing, snake handling, and trance dancing in the realm of public spectacle in urban areas of Morocco. The still-resonant *salafi* reformist roots of the movement, a strain of which had been virulently anti-Sufi, and the nationalists' own aspirations to monopolize urban performative space were evident in the outspoken support the nationalist press gave to the protectorate administration when the residency issued a decree banning annual Isawa and Hamadsha *moussems* (saint's day celebrations) in Meknes.

During this formative period in the 1930s, urban nationalists developed a uniquely Moroccan repertoire of contention. By ritualizing anti-colonial protest, they created a performance space for the nation, using nonprint symbolic resources to communicate their countervulgate of Moroccan national identity focused around Arabic, Islam, and the Alawid monarchy. This ideology, occluded Berber (and Jewish, as discussed in the next chapter) identity. Nationalists also introduced new modes of contention that mobilized the urban population to march, sign petitions, contribute to collections for the families of protestors that had been imprisoned, close stores in support of an event, boycott certain products, or secretly distribute literature or put up posters on medina walls. One outcome of this crystallization of a nationalist repertoire of contention was that the colonial state developed patterns of response that included mass arrests and imprisonment in remote regions in the Atlas Mountains and in the Sahara. This created an interactive cycle in the mid-1930s: nationalists used the residency's repressive response to further publicize and legitimate their cause and win sympathy from the wider Moroccan public.

Istiqlal (Independence), Not a Protectorate (1937–1947)

In the late summer and fall of 1937, a more violent cycle of contention between the nationalists and the French authorities signaled the end of the reformist phase of the anti-colonial nationalist movement in Morocco. By 1938, the French administration had decapitated the movement by exiling the entire top tier of the leadership and shutting down the movement's press outlets. Morocco's cities were pacified and, as tensions rose in Europe and the sultan pledged to support France in the upcoming conflict, nationalists declared an unofficial truce with the residency. During the war, however, the domestic and international landscape began to shift in dramatic ways that created new openings. Beginning in 1944, the nationalists resumed public contention, openly calling for a transformation of the political field colonial intervention had created. They wanted the French to abrogate the Treaty of Fes and grant independence to Morocco. Although nationalists still believed in the necessity of reform and even accepted that France could have a limited role in this process, they were firmly convinced modernization had to be pursued *after* Moroccan independence had been restored.

The 1937 Cycle of Protest: Exile of the Nationalist Leadership and End of Reformism

In May 1936, the rise to power of the leftist Popular Front in the French legislative elections, the first ruling socialist coalition in French history, signaled what seemed a golden opportunity for the Moroccan nationalists. Like other nationalist movements in the French Empire, the Moroccans had close relationships with sympathetic politicians on the French Left and believed that Léon Blum's government would finally reform France's illiberal colonial policies. At this point, Morocco's nationalist leadership, like their peers elsewhere in the French Empire (Lawrence 2013), still believed they could attain their goals within the context of the rules of the game that ostensibly structured the colonial political field. They again drew up a list reiterating material and symbolic, identity-related demands from the 1934 "Plan de Réformes." They referred to this list as the National Pact and presented their requests to the protectorate authorities in Rabat and to Popular Front representatives in Paris. However, events in the summer of 1936 inside and outside the protectorate raised tensions in both the northern and southern zones and stalled any movement forward on reforms.

In June, workers in multiple sectors in the French zone, including Europeans and Moroccans, coordinated strikes with the massive wave of labor unrest in France. In July, in the northern zone, the Spanish army under General Franco mutinied, starting a three-year civil war against the Spanish Popular Front. During the conflict, the Tetouan nationalist leadership played both Spanish sides, forcing Franco to promise democratic reforms to counter the influence of Republicans. Events in the Middle East such as the Arab Revolt in Palestine, the signing of the Anglo-Egyptian treaty, and negotiations between the Syrian National Bloc and the French over independence also heightened tensions and expectations in Morocco.[58] Internally, the Moroccan nationalist leadership was rent by divisions

---

58. One of the few meaningful proposals by the Popular Front about colonial policy, the Blum-Violette proposal to grant citizenship to Algerian Muslims, was never submitted to a vote by the National Assembly and ended up being abandoned.

related to a personality conflict between the two major leaders, Allal al-Fassi and Mohamed el-Ouezzani. After al-Fassi was elected president of the National Action Bloc, Ouezzani split off to create his own organization.

That fall, the months-long failure of Léon Blum's coalition to deliver reforms led the nationalists to begin a series of meetings in late October and early November in Rabat-Salé and Fes. On the eve of Throne Day 1936, security forces intervened to prevent the next meeting and arrested al-Fassi, Lyazidi, and el-Ouezzani. The arrests sparked riots in Fes, Salé, Casablanca, Oujda, and Taza, and many demonstrators were wounded and hundreds were arrested. After they had been detained for a month, the newly appointed resident general, Charles Noguès,[59] released the nationalist leadership and many demonstrators, an action the nationalists hailed as a victory (al-Fassi 1954, 161). The next spring, however, Noguès sent conflicting signals about the residency's openness to reform. He authorized the creation of several new Arabic and French periodicals, including several nationalist publications, after two and a half years during which no newspapers or journals had been allowed (Aouchar 1990, 33–35). He also declared the Kutlat al-Wataniya illegal on March 18, 1937, because it violated regulations regarding the use of membership cards and collection of dues.

That fall, the nationalists regained the initiative by exploiting a local water dispute in Meknes[60] to mobilize large-scale demonstrations in several Moroccan cities. The controversy centered on a viziriel order passed the previous spring that repartitioned rights to the Boufekrane wadi, a key source of water for French *colons* and Moroccan peasants who farmed on the fertile plain south of Meknes. Downstream, the river flowed through *habus* (*awqaf*, or Islamic foundations) domains.[61] Throughout the spring, nationalist papers decried the diversion plan and spurred a petition drive against it.[62] In August, tensions in the medina were exacerbated when the authorities refused to admit Moroccans to the municipal pool in the *ville nouvelle*. On September 1, a group of over 400 marched to the *hôtel de ville to* submit complaints to the municipal superintendent, then returned to the Zitouna mosque, chanting "Give us back our water!" The next morning police arrested five leaders,

59. In September, Noguès replaced Marcel Peyrouton, who French Leftists and Moroccan nationalists accused of being a Fascist sympathizer.

60. Guerin's (2015) nuanced analysis reveals important and previously neglected local dimensions of this episode. The stakes for the residents of Meknes had very little to do with a broader nationalist agenda; they were fighting for their own sovereignty over water and other natural resources.

61. SHD-AT, Carton 3H 250, Note sur les eaux de l'oued Bou-Fekrane, September 11, 1937.

62. *L'Action du Peuple*, June 17, 1937.

who were condemned to three months in prison. Six thousand gathered in response at the Grand Mosque and a contingent of 700 marched toward the pasha's residence. Legionnaire troops blocked their path and fired on the crowd, killing thirteen and injuring forty. Fifty-two police and one European civilian were injured in the confrontation.

The nationalists quickly capitalized on the Meknes incidents, mobilizing demonstrations and organizing the recitation of the Latif in major mosques in Casablanca, Fes, Rabat, Oujda, Marrakesh, and Meknes on September 6. Worried about the situation's volatility, French officials shut down the recently reestablished nationalist newspapers and arrested more demonstrators.[63] Protests achieved a final crescendo in several cities in the last week of September. There were riots in Marrakesh during the visit of Paul Ramadier, the French secretary of state for public works, and in Khemisset in response to plans by the Catholic Church to organize a pilgrimage to the church of Sainte-Thérése. After obtaining a confession from a detained protestor that Allal al-Fassi had ordered the riots, the police secretly arrested al-Fassi, Ahmed Mekouar, Omar Ben Abdeljalil, and Mohammed Lyazidi in Fes on September 25. The next day Hashemi al-Filali and Hassan Bouayad organized demonstrations and a strike in the medina in Fes. Huge crowds in Fes gathered in the Rcif and Qarawiyin mosques for prayers and a group of 1,500 marched out of the Rcif mosque wearing white robes (ostensibly as martyrs), chanting the Latif prayer and threatening store owners that remained open.[64] Despite a torrential downpour, demonstrators also attacked a police station at the Bab Ftouh, the principle gateway into the medina from the south. The next day troops occupied strategic points in the medina and a bolstered guard was placed at each of the medina gates for fear of an attack from surrounding the Berber tribes.[65] On September 28, the Rcif and Qarawiyin mosques were occupied by colonial troops, and as the weather cleared, airplanes were sent on patrols over the medina in subsequent days, threatening bombardment if there was further unrest.[66]

---

63. SHD-AT, Carton 3H 250, Commissariat Divisionnaire Casablanca, Note de renseignements, September 9, 1937.

64. In an interrogation following his arrest, al-Filali revealed that the nationalists had printed tracts publicizing the demonstrations on machines hidden in the homes of Hassan Bouayad (a protégé of the British), Omar Ben Abdeljalil, and Abdelwahad al-Fassi (Allal al-Fassi's father).

65. The troops the French used to occupy the medina were predominantly Berber, including the 3rd Goum of Tafrant, the 43rd Goum of Haddad, and the 18th Goum of Boulemane.

66. After an internal military investigation about the medina uprising in Fes, the military distributed new maps, put bronze plaques labeling streets in the medina, and created command centers at strategic points in the medina connected by telephone wires. Plans to quickly reoccupy the medina were also developed in 1938 and were later put to use during uprisings in the 1940s. SHD-AT, Carton 3H 250, Folder "Plan d'Occupation de la Medina de Fès," March 1938.

During the fall, protectorate authorities were extremely worried that urban protest would spread to the countryside. Although urban nationalists sent agents out to mobilize rural groups, most were intercepted by the authorities. In the *"blad,"* there were just a few scattered anti-colonial responses, including a contingent of the Ould El Hadj tribe who came to Fes to take the nationalists' oath and pay membership dues and a handful of sympathetic demonstrations in Azrou, Gigou, and Mrirt in the Middle Atlas.[67] Most of the French indigenous affairs officers reported stability, however, leading the Meknes regional commander to report: "The firm policy carried out by the protectorate has had a positive effect and has been favorably commented on by the tribes in the region."[68]

The escalated conflict between colonial authorities and the urban nationalist leadership that fall signaled a new phase in their interactions. The security forces completely shut down the nationalist press (it would not be allowed for another ten years), carried out mass arrests, and exiled virtually all of the key leaders of the nationalist movement to remote areas in the mountains or deserts of Morocco or out of the country.[69] Noguès, commenting on the events, stated:

> We no longer have a choice. The rigorous measures against the leaders of the movement, if they continue to mobilize the people against the *makhzan* and against France, are necessary, regardless of the reactions they provoke. They are the only means of assuring the future of French Morocco and of creating a new climate that permits us to follow our civilizing action.[70]

For the Moroccan nationalists, the cycle of protest and harsh crackdown by the protectorate authorities in 1937 proved the futility of the reformist platform that had been their goal since the 1930 Berber Crisis. From the late 1930s forward, their framing efforts and modes of contention stopped pressing the French to be "good" colonizers. Instead, the nationalists began to demand Moroccan independence, rejecting the legitimizing protectorate

---

67. SHD-AT, Carton 3H 250, Report of Chief Boiseaux, Commander of Gendarmerie of Fes, September 9, 1937.

68. SHD-AT, Carton 3H 250, Third Trimester Report on Meknes Region, Chef de la Région, Caillault, October 29, 1937.

69. Allal al Fassi was initially exiled to Gabon and later to French Congo; Mohamed Lyazidi, Omar Ben Abdeljalil, Ahmed Mekouar were sent to remote locations in the Sahara; and Mohamed el-Ouezzani was sent to Itzer in the High Atlas.

70. SHD-AT, Carton 3H 250, report by General Noguès to Yvon Delbos, Minister of Foreign Affairs, on Moroccan Nationalism, October 9, 1937, 31.

logics of the colonial political field and emphasizing a discourse of popular sovereignty.

World War II and Shifting Opportunity Structures

In the late 1930s, with the top-tier of its leadership interned, the Moroccan nationalist movement could muster only a low-level propaganda campaign. It continued to produce anti-French tracts, posters, and graffiti, but it staged very few open demonstrations. The nationalists, particularly the Tetouan leadership, who had more freedom under Francoist authorities, abetted German and Italian anti-French propaganda efforts in North Africa and helped produce Arabic-language broadcasts of Radio Berlin and Radio Bari (which were relayed from broadcast towers in Seville and Tetouan). They also smuggled tracts south to the French zone.[71] However, when Germany invaded Poland in September of 1939 and the war began, the nationalists and colonial powers in the southern zone entered into an unofficial truce. The sultan, Mohamed V, publicly affirmed Morocco's unequivocal support for its French "protector" in the conflict, and by 1940, close to 50,000 Moroccans were serving in the French army (Pennell 2000, 254–55).

Moroccan perceptions about their colonial overlord's strength began to shift irreversibly with France's dramatic fall to the German army in 1940 and the transition to Vichy rule. In November 1942, the Anglo-American Operation Torch invasion of North Africa overwhelmed Vichy attempts to repel the attack, though French administrations were reinstated in Morocco, Algeria, and Tunisia. Moroccans' awareness of France's weakened position relative to the rising power of the United States was strongly increased by their exposure to the large numbers of American troops based in Morocco during the war. The anti-colonial pledges about the postwar order that were made in the Anglo-American Atlantic Charter of 1941 significantly raised expectations. At the Casablanca Conference in 1943, President Roosevelt overrode objections by the residency and met individually with Mohamed V, allegedly to affirm American support for Moroccan nationalist aspirations in an off-the-record conversation.[72] In November 1943, these aspirations received further encouragement when the British and Americans

---

71. French Indigenous Affairs officers in the Souss confiscated German propaganda in the form of Tashelhit Berber phonograph disks produced by the Cairo-based Baidaphone record company. SHD-AT, Carton 3H 250, report by the Commander of Agadir Territory, "Propagande anti-française par disques de phonoghraphie," March 31, 1939.

72. See chapter 8 for a longer discussion of the Anfa Conference.

pressured de Gaulle's Free French government to tacitly recognize Lebanese independence.

Sensing an opening for renewed political engagement after the Allied invasion, Ahmed Belafrej and a few other nationalist leaders from both the Qawmiyin (Ouezzani's faction) and the Wataniyin (al-Fassi's faction) factions began to meet in secret in 1942 to plan how to resume active resistance against the protectorate. With the support and encouragement of Mohamed V, they formed the Hizb al-istiqlal, the Independence Party, in the fall of 1943. On January 11, 1944, they submitted a "Manifest de l'independence" to the sultan, Resident General Puaux, and American and British officials.[73] Signed by fifty-eight notables and high-ranking members of the *makhzan*, the declaration affirmed Morocco's commitment to the Atlantic Charter, called for the immediate recognition of Morocco's independence, and demanded Morocco's participation in the postwar peace conference. Arabic copies of the manifest that had been transcribed by students at the Guessous Free School in Rabat were distributed across the country. On January 16, the nationalists met with representatives from the residency and the palace to negotiate a reform package. However, to tamp down nationalist aspirations for immediate independence and reassure French officials, the sultan broadcast a statement on Radio Maroc reaffirming that "the evolution of Morocco will develop in a framework of French friendship and respect of the treaties."[74]

Still worried that the situation would escalate out of control, the residency arrested two high-profile nationalist leaders, Ahmed Belafrej and Mohamed Lyazidi, in Rabat on the night of January 28 for allegedly giving information to the Germans. In Fes, they took other leaders—Ahmed Mekouar, Hashemi al-Filali, and Abdelaziz Ben Driss—into custody. News of the arrests spread quickly. The next morning, medina stores in Rabat were closed in protest, and at noon, a group of 500 marched from the sanctuary of Mawlay Hassan to the royal palace, chanting "Belafrej or death!" In the *meshwar*, the large public square at the palace entrance, the grand vizier explained the military reasons for Belafrej's arrest. The crowd shouted "If Balafrej is a German, we

---

73. Churchill was actually in Marrakesh at the time; one of his favorite vacation spots was La Mamounia hotel.

74. For a detailed account (from the perspective of protectorate authorities) of the circumstances surrounding the public announcement of the independence manifesto, its dissemination, and the subsequent violent clashes that occurred in Rabat, Salé, and Fes in late January and early February 1944, see SHD-AT, Carton 3H 251, report by Resident General Gabriel Puaux, "Agitation nationaliste," 19 February 1944. This report was circulated to all of the *chefs de région* in the French zone.

are all Germans!" then pressed forward, beat up Si Mammeri, another royal counselor who had been sent out to speak with them, and threatened to enter the throne room itself. Notified of the disturbance, the residency released Mohamed Lyazidi in order to calm the crowd. When he arrived, the king gave him a tongue lashing for the crowd's savage beating of Mammeri, then Lyazidi went out to courtyard to persuade the crowd to return to the medina. There large crowds gathered in mosques to recite the Latif prayer.[75]

Several other instances of violence in Rabat and Salé were related to the demonstrations. In Rabat, during their return to the medina through the *ville nouvelle*, protestors killed a French man named Roulois. At the elite College Mawlay Youssef, students injured the director, Arsène Roux (who had been reassigned in 1936 from the Azrou Berber College), when he tried to prevent them from joining the protestors at the *meshwar*. In Salé, crowds attacked the municipal offices, killing an officer and stabbing the civil controller. Close to 5,000 protestors were involved in the Rabat protest and 3,000 protested in Salé, according to estimates by the Contrôle civile.[76] Protectorate authorities quickly responded to the disturbances, deploying tanks around the medina and making mass arrests.

In Fes, alerted security forces arrested other nationalist leaders, including Mohamed El Fassi, Mhammed Zeghari, and Mohammed Laghzaoui, on January 31. Senegalese colonial troops were sent in to occupy the medina, and thirty demonstrators were killed in a confrontation in the Derb Roum district. Reaction in other cities were mixed. The Latif was recited and stores were closed in protest in Oujda, but no demonstrations were reported in Meknes, Marrakesh, or Casablanca.[77] In the countryside, indigenous affairs officers reported that the "Berber bloc was not opened." One of the few flashpoints was the Azrou College, the pinnacle of the Berber educational system. On February 5, students at the college in communication with nationalist activists in Fes and Meknes went on strike in solidarity with the Istiqlal demonstrations and other strikes at schools in other cities.[78] In the

75. Ibid., 10.

76. MAE, CADN-Mar., Direction de l'Intérieur, Carton 347, Contrôleur civil, Chef de la région, "Rapport relative aux incidents du 29 janvier 1944 à Rabat et à Salé," February 5, 1944.

77. SHD-AT, Carton 3H 249, Commandement Supérieur des Troupes du Maroc, "Rapport Mensuel sur la politique en milieu indigène," February 1944.

78. According to Abderrahim Bouabid, a nationalist activist and signer of the independence manifesto, Mehdi Ben Barka helped create the first nationalist cells at Azrou College in 1940–1941 and later among the functionaries working in the indigenous affairs offices and tribal councils. Two tribal council officials, Abdelhamid Zemmouri and Si Amar ou Nacer, signed the manifesto in the name of "Berber youth" (Delanoë 1988, 188).

declaration they delivered to the director, the students pointedly referred to the school as the Azrou College, not using its official name, Collège Berbère d'Azrou (Benhlal 2005, 373), a protest against the ethnic divisions the French sought to maintain. The official report on the Azrou disturbances reveals French officials' intense concern about the loyalty of the "Berber bloc," which they believed was directly connected to the stance of the sultan:

> If the sultan were to align with the nationalists, he would take with him the great part of the indigenous chiefs that, for a long time, have remained indecisive and waiting for the sultan to declare himself, so they can declare themselves. We risk, then, a general uprising: twenty years of combat for the pacification taught us what that eventuality represents. The essential, urgent task is to dissociate the sultan and the nationalists, to have the prince take a public and clear position against the demand for independence, for the respect of the treaty of the protectorate. This would permit us to ensure the tranquility of the *blad* [and] limit the agitation in the cities. Two battalions of Senegalese were needed to bring the medina of Fes under control. It would take an army for us to bring the Berber mountain under control.[79]

The tense situation in Morocco finally calmed down in March, but protectorate officials remained extremely concerned about their tenuous position. In a letter to the regional heads after events in Rabat, Resident General Puaux assessed the crisis of legitimacy the French faced in Morocco and the limited viability of sustaining French control solely with force:

> However, the recourse to force cannot be a permanent procedure of a government in a protectorate country. France is imposed on Morocco by force and by prestige. We cannot maintain our place in this country by force without prestige when now we are making our protégés into a defeated adversary. It is important, then, to dedicate ourselves to the work of restoring French prestige. All of the levels of the administration must be involved.[80]

In his efforts to restore French prestige, Puaux announced plans to increase support for indigenous education, to appoint a panel to review the penal code and reform the judicial system, to admit more Moroccans into the

---

79. SHD-AT, Carton 3H 251, Section des Affaires Politique, "L'Agitation Nationaliste de Janvier-Février 1944."

80. SHD-AT, Carton 3H 251, report by Resident General Gabriel Puaux, "Agitation nationaliste," February 19, 1944.

protectorate administration, and to put a Moroccan in charge of a Muslim assistance division in the Directorate of Public Health. The Istiqlal leadership rejected the package, insisting that independence had to precede reform. The sultan reassured French authorities that his friendship with France was still strong and that the events in January were simply a surface movement directed by young activists. At the same time, he maintained clandestine contacts with these activists and had encouraged them to draft the independence manifesto.[81] Mohamed ben Youssef reaffirmed that the liberation of France was the first priority (thousands of Moroccan colonial troops were at that very moment dying for that cause in Italy and would later be deployed in Provence, the Vosges, and Alsace), but he also strongly hinted that France needed to move swiftly toward Moroccan independence after the war.

Throughout 1944, French authorities fretted about collusion between the nationalists and the sultan, particularly as the anniversary of the independence manifest came closer at the beginning of the new year.[82] Moroccans, aware that the war in Europe was drawing to close, became increasingly optimistic that independence would be granted in the postwar settlement. Later in the spring of 1945, however, the respective hopes and fears of both sides began to dissipate after Roosevelt died in March and the Moroccan delegation was excluded from the peace conference in San Francisco that founded the United Nations in April. In May, France's violent repression of protests in Syria and Algeria, including the bombings of Damascus and Setif, further dimmed prospects that the goal of *istiqlal*, or independence, was imminently achievable in Morocco. By 1946, outside pressure on the French to decolonize had dissipated; American policy objectives had shifted definitively toward maintaining Franco-American ties in the Cold War at the expense of anti-colonial pledges to the North African leaders.

Mobilizing toward Independence after the War

In the transformed postwar domestic and international context, new constraints and opportunities influenced the framing and mobilizational strategies of the Moroccan nationalist movement during the last decade of

---

81. Abdelkrim Ghallab, a young nationalist activist in the 1940s and the future editor of the Istiqlal paper *Al-'Alam*, reports that the sultan would have the nationalist leaders meet him secretly in the large car garage on the palace grounds to avoid detection by the French officials (personal communication, October 27, 2005, Rabat).

82. SHD-AT, Carton 3H 249, Commandement Supérieur des Troupes du Maroc, "Rapport Mensuel sur la politique en milieu indigène," December 1944.

the protectorate. Before the war, the nationalists had lobbied the French Left for reforms. After the war, new factors influenced the postwar international landscape, including the onset of the Cold War, the beginnings of decolonization in South Asia and the Middle East, the founding of the Arab League and the United Nations in 1945, and France's postwar attempts to reconsolidate its empire in North Africa and Southeast Asia. In response, Morocco's nationalist leaders shifted their attention to cultivating pan-Arab networks that had developed in the 1930s and tying the Arab Maghrib (Tunisia, Algeria, and Morocco) more closely to the newly independent states in the Arab East. The three nationalist movements founded the Arab Maghrib Office in Cairo to coordinate their activities in 1947. The former Rif leader, Abd el-Krim, took symbolic leadership of the office after jumping ship while being transferred from Réunion to France. Many prominent North African nationalist leaders, including Allal al-Fassi and Tunisia's Habib Bourguiba, also used Cairo as a base for greater freedom of action. Outside Cairo, the Istiqlal leadership also focused attention on the newly created United Nations in New York as an important postwar forum for communicating Morocco's claims to the United States and the nonaligned bloc.[83]

In conjunction with the reforms that were intended to relegitimize France's protector role in Morocco, the French administration relaxed restrictions on the nationalist movement in their zone. In 1947, they allowed nationalist leaders to return, including Allal al-Fassi and Mohamed el-Ouezzani, whose ten-year periods of exile had only increased their legitimacy as representatives of the nation. Their return generated widespread enthusiasm, including huge banquets and parades in Fes and Rabat, and helped the nationalists expand the membership of their organizations.

After the war, the French also eased restrictions on the nationalist press, which had been banned since 1937, authorizing a new wave of Arabic newspapers in 1946. The Spanish zone, which previously had been more liberal toward nationalist publications, shut down the Arabic press from 1947 to 1952, though the northern nationalists continued to publish out of the

---

83. On the founding of the Arab Maghreb Bureaux, Abd el-Krim's role, and the activities of North African nationalists in Cairo in the postwar period, see Benaboud and Cagne (1982). On Istiqlal's global anti-colonial diplomatic campaign, including postwar lobbying in the United States and at the United Nations, see Stenner (2012).

Tangier international zone (Aouchar 1990, 80–81).[84] In the French zone, each of the major nationalist factions published their own paper. The Istiqlal Party's primary paper, *Al-'Alam*, began publishing in November 1946, and a French version, *L'Opinion du peuple*, began publication in March 1947. In addition to Moroccan news, *Al-'Alam* devoted considerable attention to events in the United States, Europe, India, and the Middle East, particularly the deteriorating situation in Palestine. Much of the print space, including most of the front page, was dedicated to covering the activities of the royal family. Most pictures were of the king, Crown Prince Hassan, and Princess Lalla Aicha, the latter of whom were both sent out to high-profile public events.[85] The ability of the nationalist press to criticize the French administration was restrained, however, by expansive censorship powers that been granted in a decree of August 29, 1939. Due to advances in printing technology, the Directorate of the Interior could just black out individual articles instead of confiscating the whole issue of a paper (Aouchar 1990, 86).[86] Censorship intensified after the appointment of the more hardline Alphonse Juin as resident general in the summer of 1947. Juin shut down Istiqlal's French-language daily, *L'Opinion du peuple*, in June of 1948.

The most significant development in the late 1940s was the growing confluence of the nationalist movement's objectives with those of the king. As was discussed earlier in this chapter, the nationalists began to take advantage of colonial political field's legitimization logics and the king's own latent symbolic capital in the early 1930s. This linkage between nationalist demands for Moroccan independence and the king's sovereignty became more explicit as Mohamed ben Youssef himself became more proactive during and after the war. By 1947, the alignment of the king with the Istiqlal Party, so feared in the quote above by Resident General Puaux, came out fully into the open in the historic visit of the royal family to Tangier in April. The trip (discussed in detail in chapter 8) took place the day after a bloody confrontation between

---

84. The appendix in Aouchar (1990) contains a valuable compendium of the Moroccan nationalist press. The Moroccan Communist Party, which was sympathetic to nationalist cause, was allowed to begin publishing *L'Espoir*, which had made a brief appearance in 1938, in February 1945. In August 1946, Moroccans took over the editorship of the paper. Other papers that started up after the war included *L'Action Syndicale*, a French paper for the Union générale des Syndicats confédérés du Maroc (UGSCM) in Casablanca that published from January 1945 to June 1950, and another Casablanca paper, *Al-Ra'i al-'Am*, which published from April 1947 to December 1952.

85. The main Moroccan Arabic newspaper, *al-'Alam*, had a large section called "News of the Royal Family."

86. In the late 1940s, as more vociferous anti-colonial opposition began to be expressed, the front page often was mostly covered in black ink.

Senegalese colonial troops and Moroccan demonstrators in Casablanca in which scores of demonstrators were killed. As an indirect response, the king gave a speech in Tangier that enthusiastically affirmed Morocco's adherence to the Atlantic Charter, particularly its pledges about decolonization, and its strong connections to the Arab Maghrib and the Arab League. The speech pointedly omitted the obligatory affirmation of the historic partnership with the French protector that was usually reiterated in official communiqués. The sultan's subtext was clear to the French government, and the resident general, Eirick Labonne, who was viewed as too lax, was quickly sacked. He was replaced a month later with the hardline General Alphonse Juin. From this point forward, the nationalist struggle entered a new phase in which the sultan became a full player in the attempt to contest French control of the colonial state, maneuvering alongside, though not in total identification with, Istiqlal and other nationalist parties in opposition to the increasingly hostile residency.

The Moroccan nationalist movement emerged out of protests directed at a controversial 1930 decree that consolidated a separate Berber legal system. In response to the decree, urban Arabophone cultural elites attacked the ethnographic and historiographic logics underpinning the colonial political field while affirming their own nationalist countervulgate of an imagined Moroccan national community that had been unified for more than 1,000 years by Islam, Arabic, and dynastic rule. During the initial print campaign against French Berber policy in the early 1930s, Moroccan nationalists framed the legal, administrative, and educational components of the French Berber policy as a lethal threat against the unity of the Moroccan *umma*, subtly transposing an imagined ethnoreligious national political unit onto preexisting notions of Muslim collective identity. In mobilizing identity-based protests during the Berber Crisis, the nationalists also consolidated a Moroccan repertoire of anti-colonial contention that included ritualized protests such as performances of the Latif prayer and invented national anniversaries such as the commemoration of the Berber *dahir* and Throne Day. In performing the nation in these protest events, they co-opted symbols the French themselves had reinvented to legitimize their role in the protectorate, such as the Moroccan flag, the national anthem, and the sultan himself. These nonprint classification struggles that were directed back at the colonial state and laterally in society served a critical role in making the Moroccan nation a meaningful category of political identity for a mass audience. At this point, though, the nationalists' reformist political demands—that the French rule Morocco as a protectorate rather than a colony, carrying out their developmental civilizing mission with respect for Moroccan sovereignty and for the benefit of Moroccans—were framed in the rules of the game that they believed organized the colonial political field.

The French authorities' rejection of the "Plan de réformes" and the exile of the nationalist leadership in 1937 signaled the end of this phase and closed off possibilities for rapprochement. From this critical juncture forward, Moroccan nationalists began to look beyond the horizon of the French Empire and to see independence as the only alternative. France's dramatic collapse and the rise of the United States during World War II transformed the context, and Moroccan nationalist factions shifted from demanding reform of the protectorate framework to demanding its end. After the war, urban nationalists increasingly began to operate in larger postwar international fields, tying Moroccan national identity even more closely to the unity of the Arab Maghrib and to rising pan-Arab sentiment in the Mashriq, or Arab East, and framing anticolonial demands in contexts such as the United Nations in terms related to competing Cold War logics and the emerging nonaligned bloc. Most important, in the last decade of the protectorate the king himself took a leading role in pressing for Morocco's political independence. Before turning to that endgame contest over the legitimization logics of the colonial political field, two other identity-related struggles related to Morocco's transition from *umma* to *watan* must be examined. Both relate to the position of internal subaltern "others": the Jews and women of Morocco.

❧ CHAPTER 6

Negotiating Morocco's Jewish Question

This chapter considers how the ambiguous position of Morocco's Jews made their status a focal point of state- and society-based identification processes, both inclusive and exclusive, in the colonial political field.[1] It examines the external classifications and identifications that four groups used with Morocco's Jews: the colonial state, which steadfastly maintained that Jews were "subjects" of the Moroccan sultan; French Jewish leaders and associations (particularly the Alliance Israélite Universelle), which sought to assimilate them; Zionist groups that raised funds from them and tried to get them to emigrate; and the Moroccan urban nationalist movement. For the nationalists, Morocco's Jews highlighted fundamental questions about the boundaries of the Arabo-Islamic national community they imagined: Was this religious minority to be classified as *dhimmi* (a protected religious minority under Islamic law), subjects of the sultan/king, or equal citizens of the Moroccan nation? This chapter also explores internal identification struggles within Moroccan Jewish communities caught between three competing identity claims: France's attraction through linguistic and

---

1. During the protectorate period, the French used the term *les israélites marocains* to refer to Morocco's Jews. Since the time of the French Revolution, "Israélite" had been used officially rather than "Juif," which had negative connotations, in hope that the usage would promote assimilation. "Juif" continued to be used by Jews and non-Jews in France, though to a lesser extent than "Israelite" (though anti-Semites never used the term "Israélite").

cultural assimilation coupled with the elusive promise of legal naturalization; 2) Zionism's claims to their loyalties on the basis of Jewish political nationalism and, for many, religious messianism; and 3) Moroccan nationalists' appeals for them to be faithful to their Moroccan *watan*, or homeland.

The first sections consider the impact of colonial intervention, both indirect (in the nineteenth century) and direct (after 1912), on the cultural identity and economic and legal status of Morocco's Jews. I then move to an examination of competing nationalist claims on the identity of Morocco's Jews in early Zionist activity and in debates in the early Moroccan nationalist press. From the mid-1930s, the identity and loyalty of Morocco's Jews became an increasingly politicized issue exacerbated by the expansion of Zionist activity in Morocco and escalating tensions over the status of Jewish communities in Europe and in Palestine. Over the next two decades, Morocco's Jews faced successive crises, from Vichy anti-Semitic legislation to the seismic shift in Muslim-Jewish relations after Israel's independence in 1948, which permanently altered their position in Morocco. By the time of Moroccan independence in 1956, conditions had been transformed to such a degree that within a decade, virtually the entire Moroccan Jewish population had emigrated to Israel, France, or the Americas. One of the paradoxes of Morocco's Jewish Question, however, is that the presence and (perhaps more important) the memory of this religious minority continues to play an integral role in state-based and society-based Moroccan processes of national political and cultural identity (Kosansky 2003, 2011; Schroeter 2008; Kosansky and Boum 2012; Boum 2013).

Jews in Precolonial Morocco: *Dhimmis* and Protégés

Although Morocco's Jewish population has dwindled to a few thousand since independence, it numbered over 220,000 in the early 1950s, constituting the largest in a Muslim country.[2] It is also one of the most ancient Jewish communities in the world; legends claim that its origins go back to the time of King Solomon (ca. tenth century BCE), and scholars speculate that Israelites came with Phoenician traders in the seventh century BCE.[3] Whenever their origin,

---

2. This figure combines the census figures for the French and Spanish protectorate zones and Tangier. The 1951 census in the French zone reported 199,156 Jews, the 1950 census in the Spanish zones reported 7,872 Jews, and the 1952 census in Tangier reported 15,000 Jews (Service central des statistiques 1964, 8).

3. The Phoenicians established a string of colonies on the Moroccan coast including Lixis (near modern-day Larache), Tingis (Tangier), Sala (Rabat), Zili (Asilah), and Mogador (Essaouira) (Brody 2002).

by the time of the Roman Empire, Jewish communities were firmly established in the far west of North Africa.[4] These so-called *toshavim*, or original
"residents," who arrived in antiquity, are distinguished from the *megurashim*, the
"expelled" Sephardic exiles who were forced to leave the Iberian Peninsula in
the fifteenth century.[5] Although this binary, as Schroeter (2008) demonstrates,
oversimplifies the multiple and complex identifications of Jews in Morocco,
in rough terms, the *toshavim* settled in both urban and rural areas, with sizable populations in Sefrou, Marrakesh, Mogador, and in the Souss region, the
Atlas ranges, and the palm oases on the edge of the Sahara, while the self-
identifying Sephardic *megurashim* tended to be located in the northern urban
areas Tetouan, Tangier, Fes, and Rabat-Salé, where they settled alongside their
Muslim counterparts from Al-Andalus. In urban areas, Jewish communities
spoke Arabic and Hakétiya (a Judeo-Spanish Ladino-like dialect) and wrote
in Arabic, Hebrew, and Judeo-Arabic, which was written with the Hebrew
alphabet (Gottreich 2007, 6). Jews in the countryside were integrated in both
Tamazight (Middle Atlas and Central High Atlas) and Tashelhit (High Atlas
and Souss) Berber-speaking communities. Although a few communities were
monolingual Berber/Judeo-Berber speakers (in the High Atlas and Anti-Atlas),
most also spoke Arabic (Schroeter 2008, 148–49; Chetrit and Schroeter 2003).

When Muslim dynastic states rose in Morocco in the ninth century, Jews
and Christians were classified as *dhimmi*, protected religious minorities.[6]
Although *dhimmi* did not enjoy as many rights as Muslim subjects, they did
have some rights. In exchange for paying the *jizya* tax, they came under the
protection of the Muslim ruler, were not obligated to serve in the military,
and were granted a degree of administrative autonomy. By the Middle Ages,
Morocco's indigenous Christian population had more or less disappeared
and Jews constituted the sole *dhimmi* social group. With few exceptions,
most notably the Almohad persecutions,[7] this relatively tolerant system of

---

4. Haim Zafrani's *Milles ans de vie juive au Maroc* (1983) is the classic *longue durée* study of Mor-
rocco's Jews. The second French edition (1998) added another thousand years. See Schroeter (2008)
for a critical reevaluation of constructions of Moroccan Jewish identity.

5. Although this term specifically refers to those who left the Iberian Peninsula (Sepherad), it
encompasses all of the Jews who were expelled from European Christian countries in the Middle
Ages who sought refuge in North Africa. Schroeter (2008, 150) points out the cultural capital of
both Jews and Muslims in Morocco associated with Andalusia and how Jews constructed genealogies
that traced Sephardic descent even in areas with few Spanish immigrants.

6. The seventh-century Pact of Umar stipulated that "people of the book," including Jews,
Christians, and Zoroastrians, would be protected.

7. On the Almohad persecution of religious minorities, see Hirschberg (1974, 127–29) and
Dozy (1968, 223–24).

protections made Morocco and other areas of North Africa an attractive refuge for Jews fleeing persecution under Christian rule on the northern shores of the Mediterranean. The Andalusian influx in the fourteenth through the sixteenth centuries initiated a cultural florescence, and Fes became a major center for Jewish and Muslim learning. Under subsequent Marinid, Saadian, and Alawid dynasties, Jews were incorporated into the *makhzan* as key advisors. The special relationship between the sultan and the Jewish *dhimmi* became a prominent feature of urban geography in Morocco's royal cities, particularly after the creation of the first Jewish quarter, or *mellah*, in Fes in 1483.[8] Because of their linguistic skills, business contacts, and the extended networks across the Sephardic diaspora, prominent Moroccan Jews were sometimes sent on diplomatic missions to Europe in the seventeenth and eighteenth centuries.[9]

In the nineteenth century, the *dhimmi* status of Morocco's Jews began to be more ambiguous (Schroeter 2003). In the early 1800s, several major Jewish merchant families were designated as the *tujjar al-sultan*, or royal business agents, in charge of *makhzan* monopolies over key Moroccan agricultural and manufacturing sectors (Abitbol 1998; Schroeter 1988). At the same time, Jewish traders served as key intermediaries for European economic interests in Morocco, which grew steadily throughout the century. Under the agreements that multiplied between European states and the sultan in the wake of the 1856 Anglo-Moroccan commercial treaty, these protégés (which also included numerous Muslims) were granted legal and fiscal immunity (including exemption from the *jizya* taxes non-Muslims were required to pay), transforming the *dhimmi* status quo that had been in place for centuries under Islamic law (Kenbib 1994, 1996). In the 1860s, there were several Western interventions to "protect" Morocco's Jews, beginning with a visit to Marrakesh in 1863 by Sir Moses Montefiore, the prominent Jewish philanthropist, to petition the sultan to release nine Jews imprisoned in Safi. The only result of Montefiore's attempt to pressure Sultan Sidi Muhammad (r. 1859–73) to eliminate the second-tier legal status of Jews was a *dahir* that reiterated their traditional protections in the Islamic system of justice (Schroeter and Chetrit 2006, 175–76).

---

8. In Fes, the Jewish quarter was built on a salt marsh, or *mellah*. The *mellah* appeared in Marrakesh in the sixteenth century, in Meknes in the seventeenth century, and in smaller towns in the nineteenth century. Gottreich's (2007) study is an excellent critical reevaluation of conceptualizations of the Islamic city and provides invaluable background on the role of Jewish space in Morocco's urban centers.

9. García-Arenal (2003) offers a fascinating look at one such Moroccan Jewish envoy, Samuel Pallache, who was sent by Sultan Zidan Abu Maali to negotiate an alliance with the Dutch against Spain in 1608. Schroeter (2002) investigates several similar examples of Jewish diplomatic service to the Moroccan sultans.

Making Moroccan Jews into Frenchmen?
Assimilation, the Alliance Israélite Universelle,
and Protectorate Jewish Policy

In 1862, a cultural form of European interventionism vis-à-vis Morocco's Jewish communities began with the creation of the first Alliance Israélite Universelle (AIU) school in Tetouan. The Paris-based AIU grew out of French Jewry's renewed interest in the plight of their North African co-religionists, sparked by France's intervention in Algeria.[10] The AIU encouraged the "moral progress" and "emancipation" of Jews living in the Muslim world, principally through the propagation of French language and culture. In Morocco, the AIU opened schools in the 1870s and 1880s in most cities, first on the coasts and in the north and later in the interior cities, starting with Fes.[11] The schools taught a modern curriculum in the French language and actively encouraged assimilation into French culture (Laskier 1983).

Starting in 1913, the AIU mission was subsidized directly out of the colonial state's budget. Two years later, the Directorate of Public Instruction (Départment de l'instruction publique, DIP) began to centralize direct administration of European, Muslim, and Jewish education. New state-run Franco-Israélite schools were established and the AIU schools were put either directly under the jurisdiction of the DIP or under the supervision of its pedagogical review board. In 1924, however, this effort at direct administration of Jewish education was abandoned. The DIP reverted to an indirect policy, closed most Franco-Israélite schools, and increased the subsidy to the Alliance Israélite Universelle to allow it to open more schools.

However, the residency's official support for the AIU's efforts to culturally "[make] Moroccan Jews into Frenchmen," to tweak Eugen Weber's (1976) phrase, did not translate into political dividends for this community. Citing the Algerian precedent—where the 1870 Crémieux Decree unilaterally naturalized Algerian Jews as French citizens and complicated relations among newly enfranchised Jews, the settler population (some of which was overtly anti-Semitic), and Muslims who were denied citizenship—as a cautionary tale,[12] the residency, from Lyautey forward, vigorously sought to preserve what it perceived as existing social divisions, including the *indigène* status of Morocco's

---

10. The AIU was founded in 1860 with the help of Adolphe Crémieux, an antimonarchist lawyer who later authored the 1870 decree bearing his name that unilaterally naturalized Jews living in Algeria.

11. On the precolonial activities of the AIU in Tangier, see Marglin (2011).

12. On the Algerian Jews' negotiation of French intervention in the nineteenth century, see Schreier (2010). See Katz (2012) for Algerian Jewish collective memory in the twentieth century about the Crémieux Decree and Muslim-Jewish violence in Constantine in 1934.

Jews. Here it is important to clarify the firm distinction the colonial state maintained between "Moroccan Jews" and "Jews in Morocco." "Moroccan Jews" were classified as subjects of the sultan who remained under the jurisdiction of the Sharifian court system. Although their legal status as *dhimmi* was eliminated with the institution of the protectorate (Jews no longer paid *jizya* and theoretically were no longer subject to the humiliating prohibitions defined in the Pact of Umar), the Jewish religious courts lost much of their former autonomy and their competence was restricted mostly to personal status. Moroccan Jews therefore had to appear more frequently in the *makhzan* courts, which were informed by Islamic precepts. In terms of education, Moroccan Jews were separately channeled into the Franco-Israèlite or AIU schools.[13] "Jews in Morocco," who constituted a substantial population in Morocco's coastal commercial centers, included Jews with French citizenship or any other non-Moroccan nationality. These "Jews living in Morocco" were under the jurisdiction of the French legal system and had access to French system schools.

Over time, this distinction became more and more problematic for Moroccan Jews, who, as subjects of the sultan, did not have a legal or symbolic status equal to that of non–Moroccan Jews or their Muslim counterparts. As a case in point, during World War I, Moroccan Jews were severely restricted from fighting (and dying) for either Morocco or France. Although the French conscripted numerous units of North African Muslim troops to fight during World War I, the residency was hesitant to conscript Moroccan Jews. Hundreds of Moroccan Jewish youth who volunteered in 1915 were sent to work in munitions factories at Lyon instead of to the front with their Muslim co-nationals (Assaraf 2005, 294). French colonial administrators rejected numerous proposals to create North African Jewish brigades because of their concerns about Muslim sensitivities in Morocco and elsewhere in the region. In response to an inquiry in 1918 from Minister of Foreign Affairs Stephen Pinchon about counterbalancing the appeal of the British Balfour Declaration by creating a Moroccan Jewish brigade, Lyautey warned of the "deplorable effect" such a measure would have on the Moroccan Muslim community (294–95).

The status of Moroccan Jews, even at this early stage, was already beginning to be tied to sensitivities about the situation in Palestine. Francois

---

13. With the final abrogation of the system of capitulations (Britain was the last to give up its privileges in 1937), even the many Jews who had benefited from a protégé status lost these protections.

Georges-Picot, who negotiated the postwar Franco-British division of the Ottoman Empire with Mark Sykes, warned about another proposal to create a Jewish battalion from Morocco and Tunisia: "Of course, while being careful to not diminish our influence in the Jewish milieu, we must take the greater care to not give the Muslims of North Africa or of the East the sense that the achievement of the Zionist program in Palestine can hurt the material or moral position of Muslims in Palestine."[14] Other French officials dismissed the appeal of Zionism for Morocco's Jews and denigrated their military and political agency. The protectorate's director of intelligence services, Colonel Berriau, commented:

> Unused, after centuries of servitude, to any military action, they [Moroccan Jews] have no conception of how to defend their person, interests, or most importantly, their ideas, by arms. Palestine seems like a marvelous utopia to them. The offer made to them is flattering, satisfying their aspirations. It is not necessary to count on them to conquer. It is doubtful whether the Zionist exodus will take anyone other than the aged and destitute from Morocco to Jerusalem.[15]

Throughout the 1920s, Morocco's Jewish Question continued to be debated in the French metropole and among protectorate administrators. In 1927, Lyautey's replacement as resident general, Theodor Steeg, convened a commission to explore the issue of the naturalization, and in a speech that year to the central committee of the Ligue des droits de l'homme in Paris, he signaled his support for the idea: "The complete evolution of this population is very rapid, and we are looking for a means that would permit us, little by little, to let the Israelites—those who are more or less the most educated among them—to become French citizens" (quoted in Assaraf 2005, 337). The key distinction between "emancipation," or the granting of equal citizenship rights to Jews, in France versus "emancipation" in the French colonies, however, was that the latter resulted in a further distinction and separation from local society instead of integration (Schroeter and Chetrit 2006). Moroccans (both Jewish and Muslim) were well aware of this potential, and in the fall of 1928, there were widespread rumors that the naturalization of

---

14. MAE, CADN-Mar., Cabinet Diplomatique, Carton 668, Dossier 1, Ministry of Foreign Affairs to General Lyautey, Commissioner Resident General of the Republic of France, "Recrutement de volontaires israélites," 1918.

15. MAE, CADN-Mar., Cabinet Diplomatique, Carton 668, Dossier 1, Col. Berriau, head of Intelligence Service, to Adjunct Secretary General of the Protectorate, Cabinet Diplomatique, November 24, 1918.

Morocco's Jews was imminent.[16] Despite support at the highest levels in France, however, this measure was never considered viable because of the residency's worries that it would threaten the international legitimacy of the Treaty of Fes. Morocco's Jews, no matter how culturally assimilated, would officially remain *indigènes* who were technically under the authority of the sultan in the French zone.

Ironically, while formally preserving the status of Moroccan Jews as subjects of the sultan, French administrators increasingly took increasingly direct control over them, rationalizing juridical and administrative institutions to handle Jewish affairs.[17] On May 22, 1918, a *dahir* brought the Jewish courts, whose jurisdiction had been limited to personal status claims, under the direct control of the Ministry of Justice.[18] The ministry imposed a hierarchical reorganization and began to fund the rabbinical courts from the protectorate budget (under the precolonial *makhzan*, the courts had been sustained by private donations). Rabbinical courts with three judges, bailiffs, and clerks were created for larger cities. Rabbis were delegated to travel between smaller cities to judge cases, and a high appeals court was established in Rabat. The *dahir* also reorganized the previously autonomous "committees of the communities," which oversaw functions that included care for the needy, religious foundations, and synagogue services.[19] Under the new system, the grand vizier chose the members of the committees from a list created by notables in the community, then the committee elected a president, a secretary, and a treasurer. The nondemocratic nature of the appointment process and the fact that no formal structure was put in place to coordinate between the individual committees became a central demand for reform within the Moroccan Jewish community in the 1940s.

In the Spanish zone, which had a much smaller Jewish population, the much slower pace of colonial state building and the long distraction of the Rif War in the 1920s delayed similar reforms by a decade. The Spanish did not reorganize the rabbinic courts and established a high appeals court in

---

16. MAE, CADN-Mar., Direction de l'Intérieur, Questions Juives, Dossier 1. Gen. Freydenberg, commander of the Meknes region, to Plenipotentiary Delegate Minister to the Residency General, Rabat, "A/S de la naturalization éventuelle des israélite du Maroc," July 27, 1928.

17. See Schroeter and Chetrit (2006) for a detailed analysis of the French colonial state's reorganization of Jewish institutions in Morocco, including the 1918 reforms.

18. Any other civil or criminal litigation was under the Sharifian court system, which was administered by *qa'ids* or pashas. This was a significant curtailment of the autonomy the precolonial Jewish courts had enjoyed (Schroeter and Chetrit 2006).

19. This function was limited, though, due to the fact that many synagogues in Morocco were traditionally owned and maintained by private families rather than by the community at large.

Tetouan until March 1928.[20] It was in the international zone of Tangier, where they constituted 20 percent of the population, that Moroccan Jews enjoyed the greatest degree of political participation and the greatest protection of rights. There was no official *mellah* in Tangier (although the Beni Ider quarter had a concentration of more prosperous Jews), and to outside observers, Jews were indistinguishable from other inhabitants by their dress.[21] During the protectorate period, the Tangier Jewish community had a democratic, autonomous judicial and administrative system and Jews could hold positions in the city government (Assaraf 2005, 302–7). From the early 1900s, Tangier Jewish investors were also very active in the planning and financing of multiple development projects in the city (Gilson-Miller 2011).

The tenuous position of Morocco's religious minority—caught between trajectories of cultural assimilation and colonial logics of social division—was particularly evident in the legal realm, where Jews faced a complex overlay of jurisdictions that delineated vastly different rights depending upon national identity. An individual classified as a Moroccan Jew was subject to rabbinic courts for personal status law. Jews of other nationalities were subject to French law. Numerous cases illustrate how Moroccan Jews attempted to navigate the convoluted legal field the colonial state constructed. In a 1937 probate case in Salé after the death of Raphael Encaoua (who had been appointed as the first chief rabbi by protectorate officials in 1918), Raphael's son, Mikhail, claimed that the inheritance should be divided according to Mosaic (rabbinic) law rather than French law, despite the fact that his grandfather, Mardoché Encaoua, a rabbi and businessman in Salé, had been naturalized as a French citizen in 1870. This was one of the rare legal cases in which a Moroccan Jew fought in court to protect his status as a subject of the sultan. Mikhail Encaoua claimed that according to Moroccan law, naturalization applied only to his grandfather, not to any other successive generations, including his father and himself, and that they could not lose their Moroccan nationality. As a Moroccan Jew, Encaoua wanted the probate case to be tried in the rabbinic courts maintained during the protectorate.[22]

---

20. A total of around 15,000 Jews lived in the cities of Tetouan, Larache, Asilah, El Ksar el Kebir, Chefchaouen, and Nador. During the war, Jews in the Rif manufactured explosives for Abd el-Karim, a process that involved refitting undetonated bombs Spanish planes had dropped for artillery. Abd el-Krim occasionally visited the AIU school when his family took refuge in Tetouan during intraclan feuding in the Rif in 1892–1998 (Assaraf 2005, 333; Hart 1976, 371).

21. On the complexities of Tangier's social structure and the position of Jews within it in the late nineteenth and early twentieth centuries, see Gilson-Miller (2013).

22. MAE, CADN-Mar., Cabinet Diplomatique, Carton 670, Dossier General, note from Director of Sharifian Affairs, State Section, May 28, 1937.

Cases more frequently involved Moroccan Jews who fought to confirm French or another nationality, which often conferred advantageous inheritance rights. In 1938, the probate settlement in a case involving Abraham Benoliel was complicated by the multiple nationalities involved: Abraham had been a Moroccan subject; his brother Joseph and his children had been naturalized as Portuguese in 1889; and the third brother, Salomon (who passed away in 1921), had legally been a French protégé. Meir Lugassy, a Jewish businessman whose wife was Abraham's niece, wrote to protest the consul's decision regarding Benoliel's nationality because his wife's potential inheritance depended on whether rabbinic, Portuguese, or French laws applied, as all had different provisions for male and female heirs.[23]

In another case, the Diplomatic Office in Rabat tried to figure out if the daughter of a deceased Jewish man, Mr. Taieb, would inherit her father's property, which depended on whether she was legally "French" or "Jewish." Taieb had been born in Tunis in 1880 and married an Italian woman, Maria Bartoloni, in Bizerte in 1906 in a non-Jewish wedding. Their daughter was born in 1903, three years before the marriage. In 1920, the Taiebs were naturalized as French citizens in Tunisia before moving to Rabat. In the case, the French Diplomatic Office initially contended that the daughter should inherit because of how civil status was regulated by the Tunisian regency. This depended, though, on whether her father had recognized her as his legitimate daughter at the time of his marriage in 1906 or when he was naturalized in 1920. If so, she would inherit as a legitimate daughter according to French law, but if not, she would legally be under rabbinic law and would not inherit. When the authorities presented the case to the high rabbinic court for consultation, however, the court replied that *halacha* (Jewish law) did not recognize the legitimacy of a marriage consecrated by another authority, in this case the Tunisian civil court. Furthermore, even if it had been a religious marriage and the father had recognized her as his child, she would not inherit because her mother was a non-Jew at the time she was conceived. In the end, the poor woman did not inherit because as a non-Jew and as an illegitimate daughter according to French law, she had no rights to her father's estate in either jurisdiction.[24]

---

23. MAE, CADN-Mar., Cabinet Diplomatique, Carton 670, Dossier General, Avonde-Froment, Consul General of France in Tangier, to Resident General Noguès, July 4, 1938.

24. MAE, CADN-Mar., Cabinet Diplomatique, Carton 670, Dossier General, note from head of Financial Property Conservation Service, "Dévolution de la succesion de M. Achille Taieb, israélite d'origine tunisienne, naturalisé français," November 13, 1940.

The vagaries of the status of Morocco's Jews in the classificatory logics of the colonial political field were most sharply brought into relief in questions about legal jurisdiction and military service. Moroccan Jews were differentiated in the protectorate legal system from non-Jewish Europeans, from Jews with European or other nationalities, and from Arab and Berber Muslim Moroccans. Despite frequent calls inside and outside Morocco to politically and legally assimilate Moroccan Jews, the colonial state's fractious juridical structure preserved their liminal position throughout the protectorate period. They were also held in limbo on another fundamental criterion of national identity, the opportunity to die for the nation. In both world wars, they were severely restricted from fighting for France, which might have strengthened a case for their naturalization, or for Morocco, because colonial authorities feared that the creation of Moroccan Jewish brigade would provoke tensions with the sultan, creating a blasphemous innovation that contravened Islamic law and the "traditional" order of Moroccan society.[25]

Zionism and Morocco's Jews during the Protectorate

Processes of external and internal identification regarding Morocco's Jews in the colonial political field were further complicated in the 1920s and 1930s by increasing Zionist activity. Before the colonial intervention, Morocco's Jewish community had a long history of communication and interaction with colonies of Moroccan Jewish immigrants (*olim*) that had moved to the Holy Land. Strong links in the Sephardic diaspora also tied Jewish communities in Morocco to those in Palestine and elsewhere in the Ottoman Empire. One manifestation of these ties was the Shaliach Kollel (emissary of the religious institution), a triennial delegation sent to North Africa to raise benevolence funds for Jewish communities in Jerusalem, Hebron, Safed, and Tiberias. After the advent of political Zionism in the 1890s, Zionist organizations became involved in these attempts to strengthen ties between North Africa and Palestine.

---

25. Moroccan Jews were completely aware that denying them the right of military service implicitly denied that they belonged equally to the French or to the Moroccan nation. During World War II, Moroccan Jews protested being treated as "second-tier Moroccan subjects" when they were not allowed to join the French army, a reference to the fact that Muslim (mostly Berber) Moroccan colonial troops were fighting in the Allied campaigns in Italy and in France itself. MAE, CADN-Mar., Direction de l'Intérieur, Carton 111, Col. Chevroton, Head of the Meknes Region, to the Director of Political Affairs, November 15, 1944.

An early Zionist initiative was to raise funds through existing benevolence missions, including special relief collections for Moroccan Jewish communities in Palestine facing hardships caused by World War I.[26] Zionists also focused on education, creating schools that taught modern Hebrew. The first, Maghen David, was founded in Casablanca in 1920; others followed in the 1930s, including Fes in 1931, Oujda in 1935, and Sefrou in 1936. In many respects, these Zionist schools paralleled the activities of the Muslim free schools; they created a foundation for Jewish cultural nationalism through the teaching of the Hebrew language, nationalist hymns, and the use of Zionist symbols.[27]

Although Zionist outreach in North Africa was very limited in scope during this early period, it created tensions with the non-Zionist AIUs that were already firmly in place in the region. Theodor Herzl, the founder of political Zionism, directly criticized the AIU for encouraging European cultural assimilation instead of the creation of a national homeland. Nahum Sokolow, another early prominent Zionist thinker, mocked the AIUs' pedagogical *mission civilisatrice*, asking why they did not teach Turkish or Arabic and agricultural skills instead of French and Parisian bourgeois values (Laskier 1983, 195–96). In Morocco, Nahum Slousch criticized the AIU for being overly influenced by Western liberalism. Slousch, a French Orientalist and Hebraist, had been recruited in 1905 by the *Mission scientifique* to study North African Jewry, and in 1915, Lyautey commissioned him to study Jewish affairs in the French zone. His encouragement of Zionism as a form of Jewish nationalism and his attempts to organize Zionist groups in Fes and Tangier were among the factors that led to his dismissal in 1917 from the commission that was studying policy reforms regarding Morocco's Jewish community.[28]

As a general rule, the official stance of the residency toward any hint of Zionist activity was reserved, if not overtly antagonistic, due to fears that it would provoke the Moroccan Muslim population. Zionist delegations had to apply for travel permits at the French consulate in Jerusalem, and the number of recognized Palestinian benevolence societies that were active in Morocco

---

26. In the summer of 1918, the Jewish Committee of Safi sponsored a campaign to raise funds for its counterpart in Jerusalem. Funds were also collected in other Moroccan cities. MAE, CADN-Mar., Cabinet Diplomatique, Carton 668, Dossier 1, letter no. 1667 from the Civil Controller, Chief of Municipal Services, in Safi to Resident General Lyautey, June 18, 1918.

27. MAE, CADN-Mar., Cabinet Diplomatique, Carton 670, Dossier General, "Etude sur le Sionisme au Maroc," April 3, 1945, 8–9.

28. For detailed accounts on Slousch, see Goldberg (2004). On Slousch's activities in Morocco, including his reform plan and the politics of the Jewish policy in the early protectorate period, see Schroeter and Chetrit (2006).

was limited to six.[29] Although the protectorate authorized the creation of Zionist schools, it officially banned the Fédération Sioniste de France, a French Zionist organization. In March 1919, Abraham Israel, the president of the Jewish Community Committee in Fes, was able to found the Shibat Zion organization in Tetouan in the Spanish zone, but similar requests to establish branches in Fes and Oujda in the French zone were denied.

The residency's policy, from Lyautey forward, was to allow individual support for Zionism but to prohibit any Moroccan-based corporate Zionist organizations. In a letter to the French minister of foreign affairs sent on September 17, 1919, Lyautey clarified the status of Moroccan Jews under the protection of the residency and emphasized the risks of Zionist political activity:

> Moroccan Jews have no need to look for outside help to ensure the defense of their interests, of which my Residency and the Makhzan have never lost sight. The reorganization of their institutions . . . the creation of rabbinic courts and of special sections in the municipal assemblies; the granting of large indemnities for damages suffered in 1912 during the pillage of the *mellah* of Fes; the regulation of open collections for the Jews of Palestine; have given them immediate and concrete satisfaction, both on a practical and moral level. All of these are testimonies to the goodwill that the Protectorate demonstrates toward them. I will add that the sultan, the Makhzen and the higher enlightened Muslim class, on which we rely and which gives us the most solid base for the Protectorate, sees Zionist activity in the worst possible light, a fact that has been reiterated over and over again. In this, there is a political and governmental factor unique to Morocco which cannot be neglected.[30]

In Lyautey's view, Zionism was bad for Morocco's Jews and bad for Morocco's Muslims: He argued that Morocco's Jews were completely content under France's protection and had no interest in creating a national homeland somewhere else and that Zionist propaganda would only negative impact Muslim-Jewish relations. Lyautey also emphasized the threat of Zionism to

---

29. MAE, CADN-Mar., Cabinet Diplomatique, Carton 668, Dossier 2, Chief Inspector for Jewish Institutions in Morocco, Yahya Zagury, to head of Diplomatic Office, "Quêtes effectués en Afrique du Nord au profit de communautés palestiniennes."

30. MAE, CADN-Mar., Cabinet Diplomatique, Carton 668, Dossier 2, Resident General Lyautey to Minister of Foreign Affaires, "Questions israélites. Les Juifs Marocains et le Sionisme," September 17, 1919.

the legitimizing logics of the colonial political field, referring to the negative way the Moroccan sultan and political elites would interpret official support for Zionist activity.

The resulting restrictive policy in the French zone drew the ire of international Zionist organizations in the mid-1920s, particularly after the protectorate banned the Zionist paper *Ha-Olam* (The World). In a letter replying to the World Zionist Organization's demand for freedom of association for Zionist organizations and the free circulation of *Ha-Olam* in Morocco, Lyautey stressed that individuals could contribute the *shekel* (the annual donation signifying support) and belong, again as individuals, to an external Zionist organization. He also allowed a delegate of Keren Hayesod to take up collections and pledged not to block families who wanted to emigrate.[31] He warned, however, that Zionist activity in Morocco could aggravate a "fanaticism," a reference to Muslim persecution, from which the Jews had for a "long time suffered." Lyautey also stressed that it was an extremely delicate matter to allow an external movement such as Zionism to target subjects of the sultan with an appeal to another nationality; the sultan formally refused "to tolerate any propaganda which would lead to a reduction of the number of his Jewish subjects."[32]

As the situation in Palestine and Europe grew more intense during the interwar period, French administrators tightened restrictions on Zionist activities in Morocco. After the 1929 Muslim-Jewish riots in Palestine, the residency authorized Josué Cohen, a journalist and delegate of Keren Kayemet L'Israel (Jewish National Fund), to hold meetings in Casablanca and Fes to raise funds for families of the victims of the massacres in Safed and Hebron but forbade any mention of the nationalist objectives of the Zionist movement.[33] Collections were also taken in the summer of 1930 in Meknes, Oujda, Marrakesh, Fes, and Mazagan. After the Arab Revolt broke out in Palestine in 1936, vehement protests by the Muslim Moroccan community led protectorate authorities to prohibit fund-raising by the Jewish National Fund. When a French senator, Justin Godart, protested the ban, the residency responded by pointing out the contradiction of allowing a pan-Jewish political movement freedom of action in a country in which they were worried about the spread of pan-Islamism and pan-Arabism:

---

31. Keren Hayasod, which means "the Foundation Fund," was established at the 1920 World Zionist Conference in London.

32. MAE, CADN-Mar., Cabinet Diplomatique, Carton 668, Dossier 2, Resident General Lyautey to the Zionist Organization of London, June 26, 1926.

33. MAE, CADN-Mar., Cabinet Diplomatique, Carton 668, Dossier 2, Note de Renseignement, "Propagande Sioniste," May 7, 1930.

It could only cause trouble to allow Zionist organizations to carry out, with the official support of the Protectorate government, their direct propaganda in the Jewish community of Morocco, which to the present has remained outside of the pan-Jewish political movement, at the same time that we are using every means to fight against an external action by Muslim agitators who use the call of pan-Arab and pan-Islamic doctrines.[34]

From the perspective of French colonial administrators, who in Morocco and elsewhere in the empire were facing increasingly vociferous nationalist protest movements in the mid-1930s, it was difficult to see how they could condone Jewish nationalist activity and not let the same thing occur on the Muslim side.

In the fall of 1936, as the Arab Revolt in Palestine and the rise of Nazi Germany exacerbated tensions in French North Africa, Resident General Noguès emphasized the delicate position of Jews in Morocco and French reluctance to countenance attempts to politically mobilize them in a report to the Ministry of Foreign Affairs:

It is necessary to not lose sight of the unique position of Moroccan Jews, submitted to strict obedience to the sultan, subject to the same regulations as Moroccan Muslims in terms of nationality and naturalization, forming, in the interior of Morocco, large communities in constant contact with Muslim communities. In the terms of the protectorate treaty, we have formally undertaken the responsibility of safeguarding and respecting the traditional prestige of the sultan. This pledge not only obliges us to maintain harmony between Jews and Muslims, which is often fragile due to the latent antagonism that traditionally opposes these two elements of the Moroccan population, and which recent events, whether in Germany or Palestine, have a tendency to reawaken. We must also avert all propaganda liable to arouse in the Jewish communities [that are] subject to the sultan any hint of independence, any separatist aspiration that could soon be exploited against us.[35]

Here Noguès explicitly referred to the formal legitimization logics of the colonial political field. He also emphasized the strategic position of

---

34. MAE, CADN-Mar., Cabinet Diplomatique, Carton 668, Dossier 2, Counselor to the Sharifian Government to the head of the Diplomatic Office in Rabat, "Objet: Propagande sioniste au Maroc."

35. MAE, CADN-Mar., Cabinet Diplomatique, Carton 668, Dossier 2, Resident General Noguès to Minister of Foreign Affaires, "A/S Front national juif en Palestine," November 6, 1936.

Morocco's Jews at the intersection of competing political claims about their identity. From the perspective of colonial administrators, Zionist activity not only risked further escalating Jewish-Muslim tensions, it also threatened the protectorate fiction that legitimated their intervention in Morocco.

Jews and the Moroccan Nationalist Movement

Morocco's Jews also presented a dilemma for Moroccan nationalists, who worked from the early 1930s to defend a unitary definition of Arabo-Islamic national identity against the divisionary logics of the colonial state. How did this religious minority fit in the nation? This question was made even more problematic for the nationalists because on one side, large numbers of Moroccan Jews had culturally assimilated and in view of the Algerian precedent, might imminently be naturalized as French citizens, and on the other, Zionist groups were actively recruiting in this population. As the nationalists challenged the legitimacy of the protectorate structure, the question of who actually served as "protector" of Morocco's Jews, the residency or the sultan, also became acute.

In the early 1930s, the nationalist press served as a forum in which these questions were actively debated. One flashpoint highlighting the ambiguities of religious identity and legal jurisdictions in the colonial political field concerned the right of Moroccan Jews to convert to Islam. A 1932 article in the nationalist journal *Maghreb* focused on the case of Isaac el-Harrar, a Jew in Mogador (Essaouira) who went to municipal authorities to make his conversion to Islam official after practicing the religion for ten years. According to the article, the French authorities in Mogador rejected his request, saying it was a personal matter, and el-Harrar had to go to Rabat to get his conversion registered. When he returned to Mogador, four policemen had to be stationed at his house to guard him from attacks from the Jewish community. In accordance with Jewish law, his cousins then petitioned to make el-Harrar divorce his wife (with whom he had five children) and return a dowry of 50,000 francs. The adjunct civil controller in Mogador rejected el-Harrar's appeal that as a Muslim, he was not under Jewish law and that the matter should be decided in the Islamic court. The article reports that the controller forced him to give up his property, forbade him to see his children, and expelled him from the city. Caught between the French administration, the Sharifian *makhzan*, and Jewish authorities in Mogador and Rabat, el-Harrar eventually had to appeal to the sultan to resolve his case.[36]

---

36. "Le scandale Abdellah ben Mohammed," *Maghreb*, December 1932, 17–19.

Moroccan nationalists also voiced concerns about the prospect of the French unilaterally naturalizing Morocco's Jews, as had been done in Algeria. In the Fes-based *L'Action du Peuple*, Mohamed el-Ouezzani equated initiatives to naturalize Morocco's Jews as French citizens to the policies expressed in the 1930 Berber *dahir*. He warned that Arabs themselves would end up a persecuted minority:

> There will be an exceptional jurisdiction for the Arab if France continues to follow the present course towards granting Jews the right of naturalization. He [the Arab] will become a minority, and, like every minority, will be repressed because he is kept in an inferior position vis-à-vis the Berber, the Jew, and the European.

Ouezzani urged France to instead give all Moroccans equal guarantees safeguarding individual liberty in the realm of penal law while still maintaining distinctions in civil law between Muslims (Arab and Berber) under shariʻa and Jews under "Hebraic law."[37]

In the early nationalist press, Moroccan Arab nationalists and Jewish leaders also engaged directly with questions related to the status of Jews in the nationalists' framework of Moroccan national identity. After protests in 1932 following the arrest of Isaac el-Harrar, the Moroccan Jew who converted to Islam, Mohamed Kholti, one of the nationalist contributors to *L'Action du people*, wrote an article to address concerns in the Moroccan Jewish community. He contrasted the European Christian anti-Semitism displayed in the "pogroms of the Romanians" and the "Hitlerian inquisition in Germany" with the historic solidarity, tolerance, and freedom Jews had enjoyed since they took refuge in Morocco. Kholti emphasized the importance of continuing this solidarity in the context of protesting the injustice of French colonialism. He also issued a note of warning against supporting campaigns to get Morocco's Jews naturalized as French citizens, arguing that such a move would violate the 1912 treaty and foment discord between the two races.[38]

Several articles by Jews and Muslims published in subsequent months positively affirmed Moroccan Muslim-Jewish unity. In a letter to the editor, a young Moroccan Jew agreed that Jews should not forget the hospitality "extended to our fathers when they were expelled from Spain and Portugal" and pointed out that an Arab delegation had stood guard on the ramparts by the gate of the *mellah* to protect Jews against rebel tribes that attacked Fes

---

37. Mohamed el-Ouezzani, "La Politique berbère," *L'Action du people*, August 18, 1933, 2.

38. Mohamed Kholti, "Les israélites et nous," *L'Action du people*, August 18, 1933, 4.

in 1911. An article titled "Judeo-Muslim Friendship" reported a joint statement from Jewish and Muslim notables in the Spanish zone that celebrated
the historic tolerance and friendship between the groups and rejected propaganda that encouraged Jews to assimilate. The article then called on Jews
to remember the centuries of tolerance and shelter the Moroccan Muslim
people had provided for them.[39] In a September 8, 1933, piece, a Jewish
leader in Fes, Isaac Bendayan, lamented the French authorities' decision in
1928 to prohibit the creation of a Muslim-Jewish association, El Tsihad el
Chabiba Islamia Israeilia el Magribia (Union of Moroccan Muslim-Jewish
Youth). He also lamented that in the protectorate's divided educational structure, Jews were taught virtually no Arabic language, history, or Moroccan
geography. He concluded the piece by declaring his opposition to a "Moroccan Crémieux Decree," but he also expressed concern about the spread of
anti-Semitism in Europe and in the protectorate and called on the "Young
Moroccans" (the nationalists publishing the paper) to denounce it.[40]

For Moroccan nationalists, efforts to reinforce Muslim-Jewish unity were
threatened by ambiguities about Moroccan Jews' loyalties, which were exacerbated by the continuing possibility of French naturalization and by increasing tensions about Zionist activity in Palestine. Another article by Mohamed
Kholti in January 1934 titled "The Role of Jewish Youth in Moroccan Evolution" affirmed Moroccan Muslim-Jewish solidarity but warned:

> Zionism must be discarded by the Jewish youth as a sentiment of
> oppression. We will never allow it in our relationship. A Moroccan
> who loves his country must aspire to work for it. . . . Zionism is a fac-
> tor of outside domination and disorder in Morocco.[41]

Later in March, Kholti warned about the dangers of French naturalization
initiatives that would give Moroccan Jews legal advantages over their Muslim countrymen. He then affirmed a liberal vision of equal rights for Jews
and Muslims in Morocco, critiquing colonial policies of differentiation as
"annulling" the Treaty of Fes:

> For I consider that he [the Jew] is Moroccan, and that he must be
> treated like other Moroccans without consideration of religious ideas
> that he professes, which remain for me an element of personal belief
> which does not affect the will of us who want to see our country

---

39. "L'amitié Judéo-Musulmane," *L'Action du peuple*, September 1, 1933, 2.

40. Isaac Bendayan, "Lettre ouvert à M. Kholti," *L'Action du peuple*, September 8, 1933.

41. Mohamed Kholti, "Le rôle de la Jeunesse Israélite dans l'évolution marocaine," *L'Action du
peuple*, January 26, 1934.

unified under the reciprocal tolerance of a penetrating liberalism. The
Jews born and living in Morocco are Moroccans. The international
and political contingencies created by the Metropole cannot be decided
otherwise without annulling the contract with the sultan.[42]

Here, Kholti directly appealed to the formal legitimizing logics of the protectorate, or symbolic "rules of the game" set up for this unit of the French
empire, to counter arguments in France itself for the naturalization of Morocco's Jews. Kholti concluded this section of the article by turning to the other
"threat" related to the political identity of Morocco's Jews: "For us, Zionism,
in its nationalist form, cannot be accommodated with the Moroccan nation."
This civic version of Moroccan national identity (which, in context, was
critiquing the possibility of unequal treatment of Jews and Muslims by the
colonial power) excluded any other national political loyalties.

Another column from April 1934 rejected Zionism as an option for
Morocco's Jews, reiterating that their historical position was exceptional
compared to that of Jews in Europe and elsewhere. This author clearly felt
that Moroccan Jewish support for Zionism was a betrayal:

> The Jews can be Zionists as much as they want outside of Morocco. . . .
> But in a country where they have lived for centuries and where they
> are called to benefit at the same time as Muslims from the advantages
> of social evolution, to show less zeal and more discretion towards what
> I may call the Zionist "proselytism" becomes an absolute necessity![43]

That issue of *L'Action du people* also related a news story about Jewish Scouts
who upon their return from a trip to Gibraltar marched through the streets
of Tangier carrying a Zionist flag and sang Zionist songs. In response, a
group of 400 Moroccan Muslims approached the *mandub* (the sultan's delegate in the Tangier International Zone) to protest, saying, "The Jews, here,
only have one flag: the flag of Morocco. How can they carry another without considering the consequences of these gestures?"[44]

Questions about the legal status and political identity of Morocco's religious minority exposed tensions between the ethnoreligious and civic dimensions of the national community Moroccan nationalists were imagining and
attempting to mobilize in 1930s. The "Plan de réformes" the nationalists presented to the resident general and to the French government in Paris in 1934

---

42. Mohamed El Kholti, "Sionisme et patriotisme marocain," *L'Action du peuple*, March 2, 1934.
43. "Le Sionisme au Maroc sur la défensive," *L'Action du Peuple*, April 13, 1934.
44. "Rapport de Tangier," *L'Action du Peuple*, April 13, 1934.

sketched out a synthesis the nationalists were trying to achieve in defining a Muslim yet liberal polity. The plan called for the unification of civil, commercial, and penal jurisdictions under a single legal code inspired by Muslim law and included provisions included for the continuance of separate rabbinic courts to rule on civil status questions for Morocco's Jews. The plan proposed granting equal civic rights to all Moroccans, both Muslims and Jews, and called for universal suffrage without distinction regarding religion in the election of Moroccan representative councils at the municipal and national levels.

Moroccan nationalists were tempted to sharpen the boundary of Arabo-Islamic identity by targeting Moroccan Jews as an internal religious other when they rallied popular support for their cause in mass demonstrations. On the eve of the 1933 commemorations of the Berber *dahir*, for example, nationalists distributed tracts and delivered speeches calling for demonstrations against the impiety of Jews in Morocco and their affront against tradition.[45] In the mid-1930s, Muslim-Jewish relations in Morocco continued to grow more tense because of internal and external developments such as the outbreak of Muslim-Jewish violence in Constantine in August 1934 in Algeria,[46] growing antagonism between the political Left and Right among the French *colon* population in 1935,[47] increasing anti-Semitism among some of the European settlers, the outbreak of the Arab Revolt in Palestine in 1936, and the historic victory of the Popular Front in France in June 1936.

When the nationalist press was allowed to publish again in 1936 (after being shut down by the French in 1934), another round of Muslim-Jewish dialog commenced about definitions of Moroccan national identity. Moroccan Arab nationalists urged Moroccan Jews who were excited about the rise of the French Left and worried about rising Nazi anti-Semitism to remain loyal to their own *patrie*. Reporting on a meeting of the Ligue Internationale Contre L'Antisémitisme (International League against Anti-Semitism), Ahmed Bouhlal, a Moroccan nationalist activist, stated:

---

45. SHD-AT, Carton 3H 247, Office de Liaison, Rabat, "Renseignement: A/S Agitation musulmane-israélite," May 15, 1933.

46. After a Jewish man was accused of urinating on the wall of the Sidi Lakhdar mosque, simmering Muslim-Jewish tensions broke out, culminating in an attack against the city's Jewish population (Attal 2002).

47. Most Moroccan Jews were aligned with the Socialist Party and enthusiastically supported the rise of Léon Blum's Popular Front. In 1935, tensions were high between the French Left and Right in Morocco partly because the resident general, Marcel Peyrouton, was a notorious anti-Semite. (Peyrouton later served as a Vichy minister.) While the Left called for his dismissal, he enjoyed the support of the Croix de Feu and other French rightist parties formed in Morocco during the protectorate.

We have called to them and we will not cease to call to them to remain in this great family that is the Moroccan nation, where, under the protection of Muslim monarchs, from the weakest to the strongest, they have lived in mutual understanding with their Muslim compatriots.

Bouhlal exhorted Moroccan Jews to preserve the "indissoluble union between Muslims and Jews, in a strictly Moroccan national framework, for the good of our common *patrie*, for the general interest of our collectivity."[48] Two months later, another nationalist chastised young Moroccan Jews for being enamored with socialism:

> Young Jewish comrades, whose cries of enthusiasm are "Vive Trotsky! Vive Léon Blum!," should dedicate some to our sovereign Sidi Mohamed and our young prince Mawlay Hassan. Young comrades, be conscious of your duties as Moroccan citizens, try to understand your Muslim compatriots, create sporting groups and clubs where the Moroccan youth can learn of the duties of man.[49]

This article, which was titled "The Jews and Us," illustrates the ambiguities of Moroccan Jewish identity in the interwar period. At the same time that the author urges Morocco's Jews to recognize a common sovereign who symbolized the unity of the Moroccan people and to create "Moroccan" rather than "Jewish" sports teams and clubs, he also distinguishes the Jews from "us." In a very similar way to how the Latif refrain "do not separate us from our brothers, the Berbers" recognized but elided an internal "ethnic" other, this phrase about the "Jews and us" demonstrates how the Arab nationalist framework of Moroccan identity simultaneously included and excluded the internal "religious" other.

In the next issue of the journal, A. Samoun, the secretary general of Morocco's Ligue Internationale Contre L'Antisémitisme, responded to Bouhlal with an article describing the perspective of Moroccan Jews and their insecurity in both the French and Moroccan nationalist frameworks of political identity: "We are neither Moroccan nor French. We have the situation of being Moroccans to whom you freely attribute burdens but not the least privileges. The day when you tell us exactly what we are, attributing to us our duties as well as our privileges as a citizen, will be the day we will take a position."[50] Although Jewish Moroccan nationality was legally defined

---

48. Ahmed Bouhlal, "En marge du meeting de la L.I.C.A.," *L'Action du Peuple*, May 6, 1937, 3.

49. El Mesquine (a pseudonym), "Les Juifs et Nous," *L'Action du Peuple*, June 17, 1937, 5.

50. A. Samoun, "Pour l'entente judéo-arabe au Maroc," *L'Action du Peuple*, July 1, 1937.

as Moroccan, Samoun noted that was it second-class. He also chided the "Young Moroccans" (Arab nationalists) in the French zone for not taking a strong enough stand against anti-Semitism, pointing out that Moroccan nationalists in Tetouan had sent an Arabic translation of Nazi propaganda written by Goebbels via the British post and that it was circulating in the Fes medina.

A nationalists' response to Samoun's letter, written under the pseudonym "El Mesquine," critiqued his argument on multiple points:

> We cannot, in effect, accept that there is a difference between Arabs, Berbers, and Jews from a national point of view. We want all to be Moroccans. And this title we freely attribute to you. You also said that a November 21 *dahir* fixed your nationality. But, it is not possible to declare: 'We are neither Moroccan nor French.' Moroccans you are. French? That is not even a question. France, by the way, is not here in order to make the Jews of Morocco into French citizens, but to help our country in its national reform and to help the sultan consolidate his authority over the whole empire. You must recognize that authority. And, when you blurt out that 'the sultan is nothing but a figure-head,' we start to understand you.[51]

The nationalists were sensitive to Moroccan Jews' wavering identification with the sultan and the Moroccan nation and reacted strongly against France's assimilationist pull. They appealed to the protectorate's legitimization logics in exasperation: the point was not to make Moroccan Jews French; it was to carry out state and nation-building on behalf of the sultan.

On the other side, the Moroccan Jewish community was extremely sensitive, as evidenced in Samoun's comments above, about the apparent collusion of Tetouan-based Moroccan nationalists in disseminating anti-Semitic tracts and publishing anti-Semitic columns in their journals. There were also complaints about the circulation of anti-Semitic propaganda in the French zone. In August 1936, after the election of the Popular Front with Léon Blum (who was Jewish) as prime minister, a tract that Mohamed Lyazidi allegedly gave to a former editor of *Es-Sa'ada* for distribution was reportedly circulated in the Rabat medina that warned "Muslim brothers" that France had fallen into the hands of Jews and that Jews were "assassinating Arabs after despoiling them

---

51. El Mesquine, "L'entente islamo-judaïque ne peut se faire que dans le cadre nationale?" *L'Action du Peuple,* July 15, 1937, 3.

of their lands" in Palestine under British protection.[52] Lyazidi's authorship of this type of document seems doubtful; it is much more likely it was produced by French right-wing parties upset about the elections. During the summer of 1936, Moroccan nationalists were doing their utmost to curry favor with Blum's administration, not spreading anti-Semitic propaganda against it.

The statements about the plight of Palestinian Arabs, however, did accurately reflect the nationalists' concerns, particularly after the outbreak of the Arab Revolt in 1936. Literature from the Middle East detailing the threat of Jewish immigration and settlement in Palestine circulated widely in the medinas, and Moroccan pilgrims who had performed the hajj to Mecca that year brought back tracts written by the Committee for the Protection of the Al-Aqsa Mosque and Holy Places of Islam in Jerusalem that warned of the Zionist threat.[53] In Meknes, Muslim-Jewish relations were strained further by water riots at the beginning of September 1937. Muslim demonstrators returning from the confrontation with the municipality turned on the Jewish quarter, the *mellah*, damaging forty-three businesses.

Increasing anti-Semitic activity by rightist French organizations in Morocco also increased feelings of insecurity among Morocco's Jews in different parts of the country. In Meknes, one of the fascist strongholds for the French *colon* population, anti-Jewish graffiti was repeatedly written on the city walls in the *ville nouvelle* and the medina. It included slogans such as "Here is a Jewish house, a house of profiteers"; "Jews belong to a different race than ours; they form a vast nation of exploiters and thieves"; and "The Jewish congregation has taken more than half of our riches. We must confiscate the fortune of the Jews, made through exploitation and thievery, to pay back the French workers."[54] The Moroccan Jewish community was also extremely concerned about the increasing anti-Semitic repression in Germany and the seeming inevitably of war in Europe. The International League Against Anti-Semitism, founded in Paris in 1927, was able to found committees in 1935 in Fes, Rabat, Casablanca, Meknes, Mogador, Marrakesh, Oujda, and Tangier, after years of hostility from

---

52. MAE, CADN-Mar., Direction de l'Intérieur, Questions juives, Dossier 24, Report from Civil Controller, Région de Rabat, to Director of Political Affairs, no. 605, "A/S Tracts anti-juifs," August 7, 1936.

53. The tract was taken from a Tijani sharif of the Gzennaia tribe, Si Mohamed Zemrani, who had picked it up during a visit to Fes. Pilgrims returning from Mecca had apparently brought it back. MAE, CADN-Mar., Direction de l'Intérieur, Questions juives, Dossier 24, Report from General Lauzanne, Région de Taza, to Director of Indigenous Affairs, May 25, 1938.

54. MAE, CADN-Mar., Direction de l'Intérieur, Questions juives, Dossier 24, Renseignements no. 559, May 18, 1938.

the residency. One of its first initiatives was to call for a boycott of German products following the issuance of the Nuremberg laws.[55] The organization was aligned with other leftist organizations such as the League for the Rights of Man and Citizen (Ligue des Droits de l'Homme et du Citoyen) and the Socialist Party and made several efforts to network with Muslim organizations, but these lost momentum as the conflict escalated in Palestine.

As it became clear that war in Europe was imminent, Moroccan Jews clearly put their hopes in the protectorate power, France, to forestall the Nazi threat. An anti-German tract distributed in the French zone in December of 1938 said:

> You must know that:
> Those that work with Germany are responsible for the massacre of
>   your brothers.
> Each one who gives a penny to Hitler forges a weapon against you.
> Every purchase from Germany prepares your death.
> The boycott against German products, that is your motto, as noble as
>   it is sacred.
> Buy French and you help the free nation that protects and defends you.[56]

That year a boycott of German and Japanese products was organized and a campaign against Nazi propaganda was coordinated in the Spanish zone. In 1940, however, when the war finally broke out for France and its empire, Jews in Morocco faced a quick transition to Vichy rule that further troubled questions about their identity, eroded trust in the colonial protector, and damaged hopes that cultural assimilation would yield political rights.

Vichy and the Statut des Juifs:
Jews, Not Frenchmen

After Germany invaded Poland in September 1939, the lead-up to France's entry into the war reactivated debates about whether Moroccan Jews would be allowed to serve in battle for France or Morocco. In October, a campaign to sign up Jewish volunteers for the army in the French zone was launched by S. D. Levy, a businessman, Raphael Benzaref, a journalist, and Helen Cazes-Benattar, a lawyer. Over 1,300 signed up in Casablanca and more offices were opened

---

55. MAE, CADN-Mar., Cabinet Diplomatique, Carton 29, Newspaper issue, "Prés de 400 délégués, venus de toute la France et de l'Afrique du Nord, consacrent le triomphe du VIIème Congrés National de la L.I.C.A.," *Le droit de vivre,* November 28, 1936.

56. MAE, CADN-Mar., Cabinet Diplomatique, Carton 670, Note de renseignements: Politique anti-allemande, December 30, 1938.

in major cities. In response to this large-scale enlistment campaign, the French Ministry of National Defense sent out a memo to the commanders in North Africa that specified that unnaturalized Jews, primarily those in Tunisia and Morocco, had the same status as "native Muslims" and could not be directly incorporated into French units in the military. An exception was eventually made so Tunisian Jews could be admitted to the infantry division being formed in Narbonne, but Moroccan Jews, who were formally classified as "subjects" of the sultan, were prohibited from joining French forces. They were also not allowed to join Moroccan regiments being formed with Muslim conscripts.[57]

The same month, Robert Montagne, the noted French colonial sociologist, submitted a feasibility study about using Moroccan Jews in the army that was generally favorable to the idea but expressed concerns about where they would be placed. As subjects of the sultan, they could not be incorporated into French metropolitan units. He felt that it would also be difficult to integrate Moroccan Jews with Moroccan Muslim units of *tirailleurs* (indigenous sharpshooter regiments) or *spahis* (indigenous light cavalry units) because of their different "mentality," which he argued would require different modes of instruction. Montagne argued that it would be impractical to create a Moroccan Jewish regiment because it would take too much time, and he advised against putting them in the Foreign Legion.[58] Ultimately, the residency informed Moroccan Jewish volunteers at the end of 1939 that they would not be able to serve anywhere.

The swift fall of France in 1940 made military service a nonissue. Germany's lightning-fast victory in May and June shattered myths about France's military prowess throughout the empire. For North African Jews, the racist legislation that ensued in the Vichy regime over the following months dealt a devastating blow to France's self-image as a liberal beacon of human rights and emancipation. The French government moved quickly to redefine national identity along ethnic lines. On August 27, 1940, the Vichy government repealed the Marchandeau Act, which punished those who attacked racial or religious groups. This opened the door to anti-Semitic vitriol in the French press. On October 3, the Vichy government passed the first comprehensive anti-Jewish legislation in France, the Statut des Juifs. This law created

---

57. MAE, CADN-Mar., Direction de l'Intérieur, Carton 111, circular letter from Ministry of National Defense, of War, and Foreign Affairs, "Indigènes israélites nord-africaines," October 25, 1939.

58. Robert Montagne, "Étude sur l'utilisation à la guerre des israélites marocains," quoted in Assaraf (2006, 391).

a second-class category of citizenship for French Jews that forbade nearly all Jewish participation in public life.[59] Essentially Nuremberg Laws *à la française*, the decree delineated a racial classificatory system that defined a Jew as an individual with three Jewish grandparents (or just two if one's spouse was also Jewish) and banned Jews from holding any posts in the government and the military (except World War I veterans and those who had distinguished themselves in battle in 1939–1940) or any other positions of public influence, including in the media.

In French North Africa, the Jewish status law was implemented unevenly, differing according to the legitimization structures the three colonial units used.[60] It was put into effect most swiftly and comprehensively in *l'Algèrie française*, the settler colony. Just four days after the Statut des Juifs was passed in France, the Crémieux Decree was abolished in Algeria, immediately depriving Algerians Jews of their French nationality.[61] In many respects, Vichy's anti-Semitic legislation only laid bare the tiered colonial system already in place in which economic, political, and legal rights were tied to ethnic status. Well before and after the Vichy period, access to education, jobs, legal systems, and even health care in North Africa was determined according to a person's classification as French, non-French European, indigenous Jew, or indigenous Muslim (Berber or Arab), not to mention restrictions based on gender. Revoking Algerian Jews' French citizenship reclassified them at a lower rung in the social hierarchy: they could no longer enroll in French schools, be under French legal jurisdiction, or even be admitted into European hospitals. Instead, they had to use the "native" health care facilities, unless there were extenuating circumstances in which a certain type of care was only available in the European medical system or there were political priorities that necessitated special treatment.[62]

---

59. Provisions were made in the *statut* for Jewish veterans of World War I, or those who fought in the Battle of France between 1939 and 1940, to retain their French citizenship. However, in February 1942, stipulations about these provisions were tightened so that only decorated veterans or those who had been injured (and their progeny) could retain their status as French citizens.

60. Schroeter's (forthcoming) study of Vichy Morocco, which is based on archival research, stands out as the most extensive treatment of this understudied but critical period.

61. In Morocco, security reports state that many French and other Europeans in Meknes and Oujda felt that the decision put Jews "back in their place at last." Muslims who resented the double standard applied to Algerian Jews echoed this sentiment, and there was some sense of satisfaction among Moroccan Jews that Algerian Jews were now in the same predicament as them. MAE, CADN-Mar., Direction de l'Intérieur, Statut des Juifs, Dossier 5, Notes de Renseignements, nos. 217 and 432.

62. MAE, CADN-Mar., Direction de l'Intérieur, Statut des Juifs, Dossier 5, circular letter from Direction de la Santé Publique et de la jeunesse, "Hospitalisation des juifs algériens," June 16, 1941.

The implementation of the Statut des Juifs was delayed until October 31, 1940 in protectorate Morocco.[63] More significantly, the definition of Jewish status that was applied in France and in Algeria was modified in Morocco. There, in a colonial irony, the formal protectorate logics by which the residency had earlier justified its refusal to issue a Moroccan "Crémieux Decree" put Moroccan Jews, as "subjects of the sultan," in a better position than Algerian Jews. In Morocco (as was the case in Tunisia), the definition of Jewish status was amended to differentiate between Moroccan Jews and other Jews living in the protectorate. This modification was highly significant because it differentiated between a *religious* classification, which was applied to Moroccan Jews (*tout israèlite marocain*), and the *racial* criteria outlined by the Statut des Juifs, which was applied to other Jews living in protectorate Morocco.

It is unclear what role, if any, the Moroccan sultan played in amending the law's definition of Jewish status, but differentiating the position of "Moroccan" Jews was clearly in the interest of both the residency and the Alawid monarch.[64] The protectorate's formal legitimization was premised on the notion that France, at least nominally, would uphold the Moroccan sultan's sovereignty. Reclassifying Moroccan Jews according to racial criteria would have undercut the Muslim monarch's spiritual-political role as Commander of the Faithful, removing not only Jewish *dhimmi* subjects but also Jewish converts to Islam from under his ostensible protection. This would have made conversion to Islam meaningless. For French administrators in Morocco, an undifferentiated application of the Jewish status laws that were being used in the metropole threatened the stability of the protectorate; for the sultan, it constituted a threat against Islam and his position as a Muslim ruler.

The palace tried to use the early period of Vichy rule as an opportunity to reassert an Islamic order in which Jews' social position was more restrictively defined, at least in limited ways. In the spring of 1941, a circular letter, apparently instigated by the grand vizier, Mohamed El Mokri, was sent out that instructed pashas and *qa'ids* to enforce a decree that banned Muslim women from working in Jewish homes as domestic servants. The justification for this prohibition, which I quote at length, reveals official perspectives in the *makhzan* about Muslim-Jewish social boundaries in Moroccan society:

> This situation [Moroccan women working in Jewish homes], of which you cannot be unaware, threatens the respect of the Muslim woman

---

63. The *dahir* was published in *Bulletin Officiel* 1463 (November 8, 1940): 1054–1055. The Statut des Juifs was delayed even longer in Tunisia, where the formal sovereign, Moncef Bey, had to sign the decree.

64. For comprehensive treatment of the role of the sultan vis à vis Morocco's Jews during the Vichy period, see Schroeter (forthcoming).

and debases her dignity. In addition, it creates a reputation for her that our religion condemns and which tends to encourage Jews to disdain Muslims and forget their condition as *dhimmi*. Under no circumstances must they, under penalty of exposing them to the dangers that they apprehend, depart from their traditional life and the limits in which they have been always been placed.

In order to follow in the glorious paths of our august ancestors, may God hallow their souls, we have preserved the security of Jews; we have permitted them to live with our Muslim subjects, in an atmosphere of calm and peace.

Also, pressed in part by our wish to safeguard the dignity of the Muslim woman, and in other part, due to the fear that this situation might provoke grave troubles, we ordain you to formally prohibit Muslims from working, publicly or in secret, in the homes of Jews and to ensure that this prohibition will be rigorously and effectively observed.[65]

In the Moroccan social order envisioned in the letter, Jews were to not forget "their condition as *dhimmi*" and were not to "depart from their traditional life and the limits in which they have always been placed." This identification system differentiates between Muslim and Jewish "subjects"; the sultan preserves the security of Jews, but they have to remember their status. Significantly, the threat against the integrity of this order envisioned by Moroccan authorities derives from the "indignity" of the "Muslim woman" working in the home of a Jew, or *dhimmi*.[66]

That summer, the Vichy government ratcheted up anti-Jewish pressure. Upset about the lack of thoroughness with which the previous Statut des Juifs had been applied, Xavier Vallat, head of the newly created General Commission for Jewish Questions, issued a new version on June 2, 1941, that required a census of all Jews and their property in the Free Zone in France (this had already been done in the Nazi-controlled northern zone). Vallat also prioritized carrying out a census and fully implementing the new laws in French North Africa. In Morocco, it took until August to negotiate and publish four *dahirs* about the new laws. One of these, significantly, changed

---

65. MAE, CADN-Mar., Direction de l'Intérieur, "Statut des Juifs," Dossiers 5–6, Circulaire Viziriel no. 372, April 1, 1941.

66. The intimate connection between ethnic and religious identification and gender status and roles is explored in detail in chapter 7.

the religious definition of Jewish status (which was used only in Morocco and Tunisia) to the racial criteria used elsewhere in the French Empire. A second banned Jews from more professions (though artisanal industries were exempted because of concerns about destabilizing this critical economic sector in which many Moroccan Jews worked). Another of the decrees ordered a census in which all non-Moroccan and Moroccan Jews had to declare their "Jewish identity according to the law, their civil status, their family situation, their profession, and the state of their property." This census caused understandable consternation that fall among members of the Jewish community, who were aware of the growing violence and discrimination against Jews in Europe.[67]

However, when it came to actually implementing the stricter laws, the residency worried about disrupting an already fragile wartime protectorate economy in which Jews had influential positions in several sectors. When the census was carried out in the fall 1941, a system of appeals was created through which Moroccan and European Jews could request special dispensations. Exemptions were granted for exceptional services to France and for Jews who were functioning in professions deemed vital to the protectorate economy. The appeals process was left up to regional heads, who had wide latitude in making decisions based on the "personality, morality, activity, and influence" of the requestor and on economic considerations.[68] Officials tried to process the census data based on region and on the commercial and industrial situation in order to determine what the economic impact would be of a full application of the Statut des Juifs. These economic concerns were also linked to colonial administrators' worries about how the anti-Jewish laws might affect the Muslim native population. A 1942 report warned:

> Even if it is true that there is higher interest in eliminating the French or foreign Jews from certain professions, in Morocco, without a doubt, the Moroccan Jews form an integral part of the autochthonous

---

67. In some regions, including Fes, the census was rather random. In the Casablanca region (which had the largest Jewish population), it was much more thorough. The census taken in Casablanca from September 20 to 25, 1941, collected detailed information on the nationality, professions, and property of all Moroccan and non-Moroccan Jews. Thirty-four different nationalities were registered for Jews living in Morocco (in addition to French and Moroccan). Of these, only American Jews living in Morocco were exempted from the census and did not have to declare their property. MAE, CADN-Mar., Direction de l'Intérieur, "Statut des Juifs pendant la Seconde Guerre Mondiale (August 1940–May 1945)," Dossier 6, "Recensement des juifs, résultat des opérations," May 1, 1942.

68. MAE, CADN-Mar., Direction de l'Intérieur, "Statut des Juifs," Dossier 6, Instruction Résidentielle, "Pour l'examen des demandes de dérogation résultant de la législation en vigueur sur les juifs," November 15, 1941.

population, and we must see if it is necessary to apply the legislation with less rigor. In fact, their activity might prove indispensable for the economy of the protectorate.[69]

Many times colonial officials preferred pragmatism to a strict implementation of the *statut*. When French parents complained that a Jewish woman, Madame Poizot, was teaching at the rural French school in Inezgane, the director of public instruction responded that if he made her leave he would have to shut the school down. He wrote, "The inhabitants of Inezgane should be happy to have a teacher, even if her origins are suspect."[70]

At the same time, protectorate administrators also sent threatening signals to the Jewish community. In July 1941, the Directorate of Political Affairs devised a plan to move Jews who had moved into the *ville nouvelle* of Casablanca since 1939 back into the medina, ostensibly to solve the problem of overcrowding. The plan's authors did not expect that Muslims would protest the measure because Jews had traditionally lived in "ghettoes" in Morocco, and they hoped that this would be the first step toward getting all the Jews back into the *mellah*.[71] On August 19, 1941, French authorities issued a decree (published in the *Bulletin Officiel* on August 22) that forbade Moroccan Jews to live in the European sectors of the city if they had moved there since 1939. Implementing the plan posed a challenge, though, because most of the former residences of Jews in the *mellah* had, of course, since been occupied. While it seems that some Jews were forced to move back into the *mellah* in Fes and Meknes, the large size of the Jewish population in Casablanca created logistical problems that made the plan unfeasible.[72]

In contrast to the anti-Semitic repression in the French protectorate, Jews in the Spanish zone lost none of their rights. The Spanish government actually disseminated propaganda during the war calling on Sephardic Jews in

---

69. MAE, CADN-Mar., Direction de l'Intérieur, "Statut des Juifs," Dossier 6, Circular No. 7 from Director of Public Security Services, Cordier, to Secretary General of the Protectorate (April 20, 1942).

70. MAE, CADN-Mar., Direction de l'Intérieur, "Statut des Juifs," Dossiers 5–6, Director of Public Instruction to Secretary General of the Protectorate, "Objet: A/S de Mme Poizot," February 9, 1943.

71. MAE, CADN-Mar., Direction de l'Intérieur, "Statut des Juifs," Dossiers 5–6, Direction des Affaires Politiques, "Note au sujet de l'habitat juif dans les villes européens," July 5th, 1941.

72. The director of political affairs at the time, Augustin Guillaume, instructed municipal authorities to delay enforcing the law, which had been passed in August, until after the Jewish High Holidays in September. Another problem in Casablanca was that Jewish refugees from Syria had occupied vacant homes in the *mellah* and there was little to no room for families that had left. Guillaume was appointed resident general in 1951. MAE, CADN-Mar., Direction de l'Intérieur, "Statut des Juifs," Dossiers 5–6, "A/s recasement de certains juifs dans les mellahs," September 14, 1941.

occupied Europe and in the French zone in Morocco to apply for Spanish nationality. In a twist on *limpieza de sangre*, these appeals differentiated between "national" Spanish Jewry and "international" Jewry: only the former, Sephardic Jews, were part of the pure Spanish race and were welcome in the nation. Ironically, this racially inclusive criteria encouraged Jews to apply for Spanish nationality based on the inferior status they had been subjected to under French rule in North Africa and elsewhere in Europe. The Spanish "nationalization" of Jews mirrored the Moroccan sultan's struggle, described above, to maintain a distinction between Moroccan Jews and all other Jews and his strenuous objection to legislation that treated them the same.[73] In the French zone, this turning of the tables also created an incentive for Moroccan Jews to take refuge in their *dhimmi* status and ally themselves with the palace against the residency.

The situation for Jews in the French protectorate deteriorated further in the summer of 1942 as the shock troops of the Vichy-inspired French national revolution, the Service d'ordre légionnaire (SOL), grew in strength in Morocco. Mid-November was fixed as the start date for an active campaign against Morocco's Jewish population, and posters around Casablanca invited the public to gather outside the *mellah* on the night of November 15 to begin the process of "purifying France." One week before the campaign, on November 7, the major French newspaper, *La Vigie marocaine*, began a series of articles titled "Le S.O.L. est pour la pureté française contre la lèpre juive" (The SOL is for French purity and against Jewish leprosy) (Assaraf 2005, 455). These plans were foiled the very next day, though, by the Anglo-American invasion of North Africa. Operation Torch dramatically shifted the balance of power and forestalled the further escalation of anti-Semitic persecution.

Moroccan Jews ecstatically welcomed the arrival of American troops. The prevalent anti-French sentiment was evident in a Judeo-Arabic song that circulated through the country's *mellahs*, "Get out O French, Morocco is not yours. America has come to take it, your domination is over!" (Assaraf 2005, 466). The arrival of Anglo-American troops did not signify an end to French rule in North Africa, though, as the Allies chose to keep the French administration in place. The Jewish status laws were not immediately revoked either. It took significant pressure from Algerian Jews (who had lost the most

---

73. MAE, CADN-Mar., Direction de l'Intérieur, "Statut des Juifs," Dossiers 5–6, Director of Political Affairs to Secretary General of the Protectorate, "Objet: Statut des Juifs: Extension au Maroc de la législation métropolitaine postérieure au 2 juin 1941," May 9, 1942.

because of the Jewish status laws) to convince Allied commanders in Algiers to take action to reinstate their French nationality. American Jewish organizations also became directly interested in the plight of North African Jews after the Anglo-American invasion, and a campaign was launched to pressure President Roosevelt to force the French commander of North Africa, Henri Giraud, to break completely with Vichy. In the end, all racially discriminatory legislation was finally overturned in North Africa in March 1943, four months after the Allied troops landed.

Wartime developments gave Zionist organizations an opportunity to significantly expand their activity in North Africa. Zionist representatives sought to exploit the increased appeal, particularly for the youth, of Jewish nationalism among a population that had become disillusioned with French assimilation by Vichy's anti-Semitism. Zionist-oriented soccer and basketball teams were organized under the official auspices of the alumni organizations of the Alliance Israélite Universelle schools, and Jewish-only sections of the French Scouts were created in Rabat, Casablanca, Marrakesh, Fes, Oujda, and Mogador. Several separate scouting troops were also created for Jewish girls, and summer camps were organized in the Middle Atlas for both groups. By the late 1940s, many secret pro-Zionist organizations were functioning in Morocco, including a section of Beitar, the Revisionist Zionist youth movement, called Tel Hai.[74]

Which *Istiqlal*? Caught between Moroccan and Israeli Independence

In the years immediately after the war, Morocco's Jewish community was increasingly torn between two national identity movements, Zionist and Moroccan, that were accelerating toward independence. After the war, Zionist organizations began facilitating limited clandestine immigration from North Africa to Palestine. At the same time, Istiqlal, the Moroccan independence party created at the end of 1943 with the support of the king, resumed active anti-colonial mobilization. Despite assurances in the 1944 independence manifesto issued by Istiqlal that a future independent Moroccan state would grant equal civil rights for Jews and Muslims, the tenuous position of the Moroccan Jewish community on the boundary line of Moroccan national identity was amplified by several outbreaks of Muslim-Jewish violence from

74. MAE, CADN-Mar., Direction de l'Intérieur, Carton 670, Dossier General, "Etude sur le Sionisme au Maroc," April 3, 1945.

the time between the end of the war in 1945 and the establishment of the state of Israel in 1948.

One of these incidents occurred in 1944 in Sefrou, a small city southeast of Fes that was the home one of Morocco's most ancient Jewish communities.[75] On Sunday, July 30, while many Sefrawi Jews were participating in Tisha B'Av services commemorating the fall of the First and Second Temples in Jerusalem, there was an altercation in the *mellah* between a Jew and a Moroccan colonial soldier (*goumier*) around 11:30 a.m. when the *goumier* began beating up the Jewish man's sister. A neighbor, Ichoua Keslassi, intervened to protect the woman, and as fighting escalated, a group of 400 *goumiers* from a nearby military camp began to attack sections of the city where Jews lived with clubs and large stones. At the Em Habanim building in the *ville nouvelle*, where a large group of Jews were praying, the door was broken through just as the head of the local police arrived and fired his pistol in the air to get the *goumiers* to stop.[76] After the attacks, the pasha of Sefrou arrested over 200 Jews, condemning twenty-five to prison terms ranging from a few months to a year. Only three of the *goumiers* were given jail time. This apparent double standard provoked the Jewish community in Sefrou and other Moroccan cities to make strenuous protests to French officials.[77]

A couple of months later, the Jewish *mellah* of Meknes was targeted on Rosh Hashanah, September 23. Again, an argument, this time between a Jewish man and a Muslim policeman, catalyzed a broader, more systematic attack on houses and small shops in the Jewish quarter. Several hours later, the French municipal authorities sent in Senegalese colonial troops. On May 8, 1945, a fight broke out between Muslims and Jews in the midst of Victory in Europe Day celebrations in Casablanca that led to eight arrests. An altercation the same day in Marrakesh between Jewish and Muslim youths escalated into a huge brawl. Jews fled through the Gueliz neighborhood toward the *mellah*, where the gates had to be locked to prevent a wider riot in the medina.

---

75. Sefrou is the site where Clifford Geertz and a team of anthropologists, including his wife, Hildred, and his student from the University of Chicago, Lawrence Rosen, carried out extensive field work from 1965 to 1971 (Geertz 1979). Sefrou is also where Paul Rabinow (1977) was based for his fieldwork in the late 1960s.

76. MAE, CADN-Mar., Direction des Affaires Chérifiennes, Carton 323, "Émeutes à Sefrou," August 3, 1944.

77. MAE, CADN-Mar., Direction de l'Intérieur, Dossier 24, report from General de Division Suffren, Chef de la Région de Fès, to Director of Political Affairs, "Incident du 30 Juillet à Sefrou," September 4, 1944.

The perception that the protectorate administration was tolerant of these incidents only reinforced the Moroccan Jewish population's hostility, which had built up under Vichy, toward the French. Intelligence reports on the *état d'esprit* of the Jewish population reveal that the French were acutely aware of their loss of prestige. They also reveal worries about the appeal of Zionism because of the alienation Moroccan Jewish youth felt. A November 1944 report by the Department of Political Affairs observed: "They consider, first of all, the fact that for the moment they are deprived of a nationality, as the Muslims consider them not as Moroccans, but as simple protégés of the sultan (*dhimmis*)."[78] In an attempt to respond to Jewish concerns, the residency initiated a reform of the committees of the Jewish communities that increased the number of representatives and made them elected positions. These reforms also gave Morocco's Jews a more direct representation with the colonial state.

The postwar attempts of the French to win back Morocco's Jews had to compete with both Zionism and American Jewish organizations. In 1944, a Moroccan delegation attended the World Jewish Congress in Atlantic City, New Jersey, where they presented reports on the situation of Morocco's Jews in terms of education, housing, social problems, the reform of community organizations, and political rights. After the war, the World Jewish Congress and U.S.-based Jewish organizations applied diplomatic pressure to get France to reform the legal status of Moroccan Jews, renewing a campaign to grant Jews rights as French citizens. In a letter to the French ambassador to the United States, the secretary general of the congress, Leon Kubowitzki, complained that as subjects of the sultan with less than full citizenship rights, Moroccan Jews were actually in a worse position under the French protectorate than they had been at other times in Moroccan history. Governmental positions were reserved for Muslims and French, but Jews were prohibited from serving in the civil service. He also protested the fact that Jewish courts had lost their autonomy and called on the residency to transfer Jewish civil and commercial cases to French jurisdiction.[79]

For the Zionist movement, the importance of North Africa's Jewish population as a potential reservoir of immigrants increased greatly in the

---

78. MAE, CADN-Mar., Direction de l'Intérieur, "Questions juives," Dossier 2 (1944–1048), "Note de Direction des Affaires Politique: Au sujet de la réorganisation des comités des communautés israélites," November 30, 1944.

79. MAE, CADN-Mar., Direction de l'Intérieur, "Questions juives," Dossier 2, Dr. Leon Kubowitzki, Secretary General of World Jewish Congress, to Henri Bonnet, French ambassador to the United States, July 11, 1947.

aftermath of the Holocaust. The residency finally approved the creation of an independent Moroccan branch of the Zionist Federation after the war, and Zionist activity expanded quickly. As the situation worsened in Palestine in 1947, however, Zionists were forced to operate in secrecy because of sensitivities among the Moroccan Muslim population. Over the next two years, Morocco's Jews were caught even more acutely between contesting appeals to their identity and loyalty. During Mohamed V's landmark visit to Tangier in 1947, the city's Jewish leadership pledged their allegiance to the sovereign during a ceremonial tea. In his historic speech, though, Mohamed V's open affiliation with pan-Arabism and strong emphasis on Morocco's Muslim character reinforced fundamental ambiguities about the identity of his Jewish subjects. In private audiences, the sultan explicitly warned Jewish leaders to continue to be loyal and faithful subjects and to distance themselves from Zionism.

The Moroccan nationalist movement also increased pressure on Morocco's Jews after the announcement of the Palestine partition plan of the United Nations in December 1947. In an anti-Zionist campaign in the spring of 1948, Istiqlal distributed tracts attacking partition, affirmed Moroccan identification with the Palestinian Arabs, and criticized the residency for forbidding Moroccans to volunteer to fight in Palestine. They also organized a boycott against Jewish businesses and European business suspected of pro-Zionist sympathies, despite official proclamations from the sultan and the residency that warned against provoking anti-Jewish sentiment in Morocco. The boycott targeted Jewish-owned pharmacies, cinemas, and bus companies. After the United States recognized the state of Israel, the boycott was extended to all U.S. products. Moroccan nationalist women took a leading role in these campaigns, including the wife of Allal al-Fassi, who held regular gatherings of the notable women in Fes to encourage the boycott. Women also contributed to the cause by donating jewelry to Istiqlal's Palestine fund.[80]

The week after the Israel's declaration of independence in May 1948, the king delivered a radio address strongly cautioning against any violence against the Moroccan Jewish population and urging his Muslim subjects to distinguish between the events occurring in Palestine and the situation in Morocco:

> They [Muslim subjects] must know that the Moroccan Jews—who have resided in the country under the protection of its rulers for

---

80. MAE, CADN-Mar., Direction de l'Intérieur, "Questions juives," Dossier 26, telegram from Délégué Résidence Générale, Lacoste, to Diplomatie, Paris, no. 464–472, June 3, 1948.

centuries, receiving the best welcome, and who have faithfully testified to their complete loyalty to the Moroccan throne—are different than the uprooted Jews who have been led from all the corners of the world towards Palestine, which they have unjustly and arbitrarily seized.

In the note of warning that immediately followed this statement, however, the king sternly advised his Jewish subjects to "avoid any sensitive act of supporting the Zionist aggression or manifesting any solidarity with it, because by doing so, they will threaten not only their individual rights but also their Moroccan nationality" (quoted in Assaraf 2005, 521). Here again, this identification of Morocco's Jews emanating, in this case, from the palace emphasized their ambivalent status as an internal religious Other.

The distinction the sultan attempted to maintain between Moroccan Jews and other Jews became increasingly blurred as Moroccan nationalists used the war in Palestine to mobilize popular support. In an article in one of the newspapers of the Parti démocratique de l'indépendance (the nationalist faction under the leadership of el-Ouezzani), the author renewed the call for a blanket boycott against Jewish products in Morocco:

> From a religious point of view, does the Qur'an not say that Jews are the most implacable enemies of the believers? It is necessary to avoid all business with these Jews who exploit you and despoil you of your property and then support your enemies and the enemies of your religion. All cooperation with these impudent Jews, after their massacre of our brothers and the conspiracy against our homelands, will be an unpardonable crime.[81]

In this expression of nationalist identification of the "Jewish other," no distinction is made between "Moroccan" and outside Jews. This exclusionary discourse shifted to violence in the early summer at the eastern Moroccan border town of Oujda (the key point through which clandestine Jewish immigration passed to Palestine via Algeria and Marseille) in the most intense episode of anti-Jewish violence in Morocco during the protectorate period.[82]

---

81. MAE, CADN-Mar., Direction de l'Intérieur, "Question juives," Dossier 26, clipping from *Al-Ra'i al-'am*, May 12, 1948.

82. For an alternate reading of the events that seems to implicate the French *chef de région*, Jean Brunel, and possibly Zionist agents in instigating, at least partially, this sequence of events, see Kenbib (1994, 679–87). Katan (1990, 599–619) also writes about the Oujda-Djerada anti-Jewish riots, based primarily on protectorate archives, and Laskier (1994, 94–101) provides a thorough overview of the multiple and often contradicting perspectives of French authorities, Jewish residents, and Moroccan nationalists.

According to the official report on the events in Oujda and Djerada, police responded on the morning of June 7, 1948, to two incidents: first, to stop a group of Moroccan nationalist activists from beating up a Jewish barber, Albert Bensoussan, whom the nationalists accused of carrying hand grenades and trying to cross the nearby Algerian border en route to Israel. A little later, police investigated the stabbing of a Jewish convert to Islam by a Moroccan Jew during an argument about Palestine in the covered textile market (the *kissaria*). Rumors quickly spread from three cafés at the Attarine and Figari squares that a Jew had killed a Muslim, and groups began to pillage Jewish businesses in Oujda's *ville nouvelle* and in the *mellah*. The Mokhzani (Moroccan) troops sent to quell the attacks joined in with the rioters. At the time of the attacks, Foreign Legion troops stationed in Oujda were engaged in exercises outside of the town, and they took a while to arrive on the scene. They posted a guard around the European city before intervening in the medina. By the time the attacks were stopped, five Jews had been killed, fifteen had been injured, and 200 million francs of Jewish property had been destroyed.[83]

That evening the violence spread to the nearby mining town of Djerada. After bus passengers arriving from Oujda spread rumors that Jews had killed Arabs in Oujda and that the minaret of the Grand Mosque had been destroyed, a large crowd gathered in the market. Around eight o'clock, children began throwing rocks at two Jews at a *fundouk* (inn) and at a kiosk on the square. When a Muslim who had been sold a losing lottery ticket by the Jewish owner of the kiosk started kicking and throwing stones at the kiosk, the crowd of 2,000 that had gathered in the square erupted. They set the kiosk on fire and, armed with sticks and mining axes, began to attack and pillage Jewish establishments in the *mellah* and the *kissaria*. Many of Djerada's 117-member Jewish community took refuge with Muslim neighbors, while others fled to the European quarter. By the end of the episode, thirty-seven Jews had been killed, including ten women and ten children, and twenty-seven had been injured.[84] Elsewhere in Morocco, both of these attacks created widespread fear among Jewish communities about further attacks, particularly those living in isolated pockets in eastern Morocco, including Debdou, Taourirt, and Berkane.

---

83. MAE, CADN-Mar., Direction de l'Intérieur, "Questions juives," Dossier 26, report from Civil Controller of Oujda to Resident General Juin, June 19, 1948, 1–6.
84. Ibid., 7–12.

In the aftermath of the incidents in Oujda and Djerada, the French authorities arrested Confédération Générale des Travailleurs (General Confederation of Labor) leaders whom they believed had received an order from the Istiqlal leadership in Oujda to instigate the attacks. On June 11, the pasha of Oujda, Muhammad al-Hajawi, who had energetically fought to put down the earlier riot, delivered a speech in the name of the sultan that harshly condemned the rioters and called for a solemn homage for the dead in Djerada. After the speech, however, Muhammad ben Tuhami Berreheli, who had ties to the Istiqlal nationalist leadership in Oujda stabbed Hajawi in the back while he was kneeling to perform prayers at the Grand Mosque. When a rumor spread that the pasha had actually been attacked by a Jew disguised as a Muslim and that a bomb had been planted that was going to blow up the minaret of the Grand Mosque, the French civil controller had to immediately send town criers out to tell the truth to the population in order to avert more anti-Jewish attacks.

These incidences only further eroded the vestiges of trust Morocco's Jewish community placed in the French administration, which they blamed for failing to prevent the attacks and intervening too slowly to stop them, and in the sultan, whom they blamed for at least indirectly provoking the attacks with his speech in May about Israel's independence. After the events in Oujda and Djerada, the *makhzan* instructed *qa'ids* and pashas in Morocco's cities to meet with the Jewish committees to reassure of them that they would be protected. However, the message was mixed: they were also told to remind Moroccan Jews that they were forbidden to demonstrate in favor of Zionism or the state of Israel. The possible involvement of Istiqlal in the incidents in Oujda and Djerada negatively impacted Moroccan Jews' perceptions of the independence movement, despite an official statement the party issued that the enemy was Zionism, not Moroccan Jewry. One year later, in 1949, the rate of Jewish immigration to Palestine began to increase after the resident general legalized Zionist immigration activity. He approved the opening of a registration office in Casablanca and the opening of a transit camp at Mazagan run by Kadima, a Zionist organization that began sending more than 600 people every month to Israel.

The creation in the late nineteenth century of a protégé class of Moroccan Jews with special capitulatory privileges and the assimilationist cultural outreach of the Alliance Israélite Universelle began to transform the status of Jews in Moroccan society. Four decades of protectorate rule accelerated processes that profoundly reshaped the social, cultural, and economic position of the Moroccan Jewish population and made the question of whether this religious minority in Moroccan society should be classified as *dhimmi*, protégé, or citizen increasingly problematic. Because of the specific logics of the colonial political field in Morocco, the rapid Europeanization of much of the urban Moroccan Jewish community and cultural identification with France did not translate into political rights. Initiatives to naturalize Morocco's Jews as French citizens were steadfastly blocked by residency officials, for whom the legitimacy of a protectorate mode of colonial rule meant preserving Jews' status as subjects of the sultan. Jewish confidence in the French "protector" was severely shaken after the Vichy interlude, during which their Jewish status deprived them of most of their rights. At the same time, though Moroccan Jews were grateful for what they perceived as the efforts of the Moroccan king to shield them from these initiatives, many remained skeptical about throwing their lot in completely with the Moroccan nationalists. Doubts lingered that they would truly be included as equal members of a national community defined by an Arab and Muslim identity, despite attempts to assure them of the promise of equality particularly after multiple incidents of Muslim-Jewish violence in the late 1940s. Zionist activity that appealed to solidarity with a Jewish nation only further aggravated questions about the loyalty of Morocco's Jews.

The tensions revolving around Morocco's Jewish Question increased significantly when the state of Israel was created in 1948 and Zionists began to recruit Jewish emigration in the late 1940s and early 1950s. In the last decade of the protectorate, the Moroccan nationalist movement and the king himself clearly aligned the cause of Moroccan independence with the pan-Arab movement led by Gamal Abdel Nasser in Egypt. The entrenchment of the Arab-Israeli conflict increased the precarious position of Moroccan Jews, who were caught between Moroccan and Israeli nationalism.[85] As a group, Morocco's Jews forced questions about how the boundaries of the national community should be drawn. As an internal religious Other, they

---

85. For instance, the nationality law that the Israeli Knesset passed on July 14, 1952, naturalized all Jews living in Palestine as Israeli citizens unless they had expressed a desire to not become naturalized Israelis. This caused a diplomatic problem for the French. According to Moroccan law, Moroccan subjects, including Jewish subjects, have a perpetual allegiance to the king and could not lose their nationality even if they become Israelis. The French faced dilemmas over whether to offer diplomatic protection to Moroccan Jews living in Israel or how to respond if other Arab states started to naturalize Moroccan Muslims living in their countries. MAE, CADN-Mar., Direction des Affaires Chérifiennes, Carton 325, note no. 188 of the Cabinet Diplomatique, "Juifs marocains en Israël," June 23, 1952. This note also states that French Jews living in Israel would still retain their French nationality under the 1945 Code de la nationalité.

were simultaneously included and excluded in national identification processes carried out by the urban Arab nationalists and by the sultan-cum-king.
Although the nationalists and the king consistently affirmed that Morocco's
Jews would be guaranteed equal civil rights and duties in the Moroccan
nation, the core ethnocultural definition of Arabo-Islamic national identity
marginalized this religious minority. After independence, although a rem-
nant of Moroccan Jews continued to live in and play significant roles in
Morocco, the vast majority emigrated to Israel, France, or North America in
the 1950s and 1960s.

❧ CHAPTER 7

Gender and the Politics of Identity

Previous chapters have examined how the political salience of ethnic and religious markers of Arab, Berber, Muslim, and Jewish identity in Moroccan society was transformed by colonial intervention in the early twentieth century and the subsequent struggles among colonial and local actors during the protectorate period. This chapter turns to how gender played a fundamental role in both the legibility and legitimization logics that structured the colonial political field and the interactive identity struggles in which external and internal social boundaries were contested and negotiated in Moroccan society. This analysis builds on work that emphasizes the connections between gender and state formation (Connell 1990; Miller 1998; Adams 2005) and the substantial literature on the relationship between gender and the marking and reproduction of collective identity (e.g., Anthias and Yuval-Davis 1989). It brings the Moroccan case into conversation with broader studies on how colonial states used gender inequalities and gender-specific regulations in efforts to maintain social boundaries (Charrad 2001; Stoler 2002) and with recent work on gender, ethnicity, and national identity in the Middle East and North Africa (Badran 1995; Fleischmann 2003; Baron 2005; Baker 1998; Kozma 2003; Zayzafoon 2005). Emphasizing an actor-centered gender analysis (Clancy-Smith 1994; Thompson 2000), I focus not only on external state- and society-based identification processes in which women were the object; I also focus on how

Moroccan women themselves negotiated the changing politics of identity during the protectorate period.

The first section draws on French archival sources to explore how the colonial state's classificatory schema—how it "saw" different ethnic and religious identities—was expressed in gendered legal and educational policies. Gender differentiation in these realms was intended to stabilize Moroccan women's "traditional" position: to mark the division between Europeans and natives and to maintain distinctions among Moroccan "Arabs," "Berbers," and "Jews." The focus in the next section shifts to how Moroccan nationalist elites (both men and women) challenged this traditionalizing construction of gender and its classificatory logics by calling for the unification of an Islamic legal system and for legal and educational reforms that would advance and modernize the status of Moroccan women. In the 1940s, the sultan–cum–king joined these calls to expand educational opportunities for girls, using his daughter, Lalla Aicha, as a public symbol of the new "Moroccan woman."

For both colonial and local actors, the "Moroccan woman" functioned as a critical and contested site for maintaining and reproducing social boundaries and collective identity in Moroccan society. The legal and educational status of Moroccan women was also directly linked to rival legitimating discourses about traditionalization, authenticity, and modernization in the colonial political field. Each of these rival discourses, of course, reified the "Moroccan woman" as a unitary concept, obscuring the multiplicity of Moroccan women's experiences, perspectives, and agencies during the colonial period. The final section of the chapter focuses on the diverse ways that elite and non–elite urban and rural Moroccan women worked to actively resist, accommodate, and shape the identity politics that emerged during the protectorate period.

Gender and Colonial Governance

> "The Christian chief registered the women in his log / I attended
>   the operation.
> It was my lawful wife who was at the head of the line."
>   —*El-Buhali l-Bourezzouni el-Mtiri*[1]

The expansion of the colonial political field in the first two decades of the protectorate introduced unprecedented forms of governmentality in

---

1. Fonds Roux, file 59.1, songs of amateur poets of Beni Mtir, recorded by Roux in El Hajeb, 1914–1918.

Moroccan society. Women were affected by new state practices that affected the most intimate details of their everyday lives, from the registration of births, marriages, and deaths to the imposition of standards of hygiene and child care. The words of the Berber poet quoted above about seeing his wife at the head of the census line reveal the ambivalences Moroccans felt about the governmental practices of French "Christian chiefs." The French administration, on its side, was wary of provoking unrest in either urban or rural areas and, not surprisingly, prioritized the stabilization of a patriarchal political and social order (Charrad 2001, chapter 6) instead of pressing for any sort of emancipatory civilizing mission that would radically transform the status of women in Moroccan society. To implement traditionalizing legibility policies focused on gender, the colonial state relied on two primary mechanisms: definitions of women's legal status and educational policies directed at Moroccan girls.

Defining Moroccan Identities through Women's Legal Status

Between 1912 and the early 1920s, the rapid expansion of the colonial state's bureaucracy necessitated an attempt to systematize and codify legal systems that had previously been much more pliable.[2] These transformations had significant consequences for the status and classification of Morocco's women. The fundamental distinction in the colonial juridical field was between European and native: French courts were set up for the French and other Europeans while the indigenous Moroccan population fell under multiple jurisdictions that depended on ethnic and religious affiliations. The latter included Sharifian (or Makhzan) courts, administered by pashas or qa'ids (under colonial surveillance), which had jurisdiction over Moroccan Muslims and Jews in civil and criminal case. The native court system also included three separate jurisdictions for personal status law based on ethno-religious classifications: Islamic, or shari'a courts, supervised by a qadi, for Muslims; tribal councils that applied customary law in certain so-called Berber areas (mostly in the middle and central High Atlas, the Anti-Atlas, and parts of the Souss Valley); and rabbinical courts that ruled according to halacha, or "Mosaic" law, for the Moroccan Jewish population. All three legal systems used gender as a primary criterion in the delineation of personal status rights. Each had different provisions for men and women in matters

---

2. On the precolonial administration of Islamic law, with specific reference to cases involving women in the Middle East, see Tucker (1998). The paradigm shift entailed in the codification of Islamic law, with specific reference to how it impacted women, is addressed in Tucker (2008).

related to dowries, divorce, paternity, inheritance, testimony, and ownership, but they did this in different ways. For example, women could inherit under shariʻa (Islamic law) and *halacha* (rabbinic law), but not under *izref/ʻurf* (customary law). The distinct personal status provisions for women in the three legal traditions thereby served as primary classificatory mechanisms through which the colonial state enforced its logics of legibility.

First, women's status was a prominent feature of the colonial state's use of personal status laws to reify an ethnic division between Arabs and Berbers. A major component of the French "Berber Myth" derived from a stereotype that Berber women, who (like most rural women in Muslim societies) did not wear the veil, enjoyed a much higher degree of autonomy and rights than the Arab women who were sequestered in harems and required to wear the veil. In his 1925 book *Le Maroc de demain*, Paul Marty, an official in the education administration, emphasized the superiority of the Berber woman over the Arab woman, stressing her "liberty" and the fact that Berbers were largely monogamous.[3] The "higher" status of the Berber women signified that Berbers were much more amenable to "progress" than Arabs, who were "shackled" by the constraints of Islam:

> Do we not see, for example, such liberty for the woman, despite the severity of her civil status, and also that the monogamy practiced in Barbary ensures that the Shleuh [Berbers] have a chance for rapid social reconditioning? We well know that it is precisely this polygamy and above all the confinement and state of servitude of the woman that has kept generations of Islam, one after another, in a desperate stagnation. (Marty 1925, 196)

While Marty lauded the superior status of Berber women compared to the "confinement and state of servitude" of women under "generations of Islam," he was also aware that the "severity" of women's civil status under tribal customary law contradicted this image of a more liberated "Berber woman." In Algeria, where customary law was administered by tribal councils in the Kabylia, this gap led the governor general to convene a commission in

---

3. The Moroccan nationalists were particularly sensitive about the issue of polygamy, and by the 1940s, monogamy had become a social norm in the urban milieu. Fatima Mernissi (1994, 35) writes, "The nationalists, who were fighting the French, had promised to create a new Morocco, with equality for all. Every woman was to have the same right to education as a man, as well as the right to enjoy monogamy—a privileged, exclusive relationship with her husband. In fact, many of the nationalist leaders and their followers in Fes already had only one wife, and looked down on those who had many. Father and Uncle, who espoused nationalist views, each had only one wife."

1925 to research measures to improve the condition of the "Kabyle Woman." Under the 1900 version of customary law, Kabyle women had no inheritance rights, few or no property rights, no right to consent, no minimum marriageable age, and no right to divorce. In addition, when a husband or other male relative died, a Kabyle woman was considered part of the property included in the estate.[4] The husband could divorce without specifying any reason (as was also the case with Islamic law), could demand a "ransom" payment before his divorced wife could remarry, had no legal responsibility to provide alimony, and had total custody rights over the children.[5] Building on earlier reform proposals in 1903 and 1921, the 1925 commission recommended amendments that included setting the minimum marriageable age at fifteen, forbidding the placing of a ransom on repudiated women, allowing Kabyle women to ask for divorce, and granting women some inheritance rights. These reforms were finally passed in Algeria in 1930. In Morocco, however, where Berber customary law provided a very similar status for women, no similar reform efforts were ever made, even by the 1929 commission whose work resulted in the infamous decree of May 16, 1930, that reorganized Berber customary law courts. As will be shown in the next section, Moroccan nationalists focused on the relative inequality of Moroccan women under Berber customary law to critique the colonial political field's divisionary ethnographic logics. Appealing to both the preservationist and developmentalist frameworks that legitimated the protectorate, they pressed for the abolition of the customary legal system and the unification of a shari'a-based judiciary by emphasizing the progressive status Islamic law afforded women.

The colonial state's maintenance of separate personal status jurisdictions based on ethno-religious classifications also directly affected the everyday lives of Moroccan Jewish women. These consequences were clear in the case related in the previous chapter involving the disputed probate rights of the daughter of a Jewish man, Mr. Taieb, who had died in Rabat. Her right to inherit differed under French and Jewish law, but because of the ambiguity regarding her legitimacy, she fell under neither system and never inherited anything from her father's estate.[6] Another example involves a case that dragged out for one year in the late 1940s in the Azilal administrative circle in the central High Atlas.

---

4. In 1889, the use of customary law in the Kabyle was recognized, giving an existing state of affairs official footing (Charrad 2001, 133).

5. CAOM, Carton 10H 90, "Réforme du statut de la Femme Kabyle."

6. For a comparative treatment of these ambiguities within the French empire, see Pederson (1998).

Rachel Samhoun (née Ihouda), who was born in 1928 in the *mellah* of Foum Djemaa, was married to a Jewish man named Isaac Ben Soussane. In the summer of 1948, she was caught *en flagrant délit* with a Muslim man. After this, reportedly due to worries about repercussions from the village's Jewish community, she converted to Islam by saying the *shahada* and put herself under the protection of the village's Muslim population. Her husband proceeded to bring a case of adultery against her before the rabbinic court in Marrakesh, but she was acquitted because one of the two witnesses that were required to convict in such cases refused to testify against her. Rachel wanted a divorce so her conversion could be officially registered and so she could marry a Muslim man. Although he accused his wife of adultery, Isaac Ben Soussane (who apparently had moved to Casablanca and remarried himself) refused to divorce her. In a further twist, in August, Ben Soussane tried to have the local court forbid her from aborting the child she was carrying, claiming that the child was his. By May of the next year, the situation remained unresolved: Rachel was still "Jewish" and still married. Although the file unfortunately does not include the final outcome, this case reveals the quandaries generated by the multiple personal status jurisdictions maintained under the protectorate. At an official level, both the French civil controller and the local *qadi* were incensed at the other's actions in the case: the controller because the *qadi* had contravened a viziriel order when he unilaterally recognized the woman's conversion; the *qadi* because the controller was blocking a conversion to Islam. The ramifications were most severe, of course, for the woman involved: because French administrators refused to recognize her right to convert, Rachel Samhoun retained her status under Jewish law, had no right to pursue a divorce, and therefore could not remarry.[7]

During the protectorate, gender functioned as a critical mechanism for a colonial legibility system in which separate ethnic and religious identities were marked and maintained through legal pluralism. While French, Islamic, Berber, and Jewish law all differentiated between men and women, they differed in the rights given to women (for example in terms of property and inheritance, divorce, custody). Ethnoreligious identity was explicitly tied to a woman's legal status, both at the individual and collective levels. As the case of Rachel Samhoun clearly demonstrates, the preservationist and

---

7. SHD-AT, Carton 3H 1975. This carton contains files on all mixed marriages in the Azilal circle from 1935 to 1954, most of which were between Moroccan men who had been stationed in France and French women after World War II. The case of Rachel Samhoun was exceptional. The fact that hers was a mixed marriage between a Muslim and a Jewish convert is what generated controversy within the community.

traditionalizing forces in the colonial political field mitigated against changes in legal status and thus movement between these categories of identity. As was evident in negotiations over the Mudawana, the Moroccan personal status code, in 1957 and its reform in 2004, women's legal status and ethnoreligious and national identity have continued to be intimately linked and have continued to be objects of intense struggles since independence.

Defining Moroccan Identities by Educating Muslim Girls

In tandem with using separate legal systems, the colonial administration tried to use education to reproduce what it considered to be traditional notions of class, ethnic, and religious identities. During the protectorate's first few years, the Directorate of Public Instruction (DPI) created a separate educational system for the Moroccan *indigènes*. This included *écoles* and *collèges musulmans* for the sons of notables,[8] trade schools for the sons of the lower classes in Morocco's major cities, and a separate Berber *collège* in Azrou for sons of rural notables (which was founded in the 1920s). Between 1911 and the early 1920s, the DPI also opened schools for indigenous Moroccan girls in several cities. These were mainly for Arab-Muslim girls, since Jewish girls were channeled into the Franco-Israélite or the AIU schools and no girls' schools were opened in the "Berber" countryside. It is important, from the outset, to note that the actual scope of these initiatives in Morocco was very limited, as was generally true of other colonial school systems. In 1930, only 7.41 percent of the total protectorate budge was allocated to education, and out of that, less than 20 percent was spent on education for Moroccan Muslims (Segalla 2009b, 84). A miniscule fraction of the protectorate budged was apportioned for native education, and even less was allocated for girls' schools.

One of the pedagogical priorities of the schools the DPI opened was to standardize and systematize instruction for young girls in traditional Moroccan handicrafts that had historically been produced by women, as had been done previously in Algeria and Tunisia (Clancy-Smith 2000; Segalla 2009b, 101). It is telling that the DPI was attached to the Directorate of Beaux Arts and Antiquities, explicitly tying indigenous education to the traditionalizing and preservationist policies of the colonial state.[9] The goal of this gradualist

---

8. The most elite of these were the Collège Mawlay Idriss in Fes and the Collège Mawlay Youssef in Rabat, both of which were founded in 1916.

9. This ministry oversaw excavations, including the archaeological excavations at Volubulis; preservation projects; and zoning decisions for "protected" heritage sites such as the medina in Fes.

civilizing mission, particularly for girls, was to ensure the continuity of traditional social structures, safeguard Moroccan artisanal and handicraft industries, and very slowly modernize Moroccan society. Mixed in among these motives was a semi-altruistic desire to help Moroccan women better their position in society by maximizing their economic potential and increasing the amount of capital they could individually earn.

In Morocco, the creation of this type of Muslim girls' school was initiated through the efforts of a French woman named Louise Bouillot, a graduate of the Ecole des langues orientales vivantes in Paris who was in charge of the Arabic courses at the French girls' school in Salé.[10] In the fall of 1913, Ms. Bouillot began investigating the state of education for Muslim girls on behalf of the DPI. She reported that

> in Salé, as in all of the Muslim countries still distant from European civilization, the Arab woman carries on an existence highly conformed to tradition, that is to say, a life of seclusion. Nothing exists for her outside the familial circle, which marks the extent of her conception of the world and society and in which she spends the sum total of her practical knowledge that has been transferred from mother to daughters. Her intellectual knowledge is of limited scope, and, even if there are women superior to others in terms of rank, quality, distinction, or intelligence, they are all equals in terms of their perfect ignorance.[11]

Bouillot observed that the women of Salé did, however, "recognize our [French] superiority over them" and would willingly receive counsel, "especially in matters of hygiene and household care."

She also emphasized the economic benefit of skill-based education, particularly for lower-class women who could sell handicrafts at higher prices.[12] The women she studied sold their products for little in order to buy incidental items such as jewelry or clothes; they were not producing for a profit. Bouillot observed that Muslim girls' schools in Tunisia were getting higher

---

10. For an extended study of the workshop programs Bouillot initiated in Salé, Bazet initiated in Rabat, and Bel initiated in Fes, see Irbouh's excellent chapter (2005, 107–31) and Segalla (2009b, 101–2).

11. CADN, Direction de l'Instruction Publique, Carton 25, "Rapport sur les possibilités d'installation à Salé d'un ouvroir pour les jeunes filles musulmanes," December 19, 1913.

12. In contrast to what Russell found for Egypt (2004), note that in the in the French educational system in Morocco, initially the emphasis was on shaping the "Moroccan woman" as a producer rather than as a consumer.

prices for similar products, proving that their "real value" was much higher. Her recommendation was to standardize production: "Is there not a real economic interest in organizing, in a regular fashion, women's labor in a country in which local industry has never lost its originality?"[13] Small workshops that taught young girls textile trades already existed in most Moroccan cities, but these produced hardly anything for sale. The problem, lamented Miss Bouillot, was to convince local Muslim women there was no shame in making a living through their work. They also needed to create picturesque designs and standardize production so they could market their work abroad.

Bouillot also expressed concern about the hygienic conditions of the existing workshops that trained young Moroccan girls. In the one she visited in Salé, which was run by a woman named Mallema Slimana,[14] a group of twenty-five to thirty pupils sat on a single mat in a poorly lit and stuffy room. The girls, fearing a caning, were forced to work from morning to night without speaking or moving, except for a noon meal. Bouillot cited a litany of health problems caused by the poor working conditions. Her concluding recommendations were to first remove the social stigma attached to working, teach the women how to most effectively profit from their work, and then ensure that local production had an outlet for sales abroad. She hoped that reforming the workshop would eventually expand educational opportunities for Muslim girls: "In any case, it is important to not forget that the young Muslim girl will never enter school until after having crossed the threshold of the workshop."[15]

In a follow-up report, Bouillot cautioned that the French had to be very careful about too radically influencing Moroccan women's attitudes in ways that would upset the traditional social order from within the Moroccan home. Instead, they should encourage the most gradual evolutionary process toward Moroccan women's equality with their Western "civilized sisters."[16] She concluded with a statement that could have been the slogan of the protectorate itself: "Evolution and not revolution. This must be the watchword; for it would be unfortunate for a bit of science that still would be useless [to her], to trouble the beautiful harmony of the Moroccan home today."

---

13. CADN, Direction de l'Instruction Publique, Carton 25, "Rapport sur les possibilités d'installation à Salé d'un Ouvroir pour les jeunes Filles musulmanes," December 19, 1913.

14. A *ma'allem* is a person with a particular professional skill. In this instance, the title referred to the seamstress in charge of training the young girls.

15. CADN, Direction de l'Instruction Publique, Carton 25, "Rapport sur les possibilités d'installation à Salé d'un ouvroir pour les jeunes filles musulmanes," December 19, 1913.

16. In a letter to Lyautey, Batallion Chief Bussy quotes Bouillot's report at length. She wrote: "Since the Moroccan woman must remain the soul of her home for a long time, our duty to her is to help her and to bring her the most happiness and well-being possible. Since this home is not going to

Bouillot's recommendations had a lasting impact on educational policy over the next two decades. In a letter to Lyautey, Battalion Chief Bussy, the military adjunct for the Rabat-Salé area, commented: "I agree entirely with the ideas of Miss Bouillot on the means to use to win the indigenous female milieu over to our cause. Like her, I believe the young Muslim girl will not enter the school until after first crossing the threshold of the workshop. It is thus toward the creation of workshops that we must direct our efforts."[17] Bussy also reiterated the long-term political importance of women's education as a form of *pénétration pacifique* into the Moroccan home, remarking that "the political influence of these constant interactions with the indigenous world, with children and the women who—particularly at this point—show a curiosity about external events, cannot but be a help to French peaceful penetration."[18]

Over the next decade similar hybrid workshop-schools that offered a professional education in handicrafts and later in Arabic and basic French were opened in most Moroccan cities. These served as a means through which the Directorate of Public Instruction, Beaux Arts, and Antiquities could preserve traditional Moroccan society through a command craft economy. An official 1915 study of the handicraft industry of Meknes reported that embroidery production had almost completely ceased because of a sharp decrease in demand for traditional Meknessi patterns and because many Muslim women had begun buying European-made damasks, which previously had been a Meknessi specialty.[19] In response to (and in the face of) these market forces, the DPI in Rabat dictated the distinct local designs that schools in each city would produce.[20] These traditional textiles, carpets, and rugs were sold at an annual exposition, and the proceeds went to the protectorate's treasury. The dual developmentalist and preservationist goal of the Muslim girls' schools was aptly summarized by the director of the Oujda school: to give

---

change apart from her, and because she, herself, the faithful guardian of the spirit of her race, should not stop pleasing the young Muslim man who seems to be away, let us be careful not to divert her mentality too much by introducing the 'woman of tomorrow.' We cannot overemphasize this: she will remain what she is. We will enlighten her only on a practical level—hygiene, household care, etc. . . . Make her less totally ignorant of world events, less naïve in her judgments, more capable of entertaining herself—that is all she is in need of right now to aid in the slow evolution which, much later, will make her the equal of her 'civilized' sisters." CADN, DIP, Carton 25, Batallion Chief Bussy to Resident General, "Objet: A.S. de l'enseignement des filles musulmanes à Salé," December 5, 1913.

17. CADN, Direction de l'Instruction Publique, Carton 25, Battalion Chief Bussy to Resident General, November 20, 1913.

18. Ibid.

19. CADN, Direction de l'Instruction Publique, Carton 16, Commissioner of Indigenous Girls' Education in Fes-Meknes Regions to Director of Education, Rabat, December 16, 1915.

20. There were exceptions, though. For example, the Oujda school used designs from Tetouan, Rabat, and Salé.

"a profession to the young Muslim girls, to help them make a living, and to develop artisans capable of maintaining the reputation of Moroccan arts, the decline of which is certain without government intervention."[21]

These schools also consciously focused on reproducing the type of Moroccan wife and mother French officials believed the Moroccan household needed. In the mid-1920s, Paul Marty, an educational administrator, described how French schools should socialize the future spouses of the "Moroccan man":

> The solution is to open schools and to shape the girls who remain . . . in their traditional state, but who gain from their French teachers the qualities of order, economy, domestic labor, family education, and even elementary instruction, that they are lacking right now and which will make them the true companions of which we [men] dream. (Marty 1925, 196)

Similarly, the head of the Oujda school observed in a 1924 letter to Director of Public Instruction Louis Brunot, "What is our goal? To prepare the Muslim girl for her role as mistress of the house, in her cloistered life and in the native society, taking into account the evolution that pushes each individual toward the best she can be."[22] One of the primary elements of domestic order that educators sought to instill in the mistresses of Morocco's households concerned hygiene. A newspaper article about the Oujda girls' school from 1934 reported: "Hygiene and health are a constant concern of the directorate. A visiting nurse examines the small colony every week and is in contact with a doctor if there is need."[23] Administrators were careful to require daily showers and the frequent disinfection of clothes.

Although some school administrators experimented with introducing other subject material, including French and Arabic literacy, the dominant emphasis from 1913 to the 1920s was on household management and child care. This imperative was driven home in Brunot's response to the Oujda director's trimester report in 1924. He affirmed the school's priorities with the following points:

1. Reading and Writing: This teaching should only be done for those children whose parents have completely accepted French culture.

---

21. A. Cavel, "L'école musulmane de jeunes filles," *Le Maroc Oriental*, December 20, 1934, 1. This Oujda school, which was founded in 1924, had begun with 157 students. By 1934, that number had increased to 280 students.

22. CADN, Direction de l'Instruction Publique, Carton 17, Oujda Region, Director of Muslim Girls' School in Oujda to the Director General of Public Instruction, Beaux-arts and Antiquities, Rabat, "Organisation de l'Ecole des filles musulmanes à Oujda," October 30, 1934.

23. A. Cavel, "L'école musulmane de jeunes filles," *Le Maroc Oriental*, December 20, 1934, 1.

2. Housekeeping Education: This education must take priority. Your school is a house-keeping school.

He ended by saying, "I well know your conviction [about teaching the girls to read and write], but I must insist that you make sure never to overemphasize in this direction."[24]

Perspectives among the French administrators and Moroccan parents began to shift, though, in the 1930s, and the DPI was forced to reevaluate the exclusive curricular focus on handicrafts and housekeeping. In 1939, questionnaires were sent out in the course of an internal study about adapting an Algerian curriculum to the Moroccan context. The responses provide insight into the goals and experiences of the French women who directed these schools, including their perspectives on the "Moroccan social milieu" in which they worked. They frequently mentioned how Moroccan families were ambivalent about girls' education; they wanted a modern curriculum but were hesitant about entrusting their daughters to a French-run system. In their report, Mesdames Le Beux and Brunot, two teachers at the lycée of Fes, commented:

> It is extremely difficult to know what the Moroccan families want. For some, it seems they are ready to raise their girls like their boys, but others want to hear nothing of this. Whether they are for or against girls education, they send me their daughters for the most part, only with a great deal of repugnance, and only continue to do so with a great deal of pressure from us.[25]

A hardline response from another director, Renée Duval, reiterated that the protectorate's educational priorities were not to emancipate Moroccan women or disturb the social and class structures in place; instead, the priority was to preserve the existing order:

> We should not forget that the Moroccan girl must be raised in view of her duty which, after leaving school, is marriage and maternity. First and precious messenger of our civilization, she must bring her family the principles of a sound and sustainable evolution, and not an abrupt

24. CADN, Direction de l'Instruction Publique, Carton 17, Oujda Region, Director of Public Instruction, Bruno, to Director of Muslim Girls School, Oujda, 1924.

25. MAE-Nantes, Direction de l'Instruction Publique, Carton 85, report from Le Beau and Bruno, teachers at Fes Lycée, to Head of Muslim Education, "Program for Muslim Girls Schools," June 13, 1939.

emancipation that might easily shake up the harmony of the family and the society in which she must live.[26]

The director in El Hajeb presented a slightly different perspective drawn from the experience of working in a more rural school with Arabic- and Berber-speaking children. This school, which was created in 1932, received daughters of notables from the rural areas, but these students stayed for only a short period before they were married off or brought home for domestic work. She noted, however, that in the past year she had seen a significant increase in the number of students who were enrolled and that their parents had requested that they be taught French and math in addition to practical skills.[27]

In the midst of this review, the DPI also solicited input from the Moroccan alumni associations of the Muslim colleges in Fes and Rabat. These older "brothers" of girls in the schools wanted more from female education and strongly urged the administration to teach girls at exactly the same level as boys. The president of the Fes alumni association wrote:

> The essential goal of this program seems to be the creation of good house cleaners, able, above all else, to perfectly fulfill their domestic duties. While not denying the usefulness of this type of education, our view has always been that our girls should not just be instructed in a professional or house-keeping culture. In accordance with the opinion of our general assembly gathered on last 4 December, we conclude that instruction for Muslim girls should not be envisioned, for the primary cycle, as a different issue than that proposed for Muslim boys.[28]

Consistent with these sentiments, several French directors emphasized that Moroccan parents demanded that girls be taught Arabic and Islam. A 1945 report revealed that this pressure to reform the system and provide girls with a more comprehensive modern education continued to increase in Moroccan society. It stated that young men wanted "spouses who understand them"

---

26. MAE-Nantes, Direction de l'Instruction Publique, Carton 85, report on the Muslim Girls Schools by Madame (Renée) Maurice Duval, May 25, 1939.

27. MAE-Nantes, Direction de l'Instruction Publique, Carton 85, Director of Muslim Girls' school, El Hajeb, to Principal Inspector of Muslim Education, Rabat, May 20, 1939.

28. MAE-Nantes, Direction de l'Instruction Publique, Carton 85, President of Alumni Association of Collège Musulman of Fes to Director General of Public Instruction, Beaux-Arts, and Antiquities, Rabat, March 22, 1939.

and stated that they and the sultan himself were "ardent supporters of educa-tion for girls."[29]

Over the course of the protectorate, the type of educational opportunities available to Moroccan girls became a central concern for increasing num-bers of Moroccan parents, particularly in the cities. The question of girls' education was closely connected to ethnographic, preservationist, and devel-opmentalist legitimating logics that undergirded the colonial political field and constituted an increasingly important site for contesting the politics of Moroccan identity for the nationalist movement and the palace in the latter half of the protectorate period.

Nationalist Classification Struggles and the "Moroccan Woman"

The nationalists began addressing the Woman Question in the early 1930s. They used the status of Moroccan women in two ways: 1) to refute the colo-nial state's preservationist logics of legitimization and legibility by contesting its Arab and Berber policies; and 2) to attack the developmentalist legitimi-zation narrative of the protectorate, using women as a metric by which to prove that the French had not modernized the Moroccan state and society. This attack focused explicitly on the two pillars of French gender policy: the protectorate's legal structures and its educational systems. As the last section discussed, these constituted the two primary levers by which the colonial state sought to define and reproduce a "traditional" and docile Moroccan social, economic, and political order.

Given the initial prominence of the Berber Question for the framing and mobilizing efforts of the nationalist movement, it is not surprising that the "Berber woman" was a major focus in efforts to counter the colonial vulgate in the early nationalist press in the 1930s. Arab urban nationalist ideologues directly countered the French valorization of Berber women as "free"[30] and "liberated" because they were not veiled and enjoyed freedom to move about the countryside. To undercut this stereotype, nationalists attacked the separate legal structure the French maintained to preserve Berber identity, decrying

---

29. M. Decroux, "Féminisme en Islam: La femme dans l'Islam moderne," *CHEAM* 1071 (November 27, 1945).

30. The words Amazigh (masculine) and Tamazight (feminine) carry the meaning of "free." French Berberophiles stressed the Berber passion for freedom and autonomy, a stereotype that extended to their ideas about Berber women.

the repressed condition of women under 'urf (customary law) compared to shari'a (Islamic law). Although both Arabic and Berber speakers practiced customary law, the nationalists equated the practice of customary law with "Berber" identity.

The May 1934 edition of *Maghreb* that marked the fourth anniversary of the Berber *dahir* contained an article titled "The Berber Woman." The pseudonymous author, N. B., decried the ways that customary law infringed on the rights of Berber women and chastised the French for condoning this "barbaric" treatment of women.[31] She claimed that Berber customary law represented *jahiliyya*, the "ignorant age" before the advent of Islam and that the historic progression was for shari'a to completely replace these "barbarous customs." N. B. argued that all Moroccan women deserved the superior status Islamic law conferred. She also affirmed certain Berber customs, however, including the fact that Berber women were not veiled, controlled the internal affairs of their households, and played a vital role as custodians of Berber poetry. N. B. urged that the Arabic and Berber systems be fused to benefit Moroccan women: "If you combine the legal liberties afforded by shari'a law with the freedom of activity enjoyed by the Berber woman, you would have a truly liberated woman." The article's final line, though, reiterated that French Berber policy trapped Berber women under "barbaric tribal custom" and needed to be rejected.[32]

In another piece titled "The Berber Woman: Is She Free?," a former secretary of a Berber customary law council, Othman al-Fayache, rebutted an article in the French newspaper *Depeche de Fès* by an indigenous affairs officer, Jouffray, that lauded France's preservation of "Berber" freedom. Al-Fayache asserted that "the Berber woman, contrary to the canards of certain adversaries of Islam who try to make us believe in her perfect happiness, is not free, as Mr. Jouffray claims. On the contrary, the Berber woman is very unhappy and more of a slave than many of her sisters." Al-Fayache pointed out that she was property owned by her male relatives and proved this by citing the current bride price, which included the *l'ammargeb* (a ritual animal sacrifice and an exchange of butter, sugar, and tea), the *reshwa* (a tip a fiancé paid to his future male in-laws), and the *hadiya* (a financial gift of 250 to 1,500 francs.) He explained that a Berber woman had no right of consent to marriage

---

31. It is highly likely that author's pseudonym, N. B., stood for Nadia Benjelloun, the wife of Abdelkader Benjelloun, a nationalist activist. I have thus far been unable to confirm this, but if it is the case, she was been the first Moroccan woman to write in the nationalist press.

32. N. B. "La femme berbère," *Maghreb*, May–June 1934, 43.

and no right to divorce under customary law. He claimed that in the past fifteen months he had heard of four suicides by Berber women trapped in unwanted marriages. He concluded: "The Qur'an is more humane, more logical, and less complex, and it clearly determines the legal rights and duties of a woman."[33]

The nationalists also attacked the gender logics of the protectorate education policy. As discussed in the previous section, educational reform became an increasingly important issue in the late 1930s and early 1940s. Many parents, and brothers who had been educated in the French system demanded their daughters and sisters be taught Arabic, French, science, math, and Islam in a *primaire* and *collège* system similar to what was available to boys. (Private free schools were also established for this purpose during this period.) The nationalists took a lead in these efforts, and during the 1940s a feminist discourse oriented toward Islam became a major component of the nationalist framing of Moroccan identity.

One of the earliest Moroccan women to speak out about women's education in Morocco was Nadia Benjelloun, the wife of a nationalist leader, Abd-el-Kader Benjelloun.[34] She penned an article in February 1933 in the Paris-based *Maghreb* under the pseudonym "Romeikya" about Gandhi's reform of the status of women in India.[35] The following September, she addressed the issue of education for Muslim women.[36] In that article she emphasized the importance of the question for Moroccan women: "But today, where a burning thirst for instruction has seized the young men, the Moroccan woman cannot remain indifferent to this serious question." Other Muslim states had set an example by linking national renaissance to the education of women, showing "that the rebirth of a people must proceed in tandem with the intellectual elevation of the woman." Morocco, in her view, did not need European-style schools where girls were prepared for exams but remained ignorant of their "natural role"; it needed schools that taught practical skills where they could learn "the rationalization, the simplification of household tasks, manual labor." Girls should be taught how to raise a child in terms of hygiene and moral education, and this required Arabic literacy and a bit of history and geography. "The primary

---

33. Othman al-Fayache, "La femme berbère: est-elle libre?" *L'Action du peuple*, October 27, 1933.

34. Halstead (1967, 226), who interviewed dozens of the early nationalist leaders, confirms that the wife of Abdelkader Benjelloun wrote the articles signed "Romeikya."

35. Romeikya, "Ghandi et la femme," *Maghreb*, February 1933, 17–19.

36. Romeikya, "L'Enseignement de la femme marocaine," *L'Action du Peuple*, September, 29, 1933, 1, 3.

role of the woman inside her house and her direct influence on the development of children are alone enough to prove the absolute necessity of giving her instruction."[37] Although she castigated the residency for its failures, the pedagogy Benjelloun envisioned was very similar to the colonial version described earlier. She just wanted more schools for Muslim girls and for more Arabic and Islam to be taught to future "mothers of the nation."

In November, another article in *Maghreb* on the "condition of the Moroccan woman" drew on *salafi*-influenced explanations for why Islam dictated that women be guaranteed rights and educational opportunities. It appealed to Islamic law, the example of the early Muslim community in the seventh century, and to the women's movement in Egypt and other Arab countries as models for how to improve the place of women in Moroccan society. According to the author, the Moroccan woman should not remain intellectually inferior to men because this contravened Islam:

> If Islam has given her rights, we, the men, have usurped them, reducing them to nothing. We have made a near slave out of she who Mohamed, the legislator, designed as free. A woman is not a minor as in the Napoleonic code, but we have taken away from her every freedom of speech and movement. She is at our mercy.[38]

The author complained that even well-raised Moroccan women were not taught how to read or write for fear that they would correspond with a lover. He noted that in the past, women were able to take walks outside the medina walls, but now they had to be veiled from head to foot when they visited the cemetery outside Bab Ftouh. The rest of the week they were prisoners in their homes. Rejecting these restrictions, the author argued, "The virtue of a woman does not depend on the thickness of her veils, but on her own honesty. Give a good education to our girls and let them go free; their self-esteem will guard them from any abasement."[39]

This public forum for debating gender questions was closed when the French shut down the nationalist press and exiled most of the leadership on the eve of World War II. These questions returned to prominence, however, in 1943–1944. When the Istiqlal Party was formed and the king actively entered the nationalist cause, legal status receded as an issue of importance,

37. Romeikya, "Instruisons la femme marocaine," *L'Action du Peuple*, October 13, 1933.
38. A. M., "Condition de la femme marocain," *Maghreb*, November 1933, 17–18.
39. Ibid.

but women's education moved to the forefront. Responding to widespread urban demand, the nationalists initiated their own program of girls' education in the late 1930s, accepting girls into the free schools.[40] Girls studied alongside boys and were initially able to attain a primary certificate. The number of girls involved in the free schools was very small, however; only fifty-two Moroccan girls achieved a primary school certificate in the period 1943–1953. Most girls were taken out at age twelve or thirteen because it was considered shameful for them to be seen in public after they reached puberty.[41] In response to critics, a May 1944 article by Mohamed El 'Arbi al-Zaggari in the Tetouan-based *Al Wahdat al-maghribiya* argued that Islam supported education for girls:

> The woman is the fundamental element in society. From his mother, the child integrates the essential principles of his education; the men, who together will form the nation to come will have received their first ideas from a woman. The cultural and moral development of Morocco and of its future generations rests on the education of the Moroccan woman. They must not be ignorant. They must be given a sound, useful, and virtuous education. Islam has never denied education to women. On the contrary, it has recognized the obligation to instruct girls, provided that this education is carried out in a pure religious framework.[42]

Here, Islam and a Moroccan nationalist version of "republican motherhood" (Kerber 1976) are blended in an appeal to extend girls education.

The most influential and articulate spokesperson for the religious injunction to educate Moroccan women and reform their legal status was Allal al-Fassi, a scholar who had trained at Al-Qarawiyin University in Fes who emerged as the principal ideologue for an Islamic reformist form of Moroccan nationalism. In the decade 1946–1956, al-Fassi was in self-exile after clashes with the king and the Istiqlal leadership. During this period, wrote extensively from Cairo and Tangier in the Moroccan press, including Istiqlal's *Al-'Alam* and the Tangier-based *Risalat al-maghrib*, and in the mainstream Arabic press published in Cairo. He also published two books in 1948 that argued the case for Moroccan independence. The first, directed

---

40. Mernissi (1994) describes her own transition into the nationalist schools in *Dreams of Trespass*.

41. By 1953, the number of girls who earned a primary certificate had only risen to 150, and only four had achieved a baccalaureate degree (Baker 1998, 48).

42. Mohamed al-'Arbi Al-Zaggari, *Wahda al maghribiyya*, May 14, 1944.

at the international diplomatic community, was a history of the nationalist movements in North Africa, *Al-Harakat al-istiqlaliya fi al-maghrib al-'arabi* (The Independence Movements in the Arab Maghreb; al-Fassi 1948), which made a case for the legitimacy of nationalist claims. The second, *Al-Naqd al-dhati* (Self-Criticism; al-Fassi [1952] 1966), addressed a Moroccan audience, systematically critiquing Moroccan society and outlining a vision for *islah*, or reform, as it evolved toward independence. One the key points of the latter book was the need to ameliorate the legal and educational condition of Moroccan women.[43]

Al-Fassi addressed the Woman Question in the book's last section, "Social Thought" in which he laid out a model for a healthy Moroccan society that affirmed the nuclear family (*'usra*) as the basic unit of the nation (*watan*). In this section, he paid significant attention to the "Moroccan woman" because of her central role in the family. Al-Fassi discussed the threat of prostitution, the protection shari'a afforded the family, and the reforms related to polygamy and divorce that needed to be implemented.

In chapter 6, "The Moroccan Woman between *Jahili* Tradition (*'urf*) and Legitimate Action (*al-'amal al-shar'i*)," al-Fassi explicitly addressed the proper place of the Moroccan woman in the nation by contrasting the "Berber woman" under customary law and the "Muslim woman" under Islamic law. He began with this declaration: "The woman is the pillar of the family, and any building whose pillar is not straight will fall down" (al-Fassi 1966, 209). He then built an argument about contemporary Moroccan society by first recounting how Islam transformed the position of Arab women in the seventh century. Women's status in pre-Islamic Arabic—signified by their treatment as chattel to be bought, sold, and inherited without any right of consent—was a primary sign of *jahiliya*, the "dark ages." Al-Fassi argued the same was true of present-day Morocco and lamented the persistence of *jahiliya* in "Berber" areas: "It is unfortunate that when we look at the present, among a portion of our own country, we find that these *jahili* customs are still followed, and women in what are called customary regions are not given the least amount of respect or honor" (210).

Al-Fassi acknowledged that customary law was historically allowed to continue in the framework of relations between the precolonial *makhzan*

---

43. Al-Fassi's sections on gender are a Moroccan corollary to Ṭahar al-Ḥaddad's ([1930] 2007) earlier work on the Tunisian "Muslim Woman."

and tribal groups but argued that those customs needed to be abolished: "No reform for the Moroccan family is possible without a reform of the condition of the woman. And no reform will come to our woman while Berber customary law continues to be imposed in our country" (al-Fassi 1966, 211). The solution for Morocco was the uniform application of a reinterpreted shari'a. Al-Fassi, who was trained as an 'alim (Islamic legal scholar), used hadith (collections of recorded sayings and deeds of the Prophet Mohammed) and fiqh (Islamic jurisprudence) to flesh out what this reinterpretation (ijtihad) entailed. He explained that Islam accorded both men and women the right to consent to marriage, and said that future spouses should be able to meet before being married. He also argued that the law should require a minimum age of fifteen for both boys and girls and that before a marriage took place, the state should require that both parties be tested for infectious diseases and terminal illnesses. In regards to head covering, al-Fassi pointed out that almost all of the four Muslim legal schools permitted women to expose their face, hands, and extremities. He explained that the underlying issue concerned the threat of fitna (literally connoting a temptation or test but also referring to discord or chaos in the community) but that there was debate over whether the responsibility should devolve to women or to men. He concluded by affirming that veiling was a matter of custom rather than a clear-cut issue dictated by shari'a.

A later chapter lauded the superiority of Islamic law because it gave women more rights than other systems. Women were guaranteed property and inheritance rights under shari'a. They also retained their own "personality" in marriage, keeping their own name rather than taking that of their husband. Al-Fassi pointed out that women had equal religious duties and were enjoined to pray in mosques, as men were. In this section, al-Fassi criticized how customary law had denigrated the position of women in Morocco. He contrasted it with a true application of shari'a and urged the women be granted full religious, social, and economic rights, including the right to education (1966, 299). Having critiqued the degenerate condition of the Moroccan woman under the "corrupt" customary system maintained by the colonizer, al-Fassi called for the state to take action: "1. Give woman the place she deserves in society and in the family. 2. Free her from the bonds of jahili customs that colonization has supported in what are called the regions of Berber custom" (334). For al-Fassi and other nationalists, the advancement of the Moroccan woman in an Islamic legal framework constituted an essential pillar of the Arabo-Islamic national order they envisioned after independence.

The King and the New Moroccan Woman

In 1943, Mohamed V began to take the lead in using the issue of women's advancement to define Moroccan identity and challenge the legitimizing logics of colonial intervention. That spring, the king called a meeting of the Council of Viziers to discuss the issue of girls' education, to which the alumni association presidents from the Fes, Rabat, and Marrakesh *collèges* were invited. By 1943, the total number enrolled in Franco-Muslim girls schools had increased to 6,619 from the 450 who were enrolled in 1922, but this still represented only a tiny fraction of the Muslim female population.[44] After a long discussion, the council resolved that girls' instruction should lead to the same primary certificate offered to boys and that Arabic instruction should be standardized. Arabic professors would be chosen by the *majlis al-'ilmi* at Al-Qarawiyin University for the Fes schools, by the ulama of the Ben Youssef mosque-university for Marrakesh, and by local *qa'ids* for other areas.[45]

A month later, the king announced the signing of a *dahir* about girls' education in his November Throne Speech. He explained that the primary education system for girls would have the same curriculum as boys, including instruction in "religious culture, including the concepts of *tawhid* (unity), *fiqh* (Islamic jurisprudence), and also Arabic grammar," and assured that he personally would supervise the selection of male Arabic teachers until female teachers were trained.[46] Girls would also receive necessary instruction about child care and housekeeping. That winter, Mohamed V sent Mohamed Belarbi Alaoui, a famous and well-respected Qarawiyin theologian, and his older daughter, Princess Lalla Aicha, on a speaking tour to promote girls' education. After the princess spoke at these meetings, Alaoui would deliver a religious defense, quoting from the Qur'an and the Hadith to emphasize the religious injunction to have daughters educated (Baker 1998, 51).

By 1945, there were 7,000 girl students in Morocco and 20,000 boys. The royal family, including Crown Prince Hassan and Princess Lalla Aicha, were regularly sent out to deliver speeches at ceremonies for school openings. On October 17, 1945, the king himself inaugurated the École des filles de

---

44. MAE-Nantes, Direction de l'Instruction Publique, Carton 85, "Le publication du dahir du 10 Octobre 1943."

45. MAE-Nantes, Direction de l'Instruction Publique, Carton 85, Director of Political Affairs, Guillaume, to the Director of Public Instruction, May 24, 1943. The residency was aware that this initiative signaled a larger push by the palace to exercise more direct control over education, using the sensitive issue of girls' education to gain leverage.

46. "Khutab al-'arsh," *Es-Sa'ada*, December 19, 1943.

notables marocaines in Rabat, the sister school of the Mawlay Youssef school for the sons of notables, which opened with 200 students. The curriculum included modern instruction leading to a primary certificate, including French and Arabic; training in embroidery and lace making; and moral and religious instruction. In November, the teaching school the king had promised, the École normale d'institutrices, was opened in Rabat to train Moroccan women teachers. A similar women's teacher training school was created in Tetouan in the Spanish zone in December.

Mohamed V set the example in the education he provided his own daughter, Lalla Aicha, who was taught in the palace with a group of other girls. One of her classmates related that the school day began with prayer and the reading of the Qur'an at six, followed by bilingual instruction in Arabic and French. The girls were also taught some English and Latin.[47] In 1943, this group constituted the first cohort of Moroccan girls to receive a primary certificate of studies. In the years after the war, Lalla Aicha emerged as a high-profile advocate for women's education in Morocco, articulating an Islamic modernist justification for teaching women Arabic, Islam, and modern subjects in order to strengthen the Moroccan nation.

In April 1947, she accompanied her father and brother on the historic trip to Tangier. The day after her father's controversial speech, the seventeen-year-old also delivered a speech in Arabic, French, and English. Lalla Aicha reaffirmed Morocco's ties to the Arab east and the importance of Islam and urged the "liberation of the Moroccan woman" in the framework of Arabo-Islamic nationalism. Her speech also contained the first open allusion to Morocco's "independence" by any representative of the palace. In a deliberate symbolic gesture orchestrated by Mohamed V, the princess was not veiled when she delivered this pro-nationalist and pro–women's emancipation speech.[48] Thousands of women from Tangier, Tetouan, and other northern cities attended the speech, which was also broadcast over the radio and reprinted in all of the Moroccan newspapers.[49]

---

47. Baker's interview with Aicha Terrab, who studied with the princess in the palace (Baker 1998, 51).

48. In its issue for April 11, 1957, the Istiqlal Arabic daily *Al-'Alam* ran a picture of the princess, whom they labeled *za'ima al-nahda*, "Leader of the Renaissance," wearing a formal Western gown. The full text of the speech was printed under the picture.

49. *Time* magazine published an image of Lalla Aicha (without a veil) on the cover of its issue of November 11, 1957. The issue featured a lengthy article on the recent progress of Muslim women. In March 1965, Lalla Aicha was sent by her brother, King Hassan II, to Great Britain as the first Moroccan woman ambassador.

Moroccan Women, Agency, and Identification Processes

Moroccan women were not just the objects of state- and society-based identification struggles in the colonial political field. They also actively contributed to discursive struggles over collective identity, engaged in practices and activities that expanded their presence in the political sphere, and directly and indirectly accommodated and resisted aspects of colonial rule. While colonial and nationalist actors referred to a reified "Moroccan woman," in reality, Moroccan women occupied myriad social and economic positions in various urban and rural contexts during the protectorate. Colonial intervention impacted their lives at different times and in different ways.

In the middle and central High Atlas, Berber-speaking (illiterate) female poets were among the most publicly vocal Moroccan women during the early protectorate period. From 1907 through the early 1930s, Berber women engaged in intense intertribal and intratribal classification struggles about collective identity that hinged on the viability of a military defense, or jihad, of the Moroccan Muslim community (*umma*). As was related in chapter 3, they composed songs, sometimes in intense poetic duels, that expressed a range of opinions, from urging continued military resistance to castigating fellow tribesmen and women for submitting to the foreign "Christian" invader to countering that continuing jihad was senseless to lamenting the collective tragedy of falling under *rumi*, or Christian, rule. Gender and sexuality were often interwoven with political commentary in these public speech acts by Moroccan Berber women.

Tawgrat Walt Aissa N'Ayt Sokhman was one of the women who publicly participated in a gendered classification struggles connected to impact of the violent expansion of the colonial political field into the mountains. Tawgrat, a blind female poet of the Ait Sokhman tribe, composed resistance poetry in the 1920s and 1930s that incited women in the central High Atlas to resist the "Christian invader." In one poem, she chastised the men of the tribe for giving up:

You, Moha Urriban,
You surely stained the tribe when you escaped like a rabbit
In front of the dogs.
Keep your smithy and shut up.
You are qualified only to touch coal.
How could one be a Muslim
If you visit the unfaithful's [French indigenous affairs officer] office?
Look up Itto, Thuda, and Izza; call women to carry the flag

To war, since many Berber men have [no heart, no nerve]![50]
Young men, attack,
Attack the unfaithful!
Advance forward!
Because he who dies in Jihad,
Has a shelter in paradise,
And to his relatives
He will leave honor and glory.
Shame on you; you have no manhood,
For you love to be the slaves of the unfaithful.

(*Sadiqi 2009, 124*)

Individual poems such as this one that happened to be transcribed are a small fraction of the oral production of that period. They hint, though, at a much larger women's voice in rural and social contexts that has been historiographically marginalized due to its orality (Sadiqi 2003, 2013). Surviving texts clearly indicate that women were actively involved in the contested identification processes catalyzed in the colonial political field. As is clear in Tawgrat's poem, the external boundary between the "Christian" invading Other and the Muslim community was being negotiated ("How could one be a Muslim if you visit the unfaithful's office?"), as were internal struggles in the tribe about continuing jihad or submitting to the colonial state. Gender roles were at the center of these contentious debates, which featured threats about the masculinity of the tribe's male members and injunctions to the women to "carry the flag to war" themselves.

This last exhortation was more than just a rhetorical proposition. During the pacification, French officers cited the frequent participation of Berber women in battles. They cheered on their warriors with *you-yous* (ululations), sang poetic encouragements or threats and verbal abuse at signs of cowardice, and threw rocks or rolled boulders down on enemy troops.[51] In the 1930s, women participated in the Latif demonstrations and subsequent anti-colonial protests in Moroccan cities. Women also actively mobilized about gender-specific issues, including protectorate restrictions on their mobility or dress. For example, the residency faced intense outrage in 1937 against a proposal that would have forbidden women to go out into the city unaccompanied

---

50. In personal correspondence (June 13, 2013), Fatima Sadiqi clarified the Tamazight phrase she translates as "become inert" in the *Women Writing Africa* volume.

51. See Biarnay's notes on how Rif women participated in battle, encouraging bravery and castigating cowardice. Biarnay, "Notes sur les chants populaires du Rif," *Comité d'études berbères de Rabat* 1987 (1915): 29–30.

by a man. Other decrees that attempted to regulate the type of dress worn by Muslim women sparked vocal protests in the medinas in the late 1930s.[52]

An urban women's movement gained momentum in tandem with the mobilization of the nationalist movement in the 1930s–1940s. A very small literate women's elite engaged gender debates in the nationalist press, as was related in the previous section, contributing articles on women's legal rights and education. One of these women, Malika al-Fassi, emerged in the 1940s as a prominent nationalist spokeswoman. She was from one of the most esteemed families in Fes, a cousin of the nationalist leader Allal al-Fassi, and the wife of Mohamed al-Fassi (tutor of the crown prince, president of Al-Qarawiyin University, and future minister of education). Malika al-Fassi was educated at home in the 1920s and became politically engaged during the mobilization of the nationalist movement after the 1930 Berber *dahir*. In 1935, she was among the first Moroccan women to publish in the nationalist press, writing an article in the Arabic-language newspaper *Al Maghrib* titled, "About Girls' Education" (Baker 1998, 64). Like the examples cited above, the article justified Moroccan girls' education because women were the first teachers of the next generation: "These youth will become the women of tomorrow, the leaders who will run the country." Here al-Fassi supported a complementary understanding of gender roles rather than total equality, but she demanded (quite boldly for that time) that girls should be able to have a high school education. In response to critical letters to the editor, she asked: "How can an educated [Moroccan] youth accept a wife and be comfortable with her, and give her the reins in socializing their children, when he has dealt with knowledge and formulated ideas, and gained enough learning to make him despise an ignorant woman?" (66). In 1943, Malika al-Fassi was the sole woman signer of the Manifesto of Independence written by the newly formed Istiqlal Party.

The first Moroccan women's political associations began to be formed in the mid-1940s.[53] In 1946, Istiqlal formally recognized a women's association in the party; Malika al-Fassi was its first president. The Akhawat al-safa (Sisters of Purity) was also created shortly thereafter as a women's association

---

52. French intelligence reports note women's protests in the medina in response to regulations banning the wearing of the *jalaba* (the traditional male Moroccan outer garment that nationalist women wore) instead of the *haik* (the cumbersome and voluminous wrap traditionally worn outside of the house) and in decrees dictating what kind of shoes women could wear or not wear (Decroux 1947, 11, quoted in Baker 1998, 321).

53. The Communist Party formed one of the first women's associations in the protectorate, the Moroccan Women's Union, in 1944, although the union was composed mainly of Jewish and French women and was not affiliated with the Moroccan nationalist movement.

for the rival Parti démocratique de l'indépendance, which held its first congress in Fes in May 1947. Both organizations prioritized literacy campaigns and worked to increase access to higher education. Both also aimed to get women directly involved in the independence struggle.[54] While the women's movement in the 1940s was dominated by elites who were fortunate enough to have access to education at home or in the free schools, these early women's associations intentionally aimed to cross class barriers and create solidarity among Moroccan women of all backgrounds, although primarily only in urban areas. Meetings were organized in homes of the wives of the prominent nationalist leaders. One woman who participated, Ftoma Skalli, recollects the cross-class interaction at the home of Hajja Mekouar, the wife of Ahmed Mekouar, in Fes in the 1940s: "At our gatherings, we would have very rich women, and we would seat them next to poor women. And we used to tell them that if they didn't like it they'd better not show up the next time" (Baker 1998, 56).

In Mernissi's memoir (1994) of her childhood in the Fes medina in the 1940s, women pushed spatial and social boundaries by attending cinemas, sending daughters to nationalist schools, and wearing the *jalaba* (traditionally a male garment) as a sign of nationalist solidarity. Women also directly participated in the anti-French demonstrations in response to the arrests of Istiqlal leaders in January 1944. According to Mohamed Tazi, a Fassi nationalist, when the French occupied the Fes medina in early February, women went out en masse to the rooftops to ululate. Some also took basalt rocks that were used to hold down drying laundry and dropped them on soldiers in the streets below (Baker 1998, 25). After colonial troops attacked demonstrators, women took in the wounded and helped distribute food during the blockade of the medina. Women also were active in organizing the anti-Jewish boycott in response to the 1947 UN partition plan and the 1948 Arab-Israeli war that followed and gathered collections to aid families of arrested nationalists and for the Arab cause in Palestine.

By the early 1950s, women's political activism had moved beyond the urban bourgeoisie. Working-class women were actively involved in the Moroccan labor movement and participated in union demonstrations and strikes in the major coastal cities. In August 1952, the textile workers in Rabat, more than half of whom were women, went on strike for a month. The general strike Istiqlal declared in December was also widely supported by women working

---

54. On the formation of the early women's organizations and their affiliation with nationalist parties, see Daoud (1993).

in the labor force. When Mohamed V was exiled on August 20, 1953, women entered a new phase of active struggle. The royal family's exile provoked an outpouring of emotion across many levels of the Moroccan female population, many of whom claimed to see the king's face in the moon.[55] Beyond an intensification of emotional attachment to the Commander of the Faithful, Moroccan women joined the armed nationalist resistance that broke out over the next two years, exploiting French gender stereotypes about indigenous "Moroccan woman" to aid the struggle. Although women were largely ignored in the official post-independence nationalist histories, novelists such as Driss Chraibi (1972) and Leila Abouzeid (1989) were among the first to depict Moroccan women's agency during the independence struggle. In these depictions, which are based on the biographies of the authors' mothers, women carry weapons, grenades, and messages; organize literacy groups; and participate in street protests.[56]

As was the case in other anti-colonial nationalist movements in the Middle East and North Africa, gender was a primary site for making the nation, for both drawing the boundaries of ethnoreligious identity and indexing a Moroccan reformist Islamic modernity (Badran 1995; Abu-Lughod 1998; Baron 2005; El Shakry 2007). For Moroccan nationalists, including elite nationalist women, the goal of emancipating the "Moroccan woman" was subsidiary to emancipating the nation. Defining and improving Moroccan women's status was oriented toward making them better guardians of Moroccan identity and Moroccan social values in the family. Many Moroccan women hoped the sacrifices they made while participating in the nationalist struggle would lead to and expansion of their rights, but this generation's hopes were dashed by post-independence compromises. After independence, the "Moroccan woman" was granted greatly expanded access to education, including entry into the university system. But women's legal status was restrictively defined by a conservative interpretation of Islamic law enshrined in the 1957 Mudawana, or personal status code, the Moroccan state adopted.

This chapter used gender as a lens through which to examine the politicized identification processes at work in the colonial political field. The

---

55. Mernissi (1988, 56) writes, "In Morocco that summer of 1953, the news spread throughout the country, from the north to the south to rise up. The exiled King, symbol of dignity, of renewal, of the rebirth, appeared in the moon. He is present, he is with us, the poor. One would prevent this dream of liberation? We put it there where we could: in the moon. Look—*Mohamad al khamis fel qamar.*"

56. Also see Baker's (1998) excellent oral history of Moroccan women who were involved in the nationalist movement and the Resistance and Kozma's (2003) chapter on the historiography of women's contributions to the nationalist movement.

"Moroccan woman" was a central concern in classification struggles among French administrators, male and female nationalists, and the palace. French colonial policy defined ethnic difference through separate legal classifications based on ethnicity and religion. These legal frameworks were largely differentiated by the different rights and statuses afforded to Arab, Berber, and Jewish women. As in other colonial frameworks in North Africa and the Middle East (Thompson 2000; Abugideiri 2010), the protectorate administration pursued paternalistic policies intended to reproduce a "traditional" Moroccan social order in terms of class, ethnicity, and gender. The goal of educational institutions developed for Moroccan Muslim girls was to train them to fulfill fixed roles as handicraft producers and as mistresses of their households.

The nationalist movement and later the king directly contested these gendered legal and educational policies in their calls for reform. Instead of ethnic plurality, they supported a unitary Arabo-Islamic framing of Moroccan identity, a constituent element of which was defining women's legal status solely by Islamic law (reinterpreted for modern times) rather than "Berber" customary law, although a telling exception was made for the civil status of Jews. Nationalists prioritized women's education and literacy because they wanted Moroccan mothers to reproduce a "modern" Moroccan social order in the next generation. Gendered legal differentiation was also fundamental, however, because of the importance of the implementation of shariʿa (primarily in the realm of personal status laws) for the Islamic aspects of this configuration of national identity. Before or after independence, the implicit logic of marking Arabo-Islamic Moroccan national identity by delegating separate and unequal legal rights based on gender was never challenged. In 1957, despite its progressive stance on girls' education, the monarchy supported the codification of a very conservative family code (the Mudawana), in stark contrast to the radical version President Bourguiba instituted the same year in Tunisia. As Charrad (2001) has demonstrated, this move aligned the monarchy with the patriarchal interests of the rural tribal elites it needed to shore up its power. This chapter has shown how this move flowed directly out of the gendered politics of identity that developed in the colonial political field.

Although Moroccan women were the objects of colonial and nationalist identification struggles, in rural and urban contexts and across class and ethnoreligious boundaries, they actively voiced diverse concerns and priorities. In violent struggles against the expansion of the colonial political field (1907–1934), rural Berber women poets were not concerned with women's rights per se but with the integrity of the Muslim community. Gendered roles were assumed in discourses about collective identity, and fidelity/infidelity and bravery/impotence represented different responses to colonial military conquest and statuses vis-à-vis the colonial state. In the urban nationalist classification struggles described above, some urban elite women concurred with the dominant Arabo-Islamic pillars of Moroccan identity and urged educational rather than legal parity, believing in a complementary role for women as mothers in the strengthening of the nation. Women were later involved in labor activism and eventually in armed struggle after the king was exiled in 1953. The legacies of how gender was politicized during the protectorate, how women were both objects and agents of identification processes, have continued into the post-protectorate Moroccan political field. Most recently, this has been obvious in struggles among women's groups, Islamist actors, and the monarchy over the 2004 reforms of the Mudawana (Salime 2011; Guessous 2011).

❧ CHAPTER 8

The Sultan-cum-King and the Field's Symbolic Forces

The idea of "protectorate intervention" provided the foundational conceit that was embedded in the 1912 Treaty of Fes, symbolically legitimating the creation of a colonial political field in Morocco. The French and the Spanish pledged to "protect" the Moroccan sovereign, the Alawid sultan, by assisting him through state building (internal military pacification, infrastructural development, and administrative modernization) and economic development. Earlier chapters have probed how this protectorate imaginary was implemented under Lyautey and subsequent resident generals and have analyzed interactions among colonial and local Moroccan actors in the colonial political field. The concluding chapters turn to a final key player, the Alawid monarch, Mohamed ben Youssef, who was both an object of and key actor in identity struggles related to the legitimizing logics of the protectorate.

This chapter explores the evolution of Sidi Mohamed ben Youssef from a colonial figurehead whom the French chose to be a pliable *dahir*-stamping sovereign in the 1920s to an anti-colonial religio-political nationalist hero, the Commander of the Faithful (Amir al-mu'iminin), who embodied Moroccan aspirations for sovereignty and independence. The return of the king, figuratively in his active engagement in the nationalist cause from the 1940s and literally in his return in November 1955 from two years of exile, profoundly shaped the post-protectorate political field in Morocco. During the last two decades of the protectorate, Mohamed V deftly exploited his structural position in the formal logics of the colonial field, consolidating substantial symbolic power that enabled the monarchy to significantly influence how Moroccan national identity was defined during the anti-colonial nationalist struggle and after independence.

In tracing Mohamed V's evolution from sultan to king, these chapters emphasize the historical contingency of the monarchy's surviving colonization and decolonization. The Alawid dynasty's endurance is a remarkable exception; most ancien régime royal families that were in place prior to colonization or were installed by European control in North Africa and the Middle East did not survive anti-colonial independence struggles or revolutionary upheavals. (The Hashemites in Jordan are the other exception.) How did Mohamed V and his successors consolidate dynastic power while most other ruling monarchs in postcolonial states fell to officer-led coups (Egypt, Iraq, Libya) or to charismatic nationalist party leaders (Tunisia)? The following chapters demonstrate how the postcolonial Moroccan exception was an outcome that was produced by a historical sequence that involved the organizing forces of the colonial political field in Morocco, multiple contingencies, and the individual agency of Mohamed V.

From Sultan to King

Mohamed ben Youssef was born in Fes on August 10, 1909.[1] Three years later, on March 30, 1912, his uncle, Mawlay 'Abd al-Hafiz, was forced to sign the Treaty of Fes. At this initial critical juncture, the French decided to preserve the Alawid monarchy within the protectorate framework instead of obliterating local elites, as they had done in Algeria. When Mawlay 'Abd al-Hafiz abdicated on August 13, 1912, Lyautey chose Mawlay Youssef, Mohamed's father, as successor. He was proclaimed sultan several days later after the obligatory *bay'a*, or oath of allegiance, of the Fassi ulama. Mawlay Youssef's youngest son, Mohamed, was raised in the royal palace in Meknes with almost no contact with the outside world other than with his Algerian tutor, Si Mammeri, who taught him Arabic and French. One of the few breaks in this isolation occurred in 1926 when he joined his father on

---

1. Due to political sensitivities about the royal family, almost no official Moroccan archives about Mawlay Youssef, Mohamed V, Hassan II, or Mohamed VI are open to the public. Not surprisingly, a critical biography of Mohamed V has yet to be written. The following biographical details are drawn from works by authors with personal access to the king, including Charles-André Julien (1977), Rom Landau (1957), and the king's son, Hassan II (1978). This chapter also relies on official French archival records pertaining to the monarchy that have recently been declassified.

a state visit to France to dedicate the newly built Paris Mosque and the Islamic institute.[2] When Mawlay Youssef died unexpectedly on November 17, 1927, Mohamed ben Youssef (Mohamed V) was put forward by the resident general, Theodor Steeg. The next day, the Fassi ulama acclaimed him as sultan. He was eighteen at the time he ascended the throne, and the residency continued to restrict the young monarch to the confines of the royal palaces. State affairs were mediated to him through the experienced *makhzan* hand, the grand vizier, Mohamed el-Mokri, who was in his sixties.[3]

The Berber Crisis and the Sultan's Relationship to Nationalist Movement in the 1930s

One of the decrees that passed through the Grand Vizier to be affixed by the sultan's royal seal was the May 16, 1930, *dahir* reorganizing the customary legal system in designated "Berber" areas. The urban protests that ensued that summer precipitated the initial contact between Mohamed V and the nascent nationalist movement leadership. In September, he received the Fes delegation that presented a list of grievances related to French Berber policy. After the meeting, Mohamed V reportedly told Allal al-Fassi that he had been misled and promised "I will no longer cede a single right of our country" (Julien 1977, 214). Despite the uproar and the sultan's apparent sympathy, the customary system remained in place, with small modifications, until the end of the protectorate. Mohamed V abolished it in one of his first acts after independence.[4]

For much of the 1930s, the sultan remained sequestered from the general Moroccan population. But, as discussed in chapter 5, the Throne Day celebration the nationalists invented in 1933 began to raise Mohamed V's public profile as a mobilizing symbol. Urban nationalists also exploited the sultan's travels to various cities as an opportunity to affirm national unity, organizing large crowds to wave Moroccan flags and chant slogans to greet him. Although Mohamed V, like the nationalists, did not broach

---

2. Memories of this trip were the reason for Mawlay Ben Youssef's insistence that the young prince Hassan accompany him on his official visit to Paris in 1931 for the International Colonial Exposition (see chapter 2).

3. El-Mokri, born around 1860, served as grand vizier for the entire length of the 44-year protectorate. He died shortly after independence, in 1957 (Vermeren 2002, 210).

4. In the fall of 1930, an exception was made for tribes that chose to place themselves under Islamic law. The transfer of criminal cases to French courts, the decree's most controversial aspect, was amended in 1934 and the *makhzan*-appointed *qadis* regained their jurisdiction.

the subject of Moroccan independence before World War II, he adamantly resisted French policies that shifted the formal terms of the protectorate during the interwar years. In 1934, he vigorously protested a French proposal to move the administration of Morocco from the Ministry of Foreign Affairs to the Ministry of Overseas France. The sultan and urban nationalists interpreted this as a step toward annexing Morocco, as had been done with the three Algerian *départements* in 1848.[5] Despite his sympathy with the nationalists' reform program, the sultan did not openly ally with them in the 1930s because of concerns about provoking the French. He maintained secret contacts with the leadership, but Mohamed ben Youssef publicly remained a stolid ally of the French and enjoyed a close personal friendship with Resident General Noguès. This support was evident in 1939, when Mohamed V went on air to pledge Morocco's support for the French protector in the war, saying, "We Moroccans must all support the common cause. We must not refuse France either our human or our material resources."[6]

Toward *Istiqlal*: World War II, the Anfa Conference, and the Manifesto of Independence

World War II was an exogenous shock that radically reshaped the colonial political fields in North Africa. Although Mohamed V averred his own loyalty and that of his country to their "protector" after France declared war on Germany in the fall 1939, the fall of France the next spring and the transition to Vichy rule substantially altered his relations with the residency. Even before the landing of Allied troops in November 1942, Mohamed V began to chart a more independent course, albeit subtly, in the first years of the war. Worried about Axis propaganda and the intrusion of the German Armistice Commission, Vichy administrators relied even more on the

---

5. Ouezzani wrote in support of the sultan's vociferous opposition to the proposal: "Being, despite the protectorate regime, an autonomous and foreign country in regards to France, our country has the absolute right to suspect this type of 'reform' and to repel anything that might imperil its destiny. It does not intend to improve this destiny in a manner that profits another country or colony and wants to guarantee the character of its status by its dependence on the Ministry of Foreign Affairs." Mohamed Ouezzani, "A propos du Ministère de la France d'Outre Mer: Protectorat et Colonie," *Maghreb*, April 1934, 10.

6. Hassan (1978, 27). The complete text is available online at Feu sa majesté le roi Mohammed V (http://www.mohammed5.ma/), a commemorative website the Moroccan government created for the fiftieth anniversary of the "Revolution of the King and the People," that includes photos, news clips, audio, and transcripts of Mohamed V's speeches.

Moroccan sultan's legitimization of their rule and encouraged him to make several well-publicized trips across the French zone in 1941–1942 to bolster his image and their own.[7]

During this period, Mohamed V began to subtly reassert his prerogatives as the Moroccan sovereign. The area in which the sultan began to assert autonomy the most in the early 1940s was educational policy. The previous chapter examined how Mohamed V pressured the residency to provide higher levels of education to Muslim girls and ensure a more uniform curriculum. This proactive stance bore fruit, and the Directorate of Public Instruction put the recommended reforms into effect on October 10, 1943. Two years later, an expanded teacher training school was opened to help provide more Moroccan teachers, particularly female teachers of Arabic, for schools for Muslim children.

Less publicly, the sultan also took an interest in the modest but politically contentious Berber educational system that began in the 1920s with the opening of Franco-Berber elementary schools and the Azrou College for sons of Berber notables. On December 24, 1942, while in the resort town of Ifrane in the Middle Atlas, Mohamed V drove fifteen kilometers southwest to make an incognito visit to the Azrou College. At the school, he asked about Arabic instruction and whether the professor was French or Muslim. He also inquired about Islamic instruction and when and where prayers were performed. Afterwards French administrators worried about the sultan's intervention, remarking in reports that he could make "the particular instruction given in Berber country disappear and achieve the political and spiritual unity of the country."[8]

Mohamed V's frequent visits to his vacation home in Ifrane (a hill station in the middle of the designated region of Berber customary law) also disturbed officials in the Directorate of Political Affairs, who worried about protecting the Middle Atlas "Berber bloc" from the sultan's influence. These fears were exacerbated by plans to build a resort facility for Moroccan functionaries in the Ifrane city center. In the early 1940s, the city became a more frequent destination for Moroccan residents of Rabat and Fes, many of whom were active in the nationalist movement, making it a key node for networking

---

7. MAE, CADN-Mar., Direction de l'Intérieur, Carton 892, "Le Nationalisme sultanien," May 1945. These modern iterations of the *mahalla*, a convoy of vehicles that passed through the countryside and made periodic stops for ceremonies, became a potent means of projecting the monarchy's symbolic power. In 1941, the sultan visited the Tafilelt region, where he visited the tombs of Alawid ancestors. The next year he visited Marrakesh, Fes, and Oujda in well-publicized trips.

8. MAE, CADN-Mar., Direction de l'instruction publique, Carton 30, report by Lucien Paye, Head of Service of Muslim Education, "Note relative au college d'Azrou à la politique scolaire en pays berbère," January 23, 1943.

(Benhlal 2005, 368–69). French officials worried that the proximity of the sultan and these government officials would "make it difficult, in the near future, to guard the strictly Berber character originally given to the Azrou College."[9] These fears had some basis; Mohamed V used Ifrane as a base from which to build connections with surrounding Middle Atlas Berber chiefs, who were becoming more oriented toward Rabat. He also used the annual *hadiya* ceremonies at the palace, a ritual Lyautey reinforced in the first years of the protectorate, to build stronger ties with rural notables when they came to present tribute.[10] In the early 1940s, French officials became increasingly concerned about the viability of their Berber policy when many chiefs refused to send their children to the Franco-Berber schools. Instead, they preferred the Arabic schools in the major cities or pressured local Berber schools (in Sefrou, El Hajeb, Khemisset) to offer more Arabic and Islamic instruction.[11]

Throughout 1942, Mohamed V was also meeting secretly with nationalist leaders who had not been exiled or who had been able to reenter the country, including Ahmed Balafrej, Omar Ben Abdeljalil, Mohamed Lyazidi, Mohamed Ghazi, and Mohamed El Fassi.[12] The meetings occurred late at night in a garage or another outbuilding of the royal palace in order to avoid detection by the protectorate authorities.[13] The new objective of independence replaced the previous goal of reform in these discussions, although in the midst of the world war it was unclear how soon this could be achieved.

The Allied landings on Morocco's Atlantic coast in November 1942 reconfigured the balance of power between the sultan and the French, creating room for him to maneuver. The night of the landings he refused to withdraw inland to Fes, despite the urgings of his personal friend, Resident General Noguès. This independent course was reinforced at the 1943 Casablanca

---

9. Ibid.

10. MAE, CADN-Mar., Direction de l'Intérieur, Carton 892, "Le Nationalisme sultanien," May 1945. This report notes that the 'Aid al-mulud (celebrating the birth of the Prophet Mohamed) that was presented the sultan was "an excellent occasion to maintain the real foundations of the Empire when the *pashas* and *qa'ids* of all of the tribes gathered and were subjected to his policy of charm and attraction."

11. MAE, CADN-Mar., Direction de l'Instruction Publique, Carton 30, report by G. Germain, director of Berber College in Azrou, July 1943. Germain, who had conducted a tour of centers in the Middle Atlas (including Khenifra, Mawlay-Bouazza, Oulmès, el-Hammam, Itzer, Boumia, Tounfite, Enjil, Boulemane, Ahermoumou, Tahala, Ain Sbitt, Immouzer Kandar) to recruit new students, reported that "altogether, our tour confirmed the impression that it is difficult to get the notables to send their sons to the College, although many of the Bureaux have tried."

12. Delanoë (1988, 183) includes an appendix containing a memoire from Mohamed Bouabid, a native of Salé who was among the fifty-six signers of the Manifesto of Independence in 1944. Bouabid recounts the process leading up to the issuance of the manifest, its reception, and the reprisals and unrest that followed.

13. Abdelkrim Ghallab, personal communication, October 27, 2005, Rabat.

conference, which was held at the Anfa Hotel in January, at which Churchill, Roosevelt, and Allied military commanders (including the French leaders Giraud and de Gaulle) met to plan the North Africa military campaign. One night, after the resident general and other French officials had left the dinner party, Roosevelt and Mohamed V were left alone with a smaller group, including Churchill, Crown Prince Hassan, and an American advisor, Robert Murphy. During the conversation, Roosevelt reportedly spoke at length with the Moroccan sultan, telling him that he foresaw that Morocco would gain independence after the war and promising American diplomatic support and economic aid.[14] These personal assurances were allegedly reiterated in two letters Roosevelt sent to Mohamed V afterward (Landau 1957, 39). Whatever the specifics of the American pledges (they became a dead letter after Roosevelt's death in April 1945 and as American priorities shifted with the onset of the Cold War), this private conversation constituted the first face-to-face meeting between the sultan and a foreign head of state without the presence of a residency official. Roosevelt's warm support undoubtedly emboldened Mohamed V to reassert his prerogatives.[15]

In the fall of 1943, Mohamed V encouraged the formation of the Istiqlal Party and the drafting of the Manifesto of Independence. This was done in spite of the intransigence with which the Free French leadership had responded to other aspirations for autonomy in North Africa. In Tunisia, Mohamed El Moncef began demanding reforms from his French overlords soon after he became bey on June 19, 1942. After the Allied invasion in Morocco and Algeria in November, the Germans airlifted troops to Tunisia in order to maintain a foothold in North Africa. After the Allies occupied Tunisia in May 1943, the French leadership, including Giraud and Juin, deposed Moncef Bey and exiled him to southern France. Although ostensibly this was because he had collaborated with the Germans, the real reason for the deposition was that Moncef Bey had challenged the resident general in Tunisia by forming a national government and trying to end direct French administration.

Despite the cautionary example of Tunisia, Mohamed V urged nationalist ideologues to draft a Manifest of Independence calling for the installation of a constitutional monarchy, a national assembly elected through universal

---

14. No official transcripts were recorded of this conversation. While the United States did not give a formal pledge, according to all reports, Roosevelt personally supported Morocco's cause. King Hassan II's (1978, 31) firsthand recollection is at least as reliable as other accounts.

15. Hassan II (1978, 30) reports the effect of the meeting: "It was after the Anfa interview, and as a result of the promises that were made there to him, that my father led the Moroccan people resolutely on the road to independence."

suffrage, and local and regional assemblies (though many of these phrases were removed due to resistance from threatened *qa'ids* and pashas). The final draft called for Moroccan independence within the framework of the Atlantic Charter and intentionally did not mention France as the protectorate power. The goal was to internationalize the Moroccan question by appealing equally to the United States, Britain, France, and the Soviet Union. Reportedly, the sultan himself coordinated the delivery of the manifesto to the Allied authorities, which was done on January 11, 1944. The French reacted harshly, forcing the sultan to fire two pro-Istiqlal ministers and arresting two nationalist leaders in Rabat. These actions sparked widespread urban protests in early February 1944 that were brutally suppressed by colonial troops. The Anglo-American occupying forces made little effort to restrain the residency's crackdown, prioritizing stability over support for independence movements in Morocco or elsewhere in the French empire.[16]

At the end of the war, Charles de Gaulle invited Mohamed V to Paris to participate in the celebrations, awarding him the Cross of Liberation on June 18, 1945. De Gaulle later reported that in conversations during the visit, the sultan informed him that

> the protectorate is accepted by me as a transitory stage between the Morocco of the past and a free and modern state. After the events of yesterday, before those of tomorrow, I believe that the moment has arrived to reach another stage towards this goal. That is what my people are waiting for. (De Gaulle 1954, 127)

De Gaulle responded by affirming that France also had the goal of moving Morocco forward, which was the fundamental principle embedded in the Treaty of Fes, but stressed that this process would take time. Before Mohamed V left Paris, de Gaulle made sure to reaffirm France's prerogatives, asking the sultan: "When, at Anfa, President Roosevelt put the sparkling marvel of immediate independence in front of your Majesty, what did he propose to you, outside of his dollars and a place in his clientele?" (ibid.) Aware that the United States was not going to intervene to break up France's African empire, Mohamed V agreed, for the moment, that Morocco's progress had

---

16. As a colonial power, the British were also not inclined to validate nationalist aspirations. They did intervene, though, in Lebanon and Syria, where the demise of French imperial aspirations directly benefited their own interests.

to be accomplished within the framework of French aid (Delanoë 1998, 97–98).

In March 1946, de Gaulle appointed a much more liberal, reform-oriented resident general. Eirik Labonne, who had formerly served in Morocco under Lucien Saint, initiated a three-year plan to develop industries, expand education, and modernize the judicial system. These efforts to improve conditions for the Moroccan population generated intense resistance from *colon* population (which numbered 325,000 in the 1947 census[17]), however, and Labonne had to back off from much of his agenda. Mohamed V approached the resident general that fall to propose that he visit the Tangier zone, which had been returned to international control in September 1945 after being occupied by Spanish forces since June 1940. Although Labonne initially postponed approval, he eventually agreed that the trip could be scheduled for April 1947.

The Tangier Trip and Speech

The Tangier trip was a symbolic watershed. In 1912, Morocco's precolonial territorial space had been parceled into numerous zones (Tangier, the Spanish northern zone, the French zone, and Spain's southern holdings in Sidi Ifni, Rio de Oro, and Seguia el-Hamra). A passport was needed to travel between them during the protectorate. By traveling to Tangier, Mohamed V, the first sultan to visit the city since Mawlay Hassan in 1889, sent an overt political message that reasserted the Alawid claims to all of the subdivided territorial units that constituted the colonial political field in Morocco. Toward this end, after leaving Rabat by train on April 8, the royal cortege deliberately stopped for a ceremony in Asilah, where the sultan met the *khalifa* of the Spanish zone and spoke to a jubilant audience before continuing to Tangier.

The next day he delivered a speech in the Mendoubia Garden[18] in the center of the Tangier medina. The speech was significant not only for what the sultan said but also for what he left out. Mohamed V first stressed Morocco's strong attachment to the Arab Middle East:

> Morocco earnestly desires to acquire its full rights. It goes without saying that Morocco is a country attached by the strongest ties to the Arab countries of the East, naturally desiring that these ties grow stronger

---

17. In the 1947 census, there were 266,133 French and 58,864 other foreign nationalities residing in the French protectorate zone (Gouvernement Chérifien, Service Central des Statistiques, 1947, 13).

18. The garden surrounded the offices and residence of the *mandub*, the sultan's delegated representative in the Tangier international zone.

and stronger, since the Arab League has become an important organization that plays a great role in world politics. The Arab countries form a single nation; whether in Tangier or Damascus, this is but one nation.[19]

For the French, this open alliance with the Arab League and solidarity with the Arab nationalism emanating from the Middle East (where they had just lost their position after the postwar decolonization of Lebanon and Syria in 1945) was only the first disturbing signal. Equally offensive was the warm support Mohamed V extended to the United States, coupled with a thundering silence about the French "protector." Following the statement above, Mohamed V continued, "I have much respect for the help the American Republic has offered to the Arab countries and especially for its participation in liberating them from oppression."[20] His conclusion then omitted the obligatory phrase acknowledging the "beneficent" French government, "enamored of this liberty that steers our country towards prosperity and progress" which had been included in the original text approved by the residency.[21] This cool attitude clearly communicated Mohamed V's resentment about the tragic events days before in Casablanca, when Senegalese colonial troops went on a rampage for several hours in the medina after an argument got out of hand near the Bousbir brothel quarter, killing and injuring over 100 Moroccans before French authorities sent in troops to stop it.[22]

Two years earlier, Mohamed V had publicly hinted at his aspirations for independence. After encountering signs when entering Marrakesh that read "We do not want a foreign protectorate. By the will of Allah, Morocco claims its independence," Mohamed V responded with an understated expression of sympathy: "Be assured that everything that saddens you saddens me; and that everything that you hope for I hope for, too" (Landau 1957, 46). These comments in 1945 did not provoke the protectorate authorities (perhaps because they were made to a Moroccan audience). In 1947, however, the sultan's Tangier speech was delivered to an international and large Moroccan audience via radio broadcast, and the text was also widely published in the French

---

19. The text of the speech is quoted in Julien (1977, 221) and Delanoë (1988, 52).

20. Delanoë 1988, 52–54.

21. Ibid.

22. The United Press reported that a riot developed on April 7 after two Senegalese soldiers and an "Arab prostitute" became involved in "a street argument." "Under a hail of stones, the two Senegalese retreated to their barracks. There they recruited fifty reinforcements. The soldiers broke open the magazine of their barracks and returned to the scene with rifles and tommy guns. The Senegalese fired into the crowd. Screaming women ran for cover while Moroccans fought back with knives, pistols, and stones." "Senegalese Soldiers Kill 58 Moroccans," *New York Times*, April 9, 1947, 4.

FIGURE 11.   Mohamed V delivering a speech in the Mendoubia Garden in Tangier on April 10, 1947. MAE, CADN, Résidence générale de France au Maroc, cliché Jacques Belin, 20MA/103/137, "Tanger, 10 avril 1947. Discours de S.M. Ben Youssef."

and Arabic press. The reaction from Paris was swift and severe. President Paul Ramadier and Minister of Foreign Affairs Georges-Augustin Bidault blamed Labonne for being too lenient and summarily replaced him with a hardline resident general, Alphonse Juin, who arrived on May 14, 1947.

The Sultan of *Istiqlal* and the Protectorate's Fraying Fiction

Juin had risen in the military from modest origins. He graduated from Saint Cyr and then fought and was wounded on the Western Front in World War I. While he was posted in the Constantine region of Algeria, he married into an upper-middle-class *colon* family. He later served as a staff officer under Lyautey in Morocco. During World War II, he gained fame as the commander of the French Expeditionary Corps in the Italian campaign. When he was appointed resident general, his orders were to rein in the sultan. After four months, Juin reported back to Minister of Foreign Affairs Bidault.

> I found the country in the grip of a veritable psychosis of fear. The uneasiness created by the unbridled agitation of the nationalists, managed behind the scenes by the sultan himself, had only increased after

the spectacle and verbal demonstration at Tangier. The French controllers, civil and military, saw their authority weaken more and more with regard to the vacillations, not to mention the hostility, of many *pashas* and *qa'ids* perplexed by our cowardice and weakness, and naturally interested in safeguarding their own position.[23]

Juin's priority was to show force to reestablish the validity and authority of the 1912 Treaty and France's preponderant role in the colonial political field. He related that he had no affection for the sultan and suspected that his attempts to reconcile with the residency were simply ploys to gain time, "for he is certainly colluding with certain agents from Cairo," waiting for an incident to use at the United Nations. Juin concluded the report with a telling comment about his perception of the sultan's ambitions:

> The gravest of which is that he has detached himself from France, little by little, to the point he can no longer see us as anything but an enemy. For sure, we carry a great deal of responsibility, after having placed him on the throne as an adolescent, we let him grow up without taking care to form him properly, surrounding him with French companions of no quality.[24]

Juin acknowledged that Moroccan independence was inevitable, however, reflecting, "We are here by virtue of a protectorate treaty of which it would be childish to imagine is going to continue indefinitely through tacit agreement."[25]

The central conflict between the French administration, the sultan, and the Moroccan nationalists during the last decade of the protectorate, therefore, concerned not if but when Morocco would become independent. Juin's recommendation to Paris was to negotiate another pact that would recognize Moroccan autonomy while still guaranteeing French economic and security interests. Consistent with other postwar paternalistic attitudes expressed in French attempts to reinvent the empire as the French Union (Lewis 1962), Juin felt that Morocco had a long way to go to independence. It would take twenty to twenty-five more years, he believed, for Moroccans to progress far enough from their "medieval culture" to train the technicians and functionaries to run the government. He warned his superiors, though, that Mohamed V had more imminent aspirations to be the "Great Sultan of

---

23. SHD-AT, Carton 237 K3, Resident General Juin to Minister of Foreign Affairs Bidault, October 6, 1947.
24. Ibid.
25. Ibid.

Independence" and might need to be replaced, as Juin had done with the bey a few years earlier in Tunisia:

> It is necessary to coldly consider the possibility of pushing him aside. Certainly the operation is extremely delicate and a little undesirable, especially after the precedent of Moncef Bey. But if a serious situation occurs, that leads for example to another global conflict, no hesitation will be permitted.[26]

Throughout his term (1947–1951), Juin clashed with the sultan over proposed reforms in the municipal councils, an issue that threatened the protectorate's fundamental legitimating logics. Juin wanted to make the municipal council seats elected positions for which both French and Moroccans would be allowed to vote; the sultan argued that allowing French or other foreigners to vote violated Morocco's sovereignty under the protectorate treaty. Mohamed V wanted to extend suffrage for elected bodies to Moroccans but not to non-Moroccans.[27] In January 1948, hostilities between the residency and palace grew worse when the "Tract Affair" came to light. In December 1947, an Arabic tract was distributed by post to recipients throughout the country that claimed that the sultan was a bastard. The alleged culprit, Si Mohamed ben 'Abd al-Qadir Ferfera, was arrested on January 10 after his handwriting was matched. The fact that Ferfera worked for the Directorate of the Interior created a standoff on two fronts: the palace strongly suspected that the residency was directly involved and there was a dispute over who had jurisdiction.[28] Mohamed V claimed that under decrees dated November 11, 1913, and June 24, 1935, that forbade the disturbing of public order, Ferfera's case came under the jurisdiction of the Sharifian courts. The resident argued that Ferfera had immunity because he worked for a protectorate service.

Throughout his four-year tenure, Juin was deeply disturbed by the palace's open support for the Istiqlal Party. In his December 1949 report to Minister of Foreign Affairs Robert Schumann, Juin complained that Istiqlal's propaganda office, the Société Maghrébine d'Information, de Publicité, et de Voyages, which also served as a marketing and travel agency, mixed political messages in its Arabic print campaign for Coca-Cola. Apparently, the agency used the Sharifian imperial crown in Coke advertisements,

---

26. Ibid. Juin had deposed the Tunisian nationalist ruler in 1943.
27. SHD-AT, Carton 237 K3, the sultan to Juin, October 10, 1947.
28. SHD-AT, Carton 237 K3, Resident General Juin to Minister of Foreign Affairs Bidault, January 29, 1948.

embedding the crown as a political symbol on posters and billboards across the protectorate.[29]

In November, the French liaison with the palace brought up the issue. This time the problem was in the other direction; Coca-Cola was sponsoring the nationalists. Posters announcing a demonstration in Casablanca organized by the agency for that year's 'Aid al-'arsh (Throne Day) included a "Drink Coca-Cola" graphic. The French counselor showed the sultan one of the posters and complained it gave the impression that in celebrating Throne Day the royal family recommended that "Moroccans drink Coca-Cola" and warned that the posters could "give rise to criticisms."[30] The sultan politely responded that although he regretted that it was impossible to remove the Coca-Cola trademark, he supposed the organizers of the demonstration had to cover the costs of making the poster and that he was indifferent to criticisms it might generate. Apparently, the Moroccan nationalists and Mohamed V enjoyed the irony of provoking the French protector by allying with the American soft drink maker whose "coca-colonization" of France was generating intense opposition back in the metropole.[31]

While the anti-colonial politics of Coca-Cola's marketing campaigns were brewing in late 1949, a speech by Juin at the Academy of Colonial Sciences in Paris on November 18 further exposed the deepening rift between him and the Moroccan sultan. At his induction into the academy, Juin spoke at length in defense of the words "colonialism" and "imperialism," commenting, "Can one forget that the Sharifian Empire could not have become a national entity except by our presence?" He evoked the colonial vulgate, explaining:

> As far back as we can reach in time, the Muslim epoch in North Africa always presents the same opposition between the cities and the countryside, the same Arabo-Berber dualism which has fixed a certain field of action according to a geographic equilibrium. This left the plains

---

29. MAE, CADN-Mar., Direction de l'Intérieur, Carton 892, Resident General Juin to Minister of Foreign Affairs Robert Schuman, "Le Sultan et les partis marocains," December 3, 1949.

30. MAE, CADN-Mar., Direction de l'Intérieur, Carton 889, "Compte-rendu No. 45," November 1949, 3.

31. During World War II, the U.S. government subsidized the construction of sixty-four Coca-Cola bottling plants worldwide, and the company supplied every GI a bottle for five cents. These bottling operations were expanded in 1947 in the Netherlands, Belgium, and Luxembourg and opened in Switzerland, Italy, and France in 1949. French political opposition to Coca-Cola created a firestorm of controversy in 1949–1950, and eventually an embargo was placed on the product. Interestingly, the American company tried to bypass the embargo by exporting the concentrate to bottlers in France from its Casablanca operation. See the chapter, "Yankee Go Home: The Left, Coca-Cola, and the Cold War," in Kuisel (1993, 37–69).

FIGURE 12.   Delegation of nurses to the first meeting of the Union marocain de travail, November 19, 1955, with Coca-Cola advertisement in background. MAE, CADN, Résidence générale de France au Maroc, cliché Jacques Belin, 20MA/103/345, "Rabat 19 Nov. 1955, Premier meeting de l'Union Marocaine du Travail (Délégation des Infirmières des hôpitaux de Rabat)."

to the Arab feudalities and the mountains, the pre–Saharan, and the Saharan zones to the Berber feudalities.[32]

Juin then lauded France's *mise-en-valeur* in North Africa, citing a laundry list of developmentalist accomplishments that legitimated its intervention in Morocco: "Peace everywhere, thousands of kilometers of railroads and roads furrow the three countries. The stations, ports, and air and sea lines have put the population in direct contact with the outside world. The clinics, hospitals, and schools dispense the advantages of our science and humanism every day." In this paean to France's colonial benevolence, Juin publicly reiterated his proposal for renegotiating a "Franco-Moroccan co-sovereignty" that gave French *colons* representation in municipal councils and a Moroccan Assembly. Mohamed V remained intransigent on this issue, rejecting it as an unacceptable affront to Moroccan sovereignty. In retaliation, he used his veto power by refusing to sign *dahirs* the residency presented him.

---

32. SHD-AT, Carton 237 K3, transcript of Resident General Juin's speech to Académie des Sciences Coloniales, 18 November 1949.

In May, Juin again warned Paris that the Treaty of Fes had become anachronistic and that a new arrangement had to be worked out to safeguard Morocco's strategic value in the Cold War. He advised that Mohamed V had to be brought on board and that the Americans should be used to pressure the sultan to turn to the West for support against the "communist" threat emanating from revolutionary Moroccan urban groups hostile to the throne. If this did not work, Juin suggested using the "Berber bloc" against the sultan and the nationalists: "It is useful to also remember that there [in the interior], the great majority of the Moroccan population was not subjected to the sultan. It was to France alone that they conferred the trust to direct their destinies and never indicated that they would ever accept being subservient to an oriental minority, the authority of which they have always rejected." He warned that the *blad al-sība* would revolt against the center and that it was "precisely to avoid the renewal of internal conflict that it was necessary to try to renegotiate a constitutional monarchy."[33]

Throughout the spring and summer of 1950, the sultan blocked the approval of *qa'ids* and pashas Juin nominated. Mohamed V also demanded that more money be budgeted for education, specifically for the Moroccan free schools, and pressed for the right of Moroccans to form unions, which the French resisted because they feared that they would be used politically against them. In October, Mohamed V met with President Auriol in Paris and pressed for a restructuring of the Franco-Moroccan partnership in a manner that would quickly lead to self-administration. No tangible gains resulted, however, other than the creation of a commission to study possible reforms. In response to Juin's claim that Mohamed V was "blocking" the path to democracy, the king used the November throne speech to reiterate his support for a Moroccan democratic system, rather than one in which the political right of *colons* were acknowledged: "Not for a single moment have we lost sight of the fact that the best regime under which a sovereign and self-administered country can live is the democratic, such as we know it in the world today. A regime of that kind does not contradict the principles of Islam" (Landau 1957, 49).

The election reform issue came to a head in December during a meeting of the Government Council. Two of the Moroccan nationalist members of the council, Lyazidi and Laghzaoui, took turns criticizing the French for completely ignoring Moroccan interests in how they ran the protectorate.

---

33. SHD-AT, Carton 237 K3, Resident General Juin to Minister of Foreign Affairs Robert Schumann, May 1, 1950.

Livid at their critique, Juin expelled both from the room. The remaining nine Moroccan members (all of whom were affiliated with Istiqlal) also walked out and went directly to the palace. At the *hadiya* ceremony at the Rabat palace for the Prophet Muhammad's birthday ('Aid al-mulud), the pasha of Marrakesh, Thami el Glaoui, a stalwart ally of the residency and personal friend of Juin, came before the sultan and reportedly shouted, "Thou art no longer sultan of Morocco! Thou art the sultan of the Istiqlal! Thou art a communist and an atheist!" before being forcibly removed from the palace.[34]

After the sultan stopped signing *dahirs* again in early 1951, Juin issued an ultimatum: sign the decrees and denounce Istiqlal or abdicate.[35] On February 24, the residency colluded with Thami el Glaoui to orchestrate a dramatic warning to Mohamed V. He surrounded the Rabat palace with mounted Berber tribesmen and stationed French tanks and soldiers around them to "protect" the sultan from the "Berber revolt."[36] Under siege and fearing bloodshed in the capital, the sultan signed a document two hours later denouncing Istiqlal and saying he would sign decrees.[37] Afterward, he gave an interview to Mahmoud Azmi, a reporter for the Egyptian newspaper *Al-Ahram* in which he explained that he had agreed to the demands only under pressure.[38]

Mohamed V also eventually agreed to Juin's proposal to reorganize the government, but he continued to refuse to compromise on the matter of French *colons* voting in municipal councils. While Juin was on a trip to Indochina, Mohamed V again appealed directly to President Auriol, who

---

34. Hassan (1978, 42) comments that afterward, "the *pasha* mobilized his clients—tribes from the Atlas, pseudo-religious chiefs of communities and fraternities, hypocritical ulama and needy scribes."

35. Istiqlal and the other nationalist parties signed a memorandum creating a joint Moroccan National Front four months later, on April 9, 1951, in Tangier.

36. SHD-AT, Carton 237 K3. In a letter to Minister of Foreign Affairs Robert Schumann immediately after the incident (February 26, 1951), Juin deflected suspicion that the residency was behind the charade, saying that it was in fact a rupture between Mohamed V and his people: "It seems that in France and abroad this Istiqlal affair was a conflict between the Residency and the Palace, though this has been a long running grave difference between the sultan and his people. The incident with the *Pasha* of Marrakesh [who was banned from the throne room after chastising the "Sultan of Istiqlal"] set fire to the powder in unleashing a movement of disapproval that rapidly spread from the Berber Mountain to the Arab plains of Fes, the Gharb, the Chaouia, the Oum Er Rbia and the Doukkala. After the break in negotiations, this disapproval reached such a degree that I took measures to protect members of Istiqlal. A vast appeal was submitted by the people of the countryside and certain cities to gather in Fes to call for the deposition and replacement of the despot, hated for his politics and his greed."

37. Hassan II (1978, 40) and others report the tribesmen had no idea what their trip to Rabat was about. After hearing about the sultan's defiance, they supported him all the more.

38. SHD-AT, Carton 237 K3, Resident General Juin to Minister of Foreign Affairs Robert Schumann, February 26, 1951.

created a Franco-Moroccan commission to study the troubled protectorate relationship. The American government also voiced concerns that spring about the direction of France's North Africa policy.[39] In Paris, the Council of Ministers discussed Juin's reassignment to a position as commander in chief of Allied land forces in Central Europe.[40] Upset by the rebuke and worried that his "promotion" would be seen as a punishment, Juin pushed for the choice of his successor to clearly signal the French government's intention to continue carrying out Juin's policies. He suggested August Guillaume, "a Moroccan by training who took an active part in the pacification and who already has experience in military and indigenous affairs."[41] For his swan song, Juin published an article in *Le Monde* on September 1, 1951, that warned about the "threat" of Istiqlal's brand of Arabo-Islamic nationalism and defending France's policies in the protectorate:

> We can ask if it [Istiqlal] did not want to show, when the dissidence changed sides, that it always intended to carry on the dream of the first conquerors from the East, and to reap all of the benefits, for itself and toward the ends of Arab domination, of the unification of the Maghreb that the French accomplished for the first time in history. Already, in 1930, even before being openly spoken, it had under-handedly provoked an artificial emotion in the whole Arab world about the *dahir* regarding Berber justice, sealed by the sultan himself, which was only an official recognition of the customary jurisdiction which had been practiced throughout the ages and which the Treaty obliged us to respect. . . . France, which introduced the national idea into Morocco, cannot condemn the ideology of this party, but it can condemn its methods.[42]

At the end of the month, Juin left Morocco and was replaced by his chosen successor, Auguste Guillaume, who arrived on October 2, 1951. Guillaume had significant prior experience in Morocco, having served as the director of political affairs and having directed the formation of *goum* corps that fought in World War II and had been deployed in Indochina since 1949.

---

39. SHD-AT, Carton 237 K3, Minister of Foreign Affairs Robert Schumann to Resident General Juin, May 24, 1951. Schumann advised Juin to be more proactive in his outreach to the British and American consuls, to explain the French side and counter the nationalist lobbying against them.

40. SHD-AT, Carton 237 K3, Letter from Resident General Juin to Henri Queuille, President of the Council of Ministers, July 10, 1951.

41. Ibid.

42. SHD-AT, 237 K3, original draft of *Le Monde* article, published September 1, 1951, one month before Juin left his post as resident general in Morocco.

In a personal letter, the former resident general, Noguès, advised Guillaume that the protectorate framework would work only if it was done "in agreement with the sultan and not against the sultan."[43] He recommended that Guillaume have one-on-one private meetings to help the sultan "understand our common interests and that we can remain his best support."[44] Mohamed V and the nationalists had initial hopes that relations would improve with the change in residency, but these were dampened when Guillaume continued to press for the co-sovereignty plan. After elections for the local and municipal councils were held on October 27, 1951, which Istiqlal boycotted and the sultan openly opposed, riots in Casablanca left five dead and forty wounded.

In March, Mohamed V sent another memorandum to Paris asking the French to 1) lift the state of siege in Morocco; 2) grant Moroccans the right to public liberties and trade unions; 3) represent the government with a Moroccan head of state; and 4) allow negotiations toward independence to begin immediately. In his November 1952 Throne Day speech, Mohamed V bitterly criticized the protectorate administration for not letting Morocco progress forward. Three weeks later, on December 7, Tunisian trade union leader Ferhat Hached was assassinated and the primary Moroccan trade union called for a general strike in sympathy. On the first day of the strike, police fired on crowds in Casablanca and conducted mass arrests of Istiqlal and union leaders. Police and soldiers with machine guns fired upon a large funeral procession the next day. In the aftermath, rumors spread throughout Casablanca's *ville nouvelle* about rapes and murders of European women, and, in response, European crowds lynched Moroccan workers gathered at the union headquarters. During the episode, over fifty Moroccans were killed in the most violent episode of urban violence up to that point in the protectorate.

The next spring, Thami el Glaoui, the pasha of Marrakesh and prominent Sufi leader 'Abd el Hay Kettani, both staunch allies of the resident general, organized what became known as the "Qa'id Affair." On February 26, 1953, Glaoui assembled more than 100 *qa'ids* in Marrakesh to publicly call for the sultan's removal from power. This attempt to mobilize a Moroccan coalition against Mohamed V continued over the next several months. On March 18, he circulated a petition signed by twenty tribal chiefs and religious figures accusing Mohamed V of leading Morocco to ruin. On April

---

43. Noguès was resident general from 1936 to 1943. Having backed Darlan and Giraud, he resigned and retired to Portugal before De Gaulle arrived in Algiers. He and Guillaume maintained a regular correspondence while Guillaume was resident general, from 1951 to 1953, which is included in Guillaume's file, SHD-AT, Carton 1 K 343.

44. SHD-AT, Carton 1 K 343, Noguès to Resident General Guillaume, October 30, 1951.

4, demonstrations criticizing the sultan were organized with assistance from the residency in Fes. On May 11, to symbolically demonstrate the strength of their alliance with the "Berber bloc," the French organized a huge gathering of veterans of the colonial army on the Tizi Ntriten plateau in the Middle Atlas between Azrou and Timhadit at which Juin presented Guillaume with a marshal's baton. In June, Kettani made a formal appeal to the French in the name of the Congress of North African Confraternity in Fes to end to the "dissidence" of Istiqlal and the Sultan.

That summer, escalating tensions between the residency and the palace reached the breaking point. On August 13, police and military personnel cordoned off the palace. Mohamed V signed a co-sovereignty protocol to buy time, agreeing to the proposed reform of the municipal and regional assemblies and ceding his veto power over decrees. Three days later, Glaoui and other leaders met in Marrakesh to declare an obscure member of the Alawid family, Mohammed Ben 'Arafa, as sultan, still adhering to the formal legitimating logics of the field in which the institution, if not the person, of the Alawid monarchy was to be protected. That same day, counterdemonstrations broke out in major cities protesting the fact that the residency was holding Mohamed ben Youssef hostage in the Rabat palace. On August 20, the day before the 'Aid al-kabir holiday, Guillaume went to the palace just after the midday meal and told Mohamed V: "For reasons of security, the French government wishes you to abdicate. If you do so voluntarily, you and your family will be able to live in France in freedom, and highly esteemed" (Hassan 1978, 51). In a moment of high irony, given the pledges in the 1912 protectorate treaty that France was to ensure "internal order and general security" on the sultan's behalf, Guillaume reiterated that he was empowered to exile the sultan in order to restore "order" in the country. Mohamed V refused, responding, "I am the legitimate sovereign of Morocco. I shall never betray the mission with which my loyal and faithful people have entrusted me. France is strong. Let her act as she thinks best" (50). Surrounded by cars, tanks, cannons, and machine guns aimed at the palace, the king and his sons were marched out at gunpoint, driven to the airfield at Souissi, and flown off in a Dakota airplane at 2:45 p.m. The rest of the family joined them in Corsica and then they were all were sent to Madagascar.

Exile and Return of the King

Over the next two years, the French faced the increasingly difficult task of maintaining order in the colonial political field. A general urban insurgency broke out immediately after the sultan's exile, particularly in the coastal cities

of Casablanca and Rabat. Still adhering to the formal letter of the protectorate logics of legitimacy, colonial officials tried to buttress the new sultan, Ben
'Arafa, as a viable national symbol, albeit one with little to no real political
leverage. One of the first decrees Ben 'Arafa signed abolished Throne Day.
Another approved the municipal elections in which French settlers could
vote. A council of viziers and directors was created, with fourteen Moroccans and sixteen French, with the power to overrule the sultan. Within the
Moroccan public, the anti-'Arafa response was vigorous and included a mass
boycott of the country's mosques to protest the fact that prayers were being
said in the name of Ben 'Arafa instead of the name of Ben Youssef. There
were also numerous assassination attempts on the replacement sultan.

From 1953, Istiqlal and other secret networks that were unaffiliated with
the party began to assassinate Moroccan collaborators and sabotage public
infrastructure, including public buildings, railroads, and telephone lines.
The nationalists also launched an economic boycott against French- and
Jewish-owned cinemas, French products, and tobacco, which was under
a French-controlled monopoly. In the first days of August 1954, the Fes
medina staged a huge uprising.[45] French reports estimated that 50,000 pro-
testers, including large numbers of women and children, marched through
the streets to the royal palace to protest the "faux Sultan."[46] French colonial
troops occupied the medina, using tear gas against the crowds and opening
fire in subsequent days in confrontations with demonstrators. Simultane-
ous protests broke out in Port Lyautey (Kenitra), Rabat, and Marrakesh.
That November, Throne Day was celebrated with vigor across Morocco
in contravention of the residency's prohibition. In the Spanish zone, the
khalifa refused to recognize Ben 'Arafa, asserting that he continued to represent Mohamed V, in whose name prayers continued to be said (Landau
1957, 70).

The French also faced increasing reprobation from the international community. At the end of December 1954, the Arab League submitted a resolution to the United Nations demanding that Morocco be allowed to decide
its own destiny. In January, the league issued a resolution denouncing Ben
'Arafa as an illegitimate sovereign. The anti-French campaign received further support at the Bandung Conference of the nonaligned countries in

---

45. This episode is the setting for Paul Bowles' novel *The Spider House* (1955).

46. MAE, Afrique-Levant 1944–1959, Sous-Séries K Afrique-Maroc 1953–1959, Dossier 6.
This dossier contains telegrams from Resident General Lacoste about the situation in Fes. French
officials reported that four women and one child were killed by exposure to tear gas. The crowds
chanted for Allal al-Fassi and for Princess Lalla Aicha and called for the return of the sultan.

April 1955, at which a resolution was passed supporting "the right of the peoples of Algeria, Morocco, and Tunisia to self-determination and independence" (Hassan 1978, 56). The outbreak of open conflict in Algeria in November 1954 forced the French to look for quick resolutions to the crises in Morocco and Tunisia.

Prime Minister Mendès-France flew to Tunisia in late 1954 to announce the French were unilaterally granting the protectorate internal autonomy. The French then brokered the rest of the process of decolonization in 1955–1956 through the nationalist leader, Habib Bourguiba, rather than the technical sovereign, the Husaynid bey. For Morocco, a delegation including Dr. Dubois-Roquebert and Georges Izard, a lawyer, was sent to Madagascar to warn Mohamed V that his fortune would be seized if he did not abdicate. This heavy-handed tactic produced no results, however, and, over the summer, the French prime minister, Fauré, decided that bringing Mohamed V back constituted the best way to quickly resolve the Moroccan Crisis. The reasons for this were twofold: first, the French knew that, among the available Moroccan actors (the nationalist parties, French collaborators including Glaoui and Kettani, rural chiefs, and the urban and rural resistance movements), Mohamed V possessed an unparalleled degree of cultural capital as a national political and religious symbol that would enable him to defuse the crisis; second, they viewed Mohamed V as the best interlocutor through which to preserve their influence in the former protectorate.

A French delegation opened talks in Madrid in July with Ahmed Belafrej, but intense right-wing pressure in France and in the protectorate stalled progress. In Morocco, the rapid succession of resident generals (Lacoste, Grandval, and de la Tour) hindered progress toward defusing the violence that had broken out in retaliatory terrorist attacks between the Moroccan resistance and the French *colon* population.[47] Finally, on August 23, 1955, the French government convened Franco-Moroccan negotiations that included representatives from Istiqlal and its rival, the Parti démocratique de l'indépendance (PDI), at Aix-les-Bains. There it was agreed that Ben 'Arafa would be removed and that a Throne Council would be charged with

---

47. MAE, Afrique-Levant 1944–1959, Sous-Séries K Afrique-Maroc 1953–1959, Dossier 4. The French negotiator, La Tournelle, reported that the nationalists demanded the return of the king, a French pledge setting a limit to the protectorate regime, and a "new deal" program of education, administrative, and social reform. He also reported the nationalists counted on diplomatic support from the United States and that they believed that U.S. pledges to maintain air bases would help guarantee Moroccan independence.

Figure 13. King Mohamed V arriving at the Rabat-Salé airport on November 16, 1955. MAE, CADN, Résidence générale de France au Maroc, cliché Jacques Belin, 20MA/103/318, "16 nov 1955. Retour de S.M. Ben Youssef. Aérodrome de Rabat-Salé."

forming a Moroccan government to negotiate the terms of Sultan Mohamed ben Youssef's return.

It took until late fall, however, for this return became a reality. Ben 'Arafa resigned and was sent to Tangier on October 1. The next day, rural resistance by the Moroccan Liberation Army broke out in the Rif and the Middle Atlas. Two weeks later, a Throne Council was announced, but Istiqlal repudiated it. On October 21, Glaoui himself called for the return of Mohamed ben Youssef. The sultan was flown from Madagascar to Nice on October 31, then was taken to Paris and housed in one of the wings of the castle of Henry V at Saint-Germain-en-Laye. On November 6, 1955, the Declaration of la Celle Saint Cloud was issued in which France granted Morocco independence, but included ambivalent and controversial language about this being done in a framework of interdependence with France. The king returned to Morocco on Wednesday, November 16, 1955, landing at 11:42 a.m. at the Rabat-Salé airport, where he was greeted by jubilant crowds. The Commander of the Faithful, reinvented through forty-four years of protectorate rule by the French authorities, by Moroccan nationalists, and, most important, by Mohamed V himself, returned from exile as a reascendant king with huge reserves of symbolic capital.

Morocco's monarchical exception, that the Alawids survived coloniza-tion and decolonization, was a contingent outcome related to how the colonial political field was structured, how colonial and nationalist actors attempted to use the monarchy's symbolic potential, and how Mohamed V himself took an active role in identity struggles in the latter half of the protectorate. Morocco's strategic position on the Strait of Gibraltar delayed colonization until the late high imperial era in the late nineteenth/early twentieth centuries, when a multipolar diplomatic field of com-peting Great Powers dictated an indirect protectorate form of colonial intervention. The Alawids initially survived colonial intervention because France pursued a *makhzan* policy that structurally preserved the sultanate instead of eradicating local rule, as they had done in Algeria. Throughout the protectorate's four decades, the French remained formally tied to the legitimacy structure embedded in the Treaty of Fes. At a second junc-ture during World War II, the Alawids again benefited from Morocco's geographic position in the west and from the fact that Morocco had an Atlantic-facing coast. The Americans began the North Africa campaign by landing in Morocco in 1942, which gave the Moroccan ruler increas-ing freedom to maneuver in contrast to his peer, the Tunisian monarch, Moncef Bey, who came under German rule when the Wehrmacht dug in to hold off the Anglo-American push into Italy. After the eventual Allied victory in Tunisia, Moncef Bey, who had vigorously pushed for Tunisian autonomy, was forced to abdicate by the Free French administration in 1943. While Mohamed V was spared this fate for another decade, Moncef Bey died in exile in 1948 before he could capitalize on his popularity as a nationalist symbol.

The vagaries of historical sequence and individual agency were criti-cal factors that relate to the second question this chapter addressed: how Mohamed V also survived the process of anti-colonial nation building. In the 1930s, the fact that the colonial power had kept the sultan in place and tried to profit from his symbolic power did not delegitimize Mohamed V in the eyes of the Moroccan nationalist movement. Instead, they tried to subvert this legitimacy framework from within, emphasizing the monar-chy themselves as the symbol of national unity and sovereignty. Mohamed V thus benefited from both the colonial state-building project, which cultivated his symbolic trappings of power, and the nationalists' decision to co-opt these resources in their own efforts at nation building. In the

1940s, the war created space in which Mohamed V expanded his own sphere of agency and autonomy between these two competing camps. When he was exiled in 1953, Mohamed V completed the transformation from sultan to king. Unlike Tunisia's Moncef Bey, the Moroccan monarch was exiled late enough for him to still be in play in the decolonization endgame and early enough for him to have not compromised his credentials as an anti-colonial nationalist symbol. The next chapter turns to one remaining question: how the king won the struggle for power after independence and consolidated the dynasty's hegemony in the postcolonial Moroccan political field.

✍ CHAPTER 9

The Monarchy and Identity in Post-protectorate Morocco

> *Kifah al-malik wa al-sha'ab haqaq al-istiqlal al-kamil. Al-maghrib dawlata 'arabiya dusturiha al-islam.*
> The struggle of the king and the people has achieved complete independence. Morocco is an Arab state and its constitution is Islam.
>
> —Headline of Istiqlal paper *Al-'Alam* on November 21, 1957, in honor of the anniversary of the king's return from exile in 1955

Instead of being a singular event that culminated a four-decade struggle for complete independence, the king's return from exile was the beginning of a transitional process of decolonization. This final chapter examines the struggle for control in the post-protectorate political field during the first five years of independence, from 1956 to the death of Mohamed V and the accession of Hassan II in 1961. The analysis focuses on three critical areas in which the monarchy, in contrast to most of its regional peers,[1] had the material and symbolic power to successfully consolidate its position during this transitional phase: 1) inheriting and sustaining the military monopoly the colonial state had established; 2) defusing political threats by cultivating a multiparty system; and 3) ensuring the symbolic primacy of the monarchy in how Moroccan identity was imagined. This chapter also assesses how the three internal "Other" groups—Berbers,

---

1. In Tunisia, the Husaynid king was ousted by Bourguiba and the Neo-Destour party in 1957. Military coups eliminated dynasties in Egypt (1952), Iraq (1958), and Libya (1969). In Jordan, the first emir-cum-king, Abdullah, was assassinated by a Palestinian while visiting the Al Aqsa mosque in Jerusalem in 1951. His grandson and successor, Hussein, survived that 1951 attack, a coup attempt in 1957, and civil war with Palestinian forces in 1970. Similarly, in Morocco, Hassan II survived two officer-led coups, including an attack on his beachside palace in Skhirat in 1971 and an attack

Jews, and women—fared as Mohamed V and Hassan II laid the foundations for the Alawid monarchy's post-independence ascendance.

Territory and State Space in the Post-protectorate Political Field

Colonial intervention politicized Moroccan territory in three unprecedented ways: 1) by cartographically defining most of its borders, with the critical exception of the southern and southeastern frontier in the Sahara; 2) by subdividing the space of this field into separate zones of French, Spanish, and international control; and 3) by carrying out a decades-long military conquest that established a state-based monopoly of rule in this space. During the transitional process of decolonization, various actors that included the monarchy, the Istiqlal Party, and the Moroccan Liberation Army competed on the terrain of territorial identity politics in attempts to buttress their own leverage in the post-protectorate political field. Undoing colonial partition, irredentist claims in the Sahara, and military control were the issues at stake in these struggles.

The first concern after Mohamed V returned from exile in November 1955 was to negotiate formal independence and territorial reunification with the French and Spanish. This process took considerable time. In March 1956, French and Moroccan negotiators finally signed an official acknowledgement of Moroccan independence after resolving outstanding issues that included financial recompense for the monarchy's losses during exile.[2] One month later, in Madrid, the Moroccan king negotiated the end of the Spanish protectorate in the northern zone, which went into effect on April 7. The Tangier international zone was reincorporated into Morocco on July 8. Further territorial unification in the south took years, however. The Spanish protectorate in Tarfaya was not handed over until 1958 and Ifni took until 1970. In a controversial move in 1975, Morocco occupied the Saharan provinces of Seguia al Hamra and Rio de Oro after

---

by Moroccan F-5 fighter jets on his Boeing 727 while he was traveling back from France in 1972. Although luck is perhaps beyond the scope of sociological analysis, it also undoubtedly played some role in the survival of the monarchies in Jordan and Morocco.

2. In January, the French had agreed to pay the sultan an indemnity of 750,000,000 francs in recompense for the "injury against your personal interests during the period of Your exile." MAE, Maroc 1956–1968, Dossier 29 (1956–1960), Resident General to His Majesty Mohamed V, Sultan of Morocco, January 4, 1956.

the Spanish withdrew in response to the Green March that King Hassan II had mobilized.[3]

In this process of consolidating the post-independence territorial boundaries of the political field, the Moroccan monarchy benefited from the continuity that was maintained in the transfer of Moroccan units of the French and Spanish colonial armies to the personal command of the king in 1956–1957. Over the next five years, the newly christened Royal Armed Forces (RAF) confirmed the post-protectorate state's ability to monopolize the use of force in the space of the nation-state. This first involved ending the armed resistance movement in Morocco's urban areas, absorbing many of the irregular forces of the rural Moroccan Liberation Army (MLA) and eliminating the MLA remnants that were fighting in the south. The RAF, under the command of Crown Prince Hassan, were also used to put down insurrections in the Atlas and Rif Mountains in the late 1950s. Later, in 1963, the army waged what became known as the Sand War with Algeria over disputes about the border between Tindouf and Béchar. By that point, it was clear that military power in postcolonial Morocco was exclusively under the personal control of the monarch.

From Colonial Army to the Royal Armed Forces

As discussed in chapter 1, the successful integration of mostly Berber-speaking rural groups into the French and Spanish colonial armies constituted one of the colonial state's most significant accomplishments. These Moroccan *goumiers* did much of the subsequent work of completing pacification operations in Morocco in the late 1920s and 1930s and were used in the interwar period to put down resistance in Syria (Gershowich 2000, 82). Moroccan troops played significant roles in the Spanish Civil War in the 1930s (Balfour 2002). In World War II, they fought for the French in Italy, Corsica, Provence, the Vosges, and eventually the Rhine Valley. In the late 1940s, Moroccan troops were sent to fight in Indochina. The last *tabors* returned in 1955, on the eve of Moroccan independence (Saulay 1985).

The formal transfer of these forces to the command of the Moroccan monarchy constituted one of the most significant factors that influenced the post-independence transition. Virtually the entire officer corps of the newly formed RAF was composed of former officers in the French and Spanish colonial armies, including the highest-ranking Moroccan officer from the

---

3. The Mediterranean enclaves of Ceuta and Melilla remain under Spanish control.

French army, Brigadier General Ben Hamou Kettani, and from the Spanish army, General Mohamed Ben Mizian. In addition to an officer corps trained by the French and Spanish, the monarchy inherited units with significant combat experience that numbered 14,000 when the RAF were officially formed in the spring 1956. During the first years of independence, French officers continued to play an essential role; at the end of 1957, over 1,000 French advisors were still involved in training 27,000 Moroccan troops in the RAF (Monjib 1992, 65). The French also provided significant logistical and material support, including equipment and munitions.[4]

With the RAF, the monarchy continued the colonial state's strategy of using the rural, Berber-speaking regions of Morocco as a reinvented version of a *jaysh* tribal reservoir and ensuring the loyalty of this bloc with lines

FIGURE 14. A parade in downtown Rabat of newly created Moroccan Royal Armed Forces, May 14, 1956. Crown Prince Hassan II is in the foreground in white. King Mohamed V is sitting on the review stand. MAE, CADN, Résidence générale de France au Maroc, 20MA/103/377, "Défilé de l'Armée royale marocaine." This shot is taken from in front of the train station, looking toward St. Peter's Cathedral. The parade route proceeded through the *ville nouvelle* down what is now Avenue Mohamed V toward the medina.

---

4. See MAE, Maroc 1956–1968, Dossier 209, on Franco-Moroccan military cooperation after independence.

of patronage that flowed through the military. Significantly, the allegiance of the armed forces was directed personally to the king. The military was christened the "royal" rather than the "national" or "Moroccan" armed forces. The military's direct allegiance to the monarchy was also reinforced in the RAF's initial seal and motto, which modified the order of the Moroccan national motto—*Allah, al-Watan, al-Malik* (God, the Nation, the King)—to *Allah, al-Malik, al-Watan* (God, the King, the Nation). Beyond the army, the new Moroccan state also created an internal security apparatus that included the military and civilian police forces of the Royal Gendarmerie (1957) and National Security (1956), both of which were under the king's close supervision.

Pacifying the Resistance and the Army of Liberation

Two other armed groups were active during the transitional period of decolonization: the Resistance, which, since the king's exile in 1953, fought in Morocco's cities against French *colon* terrorist groups and Moroccan "collaborators"; and the Moroccan Liberation Army, which launched a rural insurgency in October 1955. The violent threat of both created pressures that sped the end of the protectorate, as France could ill afford the prospect of deploying thousands of troops that it needed in Algeria to repacify Morocco.

Immediately after independence, these groups' military potential constituted both a threat and an opportunity for the palace and for rival nationalist parties that sought to control them. The urban Resistance began operations immediately after the exile of the sultan in August 1953. It consisted of loosely coordinated cells organized into various groups that included Al-Munazzama al-sirriya (The Secret Organization), Al-Hilal al-aswad (The Black Rising), Usad al-tahrir (the Lions of Liberation), and the Organization of the Black Hand (Ashford 1959). Between 1953 and 1956, the Resistance engaged in 4,520 violent attacks in Morocco's cities, primarily in Casablanca, targeting infrastructure. They also attempted assassinations and terrorist bombings against the French *colon* community, where parallel clandestine organizations had been organized (Lawrence 2010, 104).[5] The leadership of

---

5. As in Algeria (famously dramatized in Pontecorvo's movie *Battle of Algiers*), women in Morocco actively participated in the resistance. An intelligence note from the summer of 1955 reports that a woman planted a bomb on a bus in Rabat, which the reporting officer believed was the first example of a terror attack by a woman in Morocco. MAE, Afrique-Levant 1944–1959, Sous-Séries K Afrique-Maroc 1953–1959, Dossier 6, Telegram no. 2019/25, June 18, 1955.

the Resistance were a new and younger generation that had only loose ties to the Istiqlal old guard. In the summer of 1955 and through the winter after the king's return in November, violent activity increased as contending factions in the Resistance attempted to eliminate rivals and collaborators. By the end of the spring of 1956, this violence had largely subsided as much of the leadership and rank-and-file members were co-opted into government posts or the police and security forces.

The process of absorbing and eliminating the rural insurgency in the Atlas and Rif took much longer. In the summer of 1955, the Arab Maghreb Liberation Committee[6] laid the groundwork for an armed campaign against the French colonial state, setting up an Algerian-Moroccan subcommittee in the Mediterranean coastal city of Nador. The nascent Moroccan Liberation Army (MLA) trained troops in the northern zone and smuggled in weapons from Egypt through the Mediterranean coast, taking advantage of the relative freedom the Spanish authorities allowed (Hughes 2001, 5). The Moroccan Liberation Army joined the struggle on October 2, 1955, a month after the French opened up negotiations at Aix-les-Bains and days after Ben 'Arafa abdicated the throne. It launched attacks on two French military posts at Aknoul and Boured on the interzonal border north of Taza. Over the next months, the MLA directed propaganda at Moroccan colonial soldiers, distributing tracts that urged them with religious injunctions and appeals to anti-colonial solidarity to desert and join the resistance army. These recruitment efforts had some success among recently decommissioned soldiers returning home from Indochina, who were attracted by the MLA's ideological appeal and financial incentives (The MLA promised clothing, supplies, and a monthly stipend of 1,000 francs.) (M'Barek 1987, 91–93).

For the French, the prospect of the "*bled*," or rural interior, going back into dissidence created pressure throughout the month of October to hasten Mohamed V's full return from exile. The return of the king to Morocco on November 16 did not signal the end of the resistance, however. The MLA actually intensified its operations that winter, refusing to lay down arms until the complete liberation of Moroccan "territory" (including Tangier, the northern zone, and disputed areas in the Sahara) had been completed. Their intransigence was also linked to the MLA leadership's resentment about not being represented in the first post-independence government King Mohamed V formed.

---

6. This organization was formed in Cairo after World War II to coordinate the nationalist struggles of the three Maghrib countries.

During this delicate transitional period, the MLA, as an unaligned and autonomous military force, was a valuable source of potential leverage for several factions struggling for influence, but it resisted being coopted. MLA leaders in the field rebuffed efforts by the Istiqlal Party to co-opt the movement through contacts from the Tetouan committee. The nationalist hero Allal al-Fassi (who was still outside the Istiqlal leadership structure after years of exile) tried to leverage his supposed influence over the MLA to reposition himself in the post-independence power struggle. The MLA initially acclaimed al-Fassi, who had broadcast calls for jihad over the radio in the days after the initial attacks in October 1955, as their nominal leader. Two weeks later, on October 17, al-Fassi returned to Tetouan from Cairo to tour the northern zone. He was greeted by enthusiastic crowds in urban centers that included Tetouan, Larache, and Ksar al-Kbir, but this publicity campaign had little direct connection to actual MLA military operations. In fact, the MLA commander Sanhaji, whom al-Fassi brought along on the tour, reported that al-Fassi never inquired into the state of the morale or physical condition of MLA troops (M'Barek 1987, 68). After a March meeting between Istiqlal and MLA leaders, al-Fassi issued a call for calm and declared an end to the jihad. The MLA high command responded with their own declaration that no one else spoke in their name or could mediate their relationship with the king.

At the end of March, the king intervened directly. He received a MLA delegation in Rabat and invited the leadership to be incorporated into the RAF. A large proportion agreed, and about 5,000 of the 10,000 men of the Moroccan Liberation Army joined the regular army. Many of the rest entered the police, took public service jobs, or returned to private life (M'Barek 1987, 113). However, a small minority refused to end the jihad and committed to fight for the complete liberation of what they deemed Moroccan territory, particularly the ill-defined Saharan regions in the south that were still under French and Spanish control. Some formed up as small units and headed south, renaming themselves the Army for the Liberation of the Sahara. In the south they began harassing Spanish forces in the Ifni and Tarfaya enclaves. Istiqlal leaders tried to use these irregular liberation army troops as political leverage to pressure the palace to act on nationalist irredentist claims in the south. In a speech in Tangier in July 1956, Allal al-Fassi had called for the full liberation of the territory of "Greater Morocco," which stretched from Tangier to Mauritania (al-Fassi 1961). The Liberation Army of the Sahara carried out sporadic attacks into the late 1950s. The French and Spanish governments applied diplomatic pressure for the RAF to refrain from offering it logistical or material support, and a joint Franco–Spanish military operation eventually eliminated the liberation army in the south in 1958.

Enforcing a Territorial Military Monopoly in the Atlas and the Rif

After absorbing/eliminating the Moroccan Liberation Army as a rival, the RAF successfully faced two tests in the late 1950s through which it proved its capacity to enforce its military monopoly in Moroccan territory: one in response to the revolt of a regional governor in the Atlas mountains and the other in response to a widespread uprising in the Rif Mountains in the north.[7] In both cases, economic and political grievances heightened tensions that broke out into open defiance of the central Moroccan state.

In January 1957, the governor of the Tafilelt province, Brahim Zedki Addi ou Bihi, who had received arms from French officers still assigned in Morocco, took action in protest against governmental officials appointed in the province by Rabat. He closed down the local offices of Istiqlal in the eastern High Atlas regional center of Midelt and blocked the north–south route from Fes and Meknes to the desert (Waterbury 1970, 236–37). In contrast to earlier forms of anti-state resistance in this region (examined in chapter 3), this conflict was not about protecting local autonomy from state intrusion (taxes, conscription, etc.) but about how the *makhzan* should function in this rural province. Addi ou Bihi, the local chief, resented the urban, bourgeois Istiqlal functionaries who had been sent down to run the regional administrative apparatus. He instead wanted direct vertical access to the king and to personally distribute the patrimonial resources of the state in his domain. The king's response was to have Crown Prince Hassan deploy two battalions to Midelt. The RAF forces successfully defused the situation, taking Addi ou Bihi into custody without any fighting and opening the road to the Tafilelt.

The second uprising, a much longer and more violent confrontation, occurred in the northern Rif Mountains, another Berber-speaking peripheral region. Again, in contrast to the anti-colonial resistance of the 1920s, the conflict did not concern *whether* but *how* the central state should project influence into the region. As in the Atlas, local actors were resentful about being marginalized while outsiders (urban Istiqlal members from the former French zone) benefited from the spoils of independence. This region,

---

7. Both of these cases have received substantial attention from Gellner (1972) and Waterbury (1970).

which had long relied on seasonal labor migration into western Algeria, faced increasingly dire economic conditions after France closed the border in 1954 following the outbreak of the war. Independence also had economic costs, as the post-protectorate Moroccan state retired the Spanish peseta as currency in the northern zone, cracked down on contraband and the trafficking of *kif* (a cannabis product), and enforced stricter forestry policies.

In 1958, these tensions were catalyzed into open revolt by the reburial of the MLA commander, Abbas el-Messadi. Messadi had been killed outside Fes in June 1956, reportedly at the order of the Istiqlal Party leader, Mehdi Ben Barka. On October 2, 1958, the third anniversary of the MLA's first anti-colonial attacks, Mahjoubi Aherdane and Abdulkarim al-Khatib, two former MLA leaders, exhumed Messadi's body near Fes and brought it north to Ajdir for a public reburial. Both were arrested for provoking a crowd of 5,000 by complaining about the dominance of Istiqlal and the MLA's lack of representation in the post-independence government. Aherdane's home region in the Middle Atlas near Oulmes also immediately revolted but was quickly subdued. In the Rif, the revolt escalated as Ait Waryaghar groups attacked the local Istiqlal Party offices in the Ait Hadhifa market (Hart 1976, 430) and targeted cars traveling through the region (Monjib 1992, 128–130; Waterbury 1970, 241–43).

The revolt, which was known in Tarifit as Assouggas N'Ouedhra, or the Year of the Mountain, had little formal shape beyond an anti-government, anti-Istiqlal agenda. The protestors remained pro-monarchy, but they also acclaimed Abd el-Krim, the exiled Rif leader who still played an important symbolic role in the north as titular head of the Maghrib Liberation Committee in Cairo. In November, a delegation of eight Rif leaders met with the king, but no cease-fire resulted. Hostilities in the Rif got worse in December, and over the next month, the RAF dropped leaflets and made radio broadcasts issuing an ultimatum from the king to disarm by January 7. After several segments of the Ait Waryaghar refused, the army began artillery and aerial bombardments. On January 9, 1959, Prince Hassan arrived in Tetouan to personally direct military operations as the army moved in to the Rif with 20,000 troops (out of a total of 28,000).[8] By the end of the month, close to 3,000 tribesmen had been killed and the state had forcefully projected its power back into the region. While the palace brutally wielded an iron fist in this episode, it blamed the Istiqlal Party for catalyzing the insurrection with heavy-handed administrative practices (Monjib 1992, 132).

---

8. For an account of the RAF's crackdown on the Ait Waryaghar, see Zartman (1964a, 86–91).

The Palace and the Political Parties

In tandem with these efforts to solidify its military monopoly, the monarchy actively strengthened its control in the political field in the late 1950s. Immediately after independence, the palace cracked down on the rural and urban elites it viewed as collaborators with the French, particularly the southern chiefs who had aligned with Glaoui during the king's exile. However, the primary challenge came from Istiqlal; the mass anti-colonial nationalist party constituted the monarchy's only viable rival for power. During the first years after independence, the palace perfected a three-pronged approach for dealing with Istiqlal and the other political parties that has since constituted its strategic political repertoire: pluralization, arbitration, and delayed democratization. By the time of Mohamed V's death in 1961, these strategies had neutralized the political threat posed by the nationalist parties. Internal divisions eventually led to a split in Istiqlal in 1959, and the monarchy was left standing as the sole dominant power player by the early 1960s.

The French actually laid the groundwork for political pluralization, when they invited representatives from Istiqlal, PDI "Youssefist" independents who were directly loyal to the king, and collaborators such as Glaoui and Kettani to participate in the negotiations at Aix-les-Bains in the summer of 1955 to end the protectorate and bring back the king (Monjib 1992, 29). Istiqlal's leverage as Morocco's largest political party was weakened when it consented to come to the conference as one among several participants. When Mohamed V formed his first government in December 1955, he replicated this strategy, offering nine posts to Istiqlal, five to the PDI and seven to rural and urban independents who were loyal to the king and were headed by Prince Hassan's childhood friend Ahmed Reda Guedira. The latter also included rural notables such as M'Barek Bekkai, a colonial army veteran and former pasha of Sefrou who had resigned in protest when the French exiled the sultan. Bekkai was named head of the first two post-independence governments in the period 1955–1958.

From the onset, the king cultivated a multiparty pluralistic political structure that inhibited challenges from a single dominant party such as Istiqlal. Monjib (1992, 55) observes that Mohamed V was a political realist who was smart enough to avoid the mistakes of King Farouq, who had hammered Egypt's Wafd party too hard, or the missteps of the Tunisian bey, who withered away in the face of a dominant nationalist *zaim*, or charismatic leader, such as Bourguiba. Instead, in the Moroccan power structure, the monarchy assumed the role of an arbiter that was above the political fray but was also pulling the strings by alternating favor among various factions (Waterbury

1970). After two years spent reining in Istiqlal, Mohamed V named one of its prominent leaders, Ahmed Belafrej, head of government in April 1958 and gave Istiqlal virtually all of the cabinet positions. This shift gave Istiqlal the upper hand against its rivals, which it used to purge other parties from government positions, particularly the PDI. By the fall of 1958, however, Istiqlal's heavy-handed tactics had contributed to a backlash in the Rif, as was discussed above. The labor movement also deeply resented Istiqlal's attempt to consolidate power. That same fall the largest union, the Union marocain de travail (UMT), asserted its autonomy by calling for a general strike.

In the late 1950s, tensions in Istiqlal also worsened between the leftist and conservative factions, represented respectively by Mehdi Ben Barka and Allal al-Fassi, who had reconsolidated his position in the party since returning from self-exile in 1956. In February 1959, these divisions, which the palace actively reinforced, led to a split: the "progressive" faction around Ben Barka, which had a more socialist orientation and ties to the labor movement, formed the Union nationales des forces populaires. The king, consistent with his strategy of alternating favor, reacted to the split by appointing Abdullah Ibrahim, the UMT labor leader, as head of the government. At this juncture, the monarchy also widened the political field, formally recognizing the Mouvement populaire that Abdulkarim al-Khatib and Mahjoubi Aherdane had formed in formed in 1957, a predominantly rural party with a Berber constituency that centered on loyalty to the throne and antagonism against Istiqlal. In May 1960, however, the king dismissed the leftist Ibrahim government and appointed himself head of government, Crown Prince Hassan as defense minister, and a cadre of independents and a few Istiqlal and Mouvement populaire members as the remaining ministers.

During this five-year process of political segmentation, the king, who had promised to form a constitutional monarchy with a separation of powers in the 1955 Throne Speech, also consistently delayed democratization. Elections and the drafting of a constitution were postponed long enough to make sure that neither could fundamentally threaten the monarchy's political supremacy. By the time the first elections were held in 1960 for local and municipal elections, the palace's strategy of pluralization and alternance had neutralized the threat that any one party could pose a viable challenge in the Moroccan political field. Similarly, when Hassan II, who ascended to the throne after his father's unexpected death in February 1961, announced a new constitution in November 1962, none of the Moroccan political parties had enough leverage to dictate or influence the formal (or informal) rules governing the exercise of power in post-independence Morocco. Instead of a British-style system that limited the sovereign to a figurehead role, in

Morocco the balance of power had shifted by the early 1960s toward a de Gaullist style of presidential monarchy with vast executive and legislative power.

The Monarchy and the Nation's Internal "Others"

The achievement of national independence in 1956 and the consolidation of power by the Alawid monarchy impacted segments of Moroccan society on the margins of the core Arabo-Islamic framing of national unity that nationalists had forged in the 1930s. During the first five years of independence, as this definition of national identity began to be reinforced through state policies, the formal status of Berbers, Jews, and women was explicitly and implicitly inscribed in legal structures and educational policies that involved varying degrees of inclusion and exclusion. In these respects, the post-protectorate field's logics of legibility and legitimization expressed both breaks and continuities with the colonial policies of legal and cultural recognition and nonrecognition for these internal "others."

Do Not Separate Us from Our Brothers, the Berbers

One of the king's first priorities immediately after independence was to abolish the judicial mechanism the colonial state used to mark an ethnic division between Berbers and Arabs. On July 13, 1956, Mohamed V made a symbolic trip to the heart of the Middle Atlas to deliver a speech that officially invalidated the Berber *dahir*.[9] He intentionally chose the Ajdir plateau near Khenifra because Thami el-Glaoui had gathered hundreds of tribal chiefs and thousands of Berber tribesmen there three years earlier to rally against the king before his exile. Before a crowd of 100,000 "Berber brothers," the king completed the framing process urban nationalists had begun in the 1930 Latif protests that unified Moroccan national identity around the concepts of Islam, love of nation, and attachment to the Alawid throne. The speech, quoted here at length, reiterated multiple themes urban Arab nationalists had underscored two decades earlier to counter the French colonial vulgate:

> It was in this region that the meeting of those that plotted against the nation and the throne was held [referring to Glaoui's 1953 rally]. Despite

---

9. Si Lahcen Youssi, the former minister of the interior, had come to prepare for the event in early June, using his influence among the tribal chiefs and elements of the Moroccan Liberation Army to gain support in the area. MAE, Maroc 1956–1968, Dossier 29 (1956–1960), Telegram no. 3250–3259 from André Louis Dubois reporting to French Minister of Foreign Affairs, June 13, 1956.

everything that these enemies of the country had decided, God made justice triumph. We are thus here with you today in this same place to make the voice of truth heard. It is natural that Moroccans, animated by a deep faith, stood against injustice and combined their efforts in the fight for the national cause. Since Islam spread its light in this country, it has cemented the union of its inhabitants and made a strong and united nation that no force in the world could divide, a unity that has been written in history for more than thirteen centuries. Our people, placed in the shadow of Islam, tolerating no discrimination between Arabs and Berbers, and with no other ideal than its love of nation, are an example of solidarity and brotherhood. It is this union that has made of us a glorious nation, which allowed our ancestors to found an empire so vaunted in history. What pain it was the day customary law was substituted for the law of Islam and placed over a portion of our subjects who were claimed to be separate from the framework of Islam and separated from their Arab brethren. Since that day you have not ceased to raise your voice in expressing your disapproval and protesting against a measure that offended your convictions, thus showing your deep attachment to Islam and your sense of national solidarity. For you, there was only one homeland, only one nation, and only one throne.

In this opening section, Mohamed V contextualized the French Berber policy in the context of the long view of Islamization processes in Morocco, which thirteen centuries earlier had "cemented" the unity of Arabs and Berbers together as one nation. He also reiterated the nationalist gloss that retroactively projected national solidarity in unified protest against France's Berber policy, lauding the "Berbers" in his audience for their attachment to Islam, nation, and king and for "not ceasing to raise their voices" against colonial divide-and-rule policies. He then announced the overturning of the Berber *dahir*, connecting his appointment of *makhzan* judges to "restore the law of Islam" in these areas to a larger narrative of national liberation and territorial unification:

Because of this, we have decided to abolish all artificial discriminatory measures and, first, restore to the law of Islam the place it deserves in your lands so that it is applied among all of our subjects. We pledge to send competent men to you to apply the law, who know your laws and customs, who are known for their integrity and their righteousness, and who will fulfill their duty to be sympathetic to your condition and deserving of your confidence and respect. Your patriotism, O faithful subjects, your piety, your attachment to the Crown, is known by all.

You have not ceased to furnish the clearest proof, especially in these past years, refuting all of the lies and slander. Thanks to the sacrifices made by us and our people, we have grasped our liberty and our independence, and accomplished our territorial unity.[10]

In the speech, the king acknowledged "Berbers" as an integral historic part of the nation and simultaneously subsumed them in a unified Islamic fraternity with their "Arab brothers." Although he nominally invoked Berbers, their markers of identity, whether cultural or linguistic, did not fit the official intertwined logics of legitimization and legibility the king intended to use to shape the post-protectorate political field.[11]

Instead, the Moroccan state's cultural and educational policy was shaped by the Islamization and Arabization nation-building program the urban nationalists had pressed for as far back as the 1930 "Berber crisis" petition described at the beginning of this book. In the first Throne Speech after independence, King Mohamed V announced: "We have as our cultural policy a national impetus to assure, to all of our youth, an education inspired by the spiritual principles of Islam and of Arab culture and a deep recognition of the history of our country. Our objective remains to be able to educate all of our children, to make this education free and mandatory for boys as well as girls. We have set a goal to Arabize the entire primary educational cycle within three years."[12]

The goal of Arabizing the education system within three years proved to be overly ambitious.[13] Under the first minister of education, Mohamed el-Fassi, the initial campaign was a resounding failure. The huge expansion in student numbers and the paucity of qualified Arabic instructors exposed the scope of the challenge. A royal commission was formed to study the issue and a group of Egyptian and Syrian teachers were brought in in 1958 to boost Arabic instruction. In 1959, the new minister of education, Abdelkarim Benjelloun, emphasized four priorities: unification of a single national educational system, Arabization, generalization of education in rural areas, and a Moroccanization of the teaching corps and curriculum. Over the next decades, however, despite multiple official pronouncements in

---

10. MAE, Maroc 1956–1968, Dossier 29 (1956–1960), Telegram no. 3260, text of July 11, 1956 speech at Ajdir, July 13, 1956.

11. On the parallel Algerian treatment of the Berber as "national signifiers," see McDougall (2006, chapter 5).

12. MAE, Maroc 1956–1968, Dossier 29 (19561960), "Discours du trône," November 18, 1956.

13. On Arabization policies in Morocco and the other Maghrib countries, see Grandguillaume (1983).

support of Arabization, actual practices oscillated between bilingual French and Arabic or monolingual Arabic instruction in the primary and secondary levels. French retained a prominent place in the upper levels and in science instruction. Similarly, in the state administration, official discourse favored Arabization but practice proved that French retained a privileged place. And although the judicial system was officially Arabized with a January 1, 1965, *dahir* on "Moroccanization, Unification, and Arabization," French continued to be used extensively in the writing of depositions and other documentation.

Although Arabic was symbolically enshrined in the official national imaginary, including a designation in the 1962 constitution as Morocco's national language, in practice it was clear that Arabization was a negotiable goal. Despite their ideological support for Arabization, the king and many of the urban nationalist elites (including Allal al-Fassi) ensured that their own children had access to a French education. Berbers still had no status in defining national identity in a post-independence Morocco in which Arabic was the official and French the unofficial language of the nation-state. In contrast to the ambivalence about Arabic and French, however, there was no question that Islam remained a nonnegotiable marker of Morocco national identity. This reality had significant consequences for Morocco's Jewish religious minority.

The Monarchy and the Jewish Question

During the transitional period from protectorate to independent Morocco, the majority of Moroccan Jews adopted a wait-and-see attitude to discern their options. As I discussed in chapter 6, Moroccan Jews occupied an ambiguous position in the core Muslim Moroccan national community imagined in the wake of the 1930 Berber *dahir*. After independence, the question remained: How did Morocco's indigenous non-Muslim population fit into the nation: as *dhimmis*, subjects, or citizens? This question was made more acute during the interwar period and after World War II as French assimilation and Zionism appealed to sectors of Morocco's Jewish community.

Throughout the post-independence transition, the monarchy continued to reaffirm the historic attachment of Morocco's Jews to the nation and to assure this population that it remained secure. In the 1955 Throne Speech delivered days after his return from exile, Mohamed V affirmed support for a separation of powers and emphasized "granting Moroccans of all faiths citizenship rights and the exercise of political and trade union freedoms. It stands to reason that the Moroccan Jews have the same rights and duties as other Moroccans" (Landau 1957, 107). In a speech almost one year later, on September 13, 1956, to the newly elected representatives on the Jewish community committees (an apparatus carried over from the protectorate to handle Jewish affairs), the king emphasized that Moroccan Jews should unite with the nation and not preserve a communitarian separate identity:

> We must direct your attention to an important point: in effect, as your president underlined, the benevolent activities of the Jewish works cannot be but provisional, as it is necessary for all Muslim and Jewish aid organizations to be combined and that they undertake a national, not [a] confessional, effort. In social matters, there is but one people who have the money. There cannot, on this point, be a distinction between Jews and Muslims. Consequently, their activities need to have a national character, because Moroccan citizens, Muslims or Jews, have the same rights and the same duties, which imply the same obligations, the same preoccupations, and the same tasks to undertake. They must combine all of their efforts and all of the means at their disposal to aid those in need.[14]

Here, the king described a trajectory of nationalization in which the provision of separate Jewish services, whether social or educational, would be eliminated; the Moroccan state would provide undifferentiated services to all of its "citizens."

Later in the same speech, the king addressed the issue of immigration, warning that this option undermined the ties of Morocco's Jews to their Moroccan national homeland:

> You must explain to your coreligionists who are thinking of immigration, who are leaving Morocco, their homeland, that this proves an absence of national feeling and [a perception] of not having faith in their own country. This is not a question of limiting the freedom of these citizens. You must also persuade those who want to leave that their place is here, that their duty demands that they stay and participate in the construction of their country. Morocco needs all of its sons.[15]

Concerned about their allegiance, the king exhorted Jewish leaders to commit to nation building in post-independence Morocco. To facilitate this, Istiqlal coordinated an official outreach to Morocco's Jewish community, under the nominal direction of Crown Prince Mawlay Hassan, through

---

14. Speech quoted in Annex 2, in Commander Honoré, "Les Israélites Marocaines et l'Independence du Maroc," *CHEAM* 2750 (November 29, 1956): 11.

15. Ibid.

the creation of a Judeo-Muslim association named Al-Wifaq (Entente). Its purpose was to organize meetings at which Jewish and Muslim speakers attempted to convince Moroccan Jews of their duty to integrate with the Moroccan community. An official declaration in 1956 against the Anglo-French-Israeli hostilities against Egypt stated the official policy of Istiqlal and the monarchy: "Here in Morocco there are only Moroccan citizens: Moroccans of the Muslim religion and Moroccans of the Jewish religion, but all are Moroccans" (quoted in Schroeter 2008, 158–59).

These appeals were relatively successful among Moroccan Jewish elites, who played active political and economic roles in independent Morocco. Several Jews held prominent positions in the post-independence Moroccan state. These included Léon Benzaquen, one of the king's physicians, who was appointed minister of post, telephone, and telegraph in the first government, and Salmon Azoulay, who was appointed a member of the Consultative Council of the Supreme Court. Moroccan Jews also played prominent roles in the leftist parties and the labor movement. Abraham Sefarty, a prominent figure in the Moroccan Communist Party, served in the late 1950s in the Ministry of Economy and later worked as director of research for the Office Chérifien des Phosphates, the mining conglomerate.[16] Immediately after independence, Jews were also allowed to serve in the RAF, although Crown Prince Hassan noted with regret that only one applied for officer candidacy in 1956.[17]

At the macrolevel, however, the exhortations from the palace and Istiqlal about Jewish assimilation and performing national duty did not staunch the steady flow leaving the nation.[18] In the 1950s–1960s, with the exception of a core community that mostly lived in Casablanca, many of Morocco's Jews living in the interior cities and the countryside emigrated for economic and ideological reasons.[19] After Mohamed V officially prohibited emigration in response to the 1956 Suez War, clandestine migration coordinated by the Mossad increased (Benros 1991, 67–68).[20] By 1960, the number of Jews

---

16. Sefarty was imprisoned and tortured in the 1970s, during Hassan II's reign, for his opposition. He was finally released in the early 1990s but was exiled from Morocco. He did not return until 2000, under the new king, Mohamed VI. He passed away in 2010.

17. Commander Honoré, "Les Israélites Marocaines et l'Independence du Maroc," *CHEAM* 2750 (November 29, 1956): 9.

18. For a comparative study of Jewish emigration from Morocco, Tunisia, and Algeria to Israel during the late colonial/early independence period, see Laskier (1994).

19. Boum's (2010) study of the migration of rural Jews from southern Morocco to Palestine indicates the relative importance of religious factors, including messianic Zionist sentiments and attachment to the Holy Land.

20. Much of this passed through the former Spanish zone and then to Israel via Gibraltar. In January 1961, the *Piscès*, a ship taking immigrants from Al Hoceima to Gibraltar, sank and forty-two died.

left in Morocco had been reduced from a peak of near 220,000 during the protectorate to 162,000 (Bensimon 1991). In the decade after 1962, when Hassan II lifted the ban on emigration, particularly after the 1967 War, much of the remaining population left Morocco for Israel, Europe, and North America. After independence, tensions over the ethnoreligious boundaries of the Moroccan nation and internal differentiation in the nation that had first come into light in dialogues in the 1930s between urban Arab nationalists and Jewish leaders (discussed in chapter 5) clearly remained salient. Despite official assurances about the equal status of this religious minority in the post-independence nation, Morocco's Jewish Question had largely become a nonissue a decade after independence due to mass emigration.

The Monarchy and Morocco's Women

The initial post-independence period also proved a critical window when the position of Morocco's women was defined. During this time precedents were established that had long-term consequences in the post-protectorate political field. As discussed in chapter 7, gender was heavily implicated in the colonial state's logics of classification, which relied on women's personal status under Islamic and customary law to differentiate between Arab and Berber (and similarly to mark Jewish identity) and on its framework of legitimization, which reinforced the practice of the traditionalizing educational curricula that was directed at Moroccan girls. In contrast, Moroccan nationalists and the king emphasized that legal and educational reform for Moroccan women was key for Morocco's national development. In this nationalist countervulgate, Moroccan women still constituted a critical site where ethnoreligious (Arabo-Islamic) identity was defined and the modern development of the nation was measured.

After independence, the king acted first on the legal front, overturning the Berber *dahir* and abolishing the customary legal system. The ostensible goal, which nationalists had championed since the 1930 Berber Crisis, was to unify a national judiciary that would implement shari'a. In practice, however, much of the existing criminal code and many of the commercial laws the French had implemented were retained with minor revisions and the area of law that was marked "Islamic" was the personal status code. In 1957, the king announced the creation of a special commission to codify the legal regulations of Moroccan family law and ground them in Islamic principles. The ten-member commission included government ministers, judges from the Islamic courts, a legal advisor from the palace, a representative from the consultative assembly, and the Istiqlal leader Allal al-Fassi. This commission drafted Morocco's Code of Personal Status, or Mudawana, which was promulgated in series of decrees published between November 1957 and March 1958.

In the Mudawana, the post-protectorate Moroccan state, like its colonial predecessor, used legal status as a primary mechanism for imposing and reinforcing linked logics of legibility and legitimacy. In this case, differentiation based on gender that allocated different legal and economic rights to men and women served an important symbolic role that reinforced the Islamic credentials of the Moroccan state. In the Mudawana, the commission upheld one of the historic pillars of the *makhzan*'s legitimacy, encoding a conservative interpretation of Maliki law that gave "men the upper hand in questions of marriage, divorce, and child custody while subjecting women to men's guardianship and permissions throughout their lives" (Salime 2011, 3). Except for minor modifications to the conditions of polygamy (a woman could include a right of option in the marriage contract that gave her legal options if her husband took a second wife), the minimum age for marriage (eighteen for men and fifteen for women instead of puberty, as prescribed in the Maliki school), and the "right of paternal constraining power" (the matrimonial guardian had to give consent to a marriage but could not force a woman into one), the code included few of the more progressive legal reforms Allal al-Fassi and others in the Istiqlal nationalist party had envisioned (Charrad 2001, 166–67).

As Salime points out, using women's status to mark Moroccan law as "Islamic" further privileged the king's role in defining national identity: "In the Moroccan case, the modernist convictions of nationalist leaders were . . . sacrificed to neo-nationalist imperatives of unity under the authority of the highly patriarchal law and a holy father-king" (Salime 2011, 4). In the struggle between the palace and Istiqlal in the late 1950s, the implementation of a conservative patriarchal expression of family law further consolidated the king's power as arbiter and ultimate power holder in the post-independence order. Charrad (2001) demonstrates how this legal move aligned the king with the rural notability at a structural level, shoring up tribal support in Morocco's interior.

How can we reconcile this conservative patriarchal turn with the monarchy's earlier progressive stance on women's advancement, the stance that constituted a hallmark of Mohamed V's anti-colonial framing in the 1940s–1950s? Here Mohamed V recapitulated Lyautey's dualist legacy by sponsoring a traditionalizing legal definition of the Moroccan woman's position in the national community in the 1957 Mudawana while simultaneously supporting a modernizing educational policy that greatly expanded

Moroccan women's access to primary and secondary schooling and for the first time giving them access to university education (Kozma 2003, 117–18). As it did in the colonial political field, gender is primary site since independence where state-based preservationist and developmentalist legitimizing logics and legibility policies of identification are focused.

In Morocco, a monarchy-centric version of Arabo-Islamic nationalism succeeded while virtually all of the other ancien régime dynasties in North Africa and the Middle East that survived colonization gave way to republican-style governments led by officer cadres or charismatic nationalist *za'ims*. This chapter has explored why and how King Mohamed V was different, examining the interacting contingencies and agencies involved in the Alawid monarchy's success in consolidating control over the space of the post-protectorate political field and over its symbolic and classificatory forces. France's choice to broker decolonization through Mohamed V—bringing him back from exile, formally transferring command to the monarchy of Moroccan colonial units, providing material support for the rechristened RAF, and paying the salaries of administrative, educational, and military functionaries that stayed on through the transitional first years after independence—was a critical reason for this outcome, as was support from the United States during the Cold War.[21]

But the Alawids' success cannot be attributed solely to these exogenous factors. Multiple endogenous processes were equally important. First, the monarchy consolidated the space of the post-protectorate political field by negotiating the unification of the former French, Spanish, and international zones and using the RAF to enforce a state-based military monopoly in this territory. Urban and rural anti-colonial insurgent groups were absorbed and episodes of rural insurrection in the Atlas and Rif were quelled in the first years after independence. Second, in the political field, the king craftily undermined Istiqlal's potential threat as a unified, mass nationalist party by insisting on a multiparty framework that enhanced his power as the arbiter and ultimate source of material and political patronage. By the late 1950s,

---

21. Despite controversy related to the military bases the Americans maintained in Morocco after independence, the monarchy allied Morocco firmly to the United States during the Cold War and received military, economic, and diplomatic support in return. As a result of NATO defense agreements arranged with the French in the early 1950s, the U.S. had air bases at Sidi Sliman, Ben Guerir, and Nouasseur and a naval station at Port Lyautey, in addition to radar and communications installations in the Atlas and at Sidi Yahya and Sidi Bouknadel. Over 10,000 American military personnel were stationed in Morocco by the late 1950s (Zartman 1964b). Although the air bases were closed by the mid-1960s, the naval station at Port-Lyautey (Kenitra) remained active until the mid-1970s.

Istiqlal had split into two parties and no single political party had the leverage to seriously challenge the monarchy's ability to dictate the rules of the game.

Finally, the monarchy successfully consolidated its control over the symbolic dimensions of the post-protectorate political field. This legitimizing logic was neatly encapsulated in the triptych that was constitutionally recognized as Morocco's national motto in 1962: *Allah* (God), *al-Watan* (Nation), *al-Malik* (King). As this study has shown, urban nationalists countered the protectorate's ethnographic logics of legibility beginning in the early 1930s by insisting on an Arabo-Islamic national imaginary that glossed over Morocco's ethnic and religious diversity. They also, from the beginning, made the monarchy a focal point for claims about national sovereignty, a role that Mohamed V increasingly took control of in the 1940s. This visibility as an anti-colonial nationalist hero gained him enormous symbolic capital during his exile and at his return in the mid-1950s. After independence, Mohamed V, as Commander of the Faithful, used his unique position to further conflate *al-watan* (nation) and *al-malik* (king), fusing the multiple components of national identity in his own person. The result was an ideological and symbolic framework of legitimacy that recapitulated Lyautey's preservationist and developmental logics of legibility, with the king exercising supreme legislative and executive power as the protector of both traditional religio-political identity and economic and political modernization in Morocco.

Conclusion

                    This book has explored how European colonial intervention politicized Moroccan identities. Emphasizing that the protectorate period was a fundamental historical rupture that cannot be parenthesized but must be integrally woven into our understanding of contemporary Morocco, I have attempted to contribute to the writing of a new colonial history that is both postcolonial and postnationalist, that avoids reproducing teleological interpretations but conveys the complexities, contingencies, nuances, and contradictions expressed during this critical transition in the country's history. I have focused on causation, but instead of unidirectional arrows—top-down colonial state formation or bottom-up national liberation or subaltern resistance—this study has traced relational mechanisms and processes.

   The making of modern Morocco was not solely carried out by either the colonial powers or local parties: it happened in interactions among them. These interactions occurred over time among elites that included colonial administrators, the Moroccan king, and urban Arab anti-colonial nationalists, but they also encompassed marginalized groups—including rural mostly Berber-speaking populations, the Jewish religious minority, and Moroccan women—who were both central objects and agents in contentious struggles over Moroccan identity. The outcome these interactions produced was the politicization, in unprecedented and lasting ways, of four identity-related poles: Moroccan territory, Moroccan Muslim and Jewish religious identities,

Moroccan Arab and Berber ethnic identities, and the Alawid monarchy. This book also demonstrated how gender was fundamental to the politics of the last three of these.

The central concept I used to capture processes related to the re-formation and politicization of Moroccan identities is the *colonial political field*. Bringing together literatures focused on colonial rule on one side and nationalist and subaltern modes of anti-colonial resistance against it on the other, this study plotted colonial and local actors together in the same field, asking how they interacted. Three basic field properties structured the book's analysis: the space of the field; the organizing forces in that space; and the struggles that played out among actors, both according to the field's rules of the game and beyond those rules.

Chapter 1 looked at the spatial expansion of a state-governed political field from the onset of French and Spanish military intervention in 1907 through the completion of pacification operations in mid-1930s. This military conquest, which progressively monopolized state control in a defined territorial unit, radically reshaped a previous political ecosystem in which multiple power centers, both state and nonstate, interpenetrated and interacted. The space of the field was cartographically defined and this territory was internally partitioned into separate subnational zones of Spanish and French control and an international zone in the immediate environs of the port city of Tangier. These processes politicized Morocco's territorial boundaries in ways that were unprecedented in its precolonial history, creating new forms of internal variation, raising the stakes for post-protectorate unification, and leaving questions open regarding Morocco's southeastern (with Algeria) and southern borders (the now-contested territory of the Western Sahara/Moroccan Sahara) in ways that have led to continued conflict since independence.

Chapter 2 turned to the intertwined legitimization and legibility logics that organized the colonial political field created in Morocco. I highlighted the importance of initial conditions—the international, metropolitan, and local contexts—that contingently determined why the French set up a formal protectorate structure through which to intervene in Morocco. Because of a constellation of factors related to the strategic and economic interests of the Great Powers, debt structures involving French banks and the Moroccan government, internal French struggles between the colonial lobby and the Ministry of Foreign Affairs, and broader transimperial shifts in the late nineteenth century toward modes of indirect rule, Morocco came into the French Empire through a treaty framework that formally preserved the sovereignty of the Alawid dynasty and included French pledges to modernize and develop the country while at the same time safeguarding its traditions.

This critical juncture at the onset of colonial intervention and the appointment of Hubert Lyautey as the protectorate's first resident general had path-dependent consequences for the organizing forces of the colonial political field. The Palace of Morocco exhibit at the 1931 International Colonial Exposition in Paris offered a window into the threefold mode of rule the colonial state implemented: 1) ethnographic—"seeing" Arabs, Berbers, and Jews; 2) preservationist—"seeing" tradition in urban space and architecture, education, religion and in the *makhzan* and palace protocols; and 3) developmentalist—"seeing" a modern economy (agriculture, mining, industry) that was distinct from the traditional "native" economy. This linkage of legibility and legitimization profoundly influenced the state-based identification processes the French implemented in Morocco. If (as they did in Algeria) the French had eradicated the indigenous ruling elite, engaged in an explicit policy of territorial annexation and settler colonization, and systematically marginalized the history and culture of the indigenous population, Moroccan identity would have been politicized in very different ways.

Colonial intervention forged the space of a political field and set up organizing logics in it. However, these factors do not fully explain the complex ways that identity became politicized in Morocco. They clarify the field's third dimension: how it functioned as an arena of struggle and competition among actors situated in it. The bulk of this study focused on this part of the story, looking beyond just colonial elite actors or their Moroccan analogs in the palace or the nationalist movement to include a wide spectrum of rural and urban Moroccan women and men. These chapters analyzed society-based internal and external identification processes through which certain features of Moroccan identity became politically salient. Chapters 3 and 4 looked at rural Berber-speaking groups in the Atlas and Rif Mountains, examining a period of three decades during which these groups militarily resisted the expansion of the colonial political field but were ultimately violently subdued by the colonial state. These chapters explored how these groups experienced and interpreted the remapping of political space. Specifically, they focused on how notions of identity—with regard to their own group, the colonial state and army, the Moroccan sultan/*makhzan*, and other groups in Moroccan society—were projected, debated, and modified through the traumas of colonial subjugation, collective defensive jihad against this threat, and the ultimate failure of this resistance and the incorporation of these groups into the colonial political field.

As the colonial political field was consolidated between 1912 and the early 1930s, its ethnographic, preservationist, and developmentalist organizing logics shaped how colonial and local actors interacted, how policies were justified, and how claims were made in this space. The protectorate framework of legitimization and the classificatory legibility the colonial state implemented set the terms of identity struggles, creating their starting points and ground rules. Moroccan actors at times played along with these rules, seeking to maximize perceived advantages provided in the protectorate's formal structure. For example, the urban Arab nationalists discussed in chapter 5 appealed to the protectorate's formal legitimization logics in their push for reforms in the 1930s, arguing that the French were supposed to be strengthening the Moroccan state instead of undermining it through divide-and-rule policies, that economic development should benefit Moroccans and not just Europeans, and that the French should not treat Morocco as a colony like Algeria because they had pledged to uphold the Moroccan sultan's sovereignty. In working to mobilize mass support, the emerging nationalist leadership exploited the monarchy's formal position in the protectorate legitimization structure, using Mohamed V as a focal point in their framing of Moroccan national identity and unity in events like Throne Day. A decade later, Mohamed V began to move in this direction himself, gradually exploiting the symbolic position both the French and nationalist had cultivated for him.

Moroccans also challenged the rules of the game, seeking to renegotiate them or use these as focal points for struggle. This was exemplified in how the urban nationalists seized on the French Berber policy as a rallying cause. In critiquing the legal and linguistic legibility practices that differentiated Berbers from Arabs, they also inflated the symbolic importance of a decree they named the Berber *dahir*, rallying public support by broadcasting a threat against Islam. The colonial politics of recognition that flowed from the ethnographic logics of the Moroccan vulgate served as a target for the nationalists' classification struggles. The counter-vulgate they and later the sultan supported instead pushed for state-based processes of linguistic and cultural homogenization. According to the logics of this rival legitimization framework, Arabic and Islamic identity formed historical axes of Moroccan unification over centuries of history and the state should support the legal unification of the country under a shari'a-based judiciary and the expansion of Islamic and Arabic instruction. French Jews and some Moroccan Jews also challenged the rules of the protectorate field. They vociferously pressed the residency to reconsider its insistence that under the protectorate's legitimization/legibility logics Morocco's Jews remained subjects of the Moroccan sultan and could not be naturalized as French citizens (as had been done in Algeria in 1870 and in limited numbers in Tunisia after 1910).

National Identity, Subaltern "Others," and Boundary Work in Colonial Contexts

This study focused on how identities function as categories of social and political practice rather than as categories of analysis. The shift in emphasis is subtle but significant. For example, instead of reifying Arabs and Berbers as units of analysis, the error of "groupism" that Brubaker (2004) critiques, I have asked how various actors—both colonial and Moroccan—used notions of collective identity (ethnic or other) in reference to themselves (internal processes of identification) and to others (external processes of identification). My argument, of course, is not that precolonial collective identities in Morocco did not exist. Rather, it is that colonial intervention catalyzed new identity-related processes through which historical, religious, ethnic, gendered, regional, and national identities came to be used by actors in historically unprecedented ways as politically relevant categories of practice. I have focused on how and why ethnic categories such as Arabic and Berber and religious identities such as Muslim and Jew emerged in the colonial political field as central sites for state- and society-based processes of internal and external identification. I have also demonstrated how gender functioned, for both the colonial state and for Moroccan actors such as the urban nationalists and the monarchy, as an essential mechanism that marked these ethnic and religious categories of identity.

This approach constituted identification as an object of analysis that exists in a processual rather than a static form. In Morocco, colonial intervention reconfigured the institutional order and incentives related to state- and society-based identity boundaries and catalyzed struggles among elite and non-elite colonial and local actors over their political implications. This study helped clarified how the making, maintenance, and contestation of social boundaries (Lamont and Molnar 2002; Wimmer 2008) functions in colonial contexts. This question is important on both theoretical and pragmatic grounds because of the preponderance of societies globally that are postcolonial. For these cases, colonial intervention was a particularly influential rupture that created or redefined the symbolic and classificatory schemas in a political field and thereby shaped subsequent identification processes in that field. A careful consideration of the colonial past is therefore imperative for understanding the contemporary constitution of ethnic and national identities, including their manifest and repressed dimensions and the varied strengths of their political salience, in myriad contemporary cases.

The nation is a configuration of identity that emerges as a product of interacting and competing state- and society-based identification processes.

Within colonial political fields, the nation is defined by a boundary with a primary Other, the colonizer. These identification processes also focus on internal boundaries in the "colonized" society, the levels of differentiated inclusion in the nation by which smaller Others (Duara 1995) are ambiguously included/excluded. This process of what Mitchell (2002) refers to as "making-other" is influenced in colonial contexts by the legibility practices the colonial state used. In Morocco, urban nationalists, emphasizing a reactionary countervulgate in which Morocco was unified by a shared history of Islamization, Arabization, and Islamic dynastic rule, set up degrees of inclusion and exclusion for the non-Arab and non-Muslim. This study examined the ambiguities embedded in this configuration, which go directly back to the modified Latif prayer first used in the anti–Berber *dahir* protests in 1930, which concluded with the phrase "do not separate *us* from our brothers the Berbers."

The paradoxes of this type of configuration, in which both unity and the implied distinction between "us" and the "Berbers" are invoked, created an even stronger ambiguity for Morocco's non-Muslim population, Jews, who were simultaneously included as citizen-subjects in the Moroccan community and distinguished as a religious minority. Chapter 8 examined how Morocco's Jews were caught in a three-way struggle between French assimilation, Zionism, and Moroccan nationalism. As the post-protectorate political field was constituted during the transition period of 1956 to 1961, a differentiated cultural and political inclusion in the nation persisted and most Moroccan Jews elected to emigrate. After independence, the unitary Arabo-Islamic configuration the urban nationalists had framed in the 1930s became the official cultural and linguistic policy for the post-independence Moroccan state. These features of Moroccan identity were officially recognized, while others—particularly Berber historical, cultural, or linguistic markers—were stigmatized and marginalized (in this case invoking the earlier purported threat against Islam posed by France's Berber policy).

One of the unique features of the field approach to identity in this study is that in writing a new type of colonial history, it moves subaltern, marginalized groups such as Berbers and Jews to the foreground. I have argued this is necessary not just as a form of historiographical affirmative action, creating a more inclusive narrative that reintegrates excluded populations (though in my opinion this represents a full justification in and of itself); it is also analytically necessary to understand how state formation and nation formation work. A field approach has helped me move away from a state-centric bias in the ways that empire and colonialism have been studied. I have emphasized not just how colonial administrators form policy but how that policy is implemented and, most important, how local actors are impacted by it: how they resist, accommodate, evade, or co-opt colonial administration.

Subaltern groups are fundamental to the identification processes that play out in the colonial political field for two reasons. First, they are objects of external identification by colonial-state elites who emphasize ethnic and religious identities in their classificatory schema. This intensifies the political stakes related to these categories of identity. Majority-group elites who challenge colonial power seek to redraw or eliminate these classifications in efforts to legitimate their own claims to national unity and sovereignty. The incentives here are often tied not to existing but to potential group identities. The stakes of these identity conflicts, in effect, concern trajectories of assimilation. In the Moroccan case, urban nationalists wanted state policies to reinforce Arab and Muslim identity, not reinforce divisions in Moroccan society. The second reason subaltern groups have to be incorporated into the scope of analysis is because they themselves actively engaged in external and internal identification struggles. This book examined how Berbers, Jews, and women were not just objects of colonialist or nationalist constructions of ethno-religious identity. They deployed identity-related categories of practice themselves that used boundaries of inclusion and exclusion in diverse ways with regard to religious, political, and regional identities and in relationship to the monarchy. These categories of self-identification related to ethnicity, religion, and gender shifted over time during the protectorate and have continued to shift during the post-independence period up to the present.

The Politics of Identity in Other Colonial Political Fields

The field analysis developed here for Morocco can be extended to studying the effects of colonial intervention elsewhere in North Africa and the Middle East, or for cases further afield (in Asia, in Africa, in the Americas, and even in Europe) where new political units were created in the framework of empire. This approach offers a framework for comparative analysis that emphasizes 1) the importance of critical junctures at which political fields come into existence and at which their space and the symbolic and classificatory forces that order them are defined; and 2) how these initial conditions influence the terms (or rules of the game) through which identification processes consequently play out. While the initial Treaty of Fes set terms in Morocco with a strong path-dependent influence on the trajectory of the protectorate, in other cases, the critical juncture at which a political field was created extended over a longer formative period. In Algeria, the first four decades of French intervention were a critical formative period in which the space of the field was being brutally extended. However, the organizing logics of legitimization and legibility that ordered this space remained ambivalently contested between supporters of direct assimilationist rule and supporters of a more indirect associationist model. The former emerged predominant after 1870, leading to results that were both similar and different than in Morocco. In terms of legitimization, the dey and other potential local leaders were eliminated, so no equivalent symbolic figure like the sultan was available for making identity claims. In terms of legibility, similar attempts to differentiate Arabs and Berbers (Kabyles) through educational and legal structures were implemented and Algerian nationalists engaged in an energetic classification struggle against this legibility policy.[1] In contrast to Morocco, though, Algeria's Jews were unilaterally naturalized as French citizens by the Crémieux Decree in 1870. The dominant configuration of Algerian national identity that eventually emerged from interactive struggles in that colonial field centered on a different triptych than Morocco's "God, Nation, King." A motto of the Algerian Association of Ulama was later adopted as the country's official slogan: "Islam is my religion, Arabic is my language, and Algeria is my nation (watan)."

A field model also offers useful insights into the different trajectories of political units created in the Middle East through the partitioning of the Ottoman Empire. Post–World War I Palestine, like Algeria, is another case where the formative period when the political field was constituted was marked by the ambivalence of the legitimization/legibility linkage. The contradictory pledges to Jews and Arabs that were built into the mandate the League of Nations awarded the British ambivalently defined both the legitimization structure and the logics of legibility of the colonial political field. Spatially the field was subdivided early in the 1920s into separate state-governed territories in Palestine and Transjordan, creating separate trajectories that took these units in very different directions. Within Palestine, the ambiguous ordering forces in this political field, which remained unresolved up until the British termination of the mandate in 1948, greatly influenced how various actors on the Jewish and Arab sides made claims. In Transjordan, the British decision in 1921 to recognize Abdullah as emir established a created a completely different legitimization framework, and in the mandate and post-independence state of Jordan, legibility policies that differentiated

---

1. See McDougall (2005) on the Algerian construction of Arabo-Islamic identity and approaches to the Berber Question.

Bedouin and sedentary groups greatly influenced the development of the colonial army and the power structure.[2] A field model could also be used to analyze the British mandate in Iraq or the French mandates in Syria and Lebanon, focusing on the consolidation of state space in these units in the face of intense resistance in the 1920s and how various local groups that were brought together in these units interacted with the formal legitimization logics and the classificatory systems the colonial administration implemented that directly politicized sectarian and ethnic group identities.

Beyond North Africa and the Middle East, this field framework offers a resource for other single case studies or for comparative studies of internal variation in an empire or among different empires, tracing the different trajectories of identity politics in various formal legitimization frameworks (colony, protectorate, mandate, territory). It also might usefully be used, even for metropolitan cases, to analyze how periods of intensified state formation when the legitimization framework of the political field was renegotiated or got locked in shaped path dependencies with regard to how legibility structures develop. As has been clear throughout this book, this type of comparative and historical analysis cannot focus only on state-based processes of identification and classification (caste, legal pluralism, sectarian representation, educational tracks). It must also account for how local actors—both elite and subaltern—were shaped by and shaped the identification processes catalyzed by structural shifts.

Colonial Legacies and Morocco's Contemporary Identity Politics

> The Kingdom of Morocco, a sovereign Muslim state attached to its national unity and territorial integrity, intends to preserve, in its plenitude and diversity, its one and indivisible national identity. Its unity, forged by the convergence of its Arabo-Islamic, Amazigh, and Saharan-Hassanian components, is nourished by its African, Andalusian, Hebrew, and Mediterranean influences. The preeminence accorded to the Muslim religion in this national reference is consistent with the attachment of the Moroccan people to the values of openness, moderation, tolerance, and dialogue for mutual comprehension among all of the cultures and civilizations of the world.
>
> —*Preamble to the 2011 Moroccan Constitution*

---

2. On the interactive process of state building and nation building in Jordan, see Massad (2001).

Finally, it is important to suggest, albeit briefly, how this analysis of the politi-cization of identities in the colonial political field can be extended in the Moroccan case, where the legacies examined in this book continue to influ-ence contemporary renegotiations of identity in the twenty-first century. As the quote of the preamble to the new 2011 Moroccan constitution clearly shows, the four pillars of Moroccan identity that emerged as primary sites of struggle during the colonial period—territory, religion, ethnicity, and the monarchy—remain the foci of both state-based and society-based identifica-tion processes in the current Moroccan political field.[3]

The continuing process of making Morocco, in which these four poles of identity remain political salient, still involves interactions and struggles among multiple elite and non-elite actors. In the 1980s, in the midst of what Moroccans refer to as Hassan II's repressive *années de plomb* (years of lead), multiple grassroots movements began to challenge various dimensions of the post-independence configuration of Moroccan national identity cen-tered on Arabo-Islamic ethno-religious unity, the Alawid throne, and the territorial integrity of the *watan*. After occupying Spanish Sahara with the "Green March" in November 1975, Morocco fought a fifteen-year war against the forces of the Frente Popular de Liberación deSaguía el Hamra y Río de Oro (Popular Front for the Liberation of Saguia el-Hamra and Río de Oro), which were seeking to establish an independent Western Sahara. The international status of the Saharan provinces remains unresolved and the "territorial integrity" the constitution's preamble refers to indicates how sen-sitive this issue remains in the Moroccan political field. Over the past three decades, the Amazigh (Berber), women's rights, and Islamist movements have been three other society-based sources of pressure to renegotiate the ethnic, gendered, and religious dimensions of Moroccan identity.[4]

The monarchy's response to these pressures has, to a large degree, func-tioned in remarkable continuity with the ethnographic, preservationist, and developmentalist logics of legitimization and legibility described in this book. Beginning in Hassan II's last decade and increasing under Mohamed VI since his succession in 1999, the palace has continued to use the strate-gic repertoire of co-optation and arbitrage it developed with respect to the politics of identity during the anti-colonial struggle. Mohamed VI's multi-culturalist pivot for redefining a bi-ethnic or multiethnic Moroccan identity

---

3. King Mohamed VI instituted the constitutional reform process in 2011 in response to the February twentieth movement protests during the "Arab Spring."

4. On the rise of Amazigh activism, see Maddy-Weitzmann (2011) and Silverstein and Craw-ford (2004). On the Moroccan women's movement, see Daoud (1993), Salime (2011), and Guessous (2011). On the Islamist challenge to the monarchy, see Tozy (1999) and Willis (2007).

was initiated in an October 2001 speech at Ajdir (the very Middle Atlas site where his grandfather overturned the Berber *dahir* in 1956), where he announced the creation of the Royal Institute for Amazigh Culture. Eighty years after the Berber *dahir* protests, the monarchy's Berber policy entails an ethnocultural politics of recognition that involves reintroducing the teaching of Tamazight in schools and, in the 2011 constitutional reform, declaring Tamazight an official state language alongside Arabic. The presence and memory of Morocco's Jews also is a critical component of a reimagined pluralistic yet unified national identity and a state-supported projection of tolerant Moroccan Islam (Kosansky and Boum 2012). The 2004 reform of women's rights in Morocco's personal status code, the Mudawana, that King Mohamed VI sponsored demonstrates how the fundamental linkage between gender and Moroccan identity continues to be contested and renegotiated. Finally, as Commander of the Faithful, the king tries to fend off Islamist challenges (and still-nascent secularist challenges) regarding the role of religion in the political field. To a remarkable degree, the monarchy continues to cultivate the dualist legitimization framework Lyautey forged at the inception of the protectorate, one that fuses traditionalization and modernization in variety of preservationist and developmentalist policies.[5]

This book looked back to the colonial period to ask why and how *Allah, al-Watan, al-Malik* (God, Country, and King) came to be written on Morocco's hillsides. The ongoing interactive process through which Moroccans struggle over this identity, "making Morocco" in the twenty-first century, is the subject of another book.

---

5. The palace party created in 2008 was called the Party of Authenticity and Modernity (Hizb al-asala wa al-mu'asara). The palace's modernization ambitions are expressed in showcase development projects such as the Tangier-Med Port, a proposed high-speed railway from Tangier to Casablanca, light railway projects in Rabat and Casablanca, and numerous large-scale real estate projects around the country.

❧ References

Archives and Libraries

France

Académie des sciences d'outre-mer. Paris
Alliance Israélite Universelle. Paris
Bibliothèque nationale de France, François-Mitterand Library. Paris
Centre des archives d'outre-mer. Aix-en-Provence (CAOM)
Institut de monde arabe. Fond Ninard. Paris
Institut de recherches et d'études sur le monde arabe et musulman (IREMAM).
    Fond Roux. Aix-en-Provence (Fond Roux)
Ministère des Affaires etrangères. La Courneuve (MAE)
Ministère des Affaires etrangères. Centre des archives diplomatiques. Nantes
    (MAE, CADN)
Service historique de la défense. Archives de l'armée de Terre. Château de Vincennes
    (SHD-AT)

Morocco

Al-Khizanat al-hassaniyya bi-l-qasr al-maliki (Hassan Archive of the Royal Palace).
    Rabat
Al-Maktabat al-wataniya li-mamlakat al-maghribiya (National Library of the King-
    dom of Morocco). Rabat
Maktabat Bennouna (Bennouna family library). Tetoutan
Maktabat Daoud (Daoud family library). Tetouan
Maktabat Qarawiyin. Fes
Al-Mandabiyat al-samiya li-quduma' al-muqawimin wa a'ada' jaysh al-tahrir (High
    Commission for the Resistance and Army of Liberation). Rabat
La Source. Rabat

Newspapers and Periodicals

Arabic

al-Chihab (Constantine), 1925–1939
al-Rif (Tetouan), 1946–1947
al-Maghreb (Rabat), 1937
al-'Alam (Rabat), 1946–1947, 1948, 1951, 1953–1957, 1961
al-Atlas (Rabat), 1937
al-Difaa (Fes), 1937
al-Huria (Tetouan), 1940, 1942
al-Wahdat al-Maghribiya (Tetouan), 1938, 1939, 1942

Risalat al-Maghrib (Tangier), 1951
al-Sa'ada (Rabat), 1911–1956

French

Annuaire Statistique du Maroc (Rabat), 1948–1953
Bulletin Officiel, Maroc (Rabat), 1915–1931
Hespéris: archives berbères et bulletin de l'Institut des hautes-études marocains (Rabat), 1921–1956
L'Action du peuple (Fes), 1933–1934
L'Action du peuple (Fes), 1937
L'Afrique française (Paris), 1930–1939
L'Avenir illustrée (Casablanca), 1926–1940
Le Maroc Catholique (Rabat), 1920–1935
La Nation Arabe (Geneva), 1930–1939
Le Courrier du Maroc (Fes), 1937
Le Journal de Maroc (Rabat), 1930
Maghreb (Paris), 1932–1935

Books and Articles

Abellán García-Muñoz, Juan. 2005. *Aviones de la aviación militar española en la Guerra de Marruecos, 1913–1928.* Madrid: Ministerio de Defensa, Secretaría General Técnica.

Abi-Mershed, Osama. 2010. *Apostles of Modernity: Saint-Simonians and the Civilizing Mission in Algeria.* Palo Alto, CA: Stanford University Press.

Abitbol, Michel. 1998. *Les commerçants du roi: Tujjār Al-Sulṭān. Une élite économique judéo-marocaine au XIXe siècle; lettres du Makhzan, traduites et annotées.* Paris: Maisonneuve et Larose.

Abouzeid, Leila. 1989. *The Year of the Elephant.* Austin, TX: Center for Middle Eastern Studies at University of Texas-Austin.

Abugideiri, Hibba. 2010. *Gender and the Making of Modern Medicine in Colonial Egypt.* Farnham, England: Ashgate Publishing.

Abu-Lughod, Janet L. 1980. *Rabat: Urban Apartheid in Morocco.* Princeton, NJ: Princeton University Press.

——. 1987. "The Islamic City—Historic Myth, Islamic Essence, and Contemporary Relevance." *International Journal of Middle East Studies* 19(2): 155–76.

Abu-Lughod, Lila. 1986. *Veiled Sentiments: Honor and Poetry in a Bedouin Society.* Berkeley: University of California Press.

——. 1990. "The Romance of Resistance: Tracing Transformations of Power through Bedouin Women." *American Ethnologist* 17(1): 41–55.

——, ed. 1998. *Remaking Women: Feminism and Modernity in the Middle East.* Princeton, NJ: Princeton University Press.

Abun-Nasr, Jamil. 1963. "The *Salafiyya* Movement in Morocco: The Religious Bases of the Moroccan Nationalist Movement." *Middle Eastern Affairs* (3): 91–105.

——. 1973. *A History of the Maghrib.* New York: Cambridge University Press.

——. 1987. *A History of the Maghrib in the Islamic Period.* New York: Cambridge University Press.

Adams, Julia. 2005. *The Familial State.* Ithaca, NY: Cornell University Press.

Ageron, Charles-Robert. 1972. *Politiques coloniales au Maghreb.* Paris: Presses universitaires de France.

Alexander, Jeffrey. 2004. "Cultural Pragmatics: Social Performance between Ritual and Strategy." *Sociological Theory* 22(4): 527–73.

Amster, Ellen. 2004. "The Many Deaths of Dr. Émile Mauchamp: Medicine, Technology, and Popular Politics in Pre-Protectorate Morocco, 1877–1912," *International Journal of Middle East Studies* 36(3): 409–28.

Anderson, Benedict. 1991. *Imagined Communities: Reflections on the Origin and Spread of Nationalism.* London: Verso.

Anderson, Matthew Smith. 1966. *The Eastern Question, 1774–1923: A Study in International Relations.* New York: Macmillan.

Anthias, Floya, Jo Campling, and Nira Yuval-Davis, eds. 1989. *Woman-Nation-State.* New York: St. Martin's Press.

Aouad, Rita. 2013. "Slavery and the Situation of Blacks in Morocco in the First Half of the Twentieth Century." In *Revisiting the Colonial Past in Morocco,* edited by Driss Maghraoui, 142–56. London: Routledge.

Aouchar, Amina. 1990. *La Presse marocaine dans la lutte pour l'indépendance (1933–1956).* Casablanca: Wallada.

———. 2002. *Colonisation et campagne berbère au Maroc.* Casablanca: Afrique Orient.

Archives marocaines: publication de la Mission scientifique du Maroc. 1904–1910. Paris: Ernest Leroux.

Ashford, Douglas. 1959. "Politics and Violence in Morocco." *Middle East Journal* 13(1): 11–25.

Assaraf, Robert. 2005. *Une certaine histoire des juifs du Maroc: 1860–1999.* Paris: Gawsewitch.

Attal, Robert. 2002. *Les Émeutes de Constantine: 5 Août 1934.* Paris: Editions Romillat.

Ayache, Germain. 1981. *Les origines de la guerre du Rif.* Rabat, Morocco: Société marocaine des éditeurs réunis.

Badran, Margot. 1995. *Feminists, Islam, and Nation: Gender and the Making of Modern Egypt.* Princeton, NJ: Princeton University Press.

Baker, Alison. 1998. *Voices of Resistance: Oral Histories of Moroccan Women.* Albany: State University of New York Press.

Balfour, Sebatian. 2002. *Deadly Embrace: Morocco and the Road to the Spanish Civil War.* New York: Oxford University Press.

Barkey, Karen. 2008. *Empire of Difference: The Ottomans in Comparative Perspective.* New York, Cambridge University Press.

Baron, Beth. 2005. *Egypt as a Woman: Nationalism, Gender, and Politics.* Berkeley: University of California Press, 2005.

Béguin, Hubert. 1974. *L'organisation de l'espace au Maroc.* Brussels: Académie royale des sciences d'outre-mer

Beissinger, Mark. 2002. *Nationalist Mobilization and the Collapse of the Soviet State.* Cambridge, UK: Cambridge University Press.

Benaboud, M., and J. Cagne. 1982. "Le Congres du Maghreb arabe de 1947 et les debuts du Bureau du Maghreb arabe au Caire: L'operation Ibn Abd-al-Karim." *Revue d'histoire maghrebine* 25–26: 17–32.

Benhlal, Mohamed. 2005. *Le collège d'Azrou: une élite berbère civile et militaire au Maroc, 1927–1959.* Aix-en-Provence, France: IREMAN.

Benros, Jonathan. 1991. *Migrations Juives Du Maroc.* Paris: Imprimerie EMF.

Bensimon, Agnès. 1991. *Hassan II et les juifs: histoire d'une émigration secrète.* Paris: Seuil.

Berger, Olivier. 2013. "Civilian Administrators in Protectorate Morocco." In *Revisiting the Colonial Past in Morocco,* edited by Driss Maghraoui, 115–27. London: Routledge.

Berque, Jacques. 1967. *French North Africa: The Maghrib between Two World Wars.* New York: Praeger.

——. 1974. *Maghreb, Histoire et Sociétés.* Gembloux, France: Duculot.

——. 1982. *Ulèmas, fondateurs, insurgés du Maghreb: XVIIe siècle.* Paris: Sindbad.

Betts, Raymond. (1960) 2005. *Assimilation and Association in French Colonial Theory, 1890–1914.* Lincoln: University of Nebraska Press.

Bhambra, Gurminder. 2007. *Rethinking Modernity: Postcolonialism and the Sociological Imagination.* Basingstoke: Palgrave MacMillan.

Bidwell, Robin. 1973. *Morocco under Colonial Rule: French Administration of Tribal Areas, 1912–1956.* London: Cass.

Bimberg, Edward L. 1999. *The Moroccan Goums: Tribal Warriors in a Modern War.* Westport, CT: Greenwood Press.

Boum, Aomar. 2010. "From 'Little Jerusalems' to the Promised Land: Zionism, Moroccan Nationalism, and Rural Jewish Emigration." *Journal of North African Studies* 15(1): 51–69.

——. 2013. *Memories of Absence: How Muslims Remember Jews in Morocco.* Stanford, CA: Stanford University Press.

Bourdieu, Pierre. 1984. *Distinction: A Social Critique of the Judgement of Taste.* Translated by Richard Nice. Cambridge, MA: Harvard University Press.

——. 1987. *Chose dits.* Paris: Editions de Minuit.

——. 1989. "Social Space and Symbolic Power." *Sociological Theory* 71(1): 14–25.

——. 1991. *Language and Symbolic Power.* Cambridge, MA: Harvard University Press.

——. 1999. "Rethinking the State: Genesis and Structure of the Bureaucratic Field." In *State/Culture: State-Formation after the Cultural Turn,* edited by George Steinmetz, 53–75. Ithaca, NY: Cornell University Press.

Bourdieu, Pierre, and Loïc J. D. Wacquant. 1992. *An Invitation to Reflexive Sociology.* Chicago, IL: University of Chicago Press.

Bourqia, Rahma. 1993. "Don et théâtralité: réflexion sur le rituel du don (hadiya) offert au sultan au XIXe siècle." *Hespéris-Tamuda* 31: 61–75.

Bourqia, Rahma, and Susan Gilson Miller, eds. 1999. *In the Shadow of the Sultan: Culture, Power, and Politics in Morocco.* Cambridge, MA: Center for Middle Eastern Studies of Harvard University, Harvard University Press.

Bowles, Paul. 1955. *The Spider House.* New York: Random House.

Brody, Aaron. 2002. "From the Hills of Adonis through the Pillars of Hercules: Recent Advances in the Archaeology of Canaan and Phoenicia." *Near Eastern Archaeology* 65(1): 69–80.

Brower, Benjamin. 2009. *A Desert Named Peace: The Violence of France's Empire in the Algerian Sahara, 1844–1902.* New York: Columbia University Press.

Brown, Kenneth. 1972. "The Impact of the *Dahir Berbère* in Salé." In *Arabs and Berbers: From Tribe to Nation in North Africa,* edited by Ernest Gellner and Charles Micaud, 201–15. Lexington, MA: Heath.

Brubaker, Rogers. 2004. *Ethnicity without Groups.* Cambridge, MA: Harvard University Press.

Brubaker, Rogers, and Frederick Cooper. 2000. "Beyond 'Identity.'" *Theory and Society* 29(1): 1–47.

Burke, Edmund, III. 1972. "The Image of Morocco in French Colonial Scholarship." In *Arabs and Berbers: From the Tribe to Nation in North Africa*, edited by Ernest Gellner and Charles Micaud, 175–99. Lexington, MA: Heath.

———.1976. *Prelude to Protectorate in Morocco: Pre-colonial Protest and Resistance, 1860–1912*. Chicago, IL: University of Chicago Press.

———. 1991. "Tribalism and Moroccan Resistance, 1890–1914: The Role of the Ait Ndhir." In *Tribe and State: Essays in Honour of David Montgomery Hart*, edited by E. George Joffe and C. R. Pennell, 119–44. Cambridgeshire, UK: Middle East and North Africa Studies Press.

———. 1998. "Theorizing the Histories of Colonialism and Nationalism in the Arab Maghrib," *Arab Studies Quarterly* 20(2): 5–19.

———. 2007. "The Creation of the Moroccan Colonial Archive, 1880–1930." *History and Anthropology* 18(1): 1–9.

———. 2014. *The Ethnographic State: France and the Invention of Moroccan Islam*. Berkeley: University of California Press.

Cachia, Pierre. 1989. *Popular Narrative Ballads of Modern Egypt*. New York: Oxford University Press.

Carlier, Omar. 1990. "Le café maure: Sociabilité masculine et effervescence citoyenne (Algérie XVIIe–XXe siècles)." *Annales ESC* 4: 976–77.

Caton, Steven. 1990. *"Peaks of Yemen I Summon": Poetry as Cultural Practice in a North Yemeni Tribe*. Berkeley: University of California Press.

Celik, Zeynep. 1992. *Displaying the Orient: Architecture of Islam at Nineteenth-Century World's Fairs*. Berkeley: University of California Press.

Centeno, Miguel. 2002. *Blood and Debt: War and the Nation-State in Latin America*. University Park: Pennsylvania State University Press.

Chandra, Uday. 2013. "Beyond Subalternity: Land, Community, and the State in Contemporary Jharkhand." *Contemporary South Asia* 21(1): 52–61.

Charrad, Mounira. 2001. *States and Women's Rights: The Making of Postcolonial Tunisia, Algeria, and Morocco*. Berkeley: University of California Press.

Chatterjee, Partha. 1993. *The Nation and Its Fragments: Colonial and Postcolonial Histories*. Princeton, NJ: Princeton University Press.

Chetrit, Joseph, and Daniel Schroeter. 2003. "Les rapports entre Juifs et Berbères en Afrique du Nord." In *Le Méditerranée des Juifs: Exodes et enracinements*, edited by Paul Balta, Caherine Dana, and Régine Dhoquois-Cohen, 75–87. Paris: L'Harmattan.

Chtatou, Mohamed. 1991. "Bin 'Abd Al-Karim Al-Khattabi in the Rifi Oral Tradition of Gzenneya." In *Tribe and State: Essays in Honour of David Montgomery Hart*, edited by E. George Joffe and C. R. Pennell, 182–212. Cambridgeshire, UK: Middle East and North Africa Studies Press.

Chraibi, Driss. 1972. *La Civilisation, ma mère*. Paris: Gallimard.

Clancy-Smith, Julia Ann. 1994. *Rebel and Saint: Muslim Notables, Populist Protest, Colonial Encounters (Algeria and Tunisia, 1800–1904)*. Berkeley: University of California Press.

———. 2000. "Envisioning Knowledge: Educating the Muslim Woman in Colonial North Africa, c. 1850–1918." In *Iran and Beyond: Essays in Middle Eastern*

History in Honor of Nikki R. Keddie, edited by R. Matthee, Beth Baron, and Nikki Keddie, 99–118. Costa Mesa, CA: Mazda Publishers.

Clement, Jean-Francois. 1992. "Les révoltes urbaines." In *Le Maroc actuel: Une modernization au miroir de la tradition?*, edited by Jean-Claude Santucci, 393–406. Aix-en-Provence: Institut de recherches et d'études sur le monde arabe et musulman.

Cleveland, William L. 1985. *Islam against the West: Shakib Arslan and the Campaign for Islamic Nationalism.* Austin: University of Texas Press.

Cohn, Bernard. 1996. *Colonialism and Its Forms of Knowledge.* Princeton, NJ: Princeton University Press.

Combs-Schilling, Elaine. 1989. *Sacred Performance: Islam, Sexuality, and Sacrifice.* New York: Columbia University Press.

Comité d'Action Marocaine. 1934. *Plan de réformes marocaines.* Paris: Imprimerie Labor.

Comité d'études berbères de Rabat. 1987. *Les Archives berbères, 1915–1916.* 2e éd. Rabat: Editions-diffusion Al Kalam.

Connell, Raewyn. 1990. "The State, Gender, and Sexual Politics: Theory and Appraisal." *Theory and Society* (19): 507–44.

Cooper, Frederick. 1994. "Conflict and Connection: Rethinking Colonial African History." *American Historical Review* 99(5): 1516–45.

Crapanzano, Vincent. 1981. *The Hamadsha: A Study in Moroccan Ethnopsychiatry.* Berkeley: University of California Press.

Cruchet, René. 1930. *La conquête pacifique du Maroc.* Paris: Editions Berger-Levrault.

Damis, John. 1970. "The Free-School Movement in Morocco, 1919–1970." PhD diss., Tufts University.

Daoud, Zakya. 1993. *Féminisme et politique au Maghreb: 1930–1992.* Paris: Maisonneuve et Larose.

Davis, Diana. 2007. *Resurrecting the Granary of Rome: Environmental History and French Colonial Expansion in North Africa.* Athens, OH: Ohio University Press.

Decroux, Paul. 1947. *Féminisme en Islam: La femme dans l'Islam moderne.* Casablanca.

De Gaulle, Charles. 1954. *Mémoires de guerre.* Paris: Plon.

Delanoë, Guy. 1988. *Lyautey, Juin, Mohammed V, fin d'un protectorat.* Paris: L'Harmattan.

Dirks, Nicholas B. 2001. *Castes of Mind: Colonialism and the Making of Modern India.* Princeton, NJ: Princeton University Press.

Dodge, Toby. 2003. *Inventing Iraq: The Failure of Nation Building and a History Denied.* New York: Columbia University Press.

Dozy, Reinhart. 1968. *The History of the Almohades.* Amsterdam: Oriental Press.

Duara, Prasenjit. 1995. *Rescuing History from the Nation: Questioning Narratives of Modern China.* Chicago, IL: University of Chicago Press.

Dunn, Ross. 1977. *Resistance in the Desert: Moroccan Responses to French Imperialism, 1881–1912.* London: Croom Helm.

——. 1980. "Bū Himāra's European Connexion: The Commercial Relations of a Moroccan Warlord." *Journal of African History* 21(2): 235–53.

Echenberg, Myron. 1991. *Colonial Conscripts: The Tirailleurs Senegalais in French West Africa, 1857–1960.* Portsmouth, NH: Heinemann.

Eickelman, Dale. 1985. *Knowledge and Power in Morocco: The Education of a Twentieth-Century Notable.* Princeton, NJ: Princeton University Press.

El Mansour, Mohammed. 1990. *Morocco in the Reign of Mawley Sulayman.* Wisbech, Cambridgeshire, UK: Middle East and North African Studies Press.

El Shakry, Omnia. 2007. *The Great Social Laboratory: Subjects of Knowledge in Colonial and Postcolonial Egypt.* Stanford, CA: Stanford University Press.

Erikson, Emily. 2014. *Between Monopoly and Free Trade: The English East India Company.* Princeton, NJ: Princeton University Press.

Ennaji, Moha. 2005. *Multilingualism, Cultural Identity, and Education in Morocco.* New York: Springer.

Fassi, Allal al-. 1948. *Al-harakat al-Istiqlaliyya fi'l-Maghrib al-'arabi.* Cairo.

———. 1954. *The Independence Movements in Arab North Africa.* Washington, DC: American Council of Learned Societies.

———. 1961. *La vérité sur les frontières du Maroc: Extraits des archives secretes de Bureaux d'affaires indigenes français en Algérie.* Tangier: M. Peretti.

———. 1966. *Al-Naqd Al-Dhati.* Bayrut: Dar al-Kashshaf lil-Nashr wa-al-Ṭiba'ah wa-al-Tawzi.

Fédération Française des Anciens Coloniaux. 1931. *Le Livre d'Or de l'Exposition Coloniale Internationale de Paris.* Paris: Librairie ancienne Honoré Champion.

Findley, Carter. 1998. "An Ottoman Occidentalist in Europe: Ahmed Midhat Meets Madame Gülnar, 1889." *American Historical Review* 103(1): 15–49.

Fleischmann, Ellen. 2003. *The Nation and Its "New" Women: The Palestinian Women's Movement, 1920–1948.* Berkeley: University of California Press.

Fligstein, Neil. 2001. "Social Skill and the Theory of Fields." *Sociological Theory* 19(2): 105–25.

Fligstein, Neil, and Doug McAdam. 2012. *A Theory of Fields.* New York: Oxford University Press.

Ford, Caroline. 2008. "Reforestation, Landscape Conservation, and the Anxieties of Empire in French Colonial Algeria." *American Historical Review* 113(2): 341–62.

Foucauld, Charles de. 1888. *Reconnaissance au Maroc, 1883–1884.* Paris: Challamel.

Fromherz, Allen. 2010. *Almohads: The Rise of an Islamic Empire.* New York: I. B. Tauris

García-Arenal, Mercedes, and Gerard Wiegers. 2003. *A Man of Three Worlds: Samuel Pallache, a Moroccan Jew in Catholic and Protestant Europe.* Baltimore, MD: Johns Hopkins University Press.

Gautier, Emile. 1927. *L'Islamisation de l'Afrique du Nord: Les siècles obscures du Maghreb.* Paris: Payot.

Geertz, Clifford. 1963. "The Integrative Revolution: Primordial Sentiments and Civil Politics in the New States." In *Old Societies and New States: The Quest for Modernity in Asia and Africa,* edited by Clifford Geertz, 105–57. New York: Free Press of Glencoe.

———. 1968. *Islam Observed: Religious Development in Morocco and Indonesia.* New Haven, CT: Yale University Press.

———. 1979. *Meaning and Order in Moroccan Society: Three Essays in Cultural Analysis.* Cambridge: Cambridge University Press.

———. 1983. *Local Knowledge: Further Essays in Interpretive Anthropology.* New York: Basic Books, Inc.

Gellner, Ernest. 1969. *Saints of the Atlas.* London: Weidenfeld and Nicolson.

———. 1983. *Nations and Nationalism.* Ithaca, NY: Cornell University Press, 1983.

Gershovich, Moshe. 2000. *French Military Rule in Morocco: Colonialism and Its Consequences.* Portland, OR: Frank Cass.

———. 2003. "Stories on the Road from Fez to Marrakesh: Oral History on the Margins of National Identity," *Journal of North African Studies* 8:43–58.

Ghazal, Amal. 2010. "The Other Frontiers of Arab Nationalism: Ibadis, Berbers, and the Arabist Salafi Press in the Interwar Period," *International Journal of Middle East Studies* 42(1): 105–22.

Gilson-Miller, Susan. 2011. "Making Tangier Modern: Ethnicity and Urban Development, 1880–1930." In *Jewish Culture and Society in North Africa,* edited by Emily Benichou Gottreich and Daniel Schroeter, 128–49. Bloomington: Indiana University Press.

———. 2013. "The Mellah without Walls: Jewish Space in a Moroccan City—Tangier, 1860–1912." In *Revisiting the Colonial Past in Morocco,* edited by Driss Maghraoui, 19–38. London: Routledge.

Go, Julian. 2008a. *American Empire and the Politics of Meaning: Elite Political Cultures in the Philippines and Puerto Rico during U.S. Colonialism.* Durham, NC: Duke University Press.

———. 2008b. "Global Fields and Imperial Forms: Field Theory and British and American Empires." *Sociological Theory* 26(3): 201–29.

———. 2009. "The 'New' Sociology of Empire and Colonialism." *Sociology Compass* 3(5): 775–88.

———. 2011. *Patterns of Empire: The British and American Empires, 1688 to the Present.* Cambridge: Cambridge University Press.

———. 2013. "For a Postcolonial Sociology." *Theory and Society* 42(1): 25–55.

Goh, Daniel. 2007. "States of Ethnography: Colonialism, Resistance and Cultural Transcription in Malaya and the Philippines, 1890s–1930s." *Comparative Studies in Society and History* 49(1): 109–42.

Goldberg, Chad. 2007. *Citizens and Paupers: Relief, Rights, and Race, from the Freedmen's Bureau to Workfare.* Chicago, IL: University of Chicago Press.

———. 2008. "T. H. Marshall Meets Pierre Bourdieu: Citizens and Paupers in the Development of the U.S. Welfare State." *Political Power and Social Theory* 19: 83–116.

Goldberg, Harvey. 2004. "The Oriental and the Orientalist: The Meeting of Mordecia Ha-Cohen and Nahum Slouschz." *Jewish Cultural and History* 7(3): 1–30.

Goodman, Jane. 2002. "Writing Empire, Underwriting Nation: Discursive Histories of Kabyle Berber 'Oral Texts.'" *American Ethnologist* 29: 86–122.

———, ed. 2013. *Bourdieu and Historical Analysis.* Durham, NC: Duke University Press

Gottreich, Emily. 2007. *The Mellah of Marrakesh: Jewish and Muslim Space in Morocco's Red City.* Bloomington: Indiana University Press.

Gouvernement Chérifien, Service Central des Statistiques. 1947. *Annuaire statistique de la Zone Française du Maroc 1945–46.* Rabat: Imprimerie Maroc-Matin.

Grandguillaume, Gilbert. 1983. *Arabisation et politique linguistique au Maghreb.* Paris: G.-P. Maisonneuve et Larose.

Gruner, Roger. 1984. *Du Maroc traditionnel au Maroc moderne : Le contrôle civil au Maroc, 1912–1956.* Paris: Nouvelles Ed. Latines.

Guennoun, Said. 1933. *La Montagne berbère: Les Ait Oumalou et le pays Zaian.* Rabat: Èditions Omnia.

———. 1934. *La Voix des Monts: Moeurs de guerre berbères*. Rabat: Èditions Omnia.

Guessous, Nadia. 2011. "Genealogies of Feminism: Leftist Feminist Subjectivity in the Wake of the Islamic Revival in Contemporary Morocco." PhD diss., Columbia University.

Guerin, Adam. 2011. "Racial Myth, Colonial Reform, and the Invention of Customary Law in Morocco, 1912–1930." *Journal of North African Studies* 16(3): 361–80.

———. 2015. "'Not a Drop for the Settlers': Reimagining Popular Protest and Anti-Colonial Nationalism in the Moroccan Protectorate." *Journal of North African Studies* 20(2): 1–22.

Guha, Ranajit. 1988. "On Some Aspects of the Historiography of Colonial India." In *Selected Subaltern Studies,* edited by R. Guha, 35–44. New York: Oxford University Press.

Guillaume, Augustin. 1946. *Les Berbères marocains et la pacification de l'Atlas central (1912–1933)*. Paris: R. Julliard.

Haddad, Tahir-al. (1930) 2007. *Muslim Women in Law and Society: Annotated Translation of al-Tāhir al-Haddād's Imra tunā fi 'l-sharī'a wa 'l-mujtama', with an Introduction*. London: Routledge.

Halstead, John. 1964. "The Changing Character of Moroccan Reformism, 1921–1934." *Journal of African History* 5(3): 435–47.

———. 1967. *Rebirth of a Nation: The Origins and Rise of Moroccan Nationalism, 1912–1944*. Cambridge, MA: Distributed for the Center for Middle Eastern Studies of Harvard University by Harvard University Press.

Hamel, Chouki El. 2010. "The Register of the Slaves of Sultan Mawlay Isma'il of Morocco at the Turn of the Eighteenth Century." *Journal of African History* 51(1):89–98.

———. 2013. *Black Morocco: A History of Slavery, Race, and Islam*. New York: Cambridge University Press.

Hammoudi, Abdellah. 1997. *Master and Disciple: The Cultural Foundations of Moroccan Authoritarianism*. Chicago, IL: University of Chicago Press.

———. 1999. "The Reinvention of Dar Al-mulk: The Moroccan Political System and Its Legitimation." In *In the Shadow of the Sultan: Culture, Power, and Politics in Morocco,* edited by Rahma Bourqia and Susan Gilson Miller, 129–75. Cambridge, MA: Harvard University Press.

Hannoum, Abdelmajid. 2008. The Historiographic State: How Algeria Once Became French." *History and Anthropology* 19(2): 91–114.

Hardy, Georges. 1925. *L'Enfant marocain*. Paris: Larose.

Harris, Walter. 1921. *Morocco that Was*. Edinburgh: W. Blackwood and Sons.

Hart, David. 1976. *The Aith Waryaghar of the Moroccan Rif: An Ethnography and History*. Tucson: University of Arizona Press.

———. 1997. "The Berber Dahir of 1930 in Colonial Morocco: Then and Now (1930–1996)." *Journal of North African Studies* 2(2): 11–33.

———. 2001. *Qabila: Tribal Profiles and Tribe-State Relations in Morocco and on the Afghanistan-Pakistan Frontier*. Amsterdam: Het Spinhuis.

Hassan II. 1978. *The Challenge: The Memoirs of King Hassan II of Morocco*. London: Macmillan.

Heggoy, A. 1986. *The French Conquest of Algiers, 1830*. Athens, OH: Ohio University Center for International Studies.

Hirschberg, Haim. 1974. *A History of the Jews in North Africa.* Leiden: Brill.

Hobsbawm, Eric, and Terrence Ranger, eds. 1983. *The Invention of Tradition.* Cambridge: Cambridge University Press.

Hoffman, Katherine. 2008a. "Purity and Contamination: Language Ideologies in French Colonial Native Policy in Morocco." *Comparative Studies in Society and History* 50(3):724–52.

——. 2008b. *We Share Walls.* Walden, MA: Blackwell Publishers.

——. 2010. "Berber Law by French Means: Customary Courts in the Moroccan Hinterlands, 1930–1956." *Comparative Studies in Society and History* 52(4): 851–80.

Hoffman, Katherine, and Susan Gilson Miller. 2010. *Berbers and Others: Beyond Tribe and Nation in the Maghrib.* Bloomington: Indiana University Press.

——. 1995. *Lyautey and the French Conquest of Morocco.* New York: St. Martin's Press.

Hughes, Stephen O. 2001. *Morocco Under King Hassan.* Reading, UK: Ithaca Press.

Huré, Antoine. 1952. *La pacification du Maroc: Dernière étape, 1931–1934.* Paris: Berger-Levrault.

Ibn Khaldun. (1958) 2005. *The Muqaddimah: An Introduction to History.* Translated by Franz Rosenthal. New York: Pantheon Books.

Irbouh, Hamid. 2005. *Art in the Service of Colonialism: French Art Education in Morocco, 1912–1956.* London: Tauris Academic Studies.

Isaac, Larry. 2008. "Movement of Movements: Culture Moves in the Long Civil Rights Struggle." *Social Forces* 87(1): 33–63.

Iskander, John. 2007. "Devout Heretics: The Barghawata in Maghribi Historiography." *Journal of North African Studies* 12(1): 37–53.

Joffe, E. G. H. 1985. "The Moroccan Nationalist Movement: Istiqlal, the Sultan, and the Country." *Journal of African History* 26(4): 289–307.

Jouad, Hassan. 1989. "Les Imdyazen, une voix de l'intellectualité rurale." *Revue du monde musulman et de la Méditerranée. Les Prédicateurs Profanes au Maghreb* 51: 100–110.

Julien, Charles. 1952. *L'Afrique du nord en marche.* Paris: R. Julliard.

——. 1978. *Le Maroc face aux impérialismes: 1415–1956.* Paris: Éditions J. A.

——, ed. 1977. *Les Africains.* Paris: Éditions J. A.

Kably, Mohammed. 1986. *Société, pouvoir et religion au Maroc à la fin du Moyen âge: XIVe–XVe siècle.* Paris: Maisonneuve et Larose.

——. 1999. "Legitimacy of State Power and Socio-Religious Variations in Medieval Morocco." In *In the Shadow of the Sultan: Culture, Power, and Politics in Morocco,* edited by Rahma Bourqia and Susan Gilson Miller, 17–29. Cambridge, MA: Harvard University Press.

Kalyvas, Stathis N. 2006. *The Logic of Violence in Civil War.* New York: Cambridge University Press.

Katan, Yvette. 1990. *Oujda, Une Ville Frontière Du Maroc, 1907–1956: Musulmans, Juifs et Chrétiens En Milieu Colonial.* Paris: L'Harmattan.

Katz, Ethan. 2012. "Between Emancipation and Persecution: Algerian Jewish Memory in the *Longue durée* (1930–1970)." *Journal of North African Studies* 17(5): 793–820.

Kenbib, Mohammed. 1994. *Juifs et Musulmans au Maroc, 1859–1948.* Rabat: Faculté des lettres et des sciences humaines-Rabat.

——. 1996. *Les Protégés. Contribution à l'histoire contemporaine du Maroc.* Casablanca: Faculté des Lettres et des Sciences Humaines.

Kerber, L. 1976. "The Republican Mother: Women and the Enlightenment—An American Perspective." *American Quarterly* 28(2): 187–205.

Khalafi, Abdeslam. 2002a. "La poésie de résistance au Rif: 1893–1926 (1ère partie)." *Tawiza* 63(Juillet). Retrieved from http://tawiza.x10.mx/Tawiza63/Khalafi.htm.

——. 2002b. "La poésie de résistance au Rif: 1893–1926 (1ère partie)." *Tawiza* 64(Août). Retrieved from http://tawiza.x10.mx/Tawiza64/Khalafi.htm.

Kosansky, Oren. 2003. "All Dear unto God: Saints, Pilgrimage and Textual Practice in Jewish Morocco." PhD diss., University of Michigan.

——. 2011. "The Real Morocco Itself: Jewish Saint Pilgrimage, Hybridity, and the Idea of the Moroccan Nation." In *Jewish Culture and Society in North Africa*, edited by Emily Gottreich and Daniel Schroeter. Bloomington: Indiana University Press.

Kosansky, Oren, and Aomar Boum. 2012. "The 'Jewish Question' in Postcolonial Moroccan Cinema." *International Journal of Middle East Studies* 44(3): 421–42.

Kozma, Liat. 2003. "Moroccan Women's Narratives of Liberation." In *Nation, Society, and Culture in North Africa*, edited by James McDougall, 112–30. London and Portland: Routledge/Frank Cass.

Kridia, Ibrahim. 1986. *Ma'rakat Anwal wa-nataijuha.* Casablanca: S. I. E.

Kudsi-Zadeh, A. 1972. "Afghani and Freemasonry in Egypt." *Journal of the American Oriental Society* 92(1): 25–35.

Kuisel, Richard. 1993. *Seducing the French: The Dilemma of Americanization.* Berkeley: University of California Press.

Kunz, Rudibert. 1990. *Giftgas gegen Abd el Krim: Deutschland, Spanien und der Gaskrieg in Spanisch-Marokko, 1922–1927.* Freiburg: Verlag Rombach.

Lafuente, Gilles. 1999. *La politique berbère de la France et le nationalisme marocain.* Paris: Harmattan.

Lahbabi, Mohamed. 1958. *Le gouvernement marocain à l'aube du XXe siècle.* Rabat: Editions Techniques Nord-Africaines.

Laitin, David. 1986. *Hegemony and Culture: Politics and Religious Change among the Yoruba.* Chicago, IL: University of Chicago Press.

Lamont, Michelle, and Virag Molnár 2002. "The Study of Boundaries in the Social Sciences." *Annual Review of Sociology* 28: 167–95.

Landau, Rom. 1957. *Mohammed V, King of Morocco.* Rabat: Morocco Publishers.

Lange, Matthew. 2005. "British Colonial State Legacies and Development Trajectories: A Statistical Analysis of Direct and Indirect Rule." In *States and Development: Historical Antecedents of Stagnation and Advance*, edited by Matthew Lange and Dietrich Rueschemeyer, 117–39. New York: Palgrave Macmillan Press.

Laroui, Abdellah. 1974. *La Crise des intellectuels arabes: Traditionalisme ou historicisme?* Paris: François Maspero.

——. 1977. *Les origines sociales et culturelles du nationalisme marocaine (1830–1912).* Paris: Maspero.

——. 1993. *Esquisses historiques.* Casablanca: Centre culturel arabe.

Laskier, Michael. 1983. *The Alliance Israélite Universelle and the Jewish Communities of Morocco, 1862–1962.* Albany: State University of New York Press.

——. 1994. *North African Jewry in the Twentieth Century: The Jews of Morocco, Tunisia, and Algeria.* New York: New York University Press.

Lawrence, Adria. 2010. "Triggering Nationalist Violence: Competition and Conflict in Uprisings against Colonial Rule." *International Security* 35(2): 88–122.

——. 2013. *Imperial Rule and the Politics of Nationalism.* New York: Cambridge University Press.

Lauzière, Henri. 2010. "The Construction of Salafiyya: Reconsidering Salafism from the Perspective of Conceptual History." *International Journal of Middle East Studies* 42(3): 369–89.

Lebovics, Herman. 1992. *True France: The Wars over Cultural Identity, 1900–1945.* Ithaca, NY: Cornell University Press.

Leclerc, René. 1931. "Le Maroc à Vincennes." In *Le Livre d'Or de l'Exposition Coloniale Internationale de Paris, 1931.* Paris: Librairie ancienne Honoré Champion.

Le Glay, Maurice. 1923. *Itto: récit marocain d'amour et de bataille.* Paris: Plon.

——. 1924. *Badda, fille berbère, et autres récits marocains.* Paris: Plon-Nourrit et cie.

——. 1930. *Trois récits marocains.* Casablanca: Les bibliophiles du Maroc.

——. 1932. *Nouveaux récits marocains de la plaine et des monts.* Paris: Berger-Levrault.

——. 1948. *Récits marocains de la plaine et des monts.* Paris: Berger-Levrault.

Le Tourneau, Roger. 1949. *Fès avant le protectorat: Étude économique et sociale d'une ville de l'occident musulman.* Casablanca: SMLE.

Lewis, Martin. D. 1962. "One Hundred Million Frenchmen: The 'Assimilation' Theory in French Colonial Policy." *Comparative Studies in Society and History* 4(2): 129–53.

Lewis, Mary. 2013. *Divided Rule: Sovereignty and Empire in French Tunisia, 1881–1938.* Berkeley: University of California Press.

Lorcin, Patricia. 1995. *Imperial Identities: Stereotyping, Prejudice and Race in Colonial Algeria.* London: I. B. Tauris, 1995.

——. 2005. *Kabyles, Arabes, Français: Identités Coloniales.* Limoges: Presses universitaires de Limoges.

Love, P. M. 2010. "The Sufris of Sijilmasa: Toward a History of the Midrarids." *Journal of North African Studies* 15(2): 173–88.

Loveman, Mara. 2005. "The Modern State and the Primitive Accumulation of Symbolic Power." *American Journal of Sociology* 110(6): 1651–83.

Lyautey, Hubert. 1891. "Du rôle social de l'officier." *Revue des Deux Mondes,* 3eme Période, 61 Année. Vol. 104, 443–59.

——. 1900. "Du rôle colonial de l'armée." *Revue des Deux Mondes,* 4e Période, 69 Année. Vol. 157, 308–28.

——. 1953. *Lyautey l'africain: Textes et lettres du maréchal Lyautey.* Paris: Plan.

M'barek, Zaki. 1987. *Resistance et armée de libération: Portée politique, liquidation, 1953–1958.* Tanger: E. T. E. I. Nord.

Madariaga, Maria Rosa de. 1992. "The Intervention of Moroccan Troops in the Spanish Civil War: A Reconsideration." *European History Quarterly* 22(1): 67–97.

——. 1999. *España y el Rif: crónica de una historia casi olvidada.* Melilla, [Spain]: Ciudad Autónoma de Melilla, UNED, Centro Asociado de Melilla.

Maghraoui, Driss. 1988. "Moroccan Colonial Soldiers: Between Selective Memory and Collective Memory." *Arab Studies Quarterly* 20(2): 21–42.

———. 2002. "'Nos goumiers Berbères': The Ambiguities of Colonial Representations in French Military Novels." *Journal of North African Studies* 7(3): 79–100.

———. 2013. *Revisiting the Colonial Past in Morocco.* London: Routledge.

Mamdani, Mahmoud. 1996. *Citizen and Subject: Contemporary Africa and the Legacy of Late Colonialism.* Princeton, NJ: Princeton University Press.

———. 2013. *Define and Rule: Native as Political Identity.* Cambridge, MA: Harvard University Press.

Mammeri, Mouloud, and Pierre Bourdieu. 1978. "Dialogue sur la poésie en Kabylie: Entretien avec Mouloud Mammeri." *Actes de la recherche en science sociales* 23: 51–66. Mann, Michael. 1986. *The Sources of Social Power.* Vol. 1. New York: Cambridge University Press.

———. 1993. *The Sources of Social Power.* Vol. 2. New York: Cambridge University Press.

Marglin, Jessica. 2011. "Modernizing Moroccan Jews: The AIU Alumni Association in Tangier, 1893–1913," *Jewish Quarterly Review* 101(4): 574–603.

Martin, John Levi. 2003. "What Is Field Theory?" *American Journal of Sociology* 109(1): 1–49.

Marty, Paul. 1925. *Le Maroc de demain.* Paris: Comité de l'Afrique française.

McLennan, Gregor. 2003. "Sociology, Eurocentrism and Postcolonial Theory." *European Journal of Social Theory* 6(1): 69–86.

McDougall, James. 2006. *History and the Culture of Nationalism in Algeria.* Cambridge: Cambridge University Press.

McNeill, John. 1992. *The Mountains of the Mediterranean World: An Environmental History.* Cambridge: Cambridge University Press.

Méraud, Marc. 1990. *Service des affaires indigènes du Maroc.* Paris: La Koumia.

Mernissi, Fatima. 1988. *Chahrazad n'est pas marocaine: Autrement, elle serait salariée!* Casablanca, Maroc: Editions le fennec.

———. 1994. *Dreams of Trespass: Tales of a Harem Girlhood.* Reading, MA: Addison-Wesley.

Michaux-Bellaire, Édouard and M. Buret. 1991. "Makhzan." In *The Encyclopaedia of Islam, New Edition.* Vol. 6, edited by C.E. Bosworth, E. Van Donzel, B. Lewis, and Ch. Pellat, 133–37. Leiden: E. J. Brill.

Miège, Jean-Louis. 1962. *Le Maroc et l'Europe.* Vol. 3. Paris: Presses universitaires de France.

Miller, Pavla. 1998. *Transformations of Patriarchy in the West, 1500–1900.* Bloomington: Indiana University Press.

Miller, Susan Gilson. 2013. *A History of Modern Morocco.* New York: Cambridge University Press.

Miller, Susan, and Katherine Hoffman, eds. 2010. *Berbers and Others: Beyond Tribe and Nation in the Maghrib.* Bloomington: Indiana University Press.

Mission Scientifique du Maroc. 1904–1933. *Archives Marocaines.* Vols. 1–19. Paris: E. Leroux.

Mitchell, Timothy. 1988. *Colonising Egypt.* New York: Cambridge University Press.

———. 1990. "Everyday Metaphors of Power." *Theory and Society* 19(5): 545–77.

———. 2002. *Rule of Experts: Egypt, Techno-Politics, Modernity.* Berkeley: University of California Press.

Monjib, Maâti. 1992. *La Monarchie Marocaine et La Lutte Pour Le Pouvoir: Hassan II Face À L'opposition Nationale, de L'indépendance À L'état D'exception.* Paris: L'Harmattan.

Montagne, Robert. 1930. *Les Berbères et le Makhzan dans le sud du Maroc; Essai sur la transformation politique des Berbères sédentaires (groupe Chleuh)*. Paris: F. Alcan.

Morton, Patricia. 2000. *Hybrid Modernities: Architecture and Representation at the 1931 Colonial Exposition, Paris*. Cambridge, MA: MIT Press.

Mounib, Mohamed. 2002. *Adhahir 'al barbari' akbar ukduba siassiya fi al-maghrib al-mu'asir*. Rabat: Dar Bou Regreg.

Munson, Henry. 1993a. "Rethinking Gellner's Segmentary Analysis of Morocco's Ait 'Atta." *Man* 28(2): 267–80.

———. 1993b. *Religion and Power in Morocco*. New Haven, CT: Yale University Press.

La Nation arabe. 1988. Farnham Common, UK: Archive Editions.

Neep, Daniel. 2012. *Occupying Syria under the French Mandate: Insurgency, Space, and State Formation*. New York: Cambridge University Press.

Nettl, J. P. 1968. "The State as a Conceptual Variable." *World Politics* 20(4): 559–92.

Nicoll, Edna L. 1931. *A travers l'Exposition coloniale*. Paris: E. L. Nicoll.

O'Callaghan, Joseph. 2011. *The Gibraltar Crusade: Castile and the Battle for the Strait*. Philadelphia: University of Pennsylvania Press.

O'Hanlon, Rosalind. 1988. "Recovering the Subject: Subaltern Studies and Histories of Resistance in Colonial South Asia Subaltern Studies." *Modern Asian Studies* 22(1): 189–224.

Ouezzani, Mohammed Hassan el-. 1982. *Mudhakirat hayah wa-jihad*. Vol. 2. Rabat: Mubat: Archive Edition.

Parsons, Frederick. 1976. *The Origins of the Morocco Question, 1880–1900*. London: Duckworth.

Paul-Margueritte, Lucie. 1935. *Chants berbères du Maroc*. Paris: Èditions Berger-Levrault.

Pedersen, Jean. 1998. "Special Customs: Paternity Suits and Citizenship in France and the Colonies, 1870–1912." In *Domesticating the Empire: Race, Gender, and Family Life in French and Dutch Colonialism*, edited by Julia Clancy-Smith and Frances Gouda, 43–64. Charlottesville, VA: University of Virginia Press.

Pennell, C. R. 1986. *A Country with a Government and a Flag: The Rif War in Morocco, 1921–1926*. Wisbech, Cambridgeshire, UK: Middle East and North African Studies Press.

———. 1991. "Makhzan and Sība in Morocco: An Examination of Early Modern Attitudes." In *Tribe and State: Essays in Honour of David Montgomery Hart*, edited by E. George Joffe and C. R. Pennell, 159–80. Cambridgeshire, UK: Middle East and North Africa Studies Press.

———. 2000. *Morocco since 1830: A History*. New York: New York University Press, 2000.

———, ed. 2001. *Bandits at Sea: A Pirate Reader*. New York: New York University Press.

Perdicaris, Ion. 1904. "In Raissuli's Hands: The Story of My Captivity and Deliverance May 18 to June 26, 1904." *Leslie's Magazine* 58 (September): 510–22.

Perkins, Kenneth. 2014. *A History of Modern Tunisia*. New York: Cambridge University Press.

Peyron, Michael. 2000. "*Amdyaz*, the Wandering Bard of Berber Poetry," *Etudes et Documents Berbères* 18: 103–10.

———. 2007. "Oralité et résistance: Dits poétiques et non-poétiques ayant pour thème le siège du Tazizaout (Haut Atlas marocain, 1932)." *Etudes et Documents Berbères* 25–26: 307–16.

Podeh, Eleh. 2011. *The Politics of National Celebrations in the Arab Middle East.* Cambridge: Cambridge University Press.

Porch, Douglas. 1983. *The Conquest of Morocco.* New York: Knopf.

Prochaska, David. 1990. *Making Algeria French: Colonialism in Bône, 1870–1920.* Cambridge: Cambridge University Press.

Rabinow, Paul. 1977. *Reflections on Fieldwork in Morocco.* Berkeley: University of California Press.

———. 1989. *French Modern: Norms and Forms of the Social Environment.* Chicago, IL: University of Chicago Press.

Rachik, Hassan. 2003. *Symboliser la nation.* Casablanca: Editions le Fennec.

Renan, Ernst. (1882) 1990. "What Is a Nation?" In *Nationalism and Narration,* edited by Homi Bhabha, 8–22. London: Routledge.

Reynier, Paul. 1930. *Taougrat, ou les Berbères racontè par eux-mêmes.* Paris: Orientaliste Paul Geuthner.

Rivet, Daniel. 1996. *Lyautey et l'institution du protectorat français au Maroc, 1912–1925.* 3 vols. Paris: L'Harmattan.

———. 1999. *Le Maroc de Lyautey à Mohammed V: Le double visage du protectorat.* Paris: Denoël.

———. 2012a. *Histoire du Maroc.* Paris: Fayard.

———. 2012b. "Blad al-sība," *Encyclopedia of Islam, 2nd edition,* edited by P. Bearman, Th. Bianquis, C.E. Bosworth, E. van Donzel, and W. P. Heinrichs, Brill Online. Retrieved from http://referenceworks.brillonline.com/entries/encyclopaedia-of-islam-2/siba-SIM_8899.

Roux, Arsène. 1928. "Les 'Imdyazen' ou aèdes berbères du groupe linguistique beraber." *Hespéris* 8: 231–51.

———. 1992. "Quelques chants berbères sur les opérations de 1931–32 dans le Maroc Central." *Etudes et Documents Berbères* 9: 165–219.

———. 2002. *Poésies Berbères de l'époque héroïque: Maroc central (1908–1932).* Edited by Michael Peyron. Aix-en-Provence: Institut de recherches et d'études sur le monde arabe et musulman.

Ruedy, John. 2005. *Modern Algeria: The Origins and Development of a Nation.* Bloomington: Indiana University Press.

Russell, Mona. 2004. *Creating the New Egyptian Woman: Consumerism, Education, and National Identity, 1863–1922.* New York: Palgrave Macmillan.

Sadiqi, Fatima. 2003. *Women, Gender, and Language in Morocco.* Leiden; Boston: Brill.

———, ed. 2009. *Women Writing Africa: Northern Region.* New York: The Feminist Press of the City University of New York.

———, ed. 2013. *Women and Knowledge in the Mediterranean.* Abingdon, Oxon; New York, NY: Routledge.

Sahli, Mohamed. 1965. *Décoloniser l'histoire: introduction à l'histoire du Maghreb.* Paris: F. Maspero.

Salime, Z. 2011. *Between Feminism and Islam: Human Rights and Sharia Law in Morocco.* Minneapolis: University of Minnesota Press.

Saulay, Jean, ed. 1985. *Histoire des Goums marocains.* [N.p.]: La Koumia; Paris: Public-réalisations.

Schreier, Joshua. 2010. *Arabs of the Jewish Faith: The Civilizing Mission in Colonial Algeria.* New Brunswick, NJ: Rutgers University Press.

Schroeter, Daniel. 1988. *Merchants of Essaouira: Urban Society and Imperialism in South-western Morocco, 1844–1886.* Cambridge: Cambridge University Press.

——. 2002. *The Sultan's Jew: Morocco and the Sephardi World.* Stanford, CA: Stanford University Press.

——. 2003. "From Dhimmis to Colonized Subjects: Moroccan Jews and the Shari-fian and French Colonial State." In *Studies in Contemporary Jewry,* vol. 19, *Jews and the State: Dangerous Alliances and the Perils of Privilege,* edited by Ezra Mendelsohn, 104–23. Oxford: Oxford University Press.

——. 2008. "The Shifting Boundaries of Moroccan Jewish Identities." *Jewish Social Studies* 15(1): 145–64.

——. Forthcoming. "Vichy in Morocco: The Residency, Mohamed V, and His Indigenous Jewish Subjects." In *Jewish History after the Imperial Turn: French and Comparative Perspectives,* edited by Ethan Katz, Lisa Leff, and Maud Mandel.

Schroeter, Daniel, and Joseph Chetrit. 2006. "Emancipation and Its Discontents: Jews at the Formative Period of Colonial Rule in Morocco." *Jewish Social Studies* 13(1): 170–206.

Scott, James. 1998. *Seeing like a State: How Certain Schemes to Improve the Human Condition Have Failed.* New Haven, CT: Yale University Press.

——. 2009. *The Art of Not Being Governed: An Anarchist History of Upland Southeast Asia.* New Haven, CT: Yale University Press.

Seddon, David. 1981. *Moroccan Peasants: A Century of Change in the Eastern Rif, 1870–1970.* Folkestone, Kent: Dawson.

Segalla, Spencer. 2003. "Georges Hardy and Educational Ethnology in French Morocco, 1920–26." *French Colonial History* 4: 171–90.

——. 2009a. *The Moroccan Soul: French Education, Colonial Ethnology, and Muslim Resistance, 1912–1956.* Lincoln: University of Nebraska Press.

——. 2009b. "'According to a Logic Befitting the Arab Soul': Cultural Policy and Popular Education in Morocco since 1912." In *Trajectories of Education in the Arab World: Legacies and Challenges,* edited by Osama Abi-Mershed, 84–108. New York: Routledge.

Service central des statistiques. 1964. *Résultats du recensement de 1960.* Rabat: Centre de documentation, Division du plan et des statistiques.

Sessions, Jennifer. 2011. *By Sword and by Plow: France and the Conquest of Algeria.* Ithaca, NY: Cornell University Press.

Shah, Alpa. 2014. "Religion and the Secular Left: Subaltern Studies, Birsa Munda and Maoists." *Anthropology of this Century* 9. Retrieved from http://aotcpress.com/articles/religion-secular-left-subaltern-studies-birsa-munda-maoists/.

Shorrock, W. 1983. "The Tunisian Question in French Policy toward Italy, 1881–1940." *International Journal of African Historical Studies* 16(4): 631–51.

Shryock, Andrew. 1997. *Nationalism and the Genealogical Imagination.* Berkeley: University of California Press.

Silverstein, Paul. 2002. "France's *Mare Nostrum*: Colonial and Post Colonial Con-structions of the French Mediterranean." *Journal of North African Studies* 7(4): 1–22.

Slavin, David H. 1998. "French Colonial Film before and after Itto: From Berber Myth to Race War." *French Historical Studies* 21(1): 125–55.

Slater, Dan, and Erica Simmons. 2010. "Informative Regress: Critical Antecedents in Comparative Politics." *Comparative Political Studies* 43(7): 886–917.

Slyomovics, Susan, and Sarah Stein. 2012. "Jews and French Colonialism in Algeria: An Introduction." *Journal of North African Studies* 17(5): 749–55.

Snyder, Richard. 2001. "Scaling Down: The Subnational Comparative Method." *Studies in Comparative International Development* 36(1): 93–110.

Souriau, Christine. 1975. *La presse, maghrébine: Libye, Tunisie, Maroc, Algérie; évolution historique, situation en 1965, organisation et problèmes actuels.* Paris: Éditions du Centre national de la recherche scientifique.

Spadola, Emilio. 2008. "The Scandal of Ecstasy: Communication, Sufi Rites, and Social Reform in 1930s Morocco." *Contemporary Islam* 2(2): 119–38.

———. 2014. *The Calls of Islam: Sufis, Islamists, and Mass Mediation in Urban Morocco.* Bloomington: Indiana University Press.

Steinmetz, George. 2003. "'The Devil's Handwriting': Pre-Colonial Discourse, Ethnographic Acuity, and Cross-Identification in German Colonialism." *Comparative Studies in Society and History* 45(1): 41–94.

———. 2007. *The Devil's Handwriting: Precoloniality and the German Colonial State in Qingdao, Samoa, and Southwest Africa.* Chicago, IL: University of Chicago Press.

———. 2008. "The Colonial State as a Social Field: Ethnographic Capital and Native Policy in the German Overseas Empire before 1914." *American Sociological Review* 73(4): 589–612.

———, ed. 2013. *Sociology and Empire: The Imperial Entanglements of a Discipline.* Durham, NC: Duke University Press.

Stenner, David. 2012. Networking for Independence: The Moroccan Nationalist Movement and its Global Campaign against French Colonialism. *Journal of North African Studies*, 17(4): 573–94.

Stewart, Charles. 1964. *The Economy of Morocco: 1912–1962.* Cambridge, MA: Center for Middle Eastern Studies by Harvard University Press.

Stoler, Ann. 2002. *Carnal Knowledge and Imperial Power: Race and the Intimate in Colonial Rule.* Berkeley: University of California Press.

Stroomer, Harry. 2001. "An Anthology of Tashelhiyt Berber Folktales (South Morocco)." *Berber Studies* Vol 2. Leiden: Rüdiger Köppe Verlag.

———. 2003. "Tashelhiyt Berber Texts from the Ayt Brayyim, Lakhsas and Guedmioua Region (South Morocco): A Linguistic Reanalysis of 'Recits, contes et legendes berberes en Tachelhiyt' by Arsene Roux with an English translation." *Berber Studies*, Vol. 5. Leiden: Rüdiger Köppe Verlag.

———. 2007. "Textes berbères du Maroc central (Textes originaux en transcription). Tome I. Récits, contes et légendes berbères dans le parler des Beni-Mtir et Choix de versions berbères (Parlers du Maroc central)." *Berber Studies*, Vol. 18. Leiden: Rüdiger Köppe Verlag.

Stroomer, Harry, and Michael Peyron. 2003. "Catalogue des archives berbères du Fond Arsène Roux." *Berber Studies*, Vol. 6. Leiden: Rüdiger Köppe Verlag.

Surdon, Georges. 1928. *Esquisses de droit coutumier berbère marocain.* Rabat: Moncho.

Taraud, Christelle. 2003. *La prostitution coloniale : Algérie, Tunisie, Maroc, 1830–1962.* Paris: Payot.

Terrasse, Henri. 1949–50. *Histoire du Maroc des origines à l'établissement du protectorat français.* 2 vols. Casablanca: Èditions Atlantides.

Taraud, Christelle. 2003. *La prostitution coloniale: Algérie, Tunisie, Maroc (1830–1962).* Paris: Payot.

Thomas, Martin. 2005. *The French Empire between the Wars: Imperialism, Politics, and Society*. Manchester, UK: Manchester University Press.

——. 2008. *Empires of Intelligence: Security Services and Colonial Disorder after 1914*. Berkeley: University of California Press.

Thompson, Elizabeth. 2000. *Colonial Citizens: Republican Rights, Paternal Privilege, and Gender in French Syria and Lebanon*. New York: Columbia University Press.

Tozy, Mohamed. 1999. *Monarchie et islam politique au Maroc*. Paris: Presses de la Fondation nationale des sciences politiques.

Trumbull, George. 2009. *An Empire of Facts: Colonial Power, Cultural Knowledge, and Islam in Algeria, 1870–1914*. New York: Cambridge University Press.

Tsur, Yaron. 2001. *Kehilah keru'ah: Yehude Maroko veha-le'umiyut, 1943–1954*. Tel Aviv: Universitat Tel Aviv.

Tucker, Judith E. 1998. *In the House of the Law: Gender and Islamic Law in Ottoman Syria and Palestine*. Berkeley: University of California Press.

——. 2008. *Women, Family, and Gender in Islamic Law*. Cambridge: Cambridge University Press.

Venier, Pascal. 1997. "French Imperialism and Pre-Colonial Rebellions in Eastern Morocco, 1903–1910." *Journal of North African Studies* 2(2): 57–67.

Waterbury, John. 1970. *The Commander of the Faithful: The Moroccan Political Elite—a Study in Segmented Politics*. New York: Columbia University Press.

Weber, Eugen. 1976. *Peasants into Frenchmen: The Modernization of Rural France, 1870–1914*. Stanford, CA: Stanford University Press.

Willis, Michael. 2007. "Justice and Development or Justice and Spirituality? The Challenge of Morocco's Nonviolent Islamist Movements." In *The Maghrib in the New Century: Identity, Religion, and Politics*, edited by Bruce Maddy-Weitzman and Daniel Zisenwine. Gainesville: University of Florida Press.

Wilson, Nicholas. 2011. "From Reflection to Refraction: State Administration in British India, circa 1770–1855." *American Journal of Sociology* 116(5): 1437–77.

Wimmer, Andreas. 2008. "The Making and Unmaking of Ethnic Boundaries: A Multilevel Process Theory." *American Journal of Sociology* 113(4): 970–1022.

Wissa, Karim. 1989. "Freemasonry in Egypt, 1798–1921," *British Society for Middle Eastern Studies* 1(2): 143–61.

Woolman, David. 1968. *Rebels in the Rif: Abd El Krim and the Rif Rebellion*. Stanford, CA: Stanford University Press.

Wright, Gwendolyn. 1991. *The Politics of Design in French Colonial Urbanism*. Chicago, IL: University of Chicago Press.

Wyrtzen, Jonathan. 2013. "Performing the Nation in Anti-Colonial Protest in Interwar Morocco." *Nations and Nationalism* 19(4): 615–34.

Young, Crawford. 1994. *The African Colonial State in Comparative Perspective*. New Haven, CT: Yale University Press.

Zafrani, Haïm. 1983. *Mille ans de vie juive au Maroc: Histoire et culture, religion et magie*. Paris: G.-P. Maisonneuve and Larose.

Zartman, I. W. 1964a. *Morocco: Problems of New Power*. New York: Atherton Press.

——. 1964b. "The Moroccan-American Base Negotiations." *Middle East Journal* 18(1): 27–40.

Zayzafoon, Lamia Ben Youssef. 2005. *The Production of the Muslim Woman: Negotiating Text, History, and Ideology.* Lanham, MD: Lexington Books.

Zubaida, Sami. 1989. *Islam, the People and the State: Essays on Political Ideas and Movements in the Middle East.* London: Routledge.

Zunes, Stephen, and Jacob Mundy. 2010. *Western Sahara: War, Nationalism, and Conflict Irresolution.* Syracuse, NY: Syracuse University Press.

❧ INDEX